KICK OFF

Publisher Simon Rosen **Editor** John Ley
Contributing Editors Johanne Springett, Mike Ivey, Frank Scimone, Marc Fiszman
Art Direction Atam Sandhu **Designers** Ian Bull, Nick Thornton, Steven Clifford,
Jeff Long, Owen Pinch, Simon Joseph
Statistics Programmers Karim Biria, Darren Tang, Sean Cronin, Kam Varma
Special Thanks to Carolyn Small

The publishers wish to confirm that the views expressed in articles and reviews
in this directory are not necessarily those of the F.A. Premier League or its clubs.
NB: The statistics relate to League matches only.

Every effort has been made to ensure that the information given in this guide
is as accurate and up-to-date as possible at the time of going to press.
Details do change, however, and the publisher cannot accept responsibility
for any consequences arising from the use of this book.
If you come across an incorrect detail that we could amend for next year, please let us know.

SIDANPRESS

Sidan Press Ltd
7 Denbigh Mews, Denbigh Street, London SW1V 2HQ
Tel: 020 7630 6446 Fax: 020 7630 5836
Email: sidanpress@btinternet.com
Registered in England No: 3174984

W elcome to what promises to be yet another thrilling season - Carling's eighth as proud sponsor of the Carling Premiership, the world's most exciting club competition.

What a season we have in store! Arsenal, with Henry, Petit, Vieira fresh back from their Euro 2000 glory, will be one of many teams looking to stop Manchester United from clinching a seventh Carling Premiership title.

Once again, Carling is very proud to be associated with Kick Off which now includes ten pages of excellent statistical analysis devoted to each club – that's two more pages than last season. Each club's stats are broken down by a home and away analysis which will certainly be enlightening for fans.

Since the inception of the Carling Premiership in 1993, we have been treated to some truly great footballing moments. Who can forget Beckham's sensational lob over Wimbledon's Neil Sullivan from inside his own half, Kanu's acute angle goal at Stamford Bridge and Poyet's superb volley against Sunderland on the first day of last season? As well as superb individual performances, we have also seen spirited team performances – Manchester United won their sixth Carling Premiership last season, finishing 18 points ahead of runners-up Arsenal. Bradford City turned out a great performance in front of their faithful on the final day of last season to keep relegation at bay. Leicester City progressed to the UEFA Cup through their victory at Wembley in the Worthington Cup Final.

We firmly believe that the Carling Premiership is the world's best club competition and that profile has been helped to a large extent by you, the fans. Your passionate support has continued to be fan-tastic, with attendances at matches continuing to rise. Kick Off is published in celebration of your passionate support and to make it easier for you when travelling to see your team play, come rain or shine! It is clear to see what a difference a Carling makes!

Will Manchester United be crowned Carling champions once more? Will Carling Player of the Year Kevin Phillips bag another 30 Carling Premiership goals? How will new boys Charlton Athletic, Ipswich Town and Manchester City fare? After playing his last game in an England shirt, Alan Shearer will be looking to please the Toon Army with Geordie goals galore. Will anyone join Matt Le Tissier - last season's latest recruit to Carling's Ton Club after scoring his 100th career goal? Let's enjoy watching all the action unfold.

Enjoy a great season!

Mark Hunter

Happy travelling
Mark Hunter, Marketing Director – Bass Brewers

Contents

Welcome to the first full season of the 21st Century and the latest edition of Kick Off, the superlative guide for all supporters of the F.A Carling Premiership.

This unique guide has become the indispensable handbook for all serious followers of the most cosmopolitan League in the world. Kick Off offers the true fan essential background to the Carling Premiership with an innovative approach to all 20 clubs.

Once again, we include all the detail today's football fan demands. If you're looking for ticket information, unique computerised stadium designs, the latest team kits, maps and guides to all Carling Premiership stadiums, Kick Off is the only football yearbook you'll need. This years edition also includes stadium diagrams plus maps and directions for all Division One teams.

We also continue to develop and improve our unique statistical database, now online at football.co.uk, which provides an unrivalled view of team performance, from the relevance of when and how goals are scored to the timing of goals and who receives most yellow and red cards.

For the 2000-2001 edition of Kick Off, we have also broken down home and away performances, to give a fascinating, in-depth breakdown of your team's season.

We believe we are close to becoming the supporter's statistical bible. We therefore invite you to contact us with suggestions for what you would like to see in future editions.

Feel free to e-mail us at sidanpress@btinternet.com with any suggestions and ideas you feel could make Kick Off an even more authorative guide to the Carling Premiership.

Good luck for the 2000-2001 season.

JOHN LEY

John Ley is a respected football writer with the Daily Telegraph. He is regarded as one of the leading statistical experts in the game, contributing to the Internet, television and radio.

What a difference a CARLING makes.

F.A. Carling Premiership Champions

1999 - 2000	Manchester United
1998 - 1999	Manchester United
1997 - 1998	Arsenal
1996 - 1997	Manchester United
1995 - 1996	Manchester United
1994 - 1995	Blackburn Rovers
1993 - 1994	Manchester United
1992 - 1993	Manchester United

WINNERS 1999-2000

Worthington Cup Fixture List 2000/2001

1st Round (1st leg)	Tuesday 22nd and Wednesday 23rd August
1st Round (2nd leg)	Tuesday 5th and Wednesday 6th September
2nd Round (1st leg)	Tuesday 21st and Wednesday 22nd September
2nd Round (2nd leg)	Tuesday 26th and Wednesday 27th September
3rd Round	Tuesday 31st October and Wednesday 1st November
4th Round	Tuesday 28th and Wednesday 29th November
5th Round	Tuesday 12th and Wednesday 13th December
Semi Final (1st leg)	Tuesday 9th and Wednesday 10th January
Semi Final (2nd leg)	Tuesday 23rd and Wednesday 24th January
Final	Sunday 25th February

Dates are subject to change

football.co.uk

If you love football,

We've got detailed statistical profiles of over 10,000 players and 40,000 matches. It is the biggest database, ever, on English football.

football.co.uk has got over one million individual records of the Beautiful Game from its birth in the 1800s to the present day.

For every match played in the Premier League, we've got:

• full team-sheets, including substitutes

• how goals were scored and why players were booked

• shots on target, corners, points and position at end of match

And that's just the beginning. The database also holds complete histories of over 20 leading English clubs as far back as 1888, featuring details of every player and every match.

But everyone knows football is more than just about the numbers.

Without the fans, the stats mean nothing.

So come and tell us what you remember of the heroes and the zeroes, the classic matches and the ones you'd rather forget. Give us your memories and reports. Tell us what makes a certain match or player special to you. Tell us why you love City and not United and exchange views with people around the world.

Use the database to prove your point and win that argument.

football.co.uk is what you need.

Come and join the most exciting online football community and write your own pages in the fans' chronicle of football. Become a part of football history.

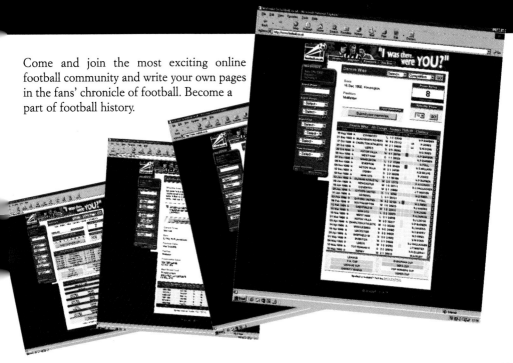

Chart and Table Explanations

The charts and tables in this year's edition of Kick Off offer a comprehensive review of each Carling Premiership team. The descriptions below explain the distinctive layout of this information and suggest ways to use the data to develop a better understanding of a team's performance. Note that statistics refer to League matches only. The charts are also broken down to show how teams performed at both home and away.

GOALS BY POSITION 1997/1998 - 1999/2000
for the latest stats and to share your memories go to football.co.uk

for the latest stats and to share your memories go to football.co.uk

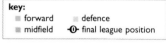

key:
- forward
- midfield
- defence
- -O- final league position

The chart tracks a team's goal-scoring record since the 1997/98 season. For each season – shown at the bottom of the chart – a team's goals are divided among forwards (orange), midfielders (green) and defenders (blue). Compare the height of the columns with the scale on the left of the chart to calculate the number of goals scored. Percentage figures reveal the distribution of goals within a season and are useful when comparing the relative goal-scoring record of a group of players across seasons. This team's midfielders, for example, claimed an increasing share of goals from 1997/98 on, moving from 35% to 40% of goals. The black line graph reveals a team's final League position for each season.

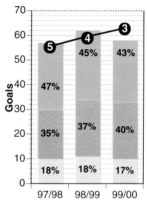

BOOKINGS BY POSITION 1997/1998 - 1999/2000
for the latest stats and to share your memories go to football.co.uk

for the latest stats and to share your memories go to football.co.uk

key:
- forward
- midfield
- defence
- goalkeeper

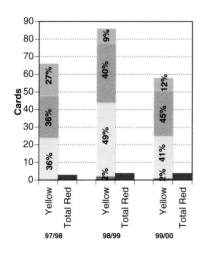

The chart tracks a team's disciplinary record since the 1997/98 season. For each season – shown at the bottom of the chart – a team's yellow cards are divided among forwards (orange), midfielders (green), defenders (blue) and goalkeepers (grey). Red cards for all positions are grouped together and are shown in the Total Red column immediately to the right of each Yellow column. Compare the height of the columns with the scale on the left of the chart to calculate the number of cards issued. Percentage figures reveal the distribution of yellow cards within a season and are useful when comparing the relative disciplinary record of a group of players across seasons. This team's midfielders, for example, claimed an increasing share of bookings from 1997/98 on, moving from 36% to 45% of yellows.

Chart and Table Explanations

key:
- ■ win ░ draw
- ■ loss -⬤- league position
home fixtures are in red

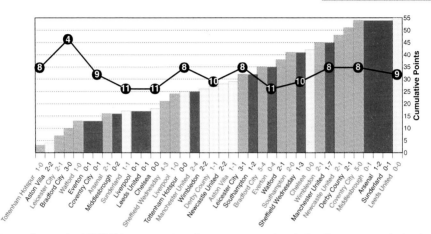

The chart refers to the 1999/2000 season only and tracks a team's results and accumulation of points. A team's 38 League games and results run in chronological order across the bottom of the chart; home games are in red, away games are in black. The score of the team in question always comes first; in this case, the team opened with an home win to Tottenham (1-0) but lost away to Everton (0-1) five games later. The colour of the column above each match indicates whether the game was a win (green), loss (red) or draw (blue). A team's total points after any game can be calculated by comparing the height of the appropriate column with the Cumulative Points scale on the left of the chart. The black line graph reveals a team's League position at various stages of the season. A team's final League position is indicated by the number above the final game of the season, in this case 9. Use the chart to spot significant runs, such as this team's four consecutive draws, starting with a 2-2 draw away to Wimbledon and ending with a 1-1 home draw against Aston Villa. This chart is also broken down into performance at home and away.

key:
- ▨ header ▨ free kick
- ░ volley ▨ inside area
- ░ penalty ░ outside area
- ░ close range* ▣ own goal

* inside six yard box

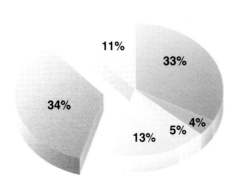

The pie chart refers to the 1999/2000 season only and indicates how a team scored and conceded their goals. The goals are divided according to the categories in the key. Percentage figures and the sizes of individual slices are used to compare the relative importance of each method of scoring or conceding goals.

13

TEAM PERFORMANCE TABLE

for the latest stats and to share your memories go to football.co.uk

Position	Club	Points Won	Percentage of points won at home	percentage of points won away	overall percentage of points won
1.	MANCHESTER UNITED	0/6			
2.	ARSENAL	3/6			
3.	LEEDS UNITED	1/6	47%	13%	30%
4.	LIVERPOOL	4/6			
5.	CHELSEA	1/6			
6.	ASTON VILLA	0/6			
7.	SUNDERLAND	2/6			
8.	LEICESTER CITY	0/6	47%	47%	47%
9.	TOTTENHAM HOTSPUR	6/6			
10.	WEST HAM UNITED	6/6			
11.	NEWCASTLE UNITED	1/6			
12.	MIDDLESBROUGH	52 pts			
13.	EVERTON	6/6	83%	33%	58%
14.	SOUTHAMPTON	4/6			
15.	COVENTRY CITY	3/6			
16.	DERBY COUNTY	3/6			
17.	BRADFORD	1/6			
18.	WIMBLEDON	4/6	33%	67%	50%
19.	SHEFFIELD WEDNESDAY	3/6			
20.	WATFORD	4/6			

The figures show a team's performance against clubs in each quarter of the final league table. The first column represents points won from the total available against each team in the league.

The chart refers to the 1999/2000 season only and measures a team's success rate against various grades of opposition. The final League table is divided into four groups of five teams, with the team in question shown with their final points total. Other teams are shown with a score out of six reflecting the number of points that the team in question earned in the two games against each opponent. A score of 6/6 against West Ham, for example, indicates home and away wins. The percentage figures provide a measure of performance against each opposition group by comparing total points gained with total points available in all matches against every team in the group, overall, at home and away. For example, this team earned nine points out of a possible 30 – 30% – against the top five teams. They won 47% of the points against the teams in sixth to tenth positions at home, and 67% away from home against the teams in the bottom five.

HALF TIME - FULL TIME COMPARATIVE CHART

for the latest stats and to share your memories go to football.co.uk

HOME				AWAY				TOTAL			
Number of Home Half Time Wins	Full Time Result W	L	D	Number of Away Half Time Wins	Full Time Result W	L	D	Total Number of Half Time Wins	Full Time Result W	L	D
9	7	1	1	7	5	0	2	16	12	1	3
Number of Home Half Time Losses	Full Time Result W	L	D	Number of Away Half Time Losses	Full Time Result W	L	D	Total Number of Half Time Losses	Full Time Result W	L	D
3	1	1	1	6	1	5	0	9	2	6	1
Number of Home Half Time Draws	Full Time Result W	L	D	Number of Away Half Time Draws	Full Time Result W	L	D	Total Number of Half Time Draws	Full Time Result W	L	D
7	6	0	1	6	2	2	2	13	8	2	3

The chart refers to the 1999/2000 season only. It shows the number of times a team was winning, losing or drawing at half time, and how many of those they went on to win, lose or draw by the final whistle. For example, this team was ahead at half time in nine of their home games, and went on to win seven, lose one and draw one of those nine matches. Away from

home, they were losing six times and went on to lose five games at full time. A total figure is shown on the right hand side of the chart, outlining the home and away figures as an overall season total. For example, this team won eight games out of the thirteen they were drawing at half time.

Chart and Table Explanations

for the latest stats and to share your memories go to football.co.uk

THE F.A. CARLING PREMIERSHIP BOOKINGS TABLE 1999/2000

The table shows the number of red and yellow cards awarded by the 18 Carling Premiership referees during the 1999/2000 season. Headings below each referee indicate matches refereed (M), red cards issued (R) and yellow cards issued (Y). A referee's activity in individual matches can be assessed, as can overall performance in all matches refereed. In this example, Bradford City were booked 5 times in the two matches refereed by A.B.Wilkie. Totals for all Carling Premiership matches can be found in the bottom right-hand corner of the table.

	A.B.Wilkie			A.G.Wiley			A.P.D'Urso			B.Knight			D.J.Gallagher			D.R.Elleray		
	M	Y	R	M	Y	R	M	Y	R	M	Y	R	M	Y	R	M	Y	R	M
Arsenal	2	6	0	1	1	0	2	4	0	1	1	0	3	6	0	2	6	2	2
Aston Villa	4	1	0	-	-	-	2	2	0	1	1	0	-	-	-	2	7	0	4
Bradford City	2	5	0	3	2	0	2	2	0	1	3	0	2	0	2	1	0	-
Chelsea	2	3	0	2	1	0	1	1	0	-	-	-	2	0	1	0	0	2
Coventry City	2	1	0	1	3	0	3	5	0	2	3	0	-	-	1	2	0	3
Derby County	2	5	1	4	9	0	3	7	0	2	0	-	-	2	4	0	2
Everton	1	0	2	3	0	4	1	0	3	4	0	1	2	0	4

for the latest stats and to share your memories go to football.co.uk

GOALS BY TIME PERIOD 1999/2000

key:  goals for   goals against

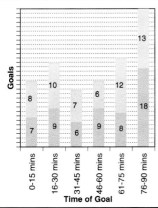

Goals

| 0-15 mins | 16-30 mins | 31-45 mins | 46-60 mins | 61-75 mins | 76-90 mins |

Time of Goal

8, 10, 13, 12, 6, 18 (goals for) / 7, 9, 6, 9, 8 (goals against) / 7

The chart refers to the 1999/2000 season only. A team's total goals for (green) and against (blue) are distributed according to when they were scored. A team's 38 League matches are divided into six 15-minute time periods and goals are allocated accordingly. Goal totals are indicated by figures on each bar. Use the chart to spot goal-scoring trends: this team, for example, managed to score more of their goals as games went on, with 26 in the final 30 minutes; but they were also defensively suspect in the same period, with 25 goals conceded.

RESULTS TABLE

for the latest stats and to share your memories go to football.co.uk

A team's 1999/2000 League matches are listed in chronological order, with home games in white and away games in blue. The following headings run across the top of the table: DATE; H/A – home or away match; OPPONENT; H/T – match score at half time (score of team in question first); F/T – final match score; POS – League position after the game; REFEREE; TEAM; SUBSTITUTES USED. Bookings are indicated by a red or yellow circle beside a player's name. Numbers beside each goal-scorer indicate times of goals. A player who was substituted has a triangle next to his name; the colour of the triangle should be matched with those in the SUBSTITUTES USED column to identify who replaced him.

M = matches refereed R = red cards Y = yellow cards

Referees A.B.Wilkie — B.Knight

Team	A.B.Wilkie M	Y	R	A.G.Wiley M	Y	R	A.P.D'Urso M	Y	R	B.Knight M	Y	R
Arsenal	2	6	0	1	1	0	2	4	0	1	1	0
Aston Villa	4	1	0	-	-	-	2	2	0	1	1	0
Bradford City	2	5	0	3	2	0	2	2	0	1	3	0
Chelsea	2	3	0	2	1	0	1	1	0	-	-	-
Coventry City	2	1	0	1	3	0	3	5	0	2	3	0
Derby County	2	5	1	4	9	0	3	7	0	2	3	0
Everton	1	1	0	2	3	0	4	10	4	1	1	0
Leeds United	-	-	-	2	5	0	2	1	1	2	6	0
Leicester City	1	2	0	3	5	0	2	1	1	1	2	0
Liverpool	2	5	0	-	-	-	1	0	0	1	0	0
Manchester United	3	2	0	1	1	0	1	1	0	-	-	-
Middlesbrough	1	2	0	2	3	0	2	2	1	3	7	0
Newcastle United	-	-	-	3	3	1	1	0	0	1	3	0
Sheffield Wednesday	1	3	1	3	1	0	2	3	0	1	3	0
Southampton	1	0	0	2	5	0	2	7	0	3	5	1
Sunderland	-	-	-	2	2	0	2	5	0	-	-	-
Tottenham Hotspur	2	7	0	3	8	0	2	3	0	-	-	-
Watford	3	6	1	3	3	0	2	4	0	1	1	0
West Ham United	1	1	0	2	4	0	1	1	0	2	4	0
Wimbledon	-	-	-	5	6	0	1	1	0	1	2	0
Total Matches	15	50	6	22	65	1	19	60	7	12	45	1

Referees D.J.Gallagher — G.Poll

Team	D.J.Gallagher M	Y	R	D.R.Elleray M	Y	R	G.P.Barber M	Y	R	G.Poll M	Y	R
Arsenal	3	6	0	2	6	2	2	3	0	4	6	0
Aston Villa	-	-	-	2	7	0	4	9	0	3	1	0
Bradford City	2	3	0	2	1	0	-	-	-	1	0	0
Chelsea	2	2	0	1	0	0	2	1	0	3	4	0
Coventry City	-	-	-	1	2	0	3	4	0	1	0	0
Derby County	-	-	-	2	4	0	2	5	0	2	9	0
Everton	1	1	0	3	4	0	1	2	0	4	4	1
Leeds United	3	4	0	2	6	0	3	7	0	2	6	0
Leicester City	1	0	0	3	3	0	3	3	0	1	3	2
Liverpool	4	7	0	2	2	0	3	5	0	4	10	0
Manchester United	3	4	1	1	0	0	1	2	1	3	6	0
Middlesbrough	2	5	0	1	3	0	2	3	0	-	-	-
Newcastle United	3	0	2	2	2	0	1	0	1	3	0	0
Sheffield Wednesday	1	1	0	-	-	-	2	4	0	2	2	0
Southampton	-	-	-	3	4	0	1	0	1	1	2	0
Sunderland	-	-	-	2	5	0	-	-	-	3	8	0
Tottenham Hotspur	-	-	-	2	5	0	1	4	0	2	2	0
Watford	1	1	0	1	2	0	-	-	-	-	-	-
West Ham United	1	0	0	2	3	1	2	3	1	2	4	0
Wimbledon	2	1	0	1	0	0	3	3	0	2	5	1
Total Matches	18	50	1	17	52	3	21	73	4	21	75	2

Referees J.T.Winter — M.R.Halsey

Team	J.T.Winter M	Y	R	M.A.Riley M	Y	R	M.D.Reed M	Y	R	M.R.Halsey M	Y	R
Arsenal	2	2	0	-	-	-	3	6	1	-	-	-
Aston Villa	1	2	1	3	5	0	-	-	-	3	3	0
Bradford City	3	3	0	-	-	-	1	0	0	2	0	1
Chelsea	3	5	1	3	4	0	3	7	2	1	2	1
Coventry City	3	4	0	1	1	0	1	1	0	2	2	0
Derby County	2	9	0	3	7	0	-	-	-	2	4	1
Everton	1	6	0	3	1	0	1	1	0	-	-	-
Leeds United	2	6	0	3	5	0	-	-	-	2	7	1
Leicester City	1	3	2	0	-	-	2	1	0	1	1	0
Liverpool	1	0	2	3	2	3	3	7	0	-	-	-
Manchester United	4	4	0	1	0	0	2	3	0	-	-	-
Middlesbrough	-	-	-	1	2	0	-	-	-	2	3	0
Newcastle United	3	7	0	1	2	1	4	3	0	2	3	0
Sheffield Wednesday	3	2	0	3	1	0	1	0	0	1	0	0
Southampton	2	7	0	2	9	1	1	1	0	3	6	0
Sunderland	1	3	0	1	1	0	1	1	1	2	2	0
Tottenham Hotspur	1	2	0	2	5	0	1	1	0	2	6	0
Watford	2	3	0	1	5	0	3	7	0	-	-	-
West Ham United	-	-	-	3	6	1	2	5	1	2	6	0
Wimbledon	2	5	1	2	4	1	2	1	0	1	1	0
Total Matches	16	42	5	19	75	7	13	40	4	20	65	1

Referees N.S.Barry — P.Jones

Team	N.S.Barry M	Y	R	P.A.Durkin M	Y	R	P.E.Alcock M	Y	R	P.Jones M	Y	R
Arsenal	1	1	0	4	6	1	1	0	0	1	1	0
Aston Villa	3	0	1	3	0	1	1	0	1	0	0	2
Bradford City	3	3	0	2	8	0	3	2	0	3	2	0
Chelsea	1	2	1	2	3	0	2	3	0	2	8	0
Coventry City	1	1	0	2	2	0	3	6	1	3	3	0
Derby County	3	7	1	1	5	1	1	3	0	2	4	0
Everton	3	1	0	1	1	0	-	-	-	3	2	0
Leeds United	1	3	0	1	0	0	2	3	0	3	6	0
Leicester City	1	1	0	3	7	0	2	2	0	0	-	-
Liverpool	2	1	0	2	0	0	-	-	-	1	6	1
Manchester United	2	3	0	4	3	0	-	-	-	4	5	0
Middlesbrough	2	3	0	3	6	0	2	4	0	1	4	1
Newcastle United	3	1	0	2	1	0	2	3	0	2	2	0
Sheffield Wednesday	2	3	0	3	2	0	2	4	0	1	1	0
Southampton	1	1	0	3	6	0	1	1	0	3	3	0
Sunderland	2	2	0	1	2	1	5	0	4	3	10	1
Tottenham Hotspur	1	2	0	2	7	0	2	2	0	2	2	0
Watford	-	-	-	2	4	0	2	4	0	2	0	0
West Ham United	3	6	1	2	5	1	2	6	0	2	1	0
Wimbledon	1	2	1	2	4	1	1	1	0	2	1	0
Total Matches	21	63	2	19	58	2	19	53	2	17	61	2

Referees R.J.Harris — U.D.Rennie & Total

Team	R.J.Harris M	Y	R	S.G.Bennett M	Y	R	S.J.Lodge M	Y	R	S.W.Dunn M	Y	R	U.D.Rennie M	Y	R	Total M	Y	R
Arsenal	-	-	-	1	1	0	3	5	0	2	3	1				38	64	5
Aston Villa	2	6	0	3	4	0	1	2	0	-	-	-	4	9	0	38	59	1
Bradford City	2	3	0	1	2	0	1	3	0	1	2	0	1	3	0	38	50	1
Chelsea	1	0	0	1	1	0	-	-	-	1	5	0	5	8	0	38	58	4
Coventry City	1	1	0	2	2	0	1	0	0	2	1	0	3	7	1	38	51	2
Derby County	1	0	2	4	0	1	4	0	1	3	0	2	3	0		38	90	4
Everton	1	1	0	2	2	0	1	1	0	2	0	0	2	5	0	38	51	6
Leeds United	3	6	0	3	3	0	2	3	0	-	-	-	1	2	0	38	75	3
Leicester City	3	7	0	2	2	0	-	-	-	2	3	0	1	0	0	38	42	3
Liverpool	2	2	0	-	-	-	1	0	0	3	6	0	3	4	0	38	60	4
Manchester United	2	3	0	-	-	-	2	4	2	3	4	0	1	0	0	38	42	4
Middlesbrough	1	1	1	0	4	12	0	2	3	0	2	6	0	4	12	0	3	3	1	38	81	3
Newcastle United	3	1	0	-	-	-	2	3	0	2	2	0	2	3	1	38	46	3
Sheffield Wednesday	2	4	0	-	-	-	1	1	0	-	-	-				38	40	1
Southampton	3	1	1	4	1	4	4	0	1	2	0	0	-	-	-	38	67	5
Sunderland	2	5	0	3	4	0	1	0	0	2	4	0	38	73	4
Tottenham Hotspur	2	2	0	1	3	0	1	4	1	1	0	0				38	81	1
Watford	2	3	1	2	3	2	1	5	0	3	7	1				38	68	4
West Ham United	2	3	1	1	2	1	1	0	1	3	0	2	1	0	2	5	1	2	3	1	38	67	8
Wimbledon	2	0	0	2	4	0	2	2	0	1	0	0	3	6	1	38	46	4
Total Matches	12	37	1	20	65	6	20	66	3	18	51	8				1211		70

Pos		Pld	W	D	L	F	A	Pts
2	Arsenal	38	22	7	9	73	43	73

Arsenal
"The Gunners"

Arsenal Stadium, Avenell Road, Highbury, London N5 1BU
Tel: 020 7704 4000
www.arsenal.co.uk

Season Review by
John Ley

The Daily Telegraph

Though Arsenal reached the UEFA Cup final and qualified for the Champions' League, the feeling persisted that even more could have been achieved with greater consistency.

The breaking up of the ubiquitous four-man defence began with Silvinho eventually settling in Nigel Winterburn's left-back berth while Tony Adams's season was again interrupted by injuries.

No fewer than nine Arsenal players were on Euro 2000 duty; after France 98 Arsenal's early season form suffered as their World Cup stars returned fatigued and Arsene Wenger will be concerned about a similar reaction.

Wenger lost Nicolas Anelka but the arrival of Thierry Henry proved a great success, with Henry matching Anelka's 17 goals in his first season at Highbury. The Gunners' Championship aspirations will be strengthened by the arrival of Lauren, a £7 million utility player from Real Mallorca, Euro 2000 winner Robert Pires and Brazilian Edu.

Useful Information

The Gunners Shop
East Stand, Arsenal Stadium
Opening Times:
Monday-Friday: 9.30am-5.00pm
Match Saturdays: 10.00am-kick off*
Match Sundays: 10.30am-kick off*
Match Evenings: 9.30am-kick off*
*closed for duration of match
Tel: 020 7704 4120
Mail Order Service: 020 7704 2020

Arsenal World of Sport
Finsbury Park Station
Opening Times:
Monday-Saturday: 9.30am-6.00pm
Match Saturdays: 9.30am-6.00pm
Match Sundays:* 10.00am-7.00pm
Match Evenings:* 9.30am-10.30pm
Tel: 020 7272 1000
Mail Order Service: 020 7704 2020
*closed for duration of match

Stadium Tours
£4 Adults, £2 Children,
£1 Junior Gunners.
Contact Iain Cook: 020 7704 4000

Corporate Hospitality
For details contact
Yvette Brown: 020 7704 4100

Literature
Programme £2
Official Arsenal magazine £2.75

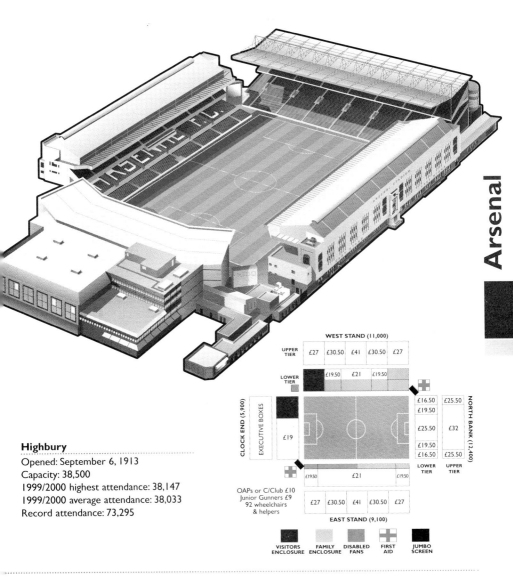

Highbury

Opened: September 6, 1913
Capacity: 38,500
1999/2000 highest attendance: 38,147
1999/2000 average attendance: 38,033
Record attendance: 73,295

WEST STAND (11,000)

| UPPER TIER | £27 | £30.50 | £41 | £30.50 | £27 |

| LOWER TIER | | £19.50 | £21 | £19.50 | |

CLOCK END (5,900)

EXECUTIVE BOXES

£19

NORTH BANK (12,400)

£16.50	£25.50
£19.50	
£25.50	£32
£19.50	
£16.50	£25.50

LOWER TIER | UPPER TIER

| | £19.50 | £21 | £19.50 | |

OAPs or C/Club £10
Junior Gunners £9
92 wheelchairs
& helpers

| £27 | £30.50 | £41 | £30.50 | £27 |

EAST STAND (9,100)

VISITORS ENCLOSURE   FAMILY ENCLOSURE   DISABLED FANS   FIRST AID   JUMBO SCREEN

Pre-Match & Half Time Entertainment

Museum open to all North Bank supporters.

Two Jumbotron screens show a full entertainment package, including highlights of previous games and an interview with the manager 20 minutes before kick off, announcing the team.

Half Time - Highlights of 1st half.
Full Time - Highlights of game.

Sports Centre

The Clock End boasts a sports centre, indoor football pitch and gymnasium, with viewing gallery and adjacent hospitality lounge. For booking details contact Ray Coventry: **020 7704 4140**

Booking Information

General Enquiries:
020 7704 4040
Credit Card Bookings:
020 7413 3366
Travel Club:
020 7704 4150
Recorded Information:
020 7704 4242

Results Breakdown

powered by **football.co.uk**

POINTS WON OR LOST AT BOTH HOME AND AWAY

for the latest stats and to share your memories go to football.co.uk

key:
- win
- draw
- loss   -0- league position
- home fixtures are in red

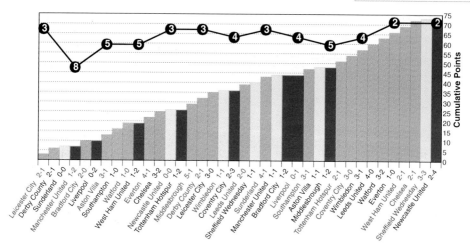

For 90 minutes in December Arsenal topped the Premiership after beating Leicester 3-0 at Filbert Street. Leeds' victory at Derby later that day returned David O'Leary's team to the top and that was as close as Arsenal got to leading the way. Defeats by Manchester United at home, and at Liverpool prevented an early charge while one win in six games between January and March effectively ended hopes of a title success.

Even an impressive sequence of eight successive victories in the final third of the season could not wrest the Championship from United though second place was, relatively speaking, a satisfying return. Wenger will be concerned with the number of goals conceded at Highbury: 17 compared to five the previous season while, away from home, Arsenal's return of 28 points was their lowest for five seasons – from December to the end of March they failed to win away.

Arsenal's 73 goals in the 1999-2000 season was their best total for eight years and five more than when they won the Carling Premiership in 1998. Only Manchester United scored more while the third highest scorers,

HOME   ### AWAY

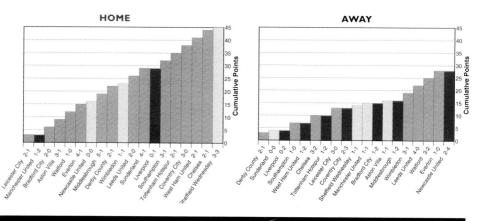

Results Table

powered by football.co.uk

Arsenal

Legend: ● = Red Card ○ = Yellow Card ▲ = Player substituted 00 = Time of goal

DATE	H/A	OPPONENT	H/T	F/T	POS	REFEREE	TEAM (Starting XI, GK →)	SUBSTITUTES USED
07/08	H	Leicester City	0:0	2:1	3	A.B.Wilkie	Manninger, Dixon, Winterburn, Keown, Grimandi, Upson, Vieira, Petit, Parlour, Ljungberg▲, Bergkamp▲65, Kanu▲	Henry▲ / Silvinho▲ / Overmars▲
10/08	A	Derby County	1:1	2:1	1	S.J.Lodge	Manninger, Dixon, Winterburn, Keown, Upson, Adams, Vieira, Petit 40, Parlour, Ljungberg, Bergkamp 47, Kanu▲	Boa Morte▲ / Silvinho▲ / Luzhny▲
14/08	A	Sunderland	0:0	0:0	2	U.D.Rennie	Manninger, Dixon, Silvinho, Keown, Upson, Adams, Vieira, Petit▲, Parlour, Ljungberg▲, Bergkamp▲, Kanu▲	Boa Morte▲ / Boa Morte▲ / Boa Morte▲
22/08	H	Manchester United	1:0	1:2	8	G.Poll	Manninger, Dixon, Silvinho, Keown, Upson, Adams, Vieira, Petit, Parlour, Henry▲, Suker, Kanu▲17	Suker▲ / Overmars▲
25/08	H	Bradford City	2:0	2:0	3	A.G.Wiley	Manninger, Vivas, Silvinho, Keown, Upson, Adams, Vieira 8, Ljungberg 41, Parlour, Henry, Suker, Kanu	Suker▲ / Overmars▲ / Upson▲
28/08	A	Liverpool	0:1	0:2	6	D.J.Gallagher	Manninger, Dixon, Winterburn, Keown, Adams, Vieira, Overmars, Petit, Parlour, Henry▲, Suker▲, Kanu▲	Silvinho▲ / Silvinho▲
11/09	H	Aston Villa	1:1	3:1	5	D.R.Elleray	Manninger, Dixon, Winterburn, Keown, Adams, Ljungberg, Vieira, Petit, Parlour, Henry, Suker 44 49, Kanu▲82	Silvinho▲ / Kanu▲82 / Henry▲
18/09	H	Southampton	0:0	1:0	3	G.P.Barber	Manninger, Dixon, Winterburn, Keown, Adams, Grimandi, Vieira, Petit, Parlour, Overmars, Suker, Henry▲79	Henry▲79 / Berg kamp▲ / Luzhny▲
25/09	A	Watford	0:1	1:2	5	P.A.Durkin	Manninger, Luzhny, Silvinho, Keown, Adams, Grimandi, Vieira▲, Ljungberg, Parlour, Overmars, Suker, Kanu▲86	Suker▲ / Bergkamp▲ / Vivas▲
03/10	H	West Ham United	0:1	1:2	3	S.W.Dunn	Seaman, Luzhny▲, Silvinho, Keown, Adams, Ljungberg, Vieira, Petit, Parlour, Henry, Suker 75, Kanu▲	Kanu▲ / Overmars▲
16/10	A	Everton	1:1	4:1	3	A.B.Wilkie	Seaman, Dixon 40, Winterburn, Keown, Adams, Grimandi, Vieira, Petit, Parlour, Overmars, Suker, Kanu 53 61 78	Kanu▲90 / Henry▲ / Ljungberg▲
23/10	H	Chelsea	0:1	3:2	2	P.Jones	Seaman, Luzhny, Silvinho, Keown●, Grimandi▲, Adams, Ljungberg, Silvinho, Parlour, Henry, Suker, Henry 73 81 90	Henry▲ / Bergkamp▲ / Vivas▲
30/10	A	Newcastle United	1:2	1:2	4	D.R.Elleray	Seaman, Dixon, Winterburn, Keown, Upson, Adams, Ljungberg, Petit, Parlour, Overmars, Suker, Kanu	Grimandi▲ / Overmars▲
07/11	A	Tottenham Hotspur	1:2	1:2	4	D.E.Elleray	Seaman, Luzhny, Winterburn, Grimandi▲, Adams, Vieira 38, Petit, Parlour, Overmars, Suker, Vivas	Grimandi▲ / Vivas▲
20/11	H	Middlesbrough	2:0	5:1	3	N.S.Barry	Seaman, Dixon, Winterburn, Keown, Upson, Adams, Ljungberg, Petit, Parlour, Overmars 25 61 78, Bergkamp 40 49, Kanu	Barrett▲ / Hughes▲
28/11	A	Derby County	1:0	3:0	2	A.P.D'Urso	Manninger, Luzhny, Winterburn, Grimandi▲, Upson, Grimandi 22, Silvinho, Petit, Parlour, Overmars 75, Henry 61, Kanu	Barrett▲ / Winterburn▲
04/12	H	Leicester City	1:0	3:0	4	D.J.Gallagher	Manninger, Dixon 52, Winterburn, Grimandi, Upson, Adams, Silvinho, Silvinho, Parlour, Silvinho, Henry 11 50, Kanu	Suker▲ / Molz▲
18/12	A	Wimbledon	0:2	2:0	2	G.P.Barber	Manninger, Dixon, Winterburn, Keown, Adams, Grimandi, Silvinho, Petit, Parlour, Henry, Hughes	Suker▲86 / Hughes▲
26/12	H	Coventry City	0:2	2:0	2	R.J.Harris	Seaman, Dixon, Silvinho, Grimandi, Adams, Ljungberg 67, Parlour, Henry 59, Suker, Kanu	Suker▲ / Winterburn▲
28/12	A	Sheffield Wednesday	1:0	1:1	3	G.Poll	Seaman, Dixon, Silvinho, Grimandi, Adams, Ljungberg 31, Silvinho, Parlour, Overmars, Suker 27 32, Kanu	Winterburn▲ / Suker▲ / Upson▲
03/01	H	Sunderland	1:0	4:1	3	M.D.Reed	Seaman, Dixon, Silvinho, Grimandi, Adams, Luzhny, Silvinho, Petit, Parlour, Hughes, Suker 3 80, Henry▲	Molz▲ / Winterburn▲
15/01	H	Sheffield Wednesday	3:0	4:1	3	P.E.Alcock	Seaman, Dixon, Luzhny, Keown, Adams, Lyungberg, Petit, Parlour, Winterburn, Suker, Ljungberg 11, Kanu	Winterburn▲ / Bergkamp▲
24/01	A	Manchester United	1:0	1:1	3	P.A.Durkin	Seaman, Dixon, Winterburn, Keown, Grimandi 78, Silvinho, Petit, Parlour, Luzhny▲79, Suker, Henry 13	Luzhny▲79 / Winterburn▲ / Suker▲
05/02	H	Bradford City	1:1	2:1	3	A.P.D'Urso	Seaman, Dixon, Silvinho, Keown, Upson, Luzhny, Silvinho, Petit, Parlour, Luzhny, Suker, Berg kamp	Bergkamp▲ / Berg kamp▲
13/02	A	Liverpool	0:1	0:1	4	S.W.Dunn	Seaman, Dixon, Silvinho, Keown, Adams, Luzhny, Silvinho, Silvinho, Parlour, Luzhny, Berg kamp	Berg kamp▲ / Suker▲
26/02	H	Southampton	2:0	3:1	3	J.T.Winter	Seaman, Dixon, Silvinho, Keown, Grimandi, Adams, Vieira, Petit, Parlour, Ljungberg 22 68, Bergkamp▲37, Kanu	Bergkamp▲37 / Berg kamp▲
04/03	H	Aston Villa	0:2	1:1	5	G.Poll	Seaman, Dixon 84, Silvinho, Keown, Silvinho, Grimandi, Vieira, Petit, Parlour, Henry, Ljungberg	Winterburn▲86 / Winterburn▲
13/03	A	Middlesbrough	1:0	2:1	5	R.J.Harris	Seaman▲, Luzhny, Winterburn, Keown, Adams, Grimandi, Vieira, Petit, Parlour, Henry, Kanu	Suker▲ / Manninger▲ / Suker▲
19/03	A	Tottenham Hotspur	3:0	2:1	4	D.J.Gallagher	Manninger, Dixon, Silvinho, Keown, Adams, Silvinho, Vieira, Silvinho, Parlour, Overmars, Berg kamp	Luzhny▲ / Winterburn▲
26/03	A	Coventry City	0:0	2:3	4	B.Knight	Seaman, Dixon, Winterburn, Keown, Adams, Luzhny, Vieira, Petit, Parlour, Henry 45 50, Berg kamp	Kanu▲79 / Luzhny▲ / Overmars▲
01/04	H	Watford	2:1	3:2	4	U.D.Rennie	Seaman, Dixon, Silvinho, Keown, Grimandi, Adams, Vieira, Petit, Parlour, Winterburn, Bergkamp, Kanu 33 41	Winterburn▲33 41 / Petit▲
16/04	A	Everton	1:0	4:0	3	S.W.Dunn	Seaman, Dixon, Winterburn, Keown, Adams, Grimandi, Vieira, Petit, Parlour, Henry 21, Bergkamp, Kanu▲82	Bergkamp▲ / Kanu▲82
29/04	A	West Ham United	3:0	2:1	4	D.J.Gallagher	Seaman, Luzhny, Silvinho, Keown, Adams, Silvinho, Vieira, Petit, Parlour, Henry 18 45, Bergkamp, Berg kamp	Block▲ / Winterburn▲
02/05	H	Chelsea	1:0	2:1	2	P.A.Durkin	Seaman, Dixon, Winterburn, Grimandi, Adams, Vieira, Petit, Parlour, Berg kamp, Henry 22 48, Kanu 22 48	Petit▲90 / Berg kamp▲ / Berg kamp▲
06/05	H	Sheffield Wednesday	1:0	3:3	2	M.D.Reed	Seaman, Dixon 29, Silvinho, Keown, Adams, Vieira, Petit, Parlour, Berg kamp, Henry 79, Berg kamp	Henry▲77 / Silvinho▲ / Silvinho▲
09/05	H	Chelsea	1:0	2:1	2	J.T.Winter	Seaman, Dixon, Winterburn▲, Grimandi, Luzhny, Vieira, Silvinho, Grimandi, Parlour, Molz 53, Henry 79, Suker	Block▲ / McGovern▲ / Vieira▲
14/05	A	Newcastle United	1:2	2:4	4	G.Poll	Manninger, Weston▲, Winterburn, Keown, Luzhny, Luzhny, Cole, Vernazza 22, Parlour, Molz, Vernazza, Suker	Suker▲ / Kanu▲7 / Gray▲

21

Goal Analysis

powered by **football.co.uk**

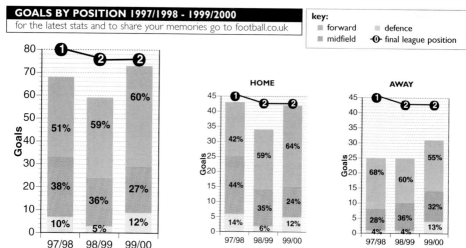

GOALS BY POSITION 1997/1998 - 1999/2000
for the latest stats and to share your memories go to football.co.uk

key:
▓ forward   ▓ defence
▓ midfield   -〇- final league position

Leeds, claimed 15 fewer than the Gunners. Thierry Henry, in his first season in English football, scored 17, matching the number scored by Nicolas Anelka the previous season, while Kanu added 12. Davor Suker scored eight but the only surprise was that Dennis Bergkamp managed only six – half his total the previous season. Importantly, the goals were shared around with 14 different players scoring in the Carling Premiership, three more than the previous term. Henry took until mid-September to score his first goal and added three before the turn of the new Millennium. But, having latched on to the pace of the Premiership, he made scoring look easy, claiming 12 in 10 successive appearances including seven consecutive Premiership games, equalling a Carling Premiership record set by Chelsea's Mark Stein (in the 1993-94 season) and repeated by Newcastle's Alan Shearer (1996-97). Only 27 percent of goals came from midfield, some way down on previous years. Though Ray Parlour claimed his first ever hat-trick, in the UEFA Cup tie at Werder Bremen, he added only one more in the League, compared to the six he scored in the 1998-1999 season.

GOALS BY TIME PERIOD 1999/2000
for the latest stats and to share your memories go to football.co.uk

key:
▓ goals for   ▓ goals against

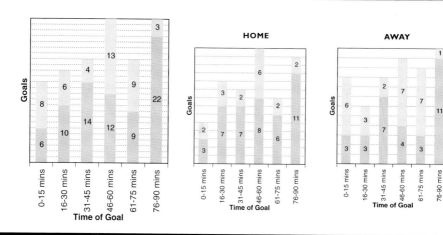

What a difference a *CARLING* makes.

Goal Analysis

powered by football.co.uk

Arsenal

HOW GOALS WERE SCORED 1999/2000
for the latest stats and to share your memories go to football.co.uk

key:
- header
- volley
- penalty
- close range*
- free kick
- inside area
- outside area
- own goal

* inside six yard box

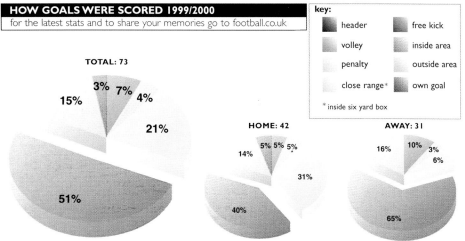

TOTAL: 73

3% 7% 4%
15%
21%
51%

HOME: 42

5% 5% 5%
14%
31%
40%

AWAY: 31

16% 10% 3%
6%
65%

Emmanuel Petit and Patrick Vieira were also disappointing in the goals department, producing only five between them (compared to the seven they scored a year earlier). However, it should be said that the Frenchmen played less games together than last term, due to various injuries and suspensions.

The defence was more productive last season; when Lee Dixon scored the first of four, against Everton in October, it was his first goal for a month short of three years. Tony Adams however, failed to score a League goal for the first time in six seasons and only the sixth time in his 17 seasons at Highbury. Arsenal seemed to be at their most dangerous in the final 15 minutes with 30 percent of their goals coming in that period. Consequently, they rarely conceded goals in the closing stages; in August Manchester United's Roy Keane and Liverpool's Patrick Berger found the Gunners vulnerable late on yet they did not concede another late goal until Gustavo Poyet scored for Chelsea in the 79th minute of the 2-1 win at Highbury in May. The period after half-time was also a busy one for Arsene Wenger's side.

HOW GOALS WERE CONCEDED 1999/2000
for the latest stats and to share your memories go to football.co.uk

key:
- header
- volley
- penalty
- close range*
- free kick
- inside area
- outside area
- own goal

* inside six yard box

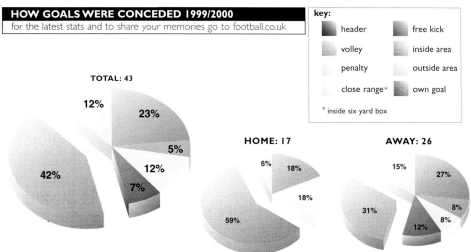

TOTAL: 43

12% 23%
5%
12%
42% 7%

HOME: 17

6% 18%
18%
59%

AWAY: 26

15% 27%
8%
31% 8%
12%

Squad and Performance

SQUAD LIST

for the latest stats and to share your memories go to football.co.uk

Position	Name	Appearances	Appearances as substitute	Goals	Clean Sheets	Yellow Cards	Red Cards
G	A.Manninger	14	1		5		
G	D.Seaman	24			5		
D	T.Adams	21				2	
D	A.Cole	1					
D	L.Dixon	28				4	3
D	G.Grimandi	27	1	2		8	1
D	M.Keown	26			1	5	1
D	O.Luzhny	16	5			2	1
D	B.McGovem		1				
D	Silvinho	23	8	1		3	
D	M.Upson	5	3			1	
D	N.Vivas	1	4			1	
D	R.Weston	1					
D	N.Winterburn	19	9			3	
M	T.Black		1				
M	J.Gray		1				
M	S.Hughes	1	1				
M	F.Ljungberg	22	4	6		2	1
M	S.Malz	2	3	1		1	
M	M.Overmars	22	9	7		1	
M	R.Parlour	29	1	1		3	
M	E.Petit	24	2	3		5	
M	P.Vernazza	1	1				
M	P.Vieira	29	1	2		8	1
F	G.Barrett		2				
F	D.Bergkamp	23	5	6		6	
F	L.Boa Morte		2				
F	T.Henry	26	5	17		5	
F	N.Kanu	25	7	12		2	
F	D.Suker	8	14	8		4	

If Arsenal were looking for reasons why they finished so far behind Manchester United they may consider their home form against poorer opposition. They should have been beating the likes of Wimbledon and Sheffield Wednesday but managed only draws. Similarly, the away defeat at Bradford proved costly.

They seemed most comfortable against the teams in the lower section of the top half, particularly at home, enjoying a 100 percent return against teams finishing in positions sixth to 10th. The record against the main rivals, those four teams finishing in the top five, was reasonable though home and away defeats against Liverpool – the fourth time in six seasons the Reds have enjoyed a double over Arsenal – must have damaged their title aspirations.

TEAM PERFORMANCE TABLE

for the latest stats and to share your memories go to football.co.uk

Position	Club	Points Won	Percentage of points won at home	percentage of points won away	overall percentage of points won
1.	MANCHESTER UNITED	1/6			
2.	ARSENAL	73 pts			
3.	LEEDS UNITED	6/6	50%	58%	54%
4.	LIVERPOOL	0/6			
5.	CHELSEA	6/6			
6.	ASTON VILLA	4/6			
7.	SUNDERLAND	4/6			
8.	LEICESTER CITY	6/6	100%	33%	67%
9.	TOTTENHAM HOTSPUR	3/6			
10.	WEST HAM UNITED	3/6			
11.	NEWCASTLE UNITED	1/6			
12.	MIDDLESBROUGH	3/6			
13.	EVERTON	6/6	87%	40%	63%
14.	SOUTHAMPTON	6/6			
15.	COVENTRY CITY	3/6			
16.	DERBY COUNTY	6/6			
17.	BRADFORD CITY	3/6			
18.	WIMBLEDON	4/6	73%	67%	70%
19.	SHEFFIELD WEDNESDAY	2/6			
20.	WATFORD	6/6			

The figures show a team's performance against clubs in each quarter of the final league table. The first column represents points won from the total available against each team in the league.

What a difference a CARLING makes.

Discipline and Season Summary

powered by football.co.uk

BOOKINGS BY POSITION 1997/1998 - 1999/2000
for the latest stats and to share your memories go to football.co.uk

key:
- forward
- midfield
- defence
- goalkeeper

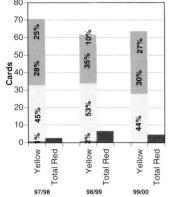

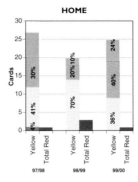

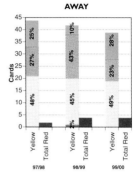

Arsenal

When Oleg Luzhny was sent-off at Wimbledon in April he became the 29th player to be dismissed in Arsene Wenger's four-year Highbury reign and also the third in four games in all competitions.

In the League, though, Arsenal received five red cards, compared to the seven collected a season earlier. The number of yellow cards received was up on the previous season; the final total of 65 cards was eight more than the previous campaign.

The worst offender was Patrick Vieira, who was cautioned no fewer than eight times while adding a dismissal at West Ham. Gilles Grimandi was also a consistent miscreant, with eight cautions and a sending off (against Tottenham at Highbury) along with another dismissal in Europe.

Arsenal collected two red cards in one game, when both Martin Keown, for a second bookable offence, and Frederik Ljungberg, for violent conduct, were ordered off during the 2-1 defeat at Tottenham.

There were times when Arsenal's discipline let them down and, arguably, cost them points; only Everton and West Ham received more red cards.

Vieira aside, the midfield was better behaved than the previous season, even claiming the lowest share of the cards away from home.

A break-down of Arsenal's record at half-time and at the end shows that when they have assumed control by the interval they are rarely vulnerable in the second half. Only once did they concede an interval lead – against Manchester United at Highbury.

HALF TIME - FULL TIME COMPARATIVE CHART
for the latest stats and to share your memories go to football.co.uk

HOME				AWAY				TOTAL			
Number of Home Half Time Wins	Full Time Result W	L	D	Number of Away Half Time Wins	Full Time Result W	L	D	Total Number of Half Time Wins	Full Time Result W	L	D
9	7	1	1	7	5	0	2	16	12	1	3
Number of Home Half Time Losses	Full Time Result W	L	D	Number of Away Half Time Losses	Full Time Result W	L	D	Total Number of Half Time Losses	Full Time Result W	L	D
3	1	1	1	6	1	5	0	9	2	6	1
Number of Home Half Time Draws	Full Time Result W	L	D	Number of Away Half Time Draws	Full Time Result W	L	D	Total Number of Half Time Draws	Full Time Result W	L	D
7	6	0	1	6	2	2	2	13	8	2	3

Maps and Directions

Arsenal are located in North London. Parking near the ground is difficult during a match as restrictions come into force. Travel by tube.

From the North:
From the M1 exit at the A1 turn-off - Junction 2/3. The A1 merges for a stretch with the A406. Keep to the A1 Archway Road and then Holloway Road. Turn left onto the A503 Seven Sisters Road and after 1 mile turn right onto the A1201 Blackstock Road which becomes Highbury Park. Turn right into Aubert Park and right again into Avenell Road.

From the North-West:
From the M40 at Junction 1 stay on the A40 for 13 miles and on the A40(M). At Paddington turn onto the A501. When the A501 becomes Pentonville Road turn left onto Baron Street, signposted as the route for the A1. Take the first right Lion Street and turn left onto the A1. At the Highbury and Islington roundabout, turn right onto St Pauls Road and then left onto the A1201 Highbury Grove. Turn left into Aubert Park and right into Avenell Road.

From the West:
Approaching on the M4 turn left onto the A406 Gunnersbury Avenue at Junction 2. At Hangar Lane turn right onto the A40. Then as route for North-West.

From the South-West:
Stay on the M3 to end and continue on A316 to Hammersmith. Turn right onto A4 for 1 1/4 miles, left onto the A3220 Warwick Road and then onto the M41. At end turn onto A40(M) and then as route for North-West.

From the East:
From the M11 turn off onto the A406 at Junction 4, and then onto the A503. After Tottenham Hale tube station, turn left into Broad Lane and then back onto the A503 Seven Sisters Road. Turn left onto the A1201 Blackstock Road and then as route for North.

Arsenal is the nearest tube station.

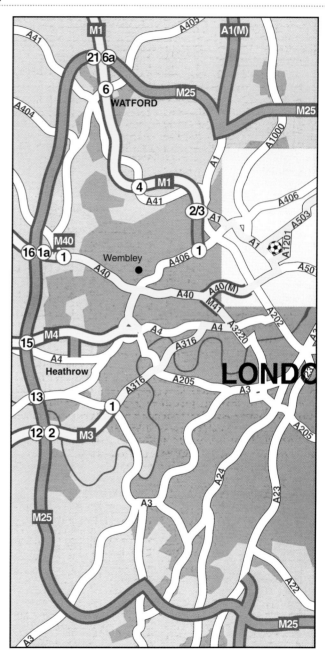

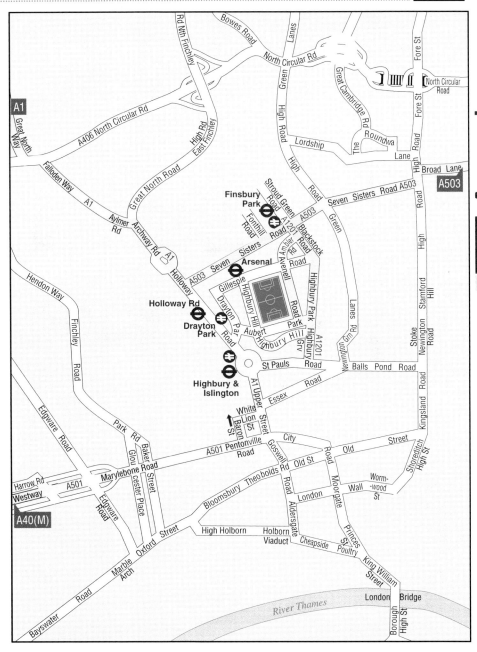

Pos		Pld	W	D	L	F	A	Pts
6	Aston Villa	38	15	13	10	46	35	58

Aston Villa

"The Villans"

Villa Park, Trinity Road,
Birmingham B6 6HE
Tel: 0121 327 2299
www.avfc.co.uk

Season Review by
John Ley

The Daily Telegraph

Expectations at Villa Park are high enough for a sixth place in the Carling Premiership to be regarded as a disappointment. But a place in the InterToto Cup and runners-up place in the FA Cup, plus a cheque for nearly £3 million for finishing so high, should not be taken lightly.

David James replaced Mark Bosnich in goal and came close to challenging for a place in England's Euro 2000 squad. George Boateng arrived from Coventry to add weight to midfield while youngsters Mark Delaney, Lee Hendrie and Gareth Barry continued to make good progress. The arrival of Benito Carbone, from Sheffield Wednesday, added fresh impetus, though Dion Dublin's career-threatening broken neck was a factor behind Villa's inconsistency.

The summer arrival of Belgian international Luc Nilis will offset the apparent unhappiness of some players who have asked for transfers including captain Gareth Southgate.

Useful Information

Villa Village

Villa Park, Aston, Birmingham B66TA
Opening Times:
Monday-Saturday: 9.00am-5.00pm
Match Saturdays: 9.00am-3.00pm*
Match Sundays: 10.00am-4.00pm*
*then 1 hour after final whistle
Midweek Matchdays: 9.00am-kick off then 3/4 hour after final whistle

Holte End Stand

Beneath Holte Pub on Witton Lane
Opening Times (matchdays only):
Saturdays: 1.30pm-3.00pm*
Sundays: 1.00pm-4.00pm*
Midweek: 6.00pm-kick off*
*then 1/2 hour after final whistle
Mail Order Service: 0121 327 5963
or 0121 327 2800

Stadium Tours

Contact Pam Bridgewater:
0121 327 2299 or **0121 326 1535**

Corporate Hospitality

A wide range of hospitality packages are available, including executive boxes, executive suites and matchday membership.
Matchball and match sponsorship also available. Contact Commercial

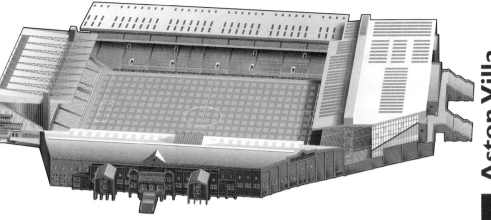

Villa Park

Opened: April 17, 1897
Capacity: 39,372
1999/2000 highest attendance: 39,217
1999/2000 average attendance: 31,697
Record attendance: 76,588

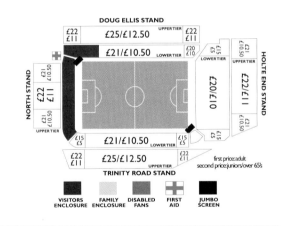

DOUG ELLIS STAND

| | £22 £11 | £25/£12.50 | UPPER TIER | £22 £11 | |
| £21 £10.50 | | | | | |

£21/£10.50 LOWER TIER

£20 £10 LOWER TIER

£15 £10.50 UPPER TIER

HOLTE END STAND

£20/£10

£22/£11

£15 £10.50

NORTH STAND

£21 £10.50

£22 £11

£21 £10.50

UPPER TIER

£15 £5

£15 £5

£21/£10.50 LOWER TIER

£5 £5

£22 £11

£25/£12.50 UPPER TIER

£22 £11

first price: adult
second price: juniors/over 65's

TRINITY ROAD STAND

VISITORS ENCLOSURE · FAMILY ENCLOSURE · DISABLED FANS · FIRST AID · JUMBO SCREEN

Department: **0121 327 5399**
Villa Park Conference Centre offers 17 function suites for 2 to 800 people. Tel: **0121 326 0388**
The Corner Flag restaurant, open for lunch Monday-Friday
Tel: **0121 326 1519**

Literature
Programme £2 Bi-monthly magazine Claret & Blue £2.50

Pre-Match & Half Time Entertainment
Programmes on video screens.

Advertising & Sponsorship
Contact Commercial Department:
0121 327 5399

Weddings at Villa Park
Contact Conference Centre:
0121 326 0388

Booking Information
General Enquiries :
0121 327 5353
Credit Card Bookings:
0121 607 8000
Official British Travel Club:
0121 327 3322

Results Breakdown

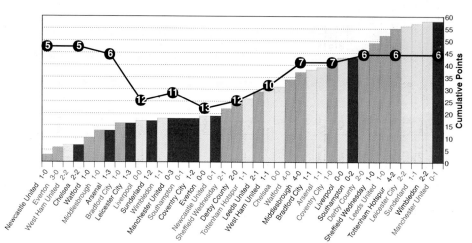

As in the previous season, John Gregory's men started strongly with four wins and a draw from the opening six but what followed saw Villa slump into the bottom half of the table while Gregory's position as manager appeared uncomfortable. From late September to mid-December Villa won three points, losing six and drawing three of nine Carling Premiership games. Had they lost to 'lucky losers' Darlington in the FA Cup, Gregory would surely have been sacked. Instead Villa embarked on the road that led to Wembley.

Villa's home form was confusing; they conceded just 12 goals at Villa Park, their best defensive record there in the top division for 105 years. Yet they managed to win just eight games at home, drawing a further eight; if those draws had been converted into wins, Villa could have finished just behind Arsenal, in third place. Their away form in the early stages of the season was also damaging; from September to November they not only lost five consecutive games, but conceded an incredible thirteen goals away from Villa Park.

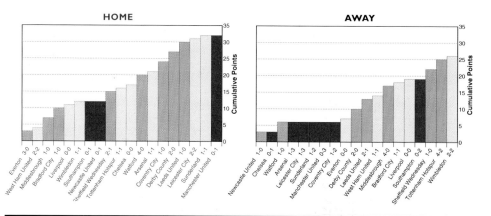

Aston Villa

Legend: ● = Red Card ○ = Yellow Card 00 = Time of goal ▲ = Player substituted

DATE	H/A	OPPONENT	H/T	F/T	POS	REFEREE	GK				Line-up & goals								Substitutes Used
07/08	A	Newcastle United	0-0	1-0	5	U.D.Rennie	James	Southgate	Ehiogu	Calderwood ▲	Wright	Booteng	Taylor	Thompson	Merson	Carbone	Joachim 75	Dublin	Stone ▲, Hendrie ▲, ·
11/08	H	Everton	1-0	3-0	1	G.P.Barber	James	Southgate	Ehiogu	Calderwood	Wright	Deloney	Taylor 85	Thompson	Booteng	Joachim 9	Dublin ▲57	Hendrie ▲	Hendrie ▲, Stone ▲, Merson ▲
16/08	A	West Ham United	1-1	2-2	2	M.A.Riley	James	Southgate	Ehiogu	Calderwood	Wright	Deloney	Taylor	Thompson	Booteng	Joachim	Dublin 5 51	Hendrie ▲	Hendrie ▲, Stone ▲, ·
21/08	H	Chelsea	0-0	0-1	5	N.S.Barry	James	Southgate	Ehiogu	Calderwood	Wright	Deloney	Taylor	Thompson	Hendrie	Joachim	Dublin		Booteng ▲, · , ·
24/08	A	Watford	0-0	1-0	2	S.G.Bennett	James	Southgate	Ehiogu	Calderwood	Wright	Deloney 68	Taylor	Thompson	Hendrie	Joachim	Dublin 5	Booteng ▲	Booteng ▲, Vassell ▲, ·
28/08	H	Middlesbrough	1-0	1-0	2	M.K.Halsey	James	Southgate	Ehiogu	Calderwood	Wright	Booteng	Taylor	Merson	Hendrie	Joachim	Dublin 5	Enckelman ▲	Enckelman ▲, Vassell ▲, ·
11/09	H	Arsenal	1-1	3-1	6	D.R.Elleray	James ▲	Southgate	Ehiogu	Calderwood	Wright	Deloney ○	Taylor	Merson	Hendrie	Joachim 44	Dublin	Stone ▲	Stone ▲, Vassell ▲, Thompson ▲
18/09	A	Bradford City	0-0	1-1	3	S.J.Lodge	Enckelman	Southgate	Ehiogu	Barry	Watson	Booteng ○	Taylor	Thompson	Hendrie	Joachim	Dublin 71	Stone ▲	Stone ▲, Merson ▲, Vassell ▲
25/09	A	Leicester City	0-1	1-3	6	J.T.Winter	Enckelman	Southgate ●	Ehiogu	Barry	Watson ▲	Booteng	Taylor	Thompson	Hendrie	Joachim	Dublin 73	Deloney ▲	Deloney ▲, Calderwood ▲, ·
02/10	H	Liverpool	0-0	0-0	12	R.J.Harris	Enckelman	Southgate	Ehiogu	Barry	Deloney	Booteng	Taylor	Thompson	Hendrie	Vassell	Dublin	Merson ▲	Merson ▲, Stone ▲, ·
18/10	A	Sunderland	1-1	1-2	12	D.R.Elleray	James	Southgate	Calderwood	Barry	Deloney	Booteng ▲	Taylor	Thompson	Hendrie	Carbone	Dublin 46	Stone ▲	Stone ▲, Merson ▲, ·
23/10	H	Wimbledon	1-1	1-1	8	U.D.Rennie	James	Southgate	Calderwood	Barry ○	Deloney	Booteng ▲	Taylor	Thompson	Hendrie	Carbone	Dublin 35	Merson ▲	Merson ▲, Ghruyib ▲, ·
30/10	A	Manchester United	0-2	0-3	11	A.B.Wilkie	James	Southgate	Calderwood	Barry ○	Deloney	Booteng ▲	Taylor	Thompson ○	Hendrie	Carbone	Dublin	Stone ▲	Stone ▲, Wright ▲, Merson ▲
06/11	H	Southampton	0-0	0-1	11	A.P.D'Urso	James	Southgate	Calderwood	Barry	Wright	Deloney	Stone	Thompson ○	Merson	Carbone	Dublin	Ghruyib ▲	Ghruyib ▲, Booteng ▲, ·
22/11	A	Coventry City	1-1	1-2	13	G.P.Barber	James	Southgate	Calderwood	Barry	Wright ▲	Booteng	Taylor	Stone	Hendrie	Joachim 41	Dublin	Watson ▲	Watson ▲, Vassell ▲, Vassell ▲
27/11	H	Everton	0-0	0-0	13	P.Jones	James	Southgate	Calderwood	Barry	Wright ▲	Booteng	Taylor	Watson	Hendrie	Joachim	Dublin	Carbone ▲	Carbone ▲, · , ·
04/12	A	Newcastle United	0-0	0-1	15	M.A.Riley	James	Southgate	Calderwood	Barry	Wright ▲	Booteng	Taylor	Deloney	Hendrie ▲	Joachim	Dublin	Joachim ▲	Joachim ▲, ▲Merson, Carbone ▲
18/12	A	Sheffield Wednesday	0-1	2-1	12	S.G.Bennett	James	Calderwood	Ehiogu	Barry	Wright ▲	Booteng ○	Taylor 70	Merson 70	Hendrie ▲	Carbone	Joachim	Stone ▲	Stone ▲, Calderwood ▲, Vassell ▲
26/12	H	Derby County	2-0	2-0	12	A.B.Wilkie	James	Southgate	Calderwood	Barry	Wright ▲	Booteng 68	Taylor 78	Watson	Merson	Carbone	Joachim	Stone ▲	Stone ▲, Vassell ▲, ·
29/12	A	Tottenham Hotspur	0-1	1-1	12	G.P.Barber	Enckelman	Southgate	Ehiogu	Barry	Wright ▲	Booteng ○	Taylor 74	Watson	Merson	Carbone	Joachim	Stone ▲	Stone ▲, Vassell ▲, ·
03/01	A	Leeds United	1-0	2-1	10	U.D.Rennie	Enckelman	Southgate	Ehiogu 19 62	Barry	Wright ▲	Booteng ○	Stone	Watson	Merson	Carbone ▲	Joachim	Vassell ▲	Vassell ▲, · , ·
15/01	H	West Ham United	1-0	1-1	10	G.Poll	James	Southgate	Ehiogu	Barry	Wright ▲	Booteng	Taylor 24	Watson	Merson	Carbone	Joachim	Deloney ▲	Deloney ▲, Vassell ▲, Vassell ▲
22/01	H	Chelsea	0-0	0-0	9	A.B.Wilkie	James	Calderwood	Ehiogu	Barry	Wright ▲	Booteng	Taylor	Watson ▲	Merson	Stone	Joachim	Carbone ▲	Carbone ▲, Vassell ▲, Stone ▲
05/02	A	Watford	4-0	4-0	8	P.Jones	James	Calderwood	Ehiogu	Barry	Wright ▲	Stone 47	Taylor	Deloney	Merson ▲57 59	Carbone	Joachim	Samuel ▲	Samuel ▲, Hendrie ▲, Walker ▲80
14/02	H	Middlesbrough	1-0	4-0	7	A.B.Wilkie	James	Southgate	Ehiogu	Barry	Wright ▲	Booteng ▲	Deloney	Merson ▲38	Carbone 11 65	Dublin 70 74	Joachim	Cutler ▲	Cutler ▲, Hendrie ▲, Taylor ▲
26/02	A	Bradford City	1-1	1-1	8	M.K.Halsey	Enckelman	Bradford City	Ehiogu	Barry	Wright ▲	Booteng ○	Deloney	Merson	Carbone	Joachim	Walker ▲63	Hendrie ▲	Hendrie ▲, Hendrie ▲, Taylor ▲
04/03	H	Arsenal	1-0	1-1	7	G.Poll	Enckelman	Southgate	Stone	Barry	Wright ▲	Stone	Taylor	Merson 48	Carbone	Joachim	Walker ▲	Walker ▲, Stone ▲, Walker ▲
11/03	A	Coventry City	1-0	1-0	7	U.D.Rennie	Enckelman	Southgate	Ehiogu 44	Barry	Wright ▲	Booteng	Taylor	Deloney	Carbone	Joachim	Stone ▲	Stone ▲, Hendrie ▲	Walker ▲
15/03	H	Liverpool	0-0	0-0	6	S.G.Bennett	Enckelman	Watson	Ehiogu	Barry	Wright ▲	Booteng ○	Stone	Samuel	Carbone	Joachim	Taylor ▲	Taylor ▲, Vassell ▲, Walker ▲
18/03	A	Southampton	0-1	0-2	6	M.A.Riley	James	Southgate	Ehiogu	Calderwood	Wright ▲	Booteng	Thompson	Hendrie	Carbone	Joachim	Thompson ▲	Thompson ▲, Hendrie ▲, Samuel ▲
25/03	H	Derby County	1-0	2-0	6	P.E.Alcock	James	Samuel	Ehiogu	Barry	Wright ▲	Booteng 57	Taylor	Deloney	Merson	Carbone ▲39	Joachim ▲39	Hendrie ▲	Hendrie ▲, Stone ▲, Dublin ▲
05/04	H	Sheffield Wednesday	1-0	1-0	6	G.Poll	James	Watson	Ehiogu	Barry	Wright ▲	Samuel	Thompson 90	Deloney ○	Merson	Walker ▲	Joachim	Ghruyib ▲	Ghruyib ▲, Joachim ▲, Stone ▲
09/04	A	Leeds United	1-0	1-0	6	B.Knight	James	Watson	Ehiogu	Barry	Wright ▲	Booteng ○	Samuel	Hendrie	Merson	Walker ▲	Joachim 40	Thompson ▲	Thompson ▲, Ghruyib ▲, Dublin ▲
15/04	H	Tottenham Hotspur	4-2	4-2	6	G.Poll	James	Watson ▲	Ehiogu	Barry	Wright 73	Booteng ○	Samuel	Merson	Carbone 69	Dublin 62 68	Joachim	Deloney ▲	Deloney ▲, Brewers ▲, ·
22/04	A	Leicester City	1-1	2-2	6	G.P.Barber	Enckelman	Watson	Ehiogu 44	Barry	Wright ▲	Booteng	Thompson ▲32	Samuel	Merson 48	Carbone	Dublin	Hendrie ▲	Hendrie ▲, Hendrie ▲, Joachim ▲
29/04	A	Sunderland	1-0	1-1	6	A.P.D'Urso	James	Southgate	Ehiogu	Barry 60	Wright	Booteng	Thompson	Deloney	Merson	Carbone	Joachim	Thompson ▲	Thompson ▲, Samuel ▲, Dublin ▲
06/05	A	Wimbledon	0-1	2-2	6	M.K.Halsey	James	Southgate	Ehiogu	Barry	Wright ▲	Deloney	Thompson	Merson 54	Carbone	Dublin ▲71	Samuel ▲71	Joachim ▲	Joachim ▲, Samuel ▲, Stone ▲
14/05	H	Manchester United	0-0	0-1	6	P.A.Durkin	Enckelman	Southgate	Ehiogu	Barry	Wright	Deloney ○	Taylor	Merson	Carbone	Dublin	Joachim	Thompson ▲	Thompson ▲, Taylor ▲, Joachim ▲

Goal Analysis

GOALS BY POSITION 1997/1998 - 1999/2000
for the latest stats and to share your memories go to football.co.uk

key:
forward · defence
midfield · -0- final league position

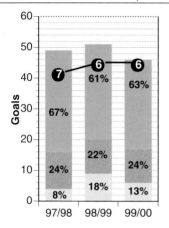

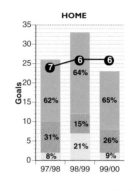
HOME

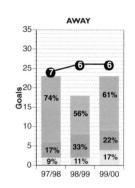
AWAY

With Dion Dublin absent for a third of the season, Villa's goals were predictably light. The 46 they scored was better than only five rivals and on a par with relegated Wimbledon. Villa have only once before scored so few Carling Premiership goals, in the 1993-94 season, when they finished in tenth position.

Crowds at Villa Park were poor and few could blame those that stayed away; Villa's total of 23 was their lowest for six seasons while the combined total by Villa and the opposition, just 35, was lower than at any time at Villa Park for 31 years.

Dublin still managed to claim 12 goals, one more than he had scored in the previous season, but the contribution from other strikers was poor with Julian Joachim, leading scorer a season earlier, managed just six while Carbone scored four in 22 starts. Still, the 29 goals from strikers represented 63 percent of Villa's goals while just 24 percent came from midfield where Hendrie managed only one goal compared to the eight he had scored in the previous campaign.

GOALS BY TIME PERIOD 1999/2000
for the latest stats and to share your memories go to football.co.uk

key:
goals for · goals against

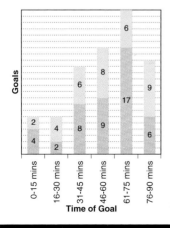

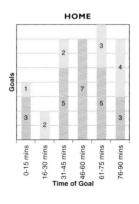
HOME

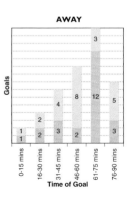
AWAY

Goal Analysis

Aston Villa

HOW GOALS WERE SCORED 1999/2000
for the latest stats and to share your memories go to football.co.uk

key:
- header
- volley
- penalty
- close range*
- free kick
- inside area
- outside area
- own goal

inside six yard box

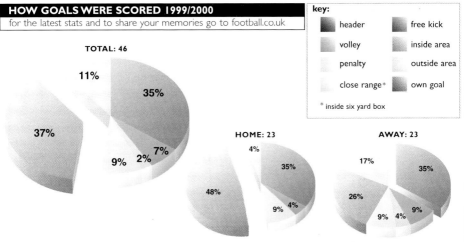

TOTAL: 46 — 11%, 35%, 37%, 9%, 2%, 7%

HOME: 23 — 4%, 35%, 48%, 9%, 4%

AWAY: 23 — 17%, 35%, 26%, 9%, 4%, 9%

Another midfielder, Ian Taylor, enjoyed a purple patch by scoring in four successive games in December and January but managed to score only once more in the league after that.

The defence again provided little contribution. Ugo Ehiogu, Mark Delaney, Gareth Barry and Alan Wright scored one each though Gareth Southgate scored twice to earn Villa precious points in a 2-1 win at Elland Road, goals which contributed to the 17 percent scored away from home by the back line.

Interestingly, it had taken the defender three seasons to score his previous two goals for Villa.

Despite being without Dion Dublin for part of the season, headed goals made up a considerable percentage of Villa's return with 35 percent coming from headers. John Gregory's men however, did show a vulnerability for conceding goals from free kicks away from home.

Villa games had little action in the first third; of their 46 goals only six were scored in this period.

HOW GOALS WERE CONCEDED 1999/2000
for the latest stats and to share your memories go to football.co.uk

key:
- header
- volley
- penalty
- close range*
- free kick
- inside area
- outside area
- own goal

inside six yard box

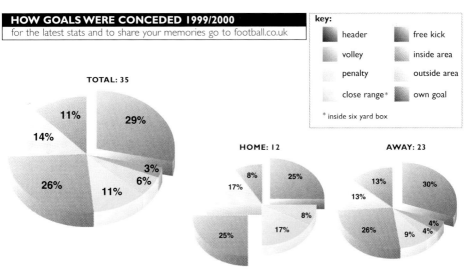

TOTAL: 35 — 11%, 29%, 14%, 3%, 6%, 26%, 11%

HOME: 12 — 8%, 25%, 17%, 8%, 17%, 25%

AWAY: 23 — 13%, 30%, 13%, 4%, 4%, 9%, 26%

Squad and Performance

SQUAD LIST

for the latest stats and to share your memories go to football.co.uk

Position	Name	Appearances	Appearances as substitute	Goals	Clean Sheets	Yellow Cards	Red Cards
G	N.Cutler		1				
G	P.Enckelman	9	1	4			
G	D.James	29		12	1		
D	G.Barry	30			1	6	
D	J.Bewers		1				
D	C.Calderwood	15	3				
D	M.Delaney	25	3	1		6	
D	U.Ehiogu	31		1		4	
D	N.Ghrayib	1	4			1	
D	G.Southgate	31		2			1
D	S.Watson	13	1			4	
D	A.Wright	31	1	1		3	
M	G.Boateng	30	3	2		9	
M	L.Hendrie	18	11	1		6	
M	J.Samuel	5	4			2	
M	S.Stone	10	13	1		1	
M	I.Taylor	25	4	5		7	
M	A.Thompson	16	5	2		7	
F	B.Carbone	22	2	4		1	
F	D.Dublin	23	3	12		1	
F	J.Joachim	27	6	6		1	
F	P.Merson	24	7	5		2	
F	D.Vassell	1	10			1	
F	R.Walker	2	3	2			

Similarly just six of the 35 goals conceded came during that same third.

They were at their most dangerous in the final 30 minutes; exactly half their goals came with an hour played while 17 came in the period between 61 and 75 minutes.

Villa used just 24 players in the Carling Premiership – only Leeds used fewer – but their inability to dominate against teams in the top half was their undoing. Though they achieved a memorable home and away double over Leeds for the first time in 23 years, they failed to claim a win home or away against the next four.

Gregory's boys were, however, comfortable against

TEAM PERFORMANCE TABLE

for the latest stats and to share your memories go to football.co.uk

Position	Club	Points Won	Percentage of points won at home	percentage of points won away	overall percentage of points won
1.	MANCHESTER UNITED	0/6			
2.	ARSENAL	1/6			
3.	LEEDS UNITED	6/6	40%	27%	**33%**
4.	LIVERPOOL	2/6			
5.	CHELSEA	1/6			
6.	ASTON VILLA	58 pts			
7.	SUNDERLAND	1/6			
8.	LEICESTER CITY	1/6	33%	33%	**33%**
9.	TOTTENHAM HOTSPUR	4/6			
10.	WEST HAM UNITED	2/6			
11.	NEWCASTLE UNITED	3/6			
12.	MIDDLESBROUGH	6/6			
13.	EVERTON	4/6	60%	47%	**53%**
14.	SOUTHAMPTON	0/6			
15.	COVENTRY CITY	3/6			
16.	DERBY COUNTY	6/6			
17.	BRADFORD CITY	4/6			
18.	WIMBLEDON	2/6	87%	73%	**80%**
19.	SHEFFIELD WEDNESDAY	6/6			
20.	WATFORD	6/6			

The figures show a team's performance against clubs in each quarter of the final league table. The first column represents points won from the total available against each team in the league.

What a difference a _CARLING_ makes.

Discipline and Season Summary

BOOKINGS BY POSITION 1997/1998 - 1999/2000
for the latest stats and to share your memories go to football.co.uk

key:
- forward
- midfield
- defence
- goalkeeper

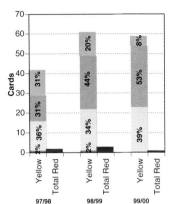

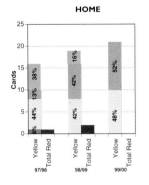
HOME

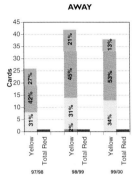
AWAY

Aston Villa

the bottom five, winning home and away against Watford, Sheffield Wednesday and Derby County. Losing to Southampton both at Villa Park and the Dell surely damaged any hopes of earning automatic entry into the UEFA Cup.

Villa received only one red card – Southgate at Leicester – while their cautions were down slightly. The 'bad boys' were in midfield where Boateng was cautioned nine times, Taylor and Thompson received seven apiece and Hendrie saw six yellow cards.

Manager John Gregory was also in trouble with the authorities; comments directed at officials cost him a 28-day touchline ban, beginning in December, but the punishment turned into a blessing, Villa did not lose again until mid-March.

Their strikers concentrated on trying to score rather than row with referees and, consequently, the front line collected just six cautions, all at Villa Park.

A positive aspect of Villa's results shows that when they are down at half time they often rally in the second period. On seven occasions they were trailing at half time but went on to lose only three while turning deficits round twice, against Sheffield Wednesday and at Tottenham, where they turned a 2-0 loss around to win 4-2 with all goals coming in the final 28 minutes.

The statistics also warn that, at home, Villa should not rest on their laurels if drawing at half time; of the 12 occasions they went into the Villa Park dressing room on level terms, they went on to win just twice.

HALF TIME - FULL TIME COMPARATIVE CHART
for the latest stats and to share your memories go to football.co.uk

HOME				AWAY				TOTAL			
Number of Home Half Time Wins	Full Time Result W	L	D	Number of Away Half Time Wins	Full Time Result W	L	D	Total Number of Half Time Wins	Full Time Result W	L	D
5	5	0	0	4	2	0	2	9	7	0	2
Number of Home Half Time Losses	Full Time Result W	L	D	Number of Away Half Time Losses	Full Time Result W	L	D	Total Number of Half Time Losses	Full Time Result W	L	D
2	1	0	1	5	1	3	1	7	2	3	2
Number of Home Half Time Draws	Full Time Result W	L	D	Number of Away Half Time Draws	Full Time Result W	L	D	Total Number of Half Time Draws	Full Time Result W	L	D
12	2	3	7	10	4	4	2	22	6	7	9

Maps and Directions

Villa Park is 2 miles north of Birmingham city centre. Please use car parks. Do not park in the streets surrounding Villa Park.

From the North:
Leave M42 junction 7 onto M6. Exit M6 at junction 6 onto the A38 (M) Aston Expressway. Take first exit right onto Victoria Road. At roundabout take right exit into Witton Road
for Villa Park.

From the South:
Take M1 to junction 19, then M6. At junction 6 turn onto the A38 (M). Then as route for North.

From the East:
Approaching on the M42, turn off at Junction 8 and get onto the M6 heading towards Birmingham. Then as route for South.

It is a 2 minute walk to the ground from Witton Station.

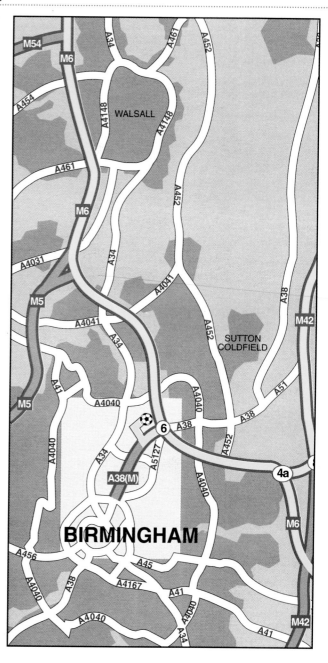

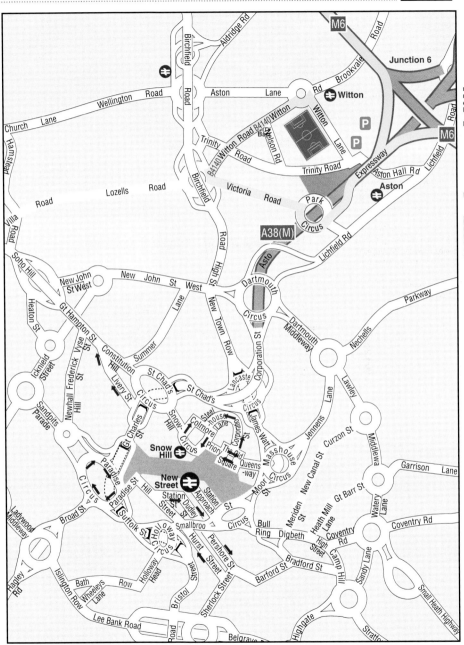

Aston Villa

Club Honours

- Division 2 Champions: 1907-08
- Division 3 Champions: 1928-29 (North), 1984-85
- FA Cup Winners: 1911

Club Records

- Victory: 11-1 v Rotherham United, Division 3 (North), August 25, 1928
- Defeat: 1-9 v Colchester United, Division 4,December 30, 1961
- League goals in a season (team): 128, Division 3 (North), 1928-29
- League goals in a season (player): 34,David Layne, Division 4, 1961-62
- Career league goals: 121, Bobby Campbell, 1979-86
- League appearances: 502, Cecil Podd, 1970-84
- Transfer fee paid: £1,400,000 to Leeds United for David Wetherall, June, 1999
- Transfer fee received: £2,000,000 from Newcastle United for Des Hamilton, March, 1997

Pos		Pld	W	D	L	F	A	Pts
17	Bradford	38	9	9	20	38	68	36

Bradford City
"The Bantams"

Bradford and Bingley Stadium, Bradford, West Yorkshire BD8 7DY
Tel: 01274 773 355
www.bradfordcityfc.co.uk

Season Review by
John Ley

The Daily Telegraph

The surprise departure of Paul Jewell will have shocked City supporters, who witnessed near-miracles at Valley Parade in their first season in the top flight for 77 years. His decision to join relegated Sheffield Wednesday will have stunned them further still. Assistant manager Chris Hutchings has been promoted to the position of manager, and will want the same solid support that Jewell received from the board, which helped Bradford to defy their critics and retain their place in the Carling Premiership on the final day of the season, sending Wimbledon into Division One. Jewell went to Leeds to sign David Wetherall, Gunnar Halle and Lee Sharpe while Neil Redfearn, Andy Myers and Matt Clarke all arrived. And just before the opening game, Dean Saunders brought his experience to Yorkshire after a spell with Benfica.

With a place in the Intertoto Cup and a reported £7 million transfer kitty, the new season will bring many challenges to the new manager, and Bradford fans should be in for another interesting season.

Useful Information

Bantams Leisure

Sunwin Stand, Asics UK Ltd.
Bradford and Bingley Stadium,
Valley Parade, Bradford BD8 7DY
Opening Times:
Monday-Saturday: 9.00am-5.00pm
Match Saturdays: 9.00am-3.00pm*
Match Sundays: 9.00am-3.00pm*
Midweek Matches: 9.00am-kick off*
*then half an hour after final whistle

Tel: 01274 770 012
Mail Order Service: 01274 770 012
The club shop is operated by Asics and stocks a wide range of leisurewear and Bradford City branded accessories.

Corporate Hospitality

Restaurant facilities available on matchdays only.

Contact Marketing Department:
01274 778 778
Matchball, match, programme and player sponsorship available.

Contact Marketing Department:
01274 778 778

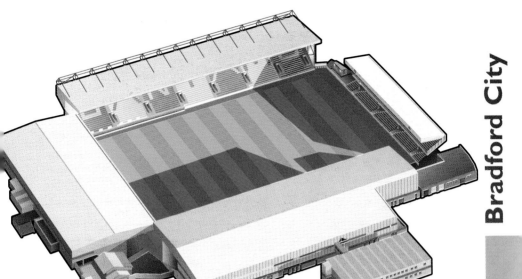

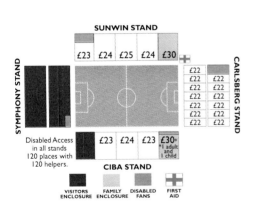

SUNWIN STAND

£23	£24	£25	£24	£30	

SYMPHONY STAND

CARLSBERG STAND

£22	
£22	£22
£22	£22
£22	£22
£22	£22
£22	£22
£22	£22
£22	£22

Disabled Access
in all stands
120 places with
120 helpers.

£23	£24	£23	£30* 1 adult and 1 child

CIBA STAND

VISITORS
ENCLOSURE

FAMILY
ENCLOSURE

DISABLED
FANS

FIRST
AID

BRADFORD & BINGLEY STADIUM

Opened: September 25, 1886
Capacity: 18,276
1999/2000 highest attendance: 18,276
1999/2000 average attendance: 18,030
Record attendance: 39,146

Literature

Programme £2

Pre-Match & Half Time Entertainment

Varies from match to match.

Miscellaneous Information

Bradford City will be opening their new Training Ground at Elm Tree Farm in Apperley Bridge on the outskirts of Bradford.

The Club have also applied for planning permission for new training facilities. These will include a state-of-the-art 60x40 yard 'fibreturf' pitch and physiotherapy suite When combined with the outdoor facilities at Elm Tree Farm Bradford City will apply for Academy Status.

Booking Information

General Enquiries:
01274 770 022
Club Fax:
01274 773 356
Credit Card Bookings:
01274 770 022

Results Breakdown

powered by **football.co.uk**

POINTS WON OR LOST AT BOTH HOME AND AWAY
for the latest stats and to share your memories go to football.co.uk

key:
- win
- draw
- loss
- -0- league position

home fixtures are in red

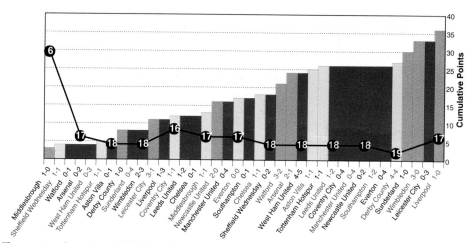

The opening day win at Middlesbrough, Saunders scoring in the 89th minute, offered hope but it was to be their last win for six games, until they won at Derby. They flirted with the relegation zone for the rest of the season, suffering a goalkeeping crisis with former Wales international Neville Southall, then 41, called upon to play against Leeds.

Bradford were rarely out of the bottom three; after their initial good start they dropped to 18th and stayed there for most of the season until they rallied at just the right time. Only twice in their first 13 home games did

they suffer defeat. Sadly, the away form, after the win at the Riverside Stadium, was not quite as clever.

They lost no fewer than 11 of their first 13 away games; a 1-1 draw at Tottenham provided City with their only point from a possible 36 away from home. In all they lost 15 away games - only Watford lost more. This was their highest number of away defeats since the 1989-90 season when they were relegated to Division Three.

But a win at Sunderland followed by a 3-0 victory over Wimbledon, took Bradford out of the relegation

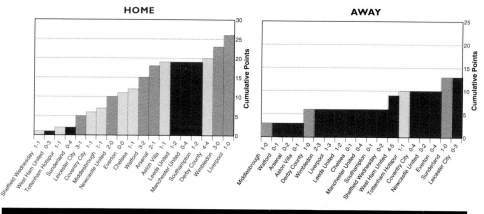

powered by

Bradford City

Legend: ● = Red Card ▲ = Player substituted ▲ = Yellow Card 00 = Time of goal

DATE	H/A	OPPONENT	H/T	F/T	POS	REFEREE	TEAM (GK)											SUBSTITUTES USED
07/08	A	Middlesbrough	0-0	1-0	6	N.S.Barry	Walsh	Wetherall	Halle	Jacobs	Redfearn	O'Brien	Dreyer	Whalley	Beagrie	Windass	Mills	Saunders ▲89
14/08	H	Sheffield Wednesday	0-1	1-1	8	D.J.Gallagher	Walsh	Wetherall	Halle	Jacobs	Redfearn	Lawrence	Dreyer	Whalley	Beagrie 89	Windass	Mills	Saunders, Gant
21/08	H	Watford	0-1	0-1	13	R.J.Harris	Walsh	Wetherall	Halle	Jacobs	Redfearn	Lawrence	Dreyer	Whalley	Beagrie	Windass	Mills	Saunders, Blake
25/08	A	Arsenal	0-2	0-2	17	A.G.Wiley	Walsh	Wetherall	Halle	Jacobs	O'Brien	Lawrence	Dreyer	Whalley	Beagrie	Windass	Saunders	Blake, McCall
28/08	H	West Ham United	0-2	0-3	18	P.Jones	Walsh	Wetherall	Halle	Jacobs	O'Brien	McCall	Mills	Whalley	Beagrie	Windass	Saunders	Blake, Mills, Redfearn
12/09	A	Tottenham Hotspur	0-0	1-1	18	A.B.Wilkie	Walsh	Wetherall	Halle	Jacobs	O'Brien	McCall 90	Mills	Whalley	Beagrie	Windass	Saunders	Blake, Myers, Rodriguez
18/09	H	Aston Villa	0-0	0-1	18	S.J.Lodge	Walsh	Wetherall	Halle	Myers	O'Brien	McCall	Mills	Whalley	Beagrie	Windass	Saunders	Rodriguez, Blake
25/09	H	Derby County	0-0	1-0	16	M.R.Halsey	Walsh	Wetherall	Halle	Myers ●	O'Brien	McCall	Mills	Whalley	Blake	Windass	Saunders	Westwood, Jacobs
02/10	A	Sunderland	1-2	2-3	18	S.G.Bennett	Walsh	Wetherall	Halle	Jacobs	O'Brien	McCall	Mills	Blake	Beagrie	Windass	Saunders	Saunders
16/10	A	Wimbledon	2-1	3-1	18	P.E.Alcock	Walsh	Wetherall	Halle	Redfearn 66	O'Brien	McCall	Redfearn	Sharpe	Blake	Windass 92	Mills 45	Saunders
23/10	H	Leicester City	1-2	1-3	16	M.D.Reed	Walsh	Wetherall	Halle	Redfearn	O'Brien	McCall	Mills 40	Sharpe	Blake	Windass	Saunders	Lawrence
01/11	H	Liverpool	1-1	1-1	18	J.T.Winter	Clarke	Wetherall	Halle	Redfearn	O'Brien	McCall	Mills	Sharpe	Blake 12	Windass 12	Saunders	Rankin, Lawrence
06/11	A	Coventry City	1-0	1-2	16	B.Knight	Clarke	Wetherall	Halle	Redfearn	O'Brien	McCall	Mills 43	Sharpe	Blake	Windass	Saunders	Lawrence, Beagrie
20/11	A	Leeds United	0-1	0-1	17	P.A.Durkin	Clarke	Wetherall	Halle	Redfearn	O'Brien	McCall	Lawrence	Sharpe	Beagrie 90	Windass	Mills	Rankin, Myers
28/11	H	Chelsea	0-1	0-1	17	A.G.Wiley	Clarke	Wetherall	Halle	Redfearn	O'Brien	McCall	Lawrence	Sharpe	Beagrie	Windass	Mills	Rankin, Blake
04/12	H	Middlesbrough	0-1	1-1	17	R.J.Harris	Clarke	Wetherall 71	Myers	Redfearn	O'Brien	McCall	Lawrence	Blake	Beagrie ●	Windass	Mills 61	Sharpe, Halle
18/12	A	Newcastle United	0-0	2-0	17	N.S.Barry	Clarke	Wetherall	Halle	Myers	O'Brien	McCall	Lawrence	Sharpe	Mills	Windass	Saunders 55	Beagrie, Blake
26/12	H	Manchester United	0-0	0-4	17	P.Jones	Clarke	Wetherall	Halle	Myers	O'Brien	McCall	Lawrence	Sharpe	Redfearn	Windass	Saunders	Saunders, Beagrie
28/12	A	Everton	0-0	0-0	18	U.D.Rennie	Clarke	Wetherall	Halle	Myers	O'Brien	McCall	Redfearn	Sharpe	Mills	Windass	Saunders	Beagrie, Blake
03/01	A	Southampton	0-0	0-2	18	D.R.Elleray	Clarke	Wetherall	Halle	Lawrence	O'Brien	McCall	Mills	Sharpe	Beagrie	Windass 57	Saunders	Beagrie, Blake
08/01	H	Chelsea	1-0	1-1	18	A.G.Wiley	Clarke	Wetherall	Halle	Myers	O'Brien	McCall	Redfearn	Blake	Beagrie	Windass	Saunders	Beagrie
15/01	H	Sheffield Wednesday	0-0	0-2	18	J.T.Winter	Clarke	Wetherall	Halle	Myers	O'Brien	McCall	Redfearn	Lawrence	Beagrie	Windass	Saunders	Mills, Redfearn
22/01	H	Watford	2-1	3-2	18	P.E.Alcock	Clarke	Wetherall	Halle	Jacobs	O'Brien 49	McCall	Redfearn	Whalley 37	Beagrie 25	Windass	Saunders	Davison
05/02	A	Arsenal	1-2	2-1	18	A.P.D'Urso	Clarke ▲	Wetherall	Halle	Jacobs	O'Brien	McCall	Dreyer	Whalley	Beagrie 45	Windass 10	Saunders	Dreyer
12/02	A	West Ham United	2-2	4-5	18	M.R.Halsey	Davison	Wetherall	Halle	Jacobs	O'Brien	Lawrence 47 50	Blake	Whalley	Mills 2	Windass 30	Saunders	Blake
26/02	H	Aston Villa	0-1	1-1	18	P.Jones	Davison	Wetherall	Halle	Jacobs	O'Brien	Lawrence 42	Blake	Whalley	Beagrie 74	Windass 76	Saunders	Dreyer
04/03	A	Tottenham Hotspur	1-1	1-1	18	P.A.Durkin	Davison	Wetherall	Halle	Jacobs	O'Brien	Lawrence	Blake	Whalley	Beagrie	Windass	Saunders	Blake, Codner
12/03	H	Leeds United	0-1	1-2	18	S.J.Lodge	Southall	Wetherall	Halle	Jacobs	O'Brien	Lawrence	Blake	Whalley	Beagrie	Windass	Saunders	Dreyer, Codner
18/03	H	Coventry City	0-2	2-4	18	G.Poll	Davison	Wetherall	Halle	Jacobs	O'Brien	Lawrence	Blake	Codner	Beagrie 27	Windass	Saunders	Sharpe, Codner
25/03	A	Manchester United	0-2	0-2	18	A.P.D'Urso	Clarke	Wetherall	Halle	Jacobs	O'Brien	Dreyer	Blake	Sharpe	Beagrie	Windass	Saunders	Bloke, Codner
08/04	A	Newcastle United	0-1	1-2	19	D.R.Elleray	Clarke	Wetherall	Halle	Jacobs	O'Brien	Blake 77	Sharpe	Sharpe	Beagrie	Windass	Codner	Ronkin
15/04	A	Everton	0-2	0-4	19	P.E.Alcock	Clarke	Wetherall	Halle	Jacobs	O'Brien	Blake	Blake	Blake	Beagrie	Windass	Saunders	Rankin
21/04	H	Derby County	4-3	4-4	19	A.B.Wilkie	Clarke	Wetherall	Halle	Jacobs	O'Brien	Blake	Dreyer	Sharpe	Beagrie 27	Windass 11 18 44 Westwood	Saunders	Sharpe
24/04	A	Sunderland	0-2	0-2	18	S.J.Lodge	Clarke	Wetherall	Halle	Jacobs	O'Brien	Blake	Dreyer 59	Sharpe	Beagrie 42 49	Windass	Westwood	Westwood
30/04	H	Wimbledon	1-0	3-0	17	J.T.Winter	Clarke	Wetherall	Halle	Jacobs	O'Brien	Blake	Dreyer	Sharpe	Beagrie ▲	Windass 82	Saunders	Rankin, Rankin
06/05	A	Leicester City	0-0	0-3	18	S.W.Dunn	Clarke	Wetherall	Halle	Jacobs	O'Brien	Lawrence	Sharpe	Sharpe	Beagrie	Windass	Saunders	Lawrence, Jacobs
14/05	H	Liverpool	1-0	1-0	17	D.J.Gallagher	Clarke	Wetherall 12	Halle	Dreyer	O'Brien	Lawrence	Sharpe	Sharpe	Beagrie ▲	Windass	Saunders	Rankin, Sharpe

41

Goal Analysis

powered by football.co.uk

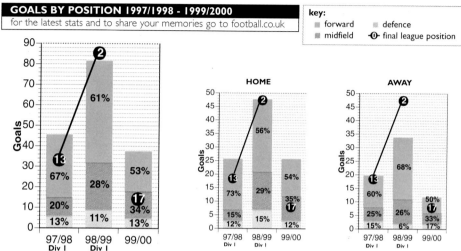

GOALS BY POSITION 1997/1998 - 1999/2000
for the latest stats and to share your memories go to football.co.uk

key:
■ forward   ■ defence
■ midfield   -●- final league position

zone for the first time since December and though they lost at Leicester, David Wetherall's goal against Liverpool on a dramatic final day kept them in the Premiership.

Only Watford scored fewer goals than Bradford, whose final tally of 38 was their poorest return since the 1924-25 season, when they scored 37. On winning promotion the previous season, City scored 82 goals, including 48 at Valley Parade. It was away from home where they were weakest, claiming less than a goal a

game – just 12 from 19. That was just one goal more than the club's all-time poorest scoring record away from home, again set 75 years earlier.

In their promotion season, top League scorer had been Lee Mills, who scored 24 in the First Division; this time around Mills found the Carling Premiership tough going and returned just four League goals, the quartet coming during a seven-game spell midway through the season. Mills, to be fair, was absent for the final third of the season with back and hamstring injuries before

GOALS BY TIME PERIOD 1999/2000
for the latest stats and to share your memories go to football.co.uk

key:
■ goals for   ■ goals against

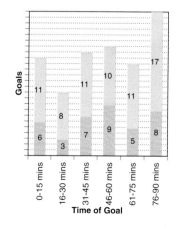

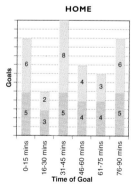

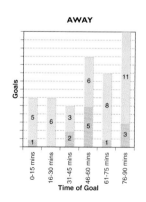

Goal Analysis

Bradford City

HOW GOALS WERE SCORED 1999/2000

for the latest stats and to share your memories go to football.co.uk

key:
- header
- volley
- penalty
- close range*
- free kick
- inside area
- outside area
- own goal

* inside six yard box

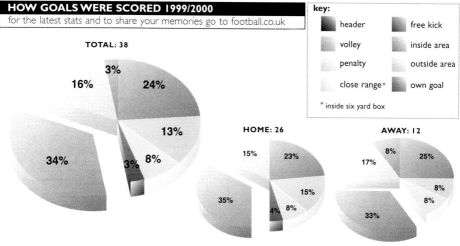

TOTAL: 38
3% — 24% — 16% — 13% — 34% — 3% — 8%

HOME: 26
15% — 23% — 35% — 4% — 8% — 15%

AWAY: 12
8% — 25% — 17% — 8% — 8% — 33%

being allowed to join Manchester City on loan in March.

Dean Windass came to City's rescue, scoring 10 League goals – more than 25 per cent of their final total. Of that tally – his best in League football for two years – three came in one of the season's more remarkable games, against Derby County in April.

City were still getting over the shock of their 5-4 defeat at West Ham six weeks earlier when they met Derby at Valley Parade in what proved to be a Good Friday epic.

A goal down after a minute, Bradford rallied to lead 4-3 in a game in which four penalties were awarded, three of them to Derby. Craig Burley scored two but missed a third when Matt Clarke made an outstanding save. All four Bradford goals came in the first half, and while a win would have gone some way to securing their safety earlier, it is a game few will forget.

Remarkably, 21 per cent of their goals came in

HOW GOALS WERE CONCEDED 1999/2000

for the latest stats and to share your memories go to football.co.uk

key:
- header
- volley
- penalty
- close range*
- free kick
- inside area
- outside area
- own goal

* inside six yard box

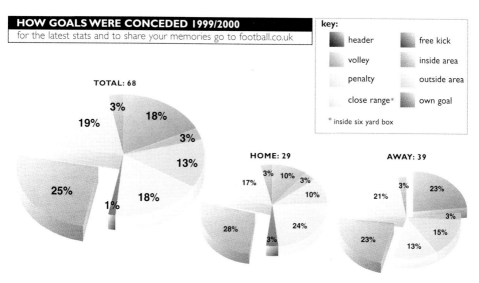

TOTAL: 68
3% — 18% — 19% — 3% — 13% — 25% — 1% — 18%

HOME: 29
3% — 10% — 3% — 17% — 10% — 28% — 3% — 24%

AWAY: 39
3% — 23% — 21% — 3% — 15% — 23% — 13%

Squad and Performance

SQUAD LIST

for the latest stats and to share your memories go to football.co.uk

Position	Name	Appearances	Appearances as substitute	Goals	Clean Sheets	Yellow Cards	Red Cards
G	M.Clarke	21			5		
G	A.Davison	5	1			1	
G	N.Southall	1					
G	G.Walsh	11			2		
D	J.Dreyer	11	3	1		4	
D	G.Halle	37	1			7	
D	W.Jacobs	22	2			3	
D	A.O'Brien	36		1		2	
D	A.Westwood	1	3			1	
D	D.Wetherall	38		2		6	
M	P.Beagrie	30	5	7		3	
M	J.Lawrence	19	4	3		3	
M	S.McCall	33	1	1		5	
M	A.Myers	10	3				1
M	N.Redfearn	14	3	1		5	
M	L.Sharpe	13	5			1	
M	G.Whalley	16		1			
F	D.Windass	36	2	10		5	
F	R.Blake	15	12	2		1	
F	J.Cadete	2	5				
F	G.Grant		1				
F	L.Mills	19	2	5		1	
F	I.Rankin		9				
F	B.Rodriguez		2				
F	D.Saunders	28	6	3		2	

those two extraordinary games against West Ham and Derby while they failed to score in 15 games.

Bradford did not show any particular preference for when they scored their goals though they were extremely vulnerable in the final 15 minutes when 17 of the 68 they conceded were scored. Away from home they were rarely a threat in the first half; they managed just three first half goals on their travels.

Bradford used four goalkeepers in the Carling Premiership but only 22 outfield players; most appearances came from Wetherall, the only ever-present at Valley Parade.

City failed to win at the homes of any of the top five though they did enjoy memorable home successes over Arsenal and Liverpool.

They were one of only two surviving teams who

TEAM PERFORMANCE TABLE

for the latest stats and to share your memories go to football.co.uk

Position	Club	Points Won	Percentage of points won at home	percentage of points won away	overall percentage of points won
1.	MANCHESTER UNITED	0/6			
2.	ARSENAL	3/6			
3.	LEEDS UNITED	0/6	47%	0%	23%
4.	LIVERPOOL	3/6			
5.	CHELSEA	1/6			
6.	ASTON VILLA	1/6			
7.	SUNDERLAND	3/6			
8.	LEICESTER CITY	3/6	33%	27%	30%
9.	TOTTENHAM HOTSPUR	2/6			
10.	WEST HAM UNITED	0/6			
11.	NEWCASTLE UNITED	3/6			
12.	MIDDLESBROUGH	4/6			
13.	EVERTON	1/6	40%	20%	30%
14.	SOUTHAMPTON	0/6			
15.	COVENTRY CITY	1/6			
16.	DERBY COUNTY	4/6			
17.	BRADFORD CITY	36 pts			
18.	WIMBLEDON	3/6	67%	25%	45%
19.	SHEFFIELD WEDNESDAY	1/6			
20.	WATFORD	3/6			

The figures show a team's performance against clubs in each quarter of the final league table. The first column represents points won from the total available against each team in the league.

Discipline and Season Summary

BOOKINGS BY POSITION 1997/1998 - 1999/2000
for the latest stats and to share your memories go to football.co.uk

key:
- forward
- defence
- midfield
- goalkeeper

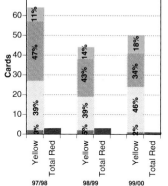

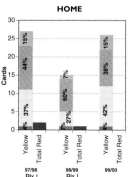

HOME

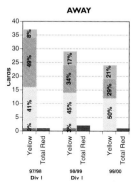

AWAY

Bradford City

failed to record a home and away double against any team; their best return came against Middlesbrough and Derby, who both surrendered four points to the Bantams. They were in best form when faced with the bottom five at home but, on their travels, they did better against teams sitting just outside the top five.

Only Andy Myers sent off, he was shown a red card for a second bookable offence during the 1-0 win over Derby at Pride Park in September. That was in stark and impressive contrast to the previous season when they received eight red cards on their way to promotion from Division One. Gunnar Halle, who missed only one game all season, collected seven cautions while David Wetherall received six yellow

cards. The attack may not have scored too many goals but they rarely troubled referees either.

On no fewer than 18 occasions last season Bradford were drawing at half time; any thoughts of comfort should have gone out of the window because they went on to lose 11, draw three and never went on to win. Similarly, a half time lead, rare though it was, was no indication of a full time success. Six times Bradford were ahead at the interval, all at Valley Parade, but they went on to win only four. Bradford also failed to recover from early set-backs on their travels; of the seven times they were behind away from home after 45 minutes, they went on to lose on each occasion.

HALF TIME - FULL TIME COMPARATIVE CHART
for the latest stats and to share your memories go to football.co.uk

HOME				AWAY				TOTAL			
Number of Home Half Time Wins	Full Time Result W	L	D	Number of Away Half Time Wins	Full Time Result W	L	D	Total Number of Half Time Wins	Full Time Result W	L	D
6	4	2		0	0	0	0	6	4	0	2
Number of Home Half Time Losses	Full Time Result W	L	D	Number of Away Half Time Losses	Full Time Result W	L	D	Total Number of Half Time Losses	Full Time Result W	L	D
7	0	4	3	7	0	7	0	14	0	11	3
Number of Home Half Time Draws	Full Time Result W	L	D	Number of Away Half Time Draws	Full Time Result W	L	D	Total Number of Half Time Draws	Full Time Result W	L	D
6	2	1	3	12	3	8	1	18	5	9	0

Maps and Directions

There is limited parking at the stadium. Street parking is for residents only. Supporters are advised to park in the city centre and walk to the ground (about 10 minutes).

All Routes:
Exit M62 at junction 26 and take M606 towards Bradford. Take last exit at end of motorway onto Rooley Lane (signposted Airport). McDonald's is on your left. At the second roundabout, turn into Wakefield Road and stay in the middle lane. Cross over the next two roundabouts staying in the middle lane (signs to Shipley & Skipton) on to Shipley Airedale Road which becomes Canal Road. Pass Staples Office Equipment showroom on your left. Turn left into Station Road and left again into Queens Road. Continue up the hill to the second traffic lights and turn left into Manningham Lane. After SAVE petrol station, take first left into Valley Parade for the Bradford and Bingley Stadium

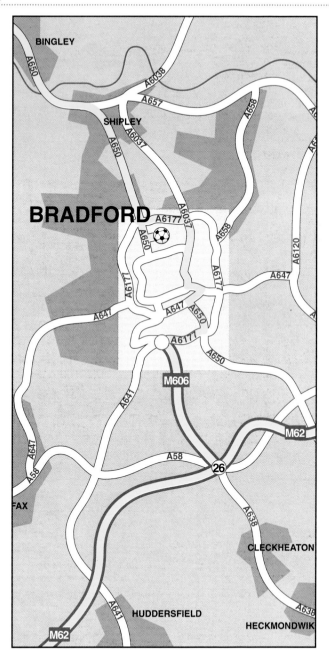

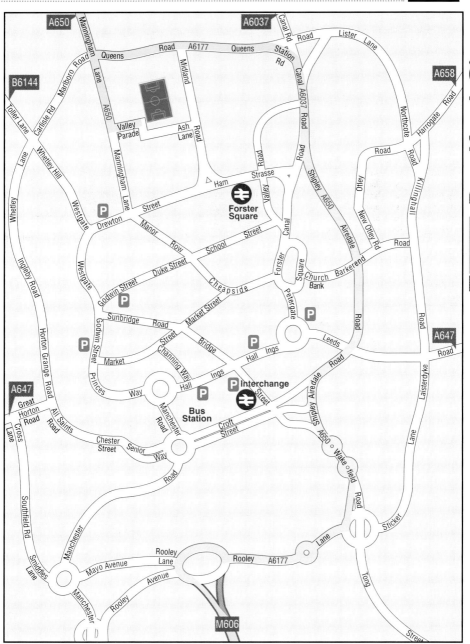

47

Club Honours

- Division 1 Champions: 1999-2000
- Division 3 Champions: 1928-29, 1934-35
- FA Cup Winners: 1947

Club Records

- Victory: 8-1 vs Middlesbrough, Division 1 September 12, 1953
- Defeat: 1-11 vs Aston Villa, Division 2 November 14, 1959
- League goals in a season (team): 107, Division 2, 1957-58
- League goals in a season (player): 32, Ralph Allen 1934-35 Division 3 (South)
- Career league goals: 153, Stuart Leary, 1953-62
- League appearances: 583, Sam Bartram 1934-56
- Transfer fee paid: £1,100,000 to Sheffield Utd for Graham Stuart, March 1999
- Transfer fee received £4,375,000 from Leeds United for Danny Mills, June 1999

Pos		Pld	W	D	L	F	A	Pts
1	Charlton	46	27	10	9	79	45	91

Charlton Athletic
"The Addicks"

The Valley, Floyd Road, Charlton
SE7 8BL
Tel:020 8333 4000
www.cafc.co.uk

Season Review by
John Ley

The Daily Telegraph

Since the Carling Premiership began only five teams have won promotion immediately after being relegated; Charlton are the latest and did so in highly impressive fashion. The Addicks made sure they had no hangovers after finishing 18th in the Carling Premiership in 1999; manager Alan Curbishley, tipped by Kevin Keegan as a potential future England coach, kept the basis of the team which had battled so gallantly, with only Danny Mills, Kevin Nicholls and Neil Redfearn departing.

Curbishley bought a new goalkeeper, spending £1 million on Bury's Dean Kiely, and his performances went some way to sending Charlton back to the Carling Premiership at the first attempt.

Later in the season John Salako arrived from Fulham, Mathias Svensson came from Crystal Palace, Andy Todd was bought for £750,000 from Bolton while the acquisition of defender Greg Shields, from Dunfermline, had the Valley buzzing. Sadly, his season was shortened by injury but if fit he could raise a few Carling Premiership eyebrows.

Useful Information

Charlton Athletic Superstore

The Valley, Floyd Road, Charlton, London SE7 8BL
Opening Times:
Monday-Friday: 10.00am-6.00pm
Saturdays: 10.00am-4.00pm
Matchday Saturdays: 10.00am-3.00pm and 4.30pm-6.00pm
Tel: **020 8333 4035**
Mail Order Service: **020 8333 4035**

Stadium Tours

Tour the facilities at The Valley with an experienced tour guide, plus a meal in Floyd's, The Valley's sports bar and diner for under £10 per adult.
Contact: **020 8333 4010**

Corporate Hospitality

There is a range of hospitality packages available some hosted by Charlton veterans.
Contact: **020 8333 4020**

Literature

Valley Review - on sale every matchday £2.50, Voice of the Yalley - on sale every matchday £1

What a difference a CARLING makes.

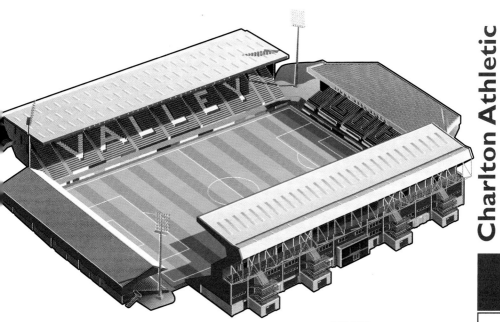

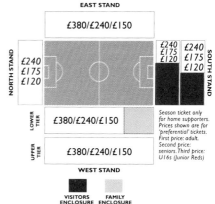

EAST STAND

£380/£240/£150

NORTH STAND		SOUTH STAND
£240 £175 £120		£240 £175 £120 / £240 £175 £120

LOWER TIER £380/£240/£150

UPPER TIER £380/£240/£150

WEST STAND

VISITORS ENCLOSURE   FAMILY ENCLOSURE

Season ticket only for home supporters. Prices shown are for 'preferential' tickets. First price: adult. Second price: seniors. Third price: U16s (Junior Reds)

The Valley
Opened: August 1, 1991
Capacity: 20,043
1999/2000 highest attendance: 20,043
1999/2000 average attendance: 19,557
Record attendance: 75,031

Pre-Match & Half Time Entertainment
Varies from match to match

Miscellaneous
Charlton Live online
live match broadcasts, and Sunday night radio shows (7-9pm) plus interviews with the stars.
Charlton Athletic run a series of coaching sessions for youngsters.

There are courses of varying lengths at many different locations, from Charlton to the South Coast. Contact the community scheme on **020 8850 2866**

Advertising & Sponsorship
Advertising and sponsorship packages available. Contact Commercial Department:
020 8333 4020

Booking Information
General Enquiries:
020 8333 4000
Credit Card Bookings:
020 8333 4010
Travel Club:
020 8265 5283
Junior Reds:
020 8265 5283

49

Results Breakdown

powered by **football.co.uk**

POINTS WON OR LOST AT BOTH HOME AND AWAY
for the latest stats and to share your memories go to football.co.uk

key:
☐ win ☐ draw
■ loss -O-league position
home fixtures are in red

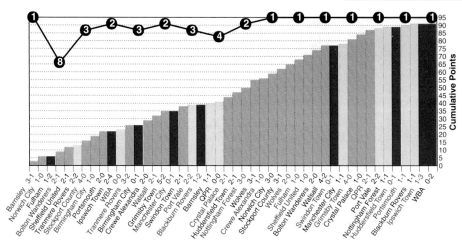

Charlton soon set the standard and when they went to the top of the First Division in January they did so by virtue of their first win – a 3-2 victory over Wolves – at Molineux for 47 years. It was a position they refused to relinquish.

That win came in a run that eventually ended in March, at home to Swindon, when a 1-0 defeat halted a club record run of 12 successive victories - two short of equalling the all time record held by Manchester United, Bristol City and Preston.

That amazing run saw Charlton run away with the

First Division lead; at one stage they were 14 points clear and with six games to play they went to Nottingham Forest capable of confirming promotion. But with nine minutes left Forest equalised Andy Hunt's goal and the champagne went on ice. In fact they failed to win in their last seven games and promotion was only confirmed when, a day after they had drawn with Portsmouth, Ipswich lost at Queens Park Rangers.

When Charlton were relegated they scored 41 goals; on their return they netted 79 and though that was nine

HOME   **AWAY**

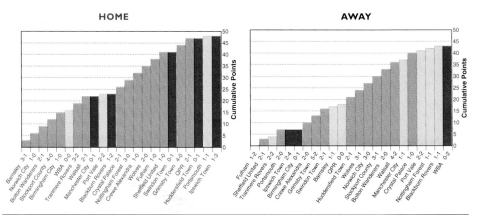

● = Red Card   = Yellow Card   ▲ = Player substituted   00= Time of goal

DATE	H/A	OPPONENT	H/T	F/T	POS	REFEREE	TEAM										SUBSTITUTES USED		
07/08	H	Barnsley	2-1	3-1	1	C.R.Wilkes	Kiely	Powell	Rufus	Youds	Brown	Newton ▲	Kinsella	Robinson	Stuart	Hunt ▲	Mendonca 6 25 81	Jones ▲	Pringle ▲	-
21/08	H	Norwich City	0-0	1-0	4	D.J.Gallagher	Kiely	Powell	Rufus 74	Youds	Brown	Newton	Kinsella	Robinson	Stuart	Hunt	Mendonca	-	-	-
28/08	A	Fulham	0-2	1-2	9	G.Poll	Kiely	Powell	Rufus	Youds	Brown ▲	Newton	Kinsella	Robinson 47	Stuart	Jones ▲	Mendonca	Hunt ▲	Parker ▲	Pringle ▲
11/09	H	Bolton Wanderers	1-1	2-1	8	J.P.Robinson	Kiely	Powell	Rufus	Youds	Shields	Newton	Kinsella	Robinson ▲	Stuart ●22	Pringle ▲	Mendonca 49	Brown ▲	Salako ▲	McCammon ▲
18/09	A	Sheffield United	1-1	2-1	7	K.A.Leach	Kiely	Konchesky	Rufus	Youds	Shields	Newton	Kinsella	Robinson ▲	Stuart ▲	Hunt 31 72	Mendonca	Brown ▲	Salako ▲	-
25/09	A	Tranmere Rovers	1-1	2-2	7	M.G.Cowburn	Kiely	Konchesky	Rufus	Youds	Shields	Newton	Kinsella 70	Robinson ▲	Parker ▲	McCammon ▲	Mendonca 24	Hunt ▲	Barness ▲	Salako ▲
28/09	H	Stockport County	0-0	4-0	3	P.S.Danson	Kiely	Powell	Rufus	Youds	Shields	Newton	Kinsella	Robinson ▲	Parker ▲	Hunt 48 89 90	Mendonca ▲65	Pringle ▲	Salako ▲	-
02/10	H	Birmingham City	1-0	1-0	1	C.J.Foy	Kiely	Powell	Rufus	Youds	Shields 28	Newton	Kinsella	Robinson ▲	Parker ▲	Hunt	Mendonca	Pringle ▲	Salako ▲	Brown ▲
16/10	A	Portsmouth	1-0	1-0	1	P.Rejer	Kiely	Powell	Rufus	Youds	Shields	Newton	Kinsella	Robinson ▲ 43	Jones	Hunt ▲	Mendonca	Salako ▲90	Pringle ▲	-
19/10	A	Ipswich Town	2-2	2-4	2	P.Dowd	Kiely	Powell ▲	Rufus	Youds	Shields	Newton	Kinsella	Robinson	Jones ▲	Hunt 7 11	Stuart ▲	Barness ▲	Salako ▲	Brown ▲
23/10	H	West Brom	0-0	0-0	2	G.P.Barber	Kiely	Konchesky	Rufus	Youds	Shields	Newton ● ▲	Kinsella	Robinson	Jones ▲	Hunt	Mendonca	Salako ▲	Stuart ▲	McCammon ▲
26/10	H	Tranmere Rovers	1-0	2-0	1	W.M.Jordan	Kiely	Konchesky	Rufus 75	Youds	Shields	Newton ▲	Stuart	Robinson 62	Jones	Hunt	Mendonca	Brown ▲48	Salako ▲	-
30/10	A	Birmingham City	0-1	0-1	3	M.D.Messias	Kiely	Powell ▲	Salako ▲	Youds	Shields	Pringle ▲	Stuart	Robinson	Jones	Hunt	Mendonca	Brown ▲	Parker ▲	-
02/11	A	Crewe Alexandra	2-0	2-0	2	J.A.Kirkby	Kiely	Powell	Brown	Youds	Shields	Pringle ▲30	Kinsella	Robinson	Jones	Hunt	Stuart 13	Newton ▲	Salako ▲	-
06/11	H	Walsall	1-1	2-1	2	P.Walton	Kiely	Powell	Rufus	Youds	Shields	Pringle ▲	Kinsella	Robinson ▲	Jones ● ▲	Hunt ▲45	Stuart 76	Pringle ▲	Brown ▲	McCammon ▲
12/11	H	Grimsby Town	2-1	5-2	2	G.B.Frankland	Ilic	Powell 76	Rufus 13 36	Youds ▲	Shields	Stuart	Kinsella	Robinson	Jones	Hunt 67	Mendonca 62	Salako ▲	Brown ▲	-
20/11	H	Manchester City	0-0	0-1	3	R.D.Furnandiz	Kiely	Powell	Rufus	Brown	Shields ▲	Stuart ▲	Kinsella	Robinson	Jones	Hunt	Mendonca	Salako ▲	Pringle ▲	-
23/11	A	Swindon Town	2-1	2-1	2	S.W.Mathieson	Kiely	Powell	Rufus	Youds	Shields	Newton ▲39	Kinsella	Robinson 24	Jones	Hunt	Mendonca	Todd ▲	Pringle ▲	-
27/11	H	Port Vale	2-0	2-2	3	M.Fletcher	Kiely	Powell	Rufus	Youds	Brown	Newton ▲	Kinsella	Robinson	Jones	Hunt	Mendonca 16 39	Salako ▲	Pringle ▲	Stuart ▲
30/11	H	Blackburn Rovers	1-1	1-2	3	R.Styles	Kiely	Powell ▲	Rufus	Youds	Brown ●	Newton 44	Kinsella	Robinson ▲	Jones ▲	Hunt	Mendonca	Pringle ▲	Salako ▲	Stuart ▲
04/12	A	Barnsley	1-1	1-1	3	A.Bates	Kiely	Powell	Rufus	Youds	Brown	Newton	Kinsella	Robinson ▲	Salako ▲	Jones 42	Mendonca	Pringle ▲	Todd ▲	-
18/12	A	QPR	0-0	0-0	4	P.Taylor	Kiely	Powell	Rufus	Youds	Shields	Newton ▲	Parker	Salako ▲	Jones	Hunt	Mendonca	Pringle ▲	Robinson ▲	-
26/12	H	Crystal Palace	2-1	2-1	3	A.G.Wiley	Kiely	Powell	Rufus	Youds	Brown	Newton	Kinsella	Salako ▲12	Jones ▲	Hunt	Pringle 13	Todd ▲	Robinson ▲	-
28/12	A	Huddersfield Town	0-0	2-0	1	M.J.Brandwood	Kiely	Powell ▲	Rufus	Youds ▲	Shields ●	Newton	Kinsella ▲	Robinson 35	Jones	Hunt 29	Pringle	Salako ▲	Brown ▲	Todd ▲
03/01	H	Nottingham Forest	1-0	3-0	1	K.M.Lynch	Kiely	Powell	Rufus	Brown	Shields 7	Newton	Todd	Robinson	Stuart ▲68	Hunt ▲79	Pringle ▲	Parker ▲	Salako ▲	McDonald ▲
11/01	A	Wolves	2-1	3-1	1	M.R.Halsey	Kiely	Powell	Rufus 42	Brown	Shields	Newton	Kinsella	Robinson ▲72	Stuart ▲	Hunt	Pringle ▲45	Salako ▲	Todd ▲	McDonald ▲
15/01	H	Crewe Alexandra	1-0	1-0	1	R.Pearson	Kiely	Konchesky	Rufus	Brown	Shields	Newton	Kinsella	Robinson	Stuart 12	Hunt	Pringle ▲	Todd ▲	-	-
22/01	A	Norwich City	1-0	3-0	1	M.J.Jones	Kiely	Powell	Rufus	Brown	Shields	Newton	Todd	Robinson	Stuart	Hunt 41 73 78	Pringle	-	-	-
05/02	A	Stockport County	2-1	3-1	1	T.A.Parkes	Kiely	Powell	Rufus	Brown	Barness	Newton	Todd	Robinson ▲	Stuart	Hunt 41 45 88	Pringle	Salako ▲	Svensson ▲	-
12/02	H	Wolves	0-0	2-0	1	D.Laws	Kiely	Powell	Rufus	Brown 69	Barness	Newton	Todd	Robinson	Stuart ▲48	Hunt	Pringle ▲	Svensson ▲	-	-
15/02	H	Fulham	0-0	1-0	1	A.R.Hall	Kiely	Powell	Rufus	Brown	Barness ▲	Newton	Todd	Robinson ● 60	Stuart	Hunt	Pringle ▲	Tiler ▲	Svensson ▲	-
26/02	H	Sheffield United	0-0	1-0	1	P.S.Danson	Kiely	Powell	Rufus	Brown	Barness ▲	Newton	Kinsella ●	Robinson ▲47	Stuart	Hunt	Svensson	Tiler ▲	Pringle ▲	Todd ▲
04/03	A	Bolton Wanderers	0-0	2-0	1	P.Dowd	Kiely	Powell ▲	Rufus	Brown	Barness	Newton	Kinsella	Robinson	Stuart	Hunt 80	Svensson ▲	Tiler ▲	Konchesky ▲	Pringle ▲79
07/03	A	Walsall	3-1	4-2	1	W.C.Burns	Kiely	Powell	Rufus	Brown	Barness	Newton	Kinsella 44 66	Robinson	Stuart ▲	Hunt 25 33	Svensson ▲	Tiler ▲	Pringle ▲	-
11/03	H	Swindon Town	0-1	0-1	1	R.J.Oliver	Kiely	Powell ▲	Rufus	Brown	Barness	Newton	Kinsella	Robinson	Stuart	Hunt	Svensson	Salako ▲	Pringle ▲	-
19/03	H	Manchester City	1-1	1-1	1	J.A.Kirkby	Kiely	Powell	Tiler	Brown	Barness	Newton	Kinsella	Robinson ▲42	Stuart	Hunt	Svensson	Salako ▲	-	-
22/03	H	Grimsby Town	1-0	4-0	1	M.L.Dean	Kiely	Powell	Rufus	Brown ▲	Barness	Newton 7	Kinsella	Robinson	Stuart	Hunt ▲60	Svensson 53	Kitson ▲	Parker ▲	Tiler ▲84
25/03	A	Crystal Palace	0-0	1-0	1	C.J.Foy	Kiely	Powell	Rufus	Tiler	Barness	Newton ▲	Kinsella	Robinson	Stuart	Hunt	Svensson	Salako ▲	Kitson ▲82	Konchesky ▲
31/03	H	QPR	0-0	2-1	1	G.B.Frankland	Kiely	Powell	Rufus	Tiler	Barness	Newton	Kinsella	Robinson	Stuart	Hunt	Svensson	-	-	-
04/04	A	Port Vale	0-0	2-2	1	W.M.Jordan	Kiely	Powell	Rufus 63	Brown	Barness	Newton	Kinsella	Robinson	Stuart	Hunt 74	Kitson ▲	Tiler ▲	Parker ▲	Svensson ▲
08/04	A	Nottingham Forest	1-0	1-1	1	G.Laws	Kiely	Powell	Rufus	Brown	Barness	Newton ▲	Kinsella	Robinson	Stuart	Hunt 40	Svensson ▲	Parker ▲	Pringle ▲	-
14/04	H	Huddersfield Town	0-1	0-1	1	M.J.Jones	Kiely	Powell ▲	Rufus	Brown	Barness	Newton	Kinsella	Robinson	Stuart 65	Hunt	Svensson	McDonald ▲	Parker ▲	-
21/04	H	Portsmouth	0-0	1-0	1	T.Heilbron	Kiely	Powell	Rufus	Brown	Barness	Newton	Kinsella	Robinson ●	Stuart	Hunt	Svensson	-	-	-
24/04	A	Blackburn Rovers	1-0	1-1	1	K.M.Lynch	Kiely	Powell	Rufus	Brown	Barness	Newton	Kinsella	Robinson	Stuart	Hunt ▲	Svensson 23	Parker ▲	Kitson ▲	-
29/04	H	Ipswich Town	0-1	1-3	1	P.R.Richards	Kiely	Powell	Rufus	Brown	Tiler	Newton	Kinsella	Robinson	Stuart	Hunt 82	Kitson ▲	Parker ▲	Svensson ▲	-
07/05	A	West Brom	0-0	0-2	1	D.Pugh	Kiely	Barness	Rufus	Konchesky	Tiler	Newton ▲	Kinsella	Robinson ●	Parker	Hunt	Svensson ▲	Stuart ▲	Salako ▲	-

Charlton Athletic

51

Goal Analysis

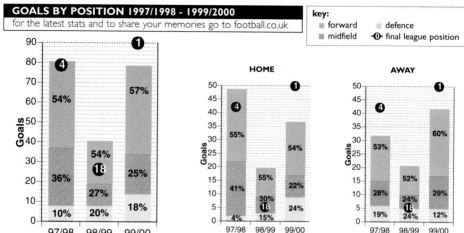

GOALS BY POSITION 1997/1998 - 1999/2000
for the latest stats and to share your memories go to football.co.uk

key:
■ forward   ■ defence
■ midfield   -0- final league position

short of Barnsley, who scored 88 First Division goals, the fact that they scored almost twice as many goals as in the previous season came as a welcome boost.

Andy Hunt, who had managed just seven goals the previous season, scored 24, one more than Clive Mendonca claimed when Charlton last won promotion to the Carling Premiership. It was, by some distance, Hunt's best season for scoring goals; his previous best League return was with West Bromwich Albion when he scored 15 in the 1996-97 season.

Hunt's goals included three hat-tricks, two of those coming in successive games, at Norwich City and Stockport County. Strangely, Hunt scored far more goals away from home than he did at The Valley. He claimed seven at home but 17 away, representing 71 per cent of all his League goals.

It is just as well Hunt kept fit – he missed only three games – because the next highest Addicks scorer was Mendonca, with nine goals in 19 starts.

Winger John Robinson was in troublesome form

GOALS BY TIME PERIOD 1999/2000
for the latest stats and to share your memories go to football.co.uk

key:
■ goals for   ■ goals against

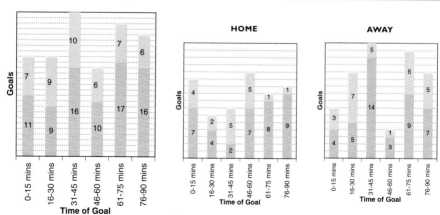

What a difference a *CARLING* makes.

Goal Analysis

powered by football.co.uk

Charlton Athletic

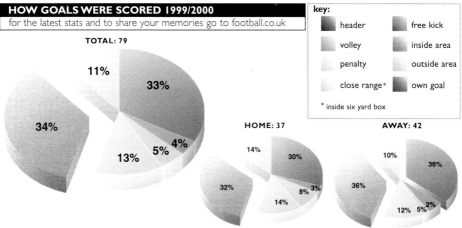

key:
- header
- volley
- penalty
- close range*
- free kick
- inside area
- outside area
- own goal

* inside six yard box

TOTAL: 79

11% · 33% · 34% · 4% · 5% · 13%

HOME: 37

14% · 30% · 32% · 3% · 8% · 14%

AWAY: 42

10% · 36% · 36% · 2% · 5% · 12%

throughout the season; the Welsh international claimed eight goals but also made a large percentage of Hunt's impressive total.

The defence offered greater contribution in the goals department with Richard Rufus using his strength and height to great effect, particularly at corners, to claim six goals - not bad for a player who had managed just one League goal in his previous five seasons with Charlton. In fact, no team in the Carling Premiership last season had a defence that provided

more goals than the 14 Charlton's back line scored. Steve Brown and Greg Shields both added two goals from defence.

Charlton conceded only 18 goals at The Valley but they were strangely vulnerable either side of half time there; in the 15 minutes before and after the interval they conceded 10, representing 55 per cent.

Goals were supplied from all areas with as many coming from headers than inside the penalty area. Similarly, Charlton were equally vulnerable from

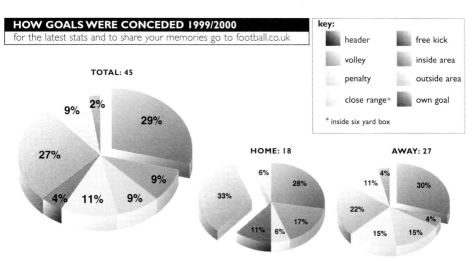

key:
- header
- volley
- penalty
- close range*
- free kick
- inside area
- outside area
- own goal

* inside six yard box

TOTAL: 45

9% · 2% · 29% · 27% · 9% · 4% · 11% · 9%

HOME: 18

6% · 28% · 33% · 17% · 11% · 6%

AWAY: 27

4% · 30% · 11% · 22% · 4% · 15% · 15%

Squad and Performance

powered by  football.co.uk

SQUAD LIST

for the latest stats and to share your memories go to football.co.uk

Position	Name	Appearances	Appearances as substitute	Goals Clean Sheets	Yellow Cards	Red Cards
G	S.Ilic	1				
G	D.Kiely	45		16	1	
D	A.Barness	17	2		1	
D	S.Brown	29	10	2	7	
D	P.Konchesky	6	2		2	
D	C.Powell	40		1	2	
D	R.Rufus	44		6	9	
D	G.Shields	21		2	1	
D	C.Tiler	4	7	1		
D	A.Todd	5	7		1	
D	E.Youds	23			8	
M	K.Jones	16	1	1	1	
M	M.Kinsella	38		3	7	
M	S.Newton	41	1	4	2	
M	S.Parker	5	10	1	1	
M	J.Robinson	43	2	9	8	
M	J.Salako	4	23	2	1	
F	A.Hunt	43	1	24	3	
F	S.Jones	1				
F	P.Kitson	2	4	1		
F	M.McCammon	1	3			
F	C.McDonald		3			
F	C.Mendonca	19		9	1	
F	M.Pringle	12	19	4	2	
F	G.Stuart	33	4	7	2	1
F	M.Svensson	13	5	2	1	

headers and penalty box assaults.

Charlton struggled against few teams, though they were beaten twice by arch-rivals Manchester City and took only one point, at Portman Road, off Ipswich. However, they did secure home and away victories over no fewer than nine teams including promotion-chasing Bolton.

Of their games against the top five rivals, Charlton's only away success came at the Reebok Stadium, where goals from Martin Pringle and Hunt gave them a valuable away victory.

While Hunt played 43 times, Dean Kiely missed only one game and kept a club record 16 clean sheets. Rufus, Robinson and the ever-improving Shaun Newton were also rarely absent offering Charlton the

TEAM PERFORMANCE TABLE

for the latest stats and to share your memories go to football.co.uk

Position	Club	Points Won	Percentage of points won at home	percentage of points won away	overall percentage of points won
1.	CHARLTON	91pts			
2.	MANCHESTER CITY	1/6			
3.	IPSWICH	0/6			
4.	BARNSLEY	4/6	60%	33%	47%
5.	BIRMINGHAM	3/6			
6.	BOLTON	6/6			
7.	WOLVES	6/6			
8.	HUDDERSFIELD	3/6			
9.	FULHAM	3/6			
10.	QPR	4/6	67%	50%	58%
11.	BLACKBURN	1/6			
12.	TRANMERE	4/6			
13.	NORWICH	6/6			
14.	NOTTINGHAM FOREST	4/6			
15.	SHEFFIELD UNITED	6/6			
16.	CRYSTAL PALACE	6/6	89%	89%	89%
17.	STOCKPORT	6/6			
18.	PORTSMOUTH	4/6			
19.	CREWE	6/6			
20.	GRIMSBY	6/6			
21.	WBA	1/6			
22.	WALSALL	6/6	61%	72%	67%
23.	PORT VALE	2/6			
24.	SWINDON	3/6			

The figures show a team's performance against clubs in each quarter of the final league table. The first column represents points won from the total available against each team in the league.

What a difference a CARLING makes.

Discipline and Season Summary

Charlton Athletic

BOOKINGS BY POSITION 1997/1998 - 1999/2000

for the latest stats and to share your memories go to football.co.uk

key:
- forward
- midfield
- defence
- goalkeeper

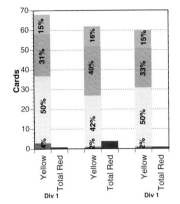

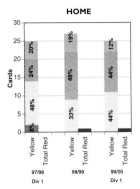

HOME

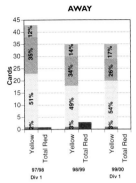

AWAY

type of consistency invaluable in chasing promotion.

Charlton's discipline was good with just one red card collected throughout 46 First Division games – only Crewe avoided any dismissals during the season in Division One. That was a vast improvement on the previous season when four red cards were administered to Charlton players.

The player with the worst bookings total was Rufus, who received nine cautions, meaning that the defence was responsible for half the total of bookings.

More cautions were received away than at home overall with midfielders booked considerably more away from The Valley than in south east London.

The records show that if Charlton are leading at half time they do not lose. On 18 occasions they led at

the interval and went on to win 15 while drawing the other three.

Of those games, eight were at The Valley and only once did they fail to claim the three points that looked likely at the interval, when they were leading 2-0 against Port Vale, with two first half strikes from Clive Mendonca, but a Martin Foyle equaliser spoiled Charlton's record.

They were also in the mood when being held at half time; on 20 occasions they were level after 45 minutes but in half of those games they turned it round their way, losing only four. But on the eight occasions they were losing at half time they went on to win just once, over-turning a 2-0 half time deficit against Tranmere to win 3-2, Rufus snatching a 75th minute winner.

HALF TIME - FULL TIME COMPARATIVE CHART

for the latest stats and to share your memories go to football.co.uk

HOME				AWAY				TOTAL			
Number of Home Half Time Wins	Full Time Result W	L	D	Number of Away Half Time Wins	Full Time Result W	L	D	Total Number of Half Time Wins	Full Time Result W	L	D
8	7	0	1	10	8	0	2	18	15	0	3
Number of Home Half Time Losses	Full Time Result W	L	D	Number of Away Half Time Losses	Full Time Result W	L	D	Total Number of Half Time Losses	Full Time Result W	L	D
5	1	3	1	3	0	2	1	8	1	5	2
Number of Home Half Time Draws	Full Time Result W	L	D	Number of Away Half Time Draws	Full Time Result W	L	D	Total Number of Half Time Draws	Full Time Result W	L	D
10	7	2	1	10	3	2	5	20	10	4	6

Maps and Directions

Charlton are located in South-East London, near the Millennium Dome and the Thames Barrier. Parking at The Valley is extremely difficult.

By Car:

Leave the M25 at Junction 2. Head towards London on the A2 and continue on this road for about ten miles. The exit signs for 'A2 Central London' should be ignored - continue along the dual carriageway. This road becomes the A102(M) Blackwall Tunnel approach road. Leave at the junction after the A2 exit (for those coming through the tunnel, this is the exit after that for the Dome). Turn right at the roundabout under the flyover (left for those coming through the tunnel) on to the A206 Woolwich Road. After the major set of traffic lights at the junction of Charlton Church Lane and Anchor and Hope Lane, turn right at the second roundabout into Charlton Lane, go across the railway crossing and take the first right, which is Harvey Gardens. This road leads to the ground.

From Central London:

Take the A13 until it becomes the East India Dock Road and take the A102 through the Blackwall Tunnel. From East London, moterists can go through Blackwall Tunnel or use the Woolwich free ferry at North Woolwich. After coming off the ferry, turn right at the roundabout and follow the Woolwich Road until Charlton Lane.

Public Transport:

Connex runs train services to Charlton railway station, which is about a two minute walk from the stadium.

There are limited services from Cannon Street (midweek) and Victoria. Other public transport links include the Docklands Light Railway (change for train or bus connections at Greenwich or Lewisham) and the North Greenwich station on the Jubilee Line. There is an extensive bus network serving the Charlton area around The Valley. The routes include the 177, 180, 472, 161, 53, and 54. The M1 service provides an overland link to Charlton train station from the North Greenwich tube station.

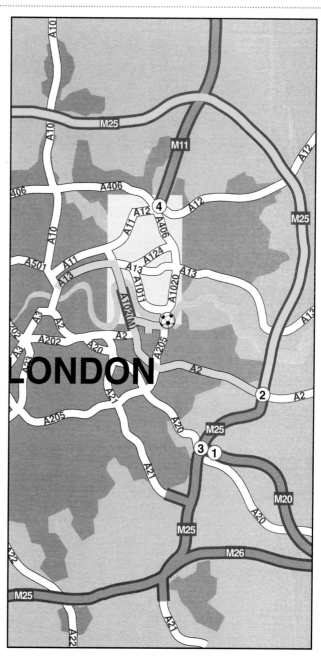

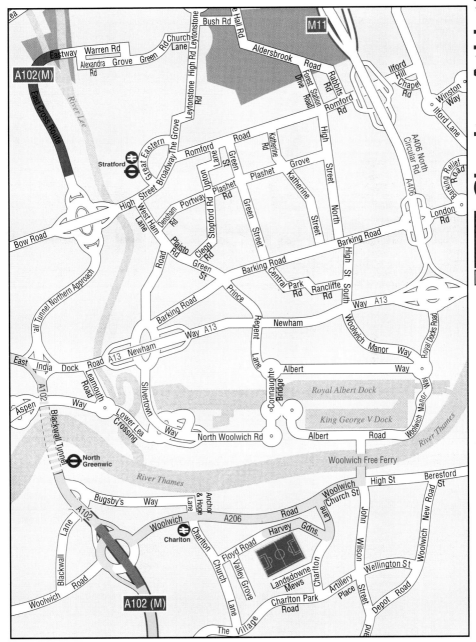

Club Honours

- Football League Champions: 1954-55
- Division 2 Champions: 1983-84, 1988-89
- FA Cup Winners: 1970, 1997, 2000
- League Cup Winners: 1965, 1998
- Full Members' Cup Winners: 1986
- Zenith Data Systems Cup Winners: 1990
- European Cup Winners' Cup Winners: 1997-98
- European Super Cup Winners: 1998

Club Records

- Victory: 13-0 v Jeunesse Hautcharage, European Cup Winners' Cup, September 29, 1971
- Defeat: 1-8 v Wolverhampton Wanderers, Division 1, September 26, 1953
- League goals in a season (team): 98, Division 1, 1960-61
- League goals in a season (player): 41, Jimmy Greaves, 1960-61
- Career league goals: 164, Bobby Tambling, 1958-70
- League appearances: 655, Ron Harris, 1962-80
- Transfer fee paid: £15,000,000 to Athletico Madrid for Jimmy Floyd Hasselbaink, June 2000
- Transfer fee received: £4,500,000 from Leeds for Michael Dubery,

Pos		Pld	W	D	L	F	A	Pts
5	Chelsea	38	18	11	9	53	34	65

Chelsea   "The Blues"

Stamford Bridge, Fulham Road,
London SW6 1HS
Tel: 020 7385 5545
www.chelseafc.co.uk

Season Review by
John Ley

𝕿𝖍𝖊 𝕯𝖆𝖎𝖑𝖞 𝕿𝖊𝖑𝖊𝖌𝖗𝖆𝖕𝖍

Gianluca Vialli will have spent the summer considering where his priorities lie. Last season his multi-national force excelled in cup competitions but at the expense of the Carling Premiership; ultimately they had to win the FA Cup to guarantee a place back in Europe. Vialli spent more than £13 million on recruitments in the summer of 1999; he topped that with one purchase a year later; the arrival of Jimmy Floyd Hasselbaink for a British record-equalling £15 million. He added to that by signing Bolton's Eidur Gudjohnsen for £4 million. Those signings should have a greater effect than the £10 million arrival of Chris Sutton, who was a huge disappointment last season. The continued absence of Pierluigi Casiraghi and injuries to Roberto Di Matteo and Graeme Le Saux also weakened Vialli's hand. The manager, who fielded the first ever all-foreign XI in the Carling Premiership at Southampton, has vowed to buy British in the future after a season of inconsistencies.

Useful Information

The Chelsea Megastore
Stamford Bridge, Chelsea Village
Opening Times:
Monday-Saturday: 10.00am-6.00pm
Sundays: 11.00am-4.00pm
Opening Times (matchdays only):
Saturdays: 10.00am-7.00pm
Sundays (3pm): 12.00pm-6.00pm*
Sundays (4pm): 10.00am-4.00pm*
Midweek: 10.00am-10.30pm*
*closed for duration of match
Tel: 020 7565 1490

The Chelsea Store
2/3 Friary Street, Guildford, Surrey
Opening Times:
Monday-Friday: 9.30am-5.30pm
Saturdays: 9.30am-6.00pm
Sundays: open in peak seasons
Tel: 01483 449 122
Fax: 01483 449 120
Mail Order Service: 0870 603 0005

Stadium Tours
Non-matchdays only.
Contact: 0870 603 0005

Corporate Hospitality
Various matchday packages, match and matchball sponsorship available.
Contact Carole Phair or Michelle Macdonald: 0171 385 7809
Conference and banqueting
Tel: 020 7385 7980

What a difference a CARLING makes.

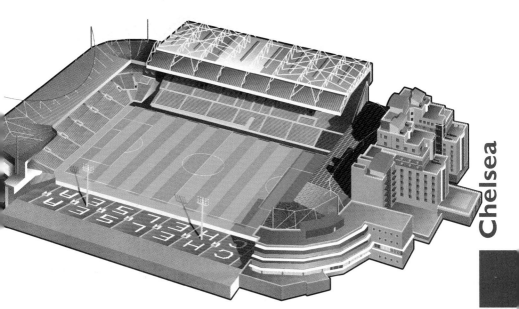

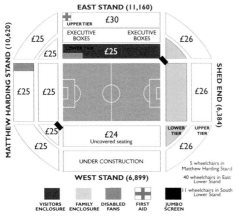

EAST STAND (11,160)

MATTHEW HARDING STAND (10,620)

£30 UPPER TIER

EXECUTIVE BOXES — EXECUTIVE BOXES

£25 — £26

£25 LOWER TIER £25

£25 £25

£25 £25

£24 Uncovered seating

£25 LOWER TIER / UPPER TIER £26

£25

SHED END (6,384)

£26

UNDER CONSTRUCTION

WEST STAND (6,899)

5 wheelchairs in Matthew Harding Stand
40 wheelchairs in East Lower Stand
11 wheelchairs in South Lower Stand

VISITORS ENCLOSURE — FAMILY ENCLOSURE — DISABLED FANS — FIRST AID — JUMBO SCREEN

Stamford Bridge

Opened: April 28, 1877 (football first played September 4, 1905)
Capacity: 35,461
1999/2000 highest attendance: 35,113
1999/2000 average attendance: 34,637
Record attendance: 82,905

Chelsea Village Hotel
Tel: **020 7565 1400**
The Court Hotel – 131 bedrooms.
Tel: **020 7565 1400**

Literature
Programme £3
Official Chelsea magazine £2.50

Matchday Commentary
Tel: **09068 121159**

Pre-Match & Half Time Entertainment
Channel Chelsea - transmitting matchdays in concourses with player interviews, match replays, fan interviews etc.

Restaurants
Fishnets (seafood): **020 7565 1430**
Arkles (Irish): **020 7565 1420**
Kings Brasserie: **020 7565 1435**

Booking Information
General Enquiries :
020 7385 5545
Credit Card Bookings:
020 7386 7799
Travel Club
(Elizabeth Duff Travel):
0345 023 243
Chelsea Village Hotel:
020 7565 1400

Results Breakdown

powered by  football.co.uk

POINTS WON OR LOST AT BOTH HOME AND AWAY

for the latest stats and to share your memories go to football.co.uk

key:
- win
- draw
- loss
- -0- league position

home fixtures are in red

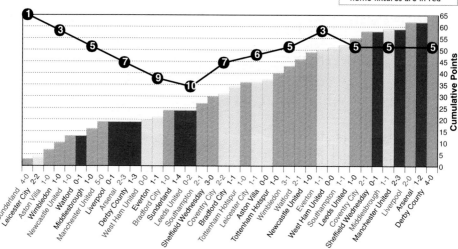

An opening day 4-0 win over newly-promoted Sunderland saw Chelsea at the top but it was the last time they would enjoy such lofty heights; five defeats and two draws from eight games over a two month spell before Christmas sent Vialli's side to 10th – their lowest position for 15 months and one from which they never really recovered.

Home defeats by title rivals Arsenal and Leeds damaged Chelsea's pride as well as their championship aspirations but it was away from home where Chelsea let slip. With minds on the extended Champions'

League programme, they struggled away from Stamford Bridge and once the FA Cup final was on the horizon, League form slumped with Chelsea losing their last three away games.

They did, however, enjoy a purple patch when they went 16 Carling Premiership games without defeat, starting from the moment they slumped to their lowly 10th position. The run began at Southampton on Boxing Day and continued right through to April, when they suffered a shock 1-0 defeat at the hands of Sheffield Wednesday.

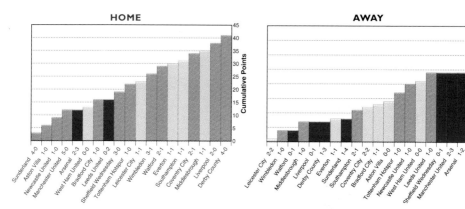

powered by football.co.uk

Chelsea

Legend: ● = Red Card ○ = Yellow Card ▲ = Player substituted 00 = Time of goal

DATE	H/A	OPPONENT	H/T	F/T	POS	REFEREE	TEAM											SUBSTITUTES USED		
07/08	H	Sunderland	2-0	4-0	1	M.A.Riley	de Goey	Ferrer	Desailly	Leboeuf	Le Saux	Petrescu ▲	Deschamps	Wise	Poyet ▲20 78	Zola 32	Sutton ▲	di Matteo ▲	Babayaro ▲	Flo ▲77
14/08	A	Leicester City	0-1	2-2	6	S.J.Lodge	de Goey	Ferrer ○	Hogh	Leboeuf	Le Saux	Petrescu ▲	Babayaro	Wise ○48	Poyet ○	Zola ▲	Flo	Goldbaek ▲	Sutton ▲	Sutton ◄
21/08	A	Aston Villa	0-0	1-0	4	N.S.Barry	de Goey	Ferrer	Desailly	Leboeuf	Babayaro	Petrescu ▲	Morris	Wise	Poyet	Zola ▲	Sutton	Goldbaek ▲	Flo ▲	Ambrosetti ◄
28/08	A	Wimbledon	0-0	1-0	3	S.W.Dunn	de Goey	Ferrer	Desailly	Leboeuf ▲78	Babayaro	Petrescu ▲78	Deschamps ▲	Wise	Poyet	Zola	Flo ▲	Ambrosetti ▲	Morris ▲	Sutton ◄
11/09	H	Newcastle United	1-0	1-0	2	G.Poll	de Goey	Ferrer ○	Desailly	Leboeuf ○37	Le Saux	Petrescu ○	Morris	Wise ○	Goldbaek ▲	Zola	Flo ▲	Petrescu ▲	Petrescu ▲	Poyet ◄
18/09	A	Watford	0-1	1-0	5	M.D.Reed	de Goey	Lambourde 55	Desailly	Hogh	Le Saux	Petrescu	Deschamps	Morris	Ambrosetti ▲	Zola	Sutton ▲	Petrescu ▲	Zola ▲	Flo ◄
25/09	A	Middlesbrough	0-0	1-0	5	P.E.Alcock	de Goey	Ferrer	Hogh	Leboeuf	Le Saux	Petrescu ▲	Deschamps	Wise	Poyet 1 54	Zola	Sutton 16	Morris ▲	Babayaro ▲	Flo ◄
03/10	H	Manchester United	2-0	5-0	5	D.J.Gallagher	de Goey	Ferrer	Desailly ●	Hogh	Babayaro	Petrescu	Deschamps ○	Wise	Poyet 81	Zola	Sutton	Morris ▲	Morris ▲80	Flo ◄
16/10	A	Liverpool	0-1	0-1	6	M.D.Reed	de Goey	Ferrer	Desailly	Leboeuf	Le Saux	Petrescu ▲	Deschamps	Wise ●	Poyet	Zola	Sutton	Le Saux ▲	Morris ▲	·
23/10	A	Arsenal	1-0	2-3	7	A.B.Wilkie	de Goey	Ferrer	Hogh ▲	Leboeuf ▲10	Babayaro	Petrescu 51	Deschamps	Morris	Poyet	Flo ▲39	Flo 15	Lambourde ▲	Le Saux ▲	Harley ◄
30/10	A	Derby County	1-1	1-3	8	R.J.Harris	de Goey	Ferrer	Desailly	Leboeuf ○	Babayaro	di Matteo	Ambrosetti ○	Wise	Ambrosetti ▲	Zola	Sutton	Lambourde ▲	Zola ▲	Hogh ◄
07/11	H	West Ham United	0-0	0-0	9	M.A.Riley	de Goey	Ferrer	Hogh	Leboeuf ●	Babayaro	Petrescu	Deschamps	Morris	Poyet	Zola ▲	Sutton ▲	Deschamps ▲	Ambrosetti ▲	·
20/11	H	Everton	0-1	1-1	9	M.R.Halsey	de Goey	Ferrer	Hogh	Hogh	Babayaro	Petrescu	Deschamps	Morris	Ambrosetti ○	Zola ▲90	Flo 43	Ambrosetti ▲	Zola ▲	·
28/11	A	Bradford City	1-0	1-0	8	A.G.Wiley	de Goey	Ferrer	Desailly ▲	Hogh	Babayaro	Harley	Deschamps	Morris	Poyet	di Matteo	Flo	Zola ▲	Wollaston ▲	Terry ◄
04/12	A	Sunderland	0-4	1-4	8	S.W.Dunn	de Goey	Lambourde	Thome	Leboeuf	Babayaro	Petrescu ▲	Morris	Wise ▲	Poyet	di Matteo	Flo ▲35	Goldbaek ▲	Hogh ▲	Zola ◄
19/12	H	Leeds United	0-0	2-0	10	J.T.Winter	de Goey	Ferrer	Thome	Leboeuf	Harley	Harley	Deschamps	Wise ▲	Poyet	Zola	Sutton ▲	Goldbaek ▲	Hogh ▲	di Matteo ◄
26/12	H	Southampton	2-0	2-1	9	P.E.Alcock	de Goey	Lambourde	Desailly	Leboeuf ▲	Babayaro	di Matteo	Deschamps	Wise	Poyet	Flo ▲	Flo 55 82	Hogh ▲	Morris ▲84	·
29/12	A	Sheffield Wednesday	2-0	3-0	7	A.P.D'Urso	de Goey	Lambourde	Thome	Thome	Babayaro	di Matteo	Deschamps ▲	Wise ▲	Poyet	di Matteo	Sutton ▲	Morris ▲	Morris ▲	·
04/01	A	Coventry City	0-0	2-2	7	P.Durkin	de Goey	Lambourde	Terry	Terry	Babayaro	di Matteo ▲	Deschamps	Wise	Poyet	Zola	Sutton ▲	Wise ▲	Zola ▲	Flo ◄
08/01	H	Bradford City	0-1	1-1	7	A.G.Wiley	de Goey	Ferrer	Terry	Terry	Babayaro	Petrescu 58	Deschamps	Wise	di Matteo	Flo	Sutton ▲	Morris ▲	Sutton ▲	Zola ◄
12/01	H	Tottenham Hotspur	1-0	1-0	6	N.S.Barry	de Goey	Ferrer	Leboeuf	Leboeuf	Harley	Petrescu	Deschamps	Wise	Poyet	Flo ▲	Sutton	Morris ▲	Weah ▲67	Zola ◄
15/01	H	Leicester City	0-1	2-1	5	G.P.Barber	de Goey	Lambourde	Thome	Leboeuf	Harley	Petrescu	Deschamps	Wise ○86	Poyet	Zola	Weah	Morris ▲	Poyet ▲	Sutton ◄
22/01	A	Aston Villa	0-0	2-1	5	A.B.Wilkie	de Goey	Lambourde 52	Desailly	Leboeuf ▲	Lambourde	Morris	Morris	Ambrosetti ▲	Poyet	Zola	Sutton ▲	Le Saux ▲	Hogh ▲	di Matteo ◄
05/02	H	Tottenham Hotspur	0-0	1-0	5	G.Poll	de Goey	Ferrer	Desailly	Desailly	Harley	Petrescu	Deschamps	Ambrosetti ▲	Poyet	Weah	Sutton ▲	Zola ▲	Flo ▲	·
12/02	H	Wimbledon	0-0	3-1	5	P.Jones	de Goey	Lambourde	Thome	Leboeuf	Harley 65	Petrescu	Deschamps	Wise	Poyet 78	Weah 80	Weah ▲2	Zola ▲	Flo ▲	Harley ◄
26/02	H	Watford	1-1	2-1	5	S.W.Dunn	de Goey	Ferrer	Thome	Leboeuf	Harley 1	Petrescu	Deschamps	Wise	Poyet	Zola	Flo	Ferrer ▲	Petrescu ▲	Hogh ◄
04/03	A	Newcastle United	0-0	1-0	5	M.A.Riley	de Goey	Ferrer	Thome	Leboeuf	Babayaro	Petrescu ▲	Morris	Wise	Poyet 21	Zola	Sutton ▲	Flo ▲	Poyet ▲	Terry ◄
11/03	A	Everton	1-0	1-1	5	D.R.Elleray	de Goey	Ferrer	Thome	Leboeuf	Harley	di Matteo	Morris	Wise ○30	di Matteo	Zola	Sutton	Flo ▲	Sutton ▲	Zola ◄
18/03	A	West Ham United	0-0	0-0	5	S.W.Dunn	de Goey	Ferrer	Thome	Leboeuf	Babayaro	Petrescu	Deschamps	Wise	Poyet	Zola	Sutton ▲	Petrescu ▲	Ambrosetti ▲	·
25/03	H	Southampton	0-0	0-0	5	D.J.Gallagher	de Goey	Ferrer	Desailly	Thome	Harley	Harley	Morris	Wise	Poyet	Weah	Sutton	Petrescu ▲	Flo ▲	·
01/04	A	Leeds United	0-1	0-0	4	J.T.Winter	de Goey	Ferrer	Thome	Leboeuf	Babayaro	Weah	Morris ▲	Morris ▲	Poyet 10	Weah	Weah	Poyet ▲	Lambourde ▲	Flo ◄
12/04	H	Coventry City	2-1	2-1	4	G.Poll	de Goey	Lambourde	Thome	Leboeuf	Harley	Harley ▲62	Morris	Wise	Ambrosetti ▲	Zola 57	Sutton	Lambourde ▲	Della Bono ▲	Deschamps ◄
15/04	A	Sheffield Wednesday	1-1	1-1	5	P.A.Durkin	de Goey	Melchiot	Thome	Desailly	Lambourde	di Matteo ▲	Deschamps	Wise	di Matteo	Zola	Sutton	Della Bono ▲	Harley ▲	Flo ◄
22/04	H	Middlesbrough	1-1	1-0	5	U.D.Rennie	de Goey	Melchiot	Thome	Thome	Babayaro	Ambrosetti	Deschamps	Wise	di Matteo	Zola	Sutton	Harley ▲	Morris ▲	Harley ◄
24/04	A	Manchester United	2-2	2-3	5	G.P.Barber	de Goey	Melchiot	Thome	Leboeuf	Babayaro	Petrescu ▲22	Deschamps ▲	Wise	Poyet ▲	Zola 36	Weah ▲2	Harley ▲	Morris ▲	Sutton ▲i
29/04	H	Liverpool	0-1	2-0	4	M.D.Reed	de Goey	Ferrer	Desailly	Leboeuf	Lambourde	Harley	Morris ▲	Wise	di Matteo	Zola	Flo	Sutton ▲	Thorne ▲	Weah ◄
06/05	A	Arsenal	0-1	1-2	5	J.T.Winter	de Goey	Melchiot	Desailly	Desailly	Babayaro	di Matteo ○69	Morris	Wise	di Matteo	Zola	Flo 90	Thorne ▲	Deschamps ▲	Poyet ▲79
14/05	H	Derby County	0-0	4-0	5	J.T.Winter	Cudicini	Ferrer ▲	Leboeuf	Leboeuf	Babayaro	di Matteo 69	Deschamps	Wise	Poyet ▲55	Zola 47	Flo 90	Terry ▲	Ambrosetti ▲	Melchiot ◄

Goal Analysis

powered by **football.co.uk**

GOALS BY POSITION 1997/1998 - 1999/2000
for the latest stats and to share your memories go to football.co.uk

key:
- forward
- midfield
- defence
- **-0-** final league position

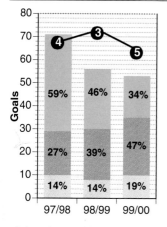

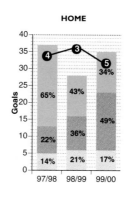

HOME

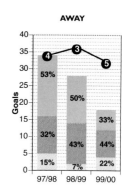

AWAY

Chelsea fans could be forgiven for going into the season believing their chief asset was their abundance of strikers. The arrival of Chris Sutton, from relegated Blackburn, only enforced the view that Chelsea would enjoy a hatful of goals. It was not to be. Sutton had scored only three times the previous season, in 17 games, but his record in his first season at Stamford Bridge was poor.

While enjoying the full support of his manager and scoring in his second game, the Champions' League qualifier against Skonto Riga, Chelsea supporters had to wait until October to see Sutton's first Carling Premiership goal. Strangely, it came in the 5-0 win over Manchester United and proved to be his only goal in 21 starts and a further seven substitute appearances.

Others struggled. Gianfranco Zola started 25 games and came on in another eight but still returned only four goals. Predictably, it was to Norwegian striker Tore Andre Flo that Chelsea turned and he responded with 10 goals from 20 starts plus a further

GOALS BY TIME PERIOD 1999/2000
for the latest stats and to share your memories go to football.co.uk

key:
- goals for
- goals against

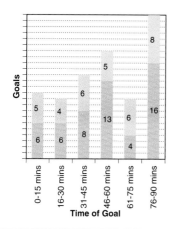

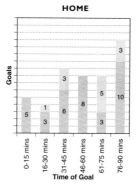

HOME

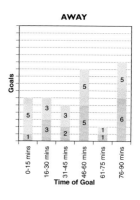

AWAY

Goal Analysis

powered by football.co.uk

Chelsea

HOW GOALS WERE SCORED 1999/2000

for the latest stats and to share your memories go to football.co.uk

key:
- header
- volley
- penalty
- close range*
- free kick
- inside area
- outside area
- own goal

* inside six yard box

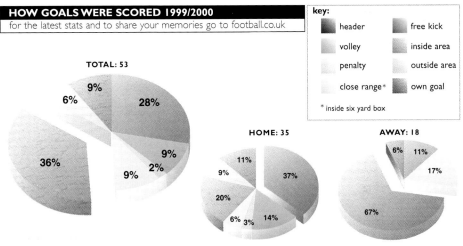

TOTAL: 53

9% · 6% · 28% · 36% · 9% · 2% · 9%

HOME: 35

11% · 9% · 37% · 20% · 6% · 3% · 14% · 9%

AWAY: 18

6% · 11% · 17% · 67%

14 substitute appearances.

Such was the concern over the lack of goals that Chelsea pulled off a coup by persuading George Weah to leave AC Milan and move to Stamford Bridge on loan for the remaining five months of the season. Weah's impact was immediate, the Liberian scoring on his debut to earn Chelsea a win over Spurs.

Such were the failures of Chelsea's attack that the strikers' contribution made up for just 34 per cent of the side's goals. But the midfield compensated for the lack of attacking goals with Gustavo Poyet matching Flo's total of 10. The Uruguayan scored twice in the opening day win over Sunderland and continued to claim valuable goals.

Overall, Chelsea scored just 53 goals, their lowest Carling Premiership total since the 1995-96 season while they managed only 18 on their travels; only six teams scored less away goals. And, of those 18, no fewer than 12 came from inside the area. They also scored a large percentage of headed goals; 37 per cent

HOW GOALS WERE CONCEDED 1999/2000

for the latest stats and to share your memories go to football.co.uk

key:
- header
- volley
- penalty
- close range*
- free kick
- inside area
- outside area
- own goal

* inside six yard box

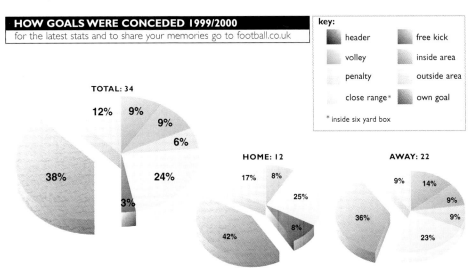

TOTAL: 34

12% · 9% · 9% · 6% · 38% · 24% · 3%

HOME: 12

17% · 8% · 25% · 42% · 8%

AWAY: 22

9% · 14% · 9% · 9% · 36% · 23%

What a difference a CARLING makes.

Squad and Performance

SQUAD LIST

for the latest stats and to share your memories go to football.co.uk

Position	Name	Appearances	Appearances as substitute	Goals	Clean Sheets	Yellow Cards	Red Cards
G	C.Cudicini	1			1		
G	E.de Goey	37			16	1	
D	C.Babayaro	23	2			3	
D	M.Desailly	23		1		2	1
D	A.Ferrer	24	1			5	
D	J.Hogh	6	3			1	
D	B.Lambourde	12	3	2		3	
D	G.Le Saux	6	2			3	
D	F.Leboeuf	28		2		7	2
D	M.Melchiot	4	1				
D	J.Terry	2	2				
D	E.Thome	18	2			1	
M	G.Ambrosetti	9	7				
M	S.Della Bona		2				
M	D.Deschamps	24	3			5	
M	R.di Matteo	14	4	2		3	
M	B.Goldbaek	2	4				
M	J.Harley	13	4	2		1	
M	J.Morris	19	11	3		4	
M	D.Petrescu	24	5	4		2	
M	G.Poyet	25	8	10		5	
M	D.Wise	29	1	4		6	1
F	T.Flo	20	14	10		1	
F	M.Forssell		1				
F	C.Sutton	21	7	1		6	
F	G.Weah	9	2	3			
F	R.Wolleaston		1				
F	G.Zola	25	8	4			

of home goals came from headers. Chelsea were also strongest in the opening 45 minutes at Stamford Bridge where they conceded only four goals all season.

Interestingly, of their 18 wins, 14 were secured without the opposition scoring and much of that was down to goalkeeper Ed de Goey who, in 37 appearances, kept 16 clean sheets. Add a further 10 in other competitions and de Goey was able to claim a club record, beating Peter Bonetti's record of 22 clean sheets 25 years ago.

What let Chelsea down most was their poor away form and in particular against the teams in the top half of the table. They won 26 points off the other top nine clubs while claiming 39 off the bottom half. They were beaten twice by Arsenal – the only team to do the

TEAM PERFORMANCE TABLE

for the latest stats and to share your memories go to football.co.uk

Position	Club	Points Won	Percentage of points won at home	percentage of points won away	overall percentage of points won
1.	MANCHESTER UNITED	3/6			
2.	ARSENAL	0/6			
3.	LEEDS UNITED	3/6	50%	25%	38%
4.	LIVERPOOL	3/6			
5.	CHELSEA	65 pts			
6.	ASTON VILLA	4/6			
7.	SUNDERLAND	3/6			
8.	LEICESTER CITY	2/6	73%	40%	57%
9.	TOTTENHAM HOTSPUR	6/6			
10.	WEST HAM UNITED	2/6			
11.	NEWCASTLE UNITED	6/6			
12.	MIDDLESBROUGH	4/6			
13.	EVERTON	2/6	60%	73%	67%
14.	SOUTHAMPTON	4/6			
15.	COVENTRY CITY	4/6			
16.	DERBY COUNTY	3/6			
17.	BRADFORD CITY	4/6			
18.	WIMBLEDON	6/6	100%	27%	63%
19.	SHEFFIELD WEDNESDAY	3/6			
20.	WATFORD	3/6			

The figures show a team's performance against clubs in each quarter of the final league table. The first column represents points won from the total available against each team in the league.

What a difference a CARLING makes.

Discipline and Season Summary

powered by football.co.uk

BOOKINGS BY POSITION 1997/1998 - 1999/2000
for the latest stats and to share your memories go to football.co.uk

key:
- forward
- defence
- midfield
- goalkeeper

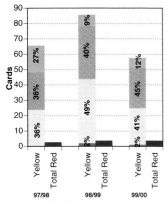

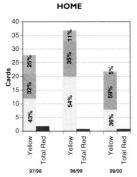
HOME

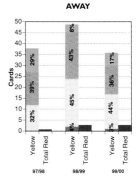
AWAY

Chelsea

double over Vialli's foreign legion – while they could manage only two draws against both Leicester City and West Ham.

Chelsea were no strangers to poor discipline; Gianluca Vialli was sent off from the bench during a Champions' League tie in Rome against Lazio while the club was fined £50,000 for a tunnel brawl with Wimbledon. Dennis Wise, the captain, was fined £7,500 for his part in that incident while receiving six cautions and a dismissal in the 1-0 defeat at Liverpool. That red card was one of four administered to Chelsea players last season, matching the previous season's total. Frank Leboeuf was sent off twice to add to the one red card he received the previous term.

Most bookings were received by the midfield; along with Wise, referees had to contend with Poyet, Jody Morris and Didier Deschamps. Even Flo was booked, for the third time in three seasons, yet received special praise from his boss after the caution for unsporting behaviour at West Ham!

Chelsea, though, showed an ability to turn adversity into strength. On seven occasions they were losing at half time yet turned five of those games round, drawing four and winning once. Similarly, of the 21 times they were drawing at the interval they avoided defeat 15 times, winning nine and drawing six. At Stamford Bridge they were particularly strong; of the two occasions they were losing at half time, they bounced back to win one and draw the other.

HALF TIME - FULL TIME COMPARATIVE CHART
for the latest stats and to share your memories go to football.co.uk

HOME

Number of Home Half Time Wins	Full Time Result W	L	D
8	6	1	1

Number of Home Half Time Losses	Full Time Result W	L	D
2	1	0	1

Number of Home Half Time Draws	Full Time Result W	L	D
9	5	1	3

AWAY

Number of Away Half Time Wins	Full Time Result W	L	D
2	2	0	0

Number of Away Half Time Losses	Full Time Result W	L	D
5	0	2	3

Number of Away Half Time Draws	Full Time Result W	L	D
12	4	5	3

TOTAL

Total Number of Half Time Wins	Full Time Result W	L	D
10	8	1	1

Total Number of Half Time Losses	Full Time Result W	L	D
7	1	2	4

Total Number of Half Time Draws	Full Time Result W	L	D
21	9	6	6

Maps and Directions

Chelsea play at Stamford Bridge in Central London. Parking restrictions during the game make it advisable to park away from the ground and travel by tube. Limited on-site matchday underground parking is available (£20 per car).

From the North:
From the M1 turn off onto the A406 North Circular Road at Junction 1. Turn off onto the A40 and stay on until the junction with the M41. Turn right onto the M41 and continue for 1 mile before turning onto the A3220 Holland Road. Follow the A3220 for 2 miles before turning right onto the A304 Fulham Road. Stamford Bridge is a quarter of a mile along on the right.

From the North-West:
From the M40 continue onto the A40 and stay on until the junction with the M41. Then as route for North.

From the West:
Get on the M4 and at Junction 1 continue along the A4 for 4 miles until it becomes the Cromwell Road. Turn right onto the A3220 Earls Court Road. Then as route for North.

From the South-West:
From the M3 turn off onto the M25 at Junction 2. Continue for 10 miles until you reach Junction 15 at which point turn off onto the M4. Then as route for West.

The nearest tube station is Fulham Broadway on the District Line.

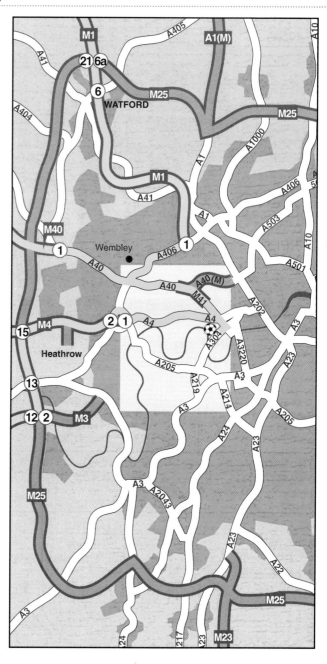

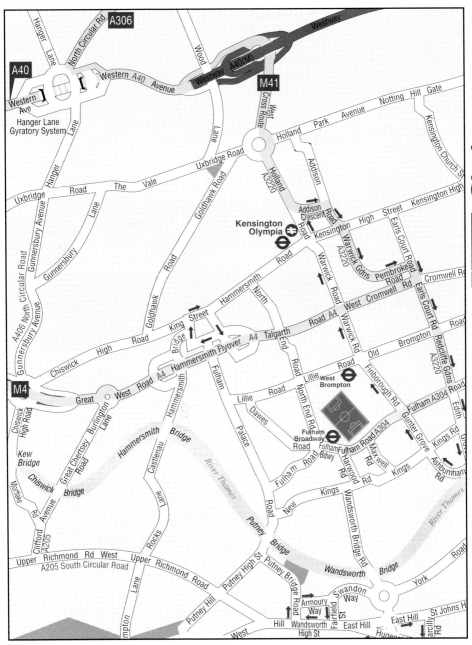

Club Honours

- Division 2 Champions: 1966-67
- Division 3 Champions:
- 1935-36 (South), 1963-64
- FA Cup Winners: 1987

Club Records

- Victory: 9-0 v Bristol City, Division 3 (South), April 28, 1934
- Defeat: 2-10 v Norwich City, Division 3 (South), March 15, 1930
- League goals in a season (team): 108, Division 3 (South), 1931-32
- League goals in a season (player): 49, Clarrie Bourton, Division 3 (South), 1931-32
- Career league goals: 171, Clarrie Bourton, 1931-37
- League appearances: 507, Steve Ogrizovic, 1984-2000
- Transfer fee paid: £6,000,000 to Wolves for Robbie Keane, August, 1999
- Transfer fee received: £5,750,000 from Aston Villa for Dion Dublin, November, 1998

Pos		Pld	W	D	L	F	A	Pts
14	Coventry	38	12	8	18	47	54	44

Coventry City
"The Sky Blues"

Highfield Road Stadium, King Ric Street, Coventry CV2 4FW
Tel: 024 76234 000
www.ccfc.co.uk

Season Review by
John Ley

The Daily Telegraph

So, once again Coventry prepare for another season of top-flight football. Given their durability, few should be surprised that the Sky Blues are the fifth longest serving team currently in the Carling Premiership and even though they have competed with the best in financial terms, they cannot shake off that tag which suggests that every August they will be one of the favourites for relegation.

Gordon Strachan spent nearly £10 million last season, more than all but six of his competitors, and at times Coventry looked like world beaters, with the Moroccan pair Mustapha Hadji and Youssef Chippo learning the English game well and Robbie Keane outstanding after his £6 million move from Wolves.

The season also saw the retirement of Steve Ogrizovic who, after 16 years in City's goal, finally hung up his gloves to take charge of the club's Under-17 Academy. 'Oggy' featured in the final home game, against Sheffield Wednesday.

Useful Information

Club Shop
Highfield Road Stadium
Opening Times:
Monday-Friday: 9.00am-5.00pm
Match Saturdays: 9.00am-3.00pm, 4.45pm-5.30pm
Match Sundays: 10.00am-6.30pm
Match Evenings: 9.00am-8.00pm, 9.45pm-10.30pm
Tel: 024 76234 030

Megastore
The West Orchards Shopping Centre, Coventry
Opening Times:
Monday-Thursday: 9.00am-5.30pm
Friday-Saturdays: 9.00am-6.00pm
Sundays: 10.30am-4.30pm
Tel: 024 76551 257
Mail Order Service: 024 76234 030

Corporate Hospitality
Premier Club
Theatre style seats, lounge location with 3-course carvery meal, complimentary programme, bar and betting facilities.

Directors Box
Directors Box seats, 4-course banquet lunch with champagne, tour of the ground, complimentary

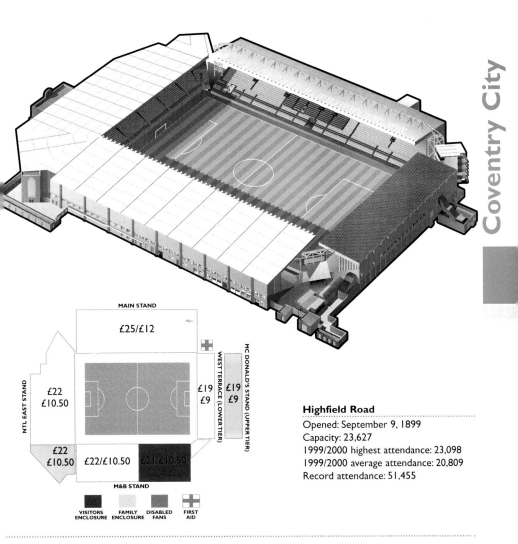

MAIN STAND

£25/£12

NTL EAST STAND

£22
£10.50

£22
£10.50

£22/£10.50

£21/£10.50

£19
£9

£19
£9

WEST TERRACE (LOWER TIER)

MC DONALD'S STAND (UPPER TIER)

M&B STAND

VISITORS
ENCLOSURE

FAMILY
ENCLOSURE

DISABLED
FANS

FIRST
AID

Highfield Road

Opened: September 9, 1899
Capacity: 23,627
1999/2000 highest attendance: 23,098
1999/2000 average attendance: 20,809
Record attendance: 51,455

programme, bar and betting facilities. Match, matchball, man of the match sponsorship packages.

Tel: **024 76234 010**

The Members Club

The Members Club cost £23 per season and offers privileges and discounts

Senior Citizen Membership

Benefits of senior citizen membership include discounts on the matches.

Literature

Programme £2

Pre-Match & Half Time Entertainment

Sky Blue Crew/Sky Blue Sam.

Restaurants

Open non-matchdays.

Tel: **024 76234 050**

Booking Information

General Enquiries :
024 76234 000
Credit Card Bookings:
024 76234 020
Travel Club:
024 76234 020
Junior Club:
024 76224 093

Results Breakdown

powered by football.co.uk

POINTS WON OR LOST AT BOTH HOME AND AWAY

for the latest stats and to share your memories go to football.co.uk

key:
- win
- draw
- loss
- -O- league position

home fixtures are in red

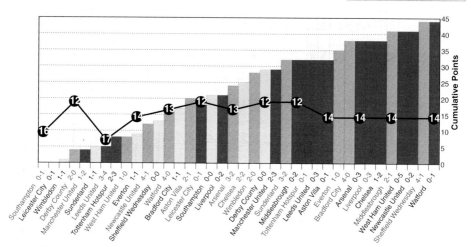

The season started badly for Coventry with just one win, over Derby, in the first eight games. Darren Huckerby was sold to Leeds, Keane arrived, and matters improved when City went seven games without defeat to move into 12th place.

Injuries played a major part in Coventry's season. Australian striker John Aloisi had scored twice in three starts when he needed a knee operation which was to halt his season as early as November. Richard Shaw, Marc Edworthy, Paul Williams, Carlton Palmer and David Burrows were also injury victims. City suffered

four successive defeats before Gary McAllister, who has now joined Liverpool, claimed the club's first goal for eight and a half hours, against Everton in March.

Sadly, for the first time in City's history they failed to win away from home, picking up just seven points on their travels, meaning they start the new season having gone 16 months without an away success.

Strachan continued to invest in his squad throughout the season, signing Cedric Roussel, Colin Hendry, Ysrael Zuniga and Tomas Gustaffson to offer promise for another defiant season.

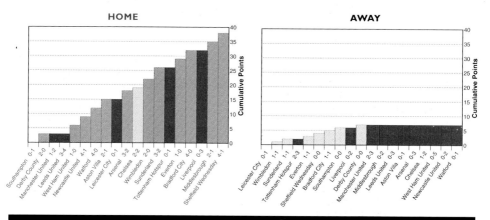

HOME

AWAY

Coventry City

DATE	H/A	OPPONENT	H/T	F/T	POS	REFEREE	Team	Substitutes Used
07/08	H	Southampton	0-0	0-1	16	P.Jones	Hedman, Edworthy, Williams, Shaw, Burrows, Telfer, Hodji, McAllister, Chippo, Whelan, Huckerby ▲	Froggatt ▲, Aloisi ▲
11/08	A	Leicester City	0-1	0-1	17	N.S.Barry	Hedman, Edworthy, Williams, Shaw, Burrows ●, Telfer, Hodji, McAllister, Chippo ●, Whelan, Froggatt ▲	Aloisi ▲
14/08	H	Wimbledon	0-0	1-1	16	M.R.Halsey	Hedman, Breen, Williams, Shaw, Burrows, Telfer, Hodji, McAllister, Chippo, Whelan, Aloisi	Froggatt ▲
21/08	H	Derby County	1-0	2-0	12	I.T.Winter	Hedman, Edworthy, Williams, Shaw, Burrows, Telfer, Hodji, McAllister, Chippo, Whelan, Keene ▲ 43 67	Froggatt ▲, Strachan ▲
25/08	H	Manchester United	0-0	0-2	16	A.B.Wilkie	Hedman, Edworthy, Williams, Shaw, Breen ▲, Froggatt, Hodji, McAllister, Chippo, Aloisi ▲, Keene	Konjic ▲, Telfer ▲, Aloisi ▲79
29/08	A	Sunderland	1-0	1-1	16	S.J.Lodge	Hedman, Edworthy, Williams, Shaw, Breen, Quinn ▲, Hodji ▲, McAllister, Chippo 54, Aloisi ▲17, Keene 32	Telfer ▲, McSheffrey ▲
11/09	A	Leeds United	2-3	3-4	17	S.W.Dunn	Hedman, Edworthy, Williams, Shaw, Quinn ▲, Froggatt ▲, Hodji ▲, McAllister 2, Chippo 54, Konjic, Keene 54	Strachan ▲, Hall ▲
19/09	H	Tottenham Hotspur	0-1	2-3	15	A.P.D'Urso	Hedman, Edworthy, Hall, Shaw, Burrows ▲, Froggatt ▲, Hodji, McAllister 74, Chippo 74, Konjic, Keene	Hall ▲, Williams ▲
25/09	H	West Ham United	1-0	1-0	15	D.R.Elleray	Hedman, Edworthy ▲, Hall, Shaw, Palmer, Telfer, Hodji 36, McAllister 11, Chippo, Konjic, Keene	McSheffrey ▲
02/10	A	Everton	1-1	1-1	14	N.S.Barry	Hedman, Edworthy ▲, Hall, Shaw, Palmer 13, Telfer, Hodji, McAllister, Chippo ▲, Hall, Keene	Williams ▲, Roussel ▲
16/10	H	Newcastle United	3-0	4-1	12	A.G.Wiley	Hedman, Hall, Williams 21, Shaw, Palmer, Telfer, Hodji 90, McAllister, Chippo ▲, Roussel ▲, Keene 39	Froggatt ▲
23/10	A	Sheffield Wednesday	0-0	0-0	13	M.A.Riley	Hedman, Hall, Williams, Shaw, Palmer, Telfer, Hodji, McAllister, Chippo ▲, Hall, Keene 17	Roussel ▲
31/10	H	Watford	1-1	1-1	12	B.Knight	Hedman, Hall, Williams, Breen, Palmer, Telfer, Hodji, McAllister, Froggatt 33, Froggatt, Keene	—
06/11	A	Bradford City	2-1	1-1	11	G.P.Barber	Hedman, Breen, Williams, Breen, Palmer, Telfer, Hodji, McAllister 1, Chippo ▲, Roussel ▲8, Keene 65	Burrows ▲, Whelan ▲
22/11	A	Aston Villa	1-1	0-1	12	S.J.Lodge	Hedman, Breen, Williams, Burrows ▲, Palmer, Eustace, Hodji, McAllister, Chippo ▲, Roussel ▲, Keene	Froggatt ▲, Whelan ▲
27/11	H	Leicester City	0-0	0-1	11	I.T.Winter	Hedman, Gustafsson ▲, Williams, Burrows, Palmer, Eustace, Zunigo, McAllister, Chippo ▲, Roussel ▲, Keene	Show ▲, Normann ▲
04/12	A	Southampton	0-0	0-0	13	A.P.D'Urso	Hedman, Breen, Hendry, Froggatt, Palmer, Froggatt, Hodji, McAllister, Chippo ▲, Whelan ▲, Keene 71	Normann ▲
18/12	H	Liverpool	0-0	0-0	13	R.J.Harris	Hedman, Gustafsson, Hendry, Froggatt, Palmer, Eustace, Hodji 40, McAllister 6, Chippo, Roussel, Keene	Whelan ▲
26/12	H	Chelsea	2-0	3-2	13	P.Durkin	Hedman, Gustafsson, Hendry, Breen, Strachan ▲, Telfer, Hodji, McAllister 56, Whelan, Roussel ▲54, Keene 81	Normann ▲, Quinn ▲
04/01	A	Wimbledon	2-0	2-0	12	S.G.Bennett	Hedman, Gustafsson, Williams, Breen, Palmer ▲, Telfer, Eustace, McAllister, Whelan, Roussel ▲, Keene 74	Gustafsson ▲, Quinn ▲
15/01	H	Derby County	0-0	0-0	12	G.P.Barber	Hedman, Gustafsson, Hendry, Breen, Palmer, Telfer ▲, Gustafsson, McAllister, Froggatt, Roussel 65 90, Keene	Eustace ▲, Normann ▲
22/01	A	Manchester United	0-1	2-3	12	A.B.Wilkie	Ogrizovic, Quinn, Gustafsson, Breen, Eustace, Froggatt ▲, Gustafsson, McAllister 17, Chippo ▲, Roussel 18, Keene 1	Quinn ▲, Show ▲
05/02	H	Sunderland	3-0	3-2	12	P.E.Alcock	Hedman, Breen, Gustafsson ▲, Eustace, Palmer, Burrows ▲, Hodji 10, McAllister, Chippo ▲, Whelan ▲, Keene	Quinn ▲, Burrows ▲
12/02	A	Middlesbrough	0-2	0-2	12	P.E.Alcock	Hedman, Breen, Williams, Show, Burrows, Eustace, Normann ▲, McAllister, Chippo ▲, Whelan, Keene 61	Show ▲, Eustace ▲
19/02	A	Tottenham Hotspur	0-0	0-1	12	G.P.Barber	Hedman, Breen, Hendry, Burrows, Quinn ▲, Telfer, Hodji, McAllister, Whelan, Whelan, Keene	Eustace ▲, Eustace ▲
26/02	H	Leeds United	0-2	0-3	13	P.A.Durkin	Hedman, Gustafsson, Williams, Eustace ▲, Eustace ▲, Froggatt, Zunijo 67, McAllister 86, Chippo, Roussel, Keene	Zunijo ▲, Keene ▲
04/03	A	Aston Villa	0-2	0-3	14	I.T.Winter	Hedman, Quinn, Breen, Gustafsson, Eustace ▲, Burrows, Hodji, McAllister, Chippo ▲, Whelan, Roussel	Telfer ▲, Burrows ▲
11/03	H	Bradford City	0-1	1-0	14	U.D.Rennie	Ogrizovic, Breen, Hendry, Quinn, Eustace 84, Quinn, Hodji, McAllister, Chippo ▲, Whelan 21, Roussel ▲6	Zunijo ▲86
18/03	A	Arsenal	0-0	0-3	14	M.R.Halsey	Hedman, Breen, Williams, Show, Froggatt, Eustace, Eustace, McAllister, Chippo ▲, Whelan ▲, Roussel ▲	Telfer ▲, Normann ▲
26/03	H	Liverpool	2-0	0-3	14	B.Knight	Ogrizovic, Breen, Hendry, Show, Froggatt, Telfer, Gustafsson 10, McAllister, Chippo ▲, Whelan ▲, Roussel	Normann ▲, Keene ▲
01/04	A	Chelsea	1-2	0-5	14	M.D.Reed	Hedman, Quinn, Williams, Show, Froggatt, Telfer, Hodji, McAllister, Chippo, Whelan, Keene	Quinn ▲, Keene ▲
12/04	H	Middlesbrough	1-0	2-1	14	G.Poll	Ogrizovic, Breen, Hendry ▲, Eustace, Froggatt, Telfer, Hodji, McAllister, Chippo ▲, Whelan ▲, Keene	Zunijo ▲, Burrows ▲
15/04	H	West Ham United	1-0	2-1	14	N.S.Barry	Hedman, Breen, Williams, Eustace, Burrows, Telfer, Normann ▲, McAllister, Whelan, Quinn ▲, Keene 61	Burrows ▲, Show ▲
22/04	A	Newcastle United	0-2	0-5	14	A.P.D'Urso	Hedman, Breen, Williams, Show, Roussel ▲, Telfer, Hodji 80, McAllister 17, Chippo, Whelan, Keene	Show ▲, Eustace ▲
29/04	H	Sheffield Wednesday	1-0	4-1	14	S.G.Bennett	Ogrizovic, Breen, Williams ▲, Show, Zunijo 67, Burrows, Hodji, McAllister 38 70, Chippo ▲, Roussel, Keene	Eustace ▲, Betts ▲
06/05	A	Everton	1-0	0-0	14	P.Jones	Hedman, Breen, Williams, Show, Zunijo, Quinn, Hodji, McAllister, Whelan, Whelan, Keene	Gustafsson ▲, Roussel ▲
14/05	H	Watford	0-1	0-1	14	U.D.Rennie	Hedman, Breen, Williams ▲, Show, Roussel ▲, Telfer, Hodji, McAllister, Chippo, Whelan, Keene	Normann ▲, Betts ▲

Goal Analysis

GOALS BY POSITION 1997/1998 - 1999/2000
for the latest stats and to share your memories go to football.co.uk

key:
- forward
- defence
- midfield
- -O- final league position

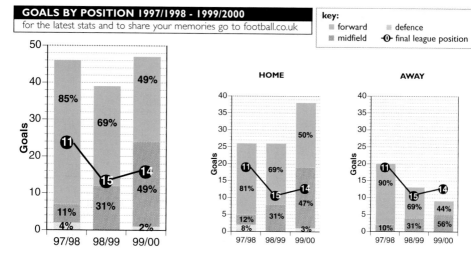

Coventry scored more goals, 47, than at any time since the inaugural Carling Premiership season (1992-93). Keane had already scored twice for Wolves when he arrived four games into the season and made an immediate impact by scoring twice on his debut, against Derby.

Keane went on to finish as the club's highest scorer with 12 Carling Premiership goals for City, his 14 goal tally beating by three his previous best total for Wolves. It also enabled him to finish as City's highest scorer

since Dion Dublin scored 18 in the 1997-98 season.

Close behind was McAllister who enjoyed what was to be his last season for the Sky Blues. Signed from Leeds in the summer of 1996, McAllister scored more goals in his fourth season at Highfield Road, 11, than over the previous three terms, when he scored nine in 81 appearances. It also equalled his best goalscoring return ever (11 for Leicester in the 1988-89 season) in his 20th season as a professional. His departure to Anfield will leave Strachan with a huge hole to fill.

GOALS BY TIME PERIOD 1999/2000
for the latest stats and to share your memories go to football.co.uk

key:
- goals for
- goals against

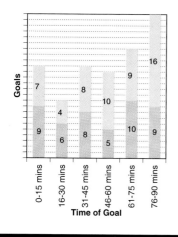

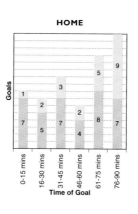

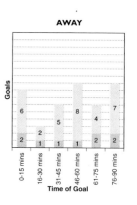

What a difference a CARLING makes.

Goal Analysis

Coventry City

HOW GOALS WERE SCORED 1999/2000
for the latest stats and to share your memories go to football.co.uk

key:
- header
- volley
- penalty
- close range*
- free kick
- inside area
- outside area
- own goal

* inside six yard box

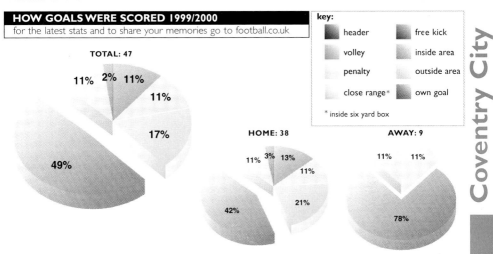

TOTAL: 47

11% 2% 11%
11%
17%
49%

HOME: 38

11% 3% 13%
11%
42% 21%

AWAY: 9

11% 11%
78%

In previous seasons, strikers have dominated the goalscoring charts for City; in the 1998-99 season, more than two thirds of their goals came from the front men with Darren Huckerby and Noel Whelan claiming most.

The season just passed, however, saw a greater percentage of their goals come from midfield than at any time since the Carling Premiership began. McAllister's efforts and a further six from Hadji meant that City had more options; indeed the goals were

scored by 12 different players compared to the eight who scored in the previous season.

The defensive contribution was minimal but at least the back line scored; in 1998-99 they failed to strike once but Paul Williams made amends by striking against Newcastle.

Coventry were clearly happier at home; their 38 Highfield Road goals was greater than at any time since 1987 but away from home it was a different story. With not one single win to celebrate, their away tally

HOW GOALS WERE CONCEDED 1999/2000
for the latest stats and to share your memories go to football.co.uk

key:
- header
- volley
- penalty
- close range*
- free kick
- inside area
- outside area
- own goal

* inside six yard box

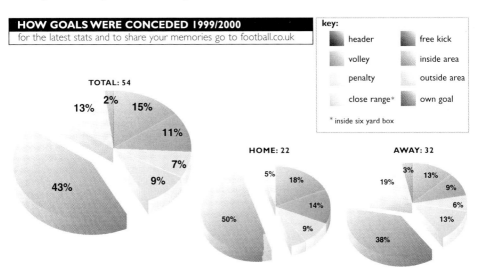

TOTAL: 54

13% 2% 15%
11%
7%
9%
43%
9%

HOME: 22

5% 18%
14%
50% 9%

AWAY: 32

3% 13%
19% 9%
6%
13%
38%

Squad and Performance

powered by  football.co.uk

SQUAD LIST

for the latest stats and to share your memories go to football.co.uk

Position	Name	Appearances	Appearances as substitute	Goals	Clean Sheets	Yellow Cards	Red Cards
G	M.Hedman	35			9		
G	S.Ogrizovic	3					
D	G.Breen	20	1			2	
D	D.Burrows	11	4				1
D	M.Edworthy	10				3	
D	T.Gustafsson	7	2			1	
D	M.Hall	7	2			1	
D	C.Hendry	9					
D	M.Konjic	3	1			1	
D	R.Shaw	27	2			3	
D	P.Williams	26	2	1		4	
M	R.Betts		2				
M	Y.Chippo	33		2		9	1
M	J.Eustace	12	4	1		2	
M	S.Froggatt	21	5	1		5	
M	M.Hadji	33		6		4	
M	G.McAllister	38		11		2	
M	R.Normann	1	7				
M	C.Palmer	15		1		3	
M	B.Quinn	5	6			2	
M	G.Strachan	1	2				
M	P.Telfer	26	4			2	
F	J.Aloisi	3	3	2		1	
F	P.Hall		1				
F	D.Huckerby	1					
F	R.Keane	30	1	12		3	
F	G.McSheffrey		3				
F	C.Roussel	18	4	6			
F	N.Whelan	20	5	1		3	
F	Y.Zunija	3	4	2			

was reduced to just nine – one short of the all-time Carling Premiership record of eight scored by Middlesbrough (1995-96) and Southampton (1998-99).

While Ogrizovic extending his club record appearance tally to 601 games, only one player was an ever present, Gary McAllister, who played in every game for the second time in his four years at Coventry. City, hampered by injuries, used 30 players – only Derby and Newcastle fielded more.

At home, City dominated the bottom sides below them in the Carling Premiership, enjoying a 100 per cent success rate, at Highfield Road, against the bottom five teams. Those sitting just below half way in the table suffered a similar fate but City were beaten home and

TEAM PERFORMANCE TABLE

for the latest stats and to share your memories go to football.co.uk

Position	Club	Points Won	Percentage of points won at home	Percentage of points won away	overall percentage of points won
1.	MANCHESTER UNITED	0/6			
2.	ARSENAL	3/6			
3.	LEEDS UNITED	0/6	27%	0%	13%
4.	LIVERPOOL	0/6			
5.	CHELSEA	1/6			
6.	ASTON VILLA	3/6			
7.	SUNDERLAND	4/6			
8.	LEICESTER CITY	0/6	60%	7%	33%
9.	TOTTENHAM HOTSPUR	0/6			
10.	WEST HAM UNITED	3/6			
11.	NEWCASTLE UNITED	3/6			
12.	MIDDLESBROUGH	3/6			
13.	EVERTON	4/6	75%	17%	46%
14.	SOUTHAMPTON	1/6			
15.	COVENTRY CITY	44 pts			
16.	DERBY COUNTY	4/6			
17.	BRADFORD CITY	4/6			
18.	WIMBLEDON	4/6	100%	27%	63%
19.	SHEFFIELD WEDNESDAY	4/6			
20.	WATFORD	3/6			

The figures show a team's performance against clubs in each quarter of the final league table. The first column represents points won from the total available against each team in the league.

What a difference a CARLING makes.

Discipline and Season Summary

BOOKINGS BY POSITION 1997/1998 - 1999/2000
for the latest stats and to share your memories go to football.co.uk

key:
■ forward   ■ defence
■ midfield   ■ goalkeeper

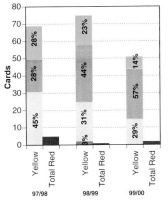

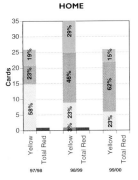

HOME

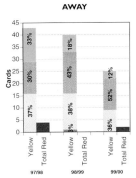

AWAY

Coventry City

away by five teams, all occupying top nine finishes. Away from home, City were atrocious and collected not one point against the top five.

City's discipline was vastly improved; just over 50 cautions was their fewest number of yellow cards for three years. The worst offender was newcomer Chippo, who collected nine yellow cards and was also one of two City players dismissed, his red card coming against Sunderland. The other was David Burrows, who was sent-off at Leicester and followed that with a Worthington Cup dismissal in the shock 5-1 defeat at Tranmere a fortnight later.

Strikers received only 14 per cent of City's cautions, their lowest percentage of front men booked since the 1995-96 season.

Coventry led twice at half time on their travels – at Sunderland and Middlesbrough – but that is as close as they got to an away win.

Of the seven points they did win away from home, none were achieved at the homes of the top five and only seven per cent – at Everton and Southampton – came against the teams in 11th to 15th place. Indeed, City lost their last nine away games – two short of the club record 11 set in the 1925-26 season.

At home though, they were more confident. Whenever they were ahead at the interval, on nine occasions, they held on to the three points. But an interval draw was not so encouraging; of the eight times they were level after 45 minutes they won only three.

HALF TIME - FULL TIME COMPARATIVE CHART
for the latest stats and to share your memories go to football.co.uk

HOME				AWAY				TOTAL			
Number of Home Half Time Wins	Full Time Result W	L	D	Number of Away Half Time Wins	Full Time Result W	L	D	Total Number of Half Time Wins	Full Time Result W	L	D
9	9	0	0	2	0	1	1	11	9	1	1
Number of Home Half Time Losses	Full Time Result W	L	D	Number of Away Half Time Losses	Full Time Result W	L	D	Total Number of Half Time Losses	Full Time Result W	L	D
2	0	2	0	9	0	9	0	11	0	11	0
Number of Home Half Time Draws	Full Time Result W	L	D	Number of Away Half Time Draws	Full Time Result W	L	D	Total Number of Half Time Draws	Full Time Result W	L	D
8	3	4	1	8	0	2	6	16	3	6	7

What a difference a CARLING makes.

Maps and Directions

Coventry City play at Highfield Road Stadium, less than a mile from the city centre. Parking is available in local side streets. Nearest car parks are Clay Lane and Pool Meadow. There is also some car parking off Kingsway.

From the North:
Take the M1 to Junction 21 and join the M69 continuing at Junction 2 onto the A4600 following signs to the centre. This road becomes the Walsgrave Road which turns right into Swan Lane. The ground is ahead on the left.

From the South:
Take the M40 to Junction 15 onto A46. Continue on A46 which changes to A444 for approx 10 miles. Then take A423 signposted city centre. After approximately 2 miles take A4600 signposted Leicester. Follow this road for half a mile and just before road bridge turn left into Swan Lane. The ground is on the left.

From the West/East:
Approaching on the M6 in either direction, turn off onto the A4600 at Junction 2. Then as route for North.

Coventry Railway Station is situated one mile from the ground. Buses leave from Trinity Street Bus Station.

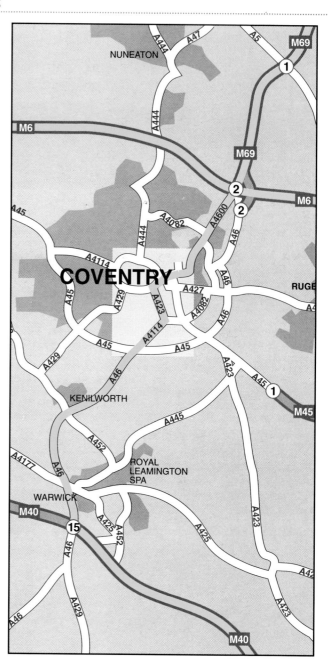

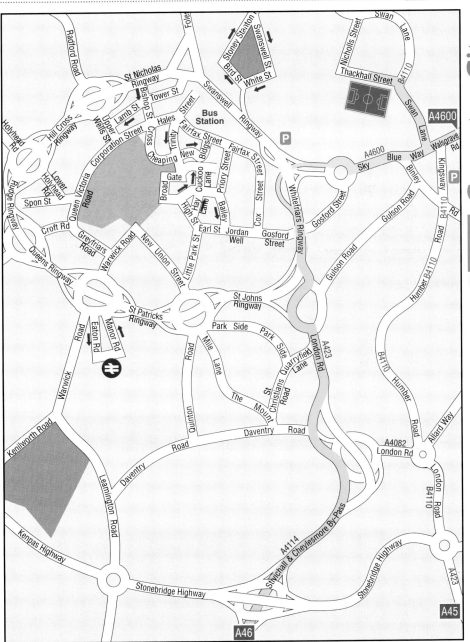

Coventry City

powered by football.co.uk

77

Club Honours

- Football League Champions: 1971-72, 1974-75
- Division 2 Champions: 1911-12, 1914-15, 1968-69, 1986-87
- Division 3 Champions (North): 1956-57
- FA Cup Winners: 1946

Club Records

- Victory: 12-0 v Finn Harps, UEFA Cup, 1st Round, 1st Leg, September 15, 1976
- Defeat: 2-11 v Everton, FA Cup 1st Round, 1889
- League goals in a season (team): 111, Division 3 (North), 1956-57
- League goals in a season (player): 37, Jack Bowers, Division 1, 1930-31; 37, Ray Straw, Division 3 (North), 1956-57
- Career league goals: 292, Steve Bloomer, 1892-1906, 1910-14
- League appearances: 486, Kevin Hector, 1966-78, 1980-82
- Transfer fee paid: £3,000,000 to Sheffield Utd for Lee Morris (rising to £4,000,000 with appearances), Oct, 1999
- Transfer fee received: £5,350,000 from Blackburn Rovers for Christian Dailly, August, 1998

Pos		Pld	W	D	L	F	A	Pts
16	Derby	38	9	11	18	44	57	38

Derby County
"The Rams"

**Pride Park Stadium,
Derby DE24 8XL
Tel: 01332 202 202
www.dcfc.co.uk**

Season Review by
John Ley

The Daily Telegraph

Before the start of the new season Jim Smith signed a new two-year extension to his contract, proof that the Pride Park board remain 100 per cent behind the 'Bald Eagle' despite a disappointing season.

Smith lost Paulo Wanchope to West Ham but fell foul of red tape while trying to sign his proposed replacement. Esteban Fuertes arrived from Argentina and, after protracted work permit problems, eventually made his debut five games into the season. He scored on his second appearance but when the club arrived back from a mid-season break abroad, he was refused re-entry over irregularities with his passport and did not play for Derby again after that.

Smith, for whom new signing Seth Johnson enjoyed a good season, was busy in the transfer market, buying Lee Morris, Branko Strupar, Craig Burley and Georgi Kinkladze, and bringing Avi Nimni in on loan, while Spencer Prior, Francesco Baiano, Vas Borbokis, Kevin Harper and Igor Stimac all left. Now will be a time for consolidation.

Useful Information

Rams Superstore

Pride Park Stadium (NE Corner)

Opening Times:

Monday-Friday: 9.00am-6.00pm

Saturdays: 9.00am-5.30pm

Sundays: 10.00am-4.00pm

Match Saturdays and Sundays 9.00am until 1 hour after final whistle Tel: **01332 209 000**

Mail Order Service: **01332 209 999**

Rams City Centre Store

St Peter's Churchyard, Derby

Opening Times:

Monday-Saturday:9.00am-5.30pm (including match Saturdays)

Closed Sundays

Tel: **01332 370 123**

Rams@East Midlands

East Midlands Airport

Tel: 01332 814932 for opening times

Stadium Tours

Contact merchandise hotline:

01332 209999

Corporate Hospitality

Contact Simon Moore or Andy Dawson:

01332 667 575

Literature

Programme £2

Quarterly magazine Rampage £2.50

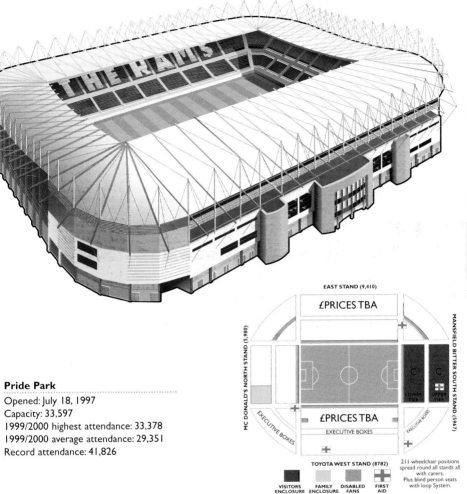

EAST STAND (9,410)

£PRICES TBA

MC DONALD'S NORTH STAND (5,980)

MANSFIELD BITTER SOUTH STAND (5967)

LOWER TIER

UPPER TIER

EXECUTIVE BOXES

£PRICES TBA

EXECUTIVE BOXES

EXECUTIVE BOXES

TOYOTA WEST STAND (8782)

211 wheelchair positions spread round all stands all with carers. Plus blind person seats with loop System.

VISITORS ENCLOSURE

FAMILY ENCLOSURE

DISABLED FANS

FIRST AID

Pride Park

Opened: July 18, 1997

Capacity: 33,597

1999/2000 highest attendance: 33,378

1999/2000 average attendance: 29,351

Record attendance: 41,826

Pre-Match & Half Time Entertainment

PA announcer plays a selection of chart and popular music.

Premium Club Prize Draw (members only) and Gold Rush Prize Draw - tickets available on matchday prices £1

Restaurants

Baseball Bar and Grill open daily 11.00am - 111.00pm (members only on matchdays). For Rammie/Rams themed birthday parties or other enquiries call **01332 667555**

Miscellaneous

Local access cable service 'Vision Rams on Cable', on channel 61 ,Derby Cable & Wireless network 6.30pm Fridays and 9am Saturdays.

Booking Information

General Enquiries :

01332 202 202

Credit Card Bookings:

01332 209 999

Travel Club:

01332 209 999

Junior Club:

01332 667 531

Results Breakdown

powered by football.co.uk

POINTS WON OR LOST AT BOTH HOME AND AWAY
for the latest stats and to share your memories go to football.co.uk

key:
■ win ■ draw
■ loss -**O**- league position
home fixtures are in red

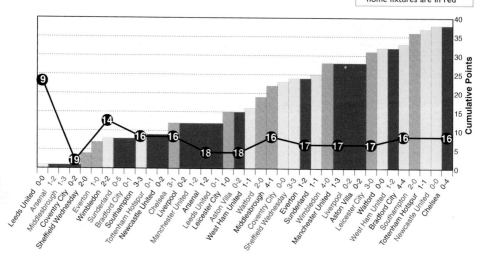

A dreadful start saw Derby drop in the bottom three as early as late August. They took five attempts before winning a game, at Sheffield Wednesday, but it was their form at Pride Park that was most disconcerting.

Of their first 10 home games, Derby won two and lost the other eight; a stadium that, previously, had seen Smith's team so strong had become their Achilles heal. By May they had won six times at home; not since the 1990-91 season, when they were relegated from the old First Division, had Derby won fewer home games. The 10 Pride Park defeats represented the club's worst ever

home record, equalling the 10 defeats at the old Baseball Ground in the 1992-93 season.

The 38 points Derby won to stave off relegation was their worst points tally for nine years. They managed to collect 17 away points, thanks to seven draws including that remarkable 4-4 stalemate at fellow strugglers Bradford, only the third time that result has been achieved in the Carling Premiership.

The 44 goals accrued by Derby was actually four more than they had scored the previous season. The 22 at home equalled the poor tally the previous season –

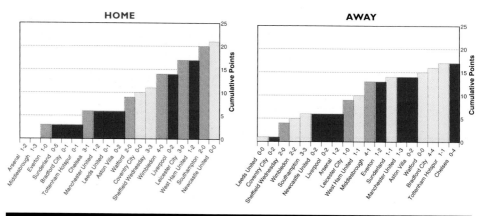

powered by football.co.uk

Derby County

Legend: ● = Red Card ○ = Yellow Card 00 = Time of goal ▲ = Player substituted

DATE	H/A	OPPONENT	H/T	F/T	POS	REFEREE	TEAM	Starting XI & notes	SUBSTITUTES USED
07/08	A	Leeds United	0-0	0-0	9	G.P.Barber	Poom	Prior○, Laursen, Carbonari, Dorigo○, Delap○, Johnson○, Powell○, Bojano▲, Eranio▲, Sturridge▲	Burton▲ Boborkis▲ Beck▲
10/08	H	Arsenal	1-1	1-2	15	S.J.Lodge	Poom	Prior○, Laursen, Carbonari, Schnoor, Delap 45, Johnson, Powell, Bojano▲, Eranio▲, Beck▲	Boborkis▲ Burton▲
14/08	H	Middlesbrough	1-2	1-3	17	S.G.Bennett	Poom	Prior▲, Laursen, Carbonari, Burton○ 41, Delap, Johnson, Powell, Bojano▲, Eranio▲, Schnoor	Schnoor● Bohinen▲
21/08	A	Coventry City	0-1	0-2	19	J.T.Winter	Poom	Prior, Laursen, Carbonari, Boborkis, Delap, Johnson, Powell, Burton, Eranio▲, Bohinen▲	Beck▲ Harper▲
25/08	A	Sheffield Wednesday	0-0	2-0	18	M.D.Reed	Hoult	Prior, Laursen, Carbonari, Schnoor, Delap 54, Johnson, Powell, Bohinen▲, Boborkis▲, Fuertes 79▲	Sturridge▲ 79 Harper▲ Beck▲
28/08	H	Everton	0-0	1-0	13	A.P.D'Urso	Hoult	Prior, Laursen, Carbonari, Schnoor, Delap, Johnson, Powell, Bohinen▲, Boborkis, Fuertes 47▲	Boano▲ 47 Eranio▲ Sturridge▲
11/09	A	Wimbledon	1-0	2-2	14	A.G.Wiley	Hoult	Prior, Laursen, Carbonari 14, Schnoor▲, Delap, Johnson○, Powell, Burton▲, Eranio▲, Fuertes	Beck▲ Boano▲ Boino▲
18/09	H	Sunderland	0-0	0-5	15	P.Jones	Hoult	Prior, Laursen, Carbonari, Schnoor▲, Delap, Johnson, Powell, Beck▲, Eranio▲, Fuertes	Harper▲ Boino▲ Boino▲
25/09	H	Bradford City	1-2	3-3	16	G.Poll	Hoult	Prior, Elliott, Carbonari, Dorigo, Delap 21, Johnson, Boborkis▲, Boano▲, Eranio▲, Sturridge	Christie▲ Harper▲ Murray▲
04/10	A	Southampton	1-2	—	18	M.R.Halsey	Hoult	Prior, Laursen ▲75, Carbonari▲, Dorigo, Delap, Johnson, Powell▲, Schnoor, Fuertes●, Sturridge	Harper▲ Boborkis▲ Beck▲ 90
16/10	H	Tottenham Hotspur	0-1	0-1	17	P.A.Durkin	Hoult	Boborkis▲, Laursen, Schnoor, Dorigo▲, Delap, Johnson, Eranio, Morris▲, Beck, Boano▲	Boano▲ Christie▲ Murray▲
25/10	A	Newcastle United	0-1	0-2	19	S.W.Dunn	Hoult	Schnoor, Laursen, Boino▲, Dorigo▲, Delap, Johnson, Powell○, Eranio○, Morris▲, Beck	Prior▲ Christie▲ Burton▲
30/10	A	Chelsea	1-1	3-1	16	K.J.Harris	Hoult	Schnoor○, Laursen▲, Carbonari, Dorigo▲, Delap 80 88, Johnson, Powell, Burton○ 7, Fuertes▲, Beck	Boborkis▲ Morris▲ Boborkis▲
06/11	H	Liverpool	0-0	0-2	17	U.D.Rennie	Hoult	Schnoor○, Laursen▲, Carbonari, Dorigo, Delap, Johnson, Powell, Eranio▲, Fuertes▲, Burton	Boborkis▲ Prior▲ Sturridge▲
20/11	H	Manchester United	1-2	1-2	8	M.D.Reed	Poom	Schnoor●, Laursen, Carbonari, Burley, Delap 90, Johnson○, Powell, Kinkladze▲, Robinson▲, Sturridge▲	Murray▲ Prior▲ Christie▲
28/11	A	Arsenal	1-1	1-2	18	A.P.D'Urso	Poom	Prior, Laursen▲, Carbonari, Dorigo, Delap 90, Johnson○, Powell, Burley▲, Sturridge 2, Sturridge	Elliott▲ Robinson▲ Kinkladze▲
05/12	H	Leeds United	0-0	0-1	18	P.E.Alcock	Poom	Elliott, Laursen▲, Elliott, Burley, Delap, Johnson, Powell 69○, Burley, Sturridge▲, Sturridge	Prior● Christie▲ Dorigo▲
18/12	A	Leicester City	0-2	0-2	18	D.R.Ellaray	Poom	Prior▲, Laursen○, Carbonari, Dorigo, Delap, Johnson, Powell○, Burley, Sturridge 3, Shpupr	Christie▲ Shpupr▲
26/12	H	Aston Villa	0-2	0-2	18	A.B.Wilkie	Poom	Prior, Laursen○, Carbonari○, Elliott, Bohinen, Nimni, Powell▲, Kinkladze, Robinson▲, Sturridge	Schnoor▲ Christie▲ Robinson▲
28/12	A	West Ham United	1-1	1-3	17	B.Knight	Poom	Elliott, Laursen, Carbonari▲, Dorigo▲, Delap, Johnson, Powell, Burley, Shpupr 3, Sturridge	Schnoor▲ Christie▲
03/01	H	Watford	1-0	2-0	17	P.E.Alcock	Poom	Elliott, Laursen, Carbonari, Dorigo▲, Bohinen▲, Nimni, Robinson▲, Burley, Shpupr 2 72, Shpupr	Schnoor▲ Robinson▲
15/01	H	Middlesbrough	1-0	4-1	16	M.R.Halsey	Poom	Elliott▲, Schnoor, Carbonari○, Bohinen▲, Johnson, Burley 90, Christie▲ 8 59, Burton 47	Nimni▲ Kinkladze▲
22/01	A	Coventry City	0-0	0-0	16	G.P.Barber	Poom	Elliott○, Laursen, Carbonari, Schnoor, Eranio▲, Bohinen, Burley, Shpupr, Shpupr 71	Christie▲ Kinkladze▲
05/02	H	Sheffield Wednesday	3-3	3-3	17	D.R.Ellaray	Poom	Elliott, Laursen, Elliott, Dorigo▲, Delap●1, Johnson○, Kinkladze, Burley 90, Christie 90	Kinkladze▲ Sturridge▲
12/02	A	Everton	0-2	1-2	17	U.D.Rennie	Poom	Prior▲, Laursen, Elliott, Dorigo▲, Eranio, Johnson, Powell 5, Burley, Shpupr, Sturridge ▲60	Nimni▲ 60 Robinson▲
26/02	A	Sunderland	0-0	1-1	17	A.G.Wiley	Poom	Elliott, Laursen, Carbonari 63, Eranio, Johnson●, Powell, Burley, Kinkladze 36 52, Sturridge▲6	Nimni▲ Schnoor▲
04/03	H	Wimbledon	0-0	4-0	17	A.P.D'Urso	Poom	Elliott▲, Laursen, Carbonari, Eranio, Johnson, Powell, Kinkladze, Kinkladze▲65, Sturridge▲	Sturridge▲90 Stupridge▲
11/03	A	Manchester United	0-1	1-3	17	J.T.Winter	Poom	Elliott●, Laursen, Carbonari▲, Dorigo●, Delap, Johnson, Schnoor, Eranio, Christie▲71	Stupridge▲66 Schnoor▲
18/03	H	Liverpool	0-1	0-2	17	B.Knight	Poom	Elliott●, Laursen○, Carbonari○▲, Eranio, Delap, Nimni▲, Powell▲, Kinkladze, Christie	Shpupr▲ Shpupr▲
25/03	H	Aston Villa	0-1	0-1	17	P.E.Alcock	Poom	Elliott▲, Laursen○▲, Carbonari, Schnoor○, Delap, Johnson, Powell, Kinkladze, Shpupr	Elliott▲ Dorigo▲
02/04	A	Leicester City	3-0	3-0	17	G.Poll	Poom	Schnoor, Laursen, Carbonari, Burley▲15, Delap 44, Johnson, Powell, Burley 36 52, Shpupr▲6	Dorigo▲ Christie▲ Murray▲
08/04	H	Watford	0-0	2-0	16	S.G.Bennett	Poom	Schnoor, Laursen, Elliott, Burley, Delap, Johnson, Powell, Kinkladze, Stupridge 84	Christie▲ Christie▲
15/04	A	West Ham United	0-2	1-2	16	M.R.Halsey	Poom	Elliott▲, Laursen, Carbonari○, Dorigo▲, Delap, Johnson, Bohinen, Burley 90, Stupridge 71	Kinkladze▲ Robinson▲
21/04	A	Bradford City	3-4	4-4	16	A.B.Wilkie	Poom	Elliott▲, Laursen, Carbonari○, Dorigo▲, Delap ●1, Johnson, Kinkladze, Burley 36 52, Shpupr ▲6	Christie 42 Kinkladze▲
24/04	H	Southampton	2-0	2-0	16	N.S.Barry	Poom	Schnoor○, Laursen, Burley, Dorigo▲, Delap, Johnson, Powell 5, Kinkladze, Shpupr	Christie▲ Boerhien▲ Murray▲
29/04	A	Tottenham Hotspur	0-1	1-1	16	A.G.Wiley	Poom	Schnoor●, Laursen○, Carbonari●, Dorigo, Murray▲, Johnson, Powell, Burton▲, Christie	Burton▲ Jackson▲ Murray▲
06/05	H	Newcastle United	0-0	0-0	16	A.G.Wiley	Poom	Elliott○, Laursen, Carbonari○, Dorigo, Delap, Burley, Bohinen■, Kinkladze▲, Burton	Bohinen▲ Jackson▲
14/05	A	Chelsea	0-0	0-4	16	J.T.Winter	Poom	Elliott▲, Laursen, Burley, Dorigo, Delap▲, Johnson, Bohinen●, Sturridge, Christie	Sturridge▲ Murray▲ Riggott▲

81

Goal Analysis

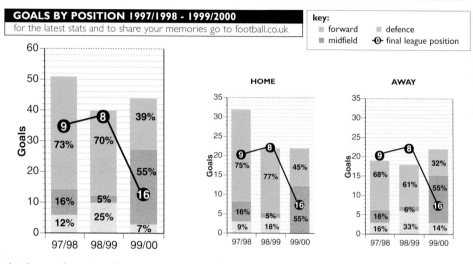

GOALS BY POSITION 1997/1998 - 1999/2000
for the latest stats and to share your memories go to football.co.uk

key:
- forward
- midfield
- defence
- -O- final league position

HOME

AWAY

their lowest at home since the 1987-88 season – but the 22 away goals was the best return on their travels for four seasons.

If the attack had matched the improvement shown from midfield, Derby could have been challenging for Europe rather than fighting against the drop. In the previous season a paltry five per cent of goals came from midfield; with Rory Delap enjoying his best ever season in goal terms with eight (he had scored just seven goals in 101 previous appearances) the

contribution from midfield was vastly improved.

But it was in attack where Derby struggled. The departure of Wanchope caused problems Derby failed to recover from; how ironic that, on his return, with West Ham, he scored both goals.

Dean Sturridge was a bit-part player and added six goals from 14 starts while Branko Strupar, who brought hundreds of loyal Belgians to Pride Park for every home game, offered promise for this season by quickly settling and showing why he was a member of his

GOALS BY TIME PERIOD 1999/2000
for the latest stats and to share your memories go to football.co.uk

key:
- goals for
- goals against

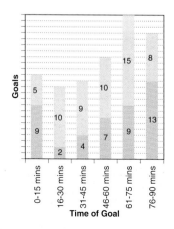

HOME

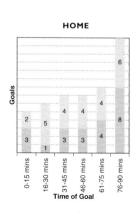

AWAY

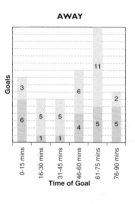

What a difference a *CARLING* makes.

Goal Analysis

Derby County

HOW GOALS WERE SCORED 1999/2000
for the latest stats and to share your memories go to football.co.uk

key:
- header
- volley
- penalty
- close range*
- free kick
- inside area
- outside area
- own goal

* inside six yard box

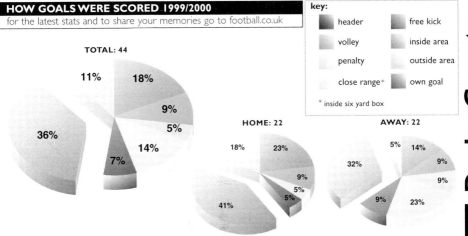

TOTAL: 44

HOME: 22

AWAY: 22

adopted country's Euro 2000 squad.

Smith spent £3 million on the Croatian-born, naturalised Belgian in December, and in only his second full game he scored twice in the 2-0 win over Watford. He also scored Derby's equaliser at Old Trafford before they lost 3-1 and offered great promise for the 2000-2001 season.

Defensively, goals were at a premium with only Horacio Carbonari and Jacob Laursen providing any goals.

It should also be noted that Mart Poom, their Estonian goalkeeper, saved two penalties, at Middlesbrough and at Manchester United.

In terms of the timing of Derby's goals, they were most dangerous in the closing half an hour when 22 of their 44 goals were scored, while 13 came in the closing 15 minutes.

They were also active in the opening 15 minutes, particularly away from home; of their 22 away goals, six came in the first 15 minutes, but then they dried

HOW GOALS WERE CONCEDED 1999/2000
for the latest stats and to share your memories go to football.co.uk

key:
- header
- volley
- penalty
- close range*
- free kick
- inside area
- outside area
- own goal

* inside six yard box

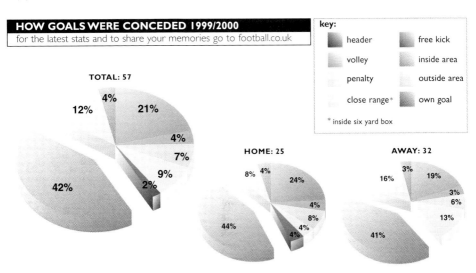

TOTAL: 57

HOME: 25

AWAY: 32

Squad and Performance

SQUAD LIST

for the latest stats and to share your memories go to football.co.uk

Position	Name	Appearances	Appearances as substitute	Goals	Clean Sheets	Yellow Cards	Red Cards
G	R.Hoult	10			2	1	
G	M.Poom	28			9	2	
D	V.Boborkis	6	6			2	
D	H.Carbonari	29		2		10	
D	T.Dorigo	20	3			4	
D	S.Elliott	18	2			1	
D	R.Jackson		2				
D	J.Laursen	36			1	5	
D	S.Prior	15	5			6	
D	C.Riggott		1				
D	S.Schnoor	22	7		4	4	2
M	P.Boertien		2				
M	L.Bohinen	8	5			1	
M	C.Burley	18		5		6	
M	M.Christie	10	11	6		2	
M	R.Delap	34		8		5	1
M	S.Eranio	17	2			3	
M	K.Harper	4				1	
M	S.Johnson	36		1		13	
M	G.Kinkladze	12	5	1		2	
M	A.Murray	1	7			1	
M	A.Nimni	2	2	1			
M	D.Powell	31		2		7	
F	F.Baiano	5	4			1	
F	M.Beck	5	6	1			
F	D.Burton	15	4	4		6	
F	E.Fuertes	8		1		2	1
F	L.Morris	2	1				
F	M.Robinson	3	5			1	
F	B.Strupar	13	2	5		1	
F	D.Sturridge	14	11	6		3	

up; 14 of the 22 away goals came in the second half.

They were most dangerous away from home when poaching goals from close range; nearly a quarter of their away goals came from within the six-yard box.

Smith's squad suffered injuries and a huge turnover over in personnel, meaning that he was forced to call upon 31 players; only Newcastle used more. Not one player was ever present, though Jacob Laursen, was absent only twice; since he arrived from Silkeborg he has played in 137 (90 per cent) of Derby's 152 Carling Premiership games.

Derby managed to beat only one team home and away – Midlands rivals Leicester – but suffered double defeats against four of the top six. Indeed, the 3-1 home win over Chelsea, when Delap scored twice in the

TEAM PERFORMANCE TABLE

for the latest stats and to share your memories go to football.co.uk

Position	Club	Points Won	Percentage of points won at home	percentage of points won away	overall percentage of points won
1.	MANCHESTER UNITED	0/6			
2.	ARSENAL	0/6			
3.	LEEDS UNITED	1/6	20%	7%	13%
4.	LIVERPOOL	0/6			
5.	CHELSEA	3/6			
6.	ASTON VILLA	0/6			
7.	SUNDERLAND	1/6			
8.	LEICESTER CITY	6/6	20%	40%	30%
9.	TOTTENHAM HOTSPUR	1/6			
10.	WEST HAM UNITED	1/6			
11.	NEWCASTLE UNITED	1/6			
12.	MIDDLESBROUGH	3/6			
13.	EVERTON	3/6	53%	27%	40%
14.	SOUTHAMPTON	4/6			
15.	COVENTRY CITY	1/6			
16.	DERBY COUNTY	38 pts			
17.	BRADFORD CITY	1/6			
18.	WIMBLEDON	4/6	58%	50%	54%
19.	SHEFFIELD WEDNESDAY	4/6			
20.	WATFORD	4/6			

The figures show a team's performance against clubs in each quarter of the final league table. The first column represents points won from the total available against each team in the league.

What a difference a CARLING makes.

Discipline and Season Summary

Derby County

BOOKINGS BY POSITION 1997/1998 - 1999/2000
for the latest stats and to share your memories go to football.co.uk

key:
- forward
- defence
- midfield
- goalkeeper

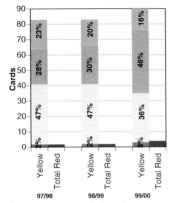

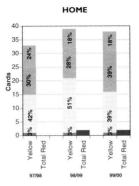

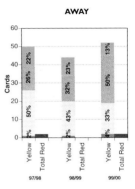

final 10 minutes, was their only success against any team in the top seven.

Derby collected more cautions than any other team in all four divisions, let alone the Carling Premiership, and more than at any time in their history. Seth Johnson, their England Under-21 midfielder, was the worst offender, receiving 13, the highest total in the top division, equal with Leeds' Lee Bowyer. In addition, Carbonari also saw double figures with 10 yellow cards. No fewer than 25 Derby players were cautioned, again the highest total in the Carling Premiership; only three players who started a League game – Avi Nimni, Mikkel Beck and Lee Morris – avoided a booking.

Derby also had four men sent off. While that was not unusual in the Carling Premiership, it was their highest ever number of red cards in a season.

Fuertes's disappointing time in England was not helped by a dismissal – and subsequent three match ban – in the 1-0 home defeat by Bradford, while Stefan Schnoor was sent off twice – in the controversial home defeat by Manchester United when Smith accused players of influencing referee Mike Reed, and at Tottenham.

Derby were predictable at home; if they were not winning at half time the chances were that they would not take the three points. Of the three occasions they were ahead at half time they went on to win but of the remaining 16 games they were either drawing or losing and only three times did they turn the game around.

HALF TIME - FULL TIME COMPARATIVE CHART
for the latest stats and to share your memories go to football.co.uk

HOME				AWAY				TOTAL			
Number of Home Half Time Wins	Full Time Result W	L	D	Number of Away Half Time Wins	Full Time Result W	L	D	Total Number of Half Time Wins	Full Time Result W	L	D
3	3	0	0	2	1	0		1	5	4	1
Number of Home Half Time Losses	Full Time Result W	L	D	Number of Away Half Time Losses	Full Time Result W	L	D	Total Number of Half Time Losses	Full Time Result W	L	D
6	0	5	1	7	0	5	2	13	0	10	3
Number of Home Half Time Draws	Full Time Result W	L	D	Number of Away Half Time Draws	Full Time Result W	L	D	Total Number of Half Time Draws	Full Time Result W	L	D
10	3	5	2	10	2	3	5	20	5	8	7

What a difference a CARLING makes.

Maps and Directions

There is no matchday parking in and around the stadium. Pride Park is a no-parking zone; people without official Derby County parking permits should park in the city of Derby and take the shuttle bus to Pride Park from Derby Bus Station on the Cockpitt Traffic Island.

From the North:
Leave the M1 at junction 28 and follow A38 into Derby. Follow signs for A52 (Nottingham) off the Pentagon Island in Derby. After 1 mile, look for a large Toys R Us store on the right. Take first left at signs for the Wyvern Shopping Centre (also signposted Pride Park Stadium) and continue to traffic island. Take second exit, passing Sainsbury's on your right, and continue to next traffic island. Take first exit over bridge into Pride Park. The stadium is on the left.

From the South:
Leave the M1 at junction 25. At the roundabout take first left signposted Derby (A52). Stay on this road for 5 miles, following signs for city centre. Look out for signs for Travel Inn on your left and a signpost for Pride Park Stadium. Take next left into the Wyvern Shopping Centre and continue to the traffic island. Take first exit over bridge into Pride Park. The stadium is on the left.

Pride Park Stadium is a 20 minute walk from Derby Midland Railway Station.

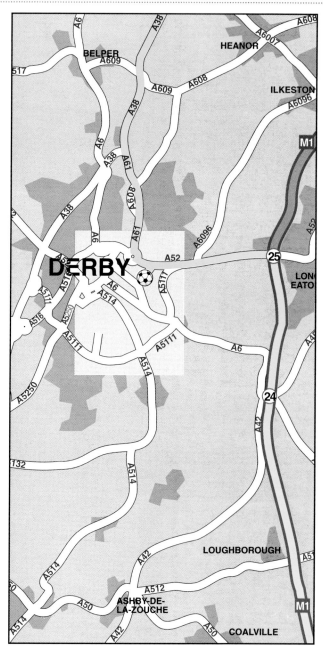

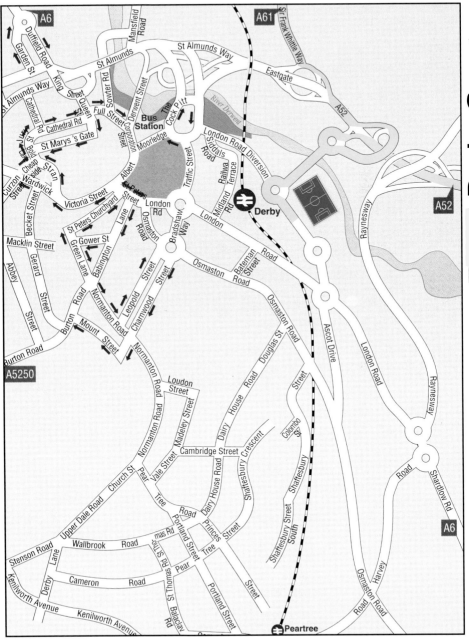

Derby County

87

Pos		Pld	W	D	L	F	A	Pts
13	Everton	38	12	14	12	59	49	50

Everton

"The Toffees"

Goodison Park, Liverpool L4 4EL
Tel: 0151 330 2200
www.evertonfc.com

Season Review by
John Ley

The Daily Telegraph

After their flirtations with relegation in previous seasons, Everton's return from the 1999-2000 season must be regarded as a success. The Toffees finished in 13th place, their best finish for four years. They won more games than at any time since the 1995-96 season and, finally, looked like a team capable of winning something.

Manager Walter Smith also had to contend with financial restraints; he kept Everton in a respectable position while making more than £12 million profit in the transfer market.

He sold Olivier Dacourt, Ibrahima Bakayoko, Marco Materazzi and Craig Short, Kevin Campbell was signed permanently and was joined by Richard Gough and Mark Pembridge. During the season Abel Xavier, Joe Max Moore, Stephen Hughes and Mark Hughes arrived but injuries were disruptive; Campbell needed a knee ligament operation, while other injury victims were Francis Jeffers, Scot Gemmill and Alex Cleland.

Useful Information

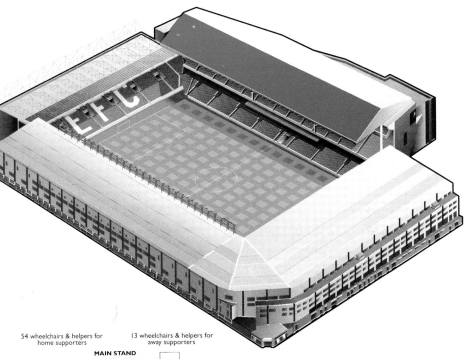

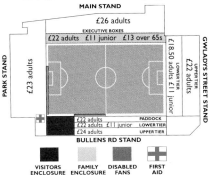

54 wheelchairs & helpers for home supporters   13 wheelchairs & helpers for away supporters

MAIN STAND

£26 adults

EXECUTIVE BOXES

£22 adults   £11 junior   £13 over 65s

PARK STAND

£23 adults

UPPER TIER £18.50 adults £11 junior
LOWER TIER £22 adults

GWLADYS STREET STAND

£22 adults   PADDOCK
£22 adults £11 junior   LOWER TIER
£24 adults   UPPER TIER

BULLENS RD STAND

VISITORS ENCLOSURE   FAMILY ENCLOSURE   DISABLED FANS   FIRST AID

Everton

Goodison Park

Opened: August 24, 1892
Capacity: 40,260
1999/2000 highest attendance: 40,052
1999/2000 average attendance: 34,775
Record attendance: 78,299

Corporate Hospitality

Hospitality package facilities include Captains Table, Joe Mercer Suite, Alex Young Lounge and Legends Sports Bar. There are also various sponsorship packages available. Contact Rita London:
0151 330 2400

Pre-Match & Half Time Entertainment

Half time draw - tickets available around the ground for £1. PA announcements and a scoreboard message service.

Miscellaneous Information

Radio Everton broadcasts on 1602 AM and on the official web site on matchdays, 12.00pm-6.00pm.

Booking Information

General Enquiries:
0151 330 2200
Supporters Club Line:
0151 330 2208
Credit Card Bookings:
0807 383 7866
Travel Club:
0151 330 2277

Results Breakdown

powered by **football.co.uk**

POINTS WON OR LOST AT BOTH HOME AND AWAY
for the latest stats and to share your memories go to football.co.uk

key:
- win
- draw
- loss -**0**-league position

home fixtures are in red

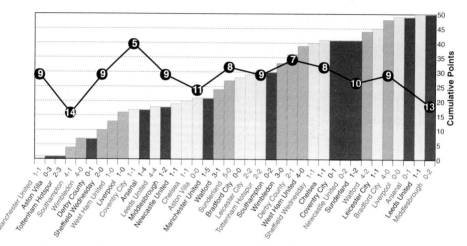

A year earlier Everton had struggled to win at Goodison Park; they had to wait seven games, into November, before their first home victory. But they responded by staying unbeaten at home last season until March when Newcastle secured a 2-0 win there. Five wins in six games soon after the start of the season took Everton into fifth place, their highest placing for seven years, but they followed that with a sequence of eight games without a win.

Indeed, but for successive victories, at Watford and home to Sunderland, and three draws they could

have slumped lower than 11th place. Between the 5-0 thumping of Sunderland in December and the 4-2 win over Watford, Everton won just three times in 12 games.

Three successive victories coincided with confirmation of the Bill Kenwright takeover though a poor finish saw Everton drop into the bottom half. Don Hutchison lost the captaincy after falling out with Smith and with it his place in the side.

Only three teams, Manchester United, Arsenal and Newcastle, scored more goals than Everton last

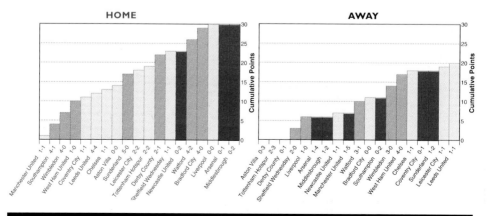

What a difference a **CARLING** makes.

Everton

● = Red Card   = Yellow Card   ▲ = Player substituted   OO = Time of goal

DATE	H/A	OPPONENT	H/T	F/T	POS	REFEREE	TEAM											SUBSTITUTES USED
08/08	H	Manchester United	0-1	1-1	9	D.J.Gallagher	Gerrard	Weir	Gough	Watson	Unsworth	Ward	Collins	Gemmill	Bornby	Hutchison	Campbell	Phelan▲ Campbell▲ Cadamarteri▲
11/08	A	Aston Villa	0-1	0-3	16	G.P.Barber	Gerrard	Ball	Gough	Watson	Unsworth	Ward	Collison●	Gemmill▲	Bornby	Hutchison	Campbell	Jeffers▲ Pembridge▲
14/08	A	Tottenham Hotspur	2-3	2-3	18	P.E.Alcock	Gerrard	Weir	Gough	Dunne	Unsworth 24 75	Ward	Collins	Gemmill▲	Bornby	Jeffers	Campbell	Cleland▲ Hutchison▲ Cadamarteri▲
21/08	H	Southampton	1-0	4-1	14	B.Knight	Gerrard	Weir	Gough 36	Dunne	Unsworth	Pembridge▲	Collins	Hutchison▲	Bornby	Jeffers▲ 48	Campbell 54	Gemmill▲ Hutchison▲ Word▲
25/08	H	Wimbledon	1-0	4-0	7	J.T.Winter	Gerrard	Weir	Gough	Dunne	Unsworth 16	Pembridge▲	Word	Hutchison	Bornby▲ 46	Jeffers▲ 50	Campbell 68	Gemmill▲ Word▲ Cadamarteri▲
28/08	A	Derby County	0-0	0-1	11	A.P.D'Urso	Gerrard	Weir	Gough	Dunne●	Unsworth	Pembridge▲	Collins	Hutchison	Bornby	Jeffers▲	Campbell	Gemmill▲ Ball▲ Cadamarteri▲
11/09	H	Sheffield Wednesday	2-0	2-0	9	M.R.Halsey	Gerrard	Weir	Gough	Watson	Unsworth▲	Pembridge▲	Word▲	Gemmill 18	Bornby 15	Jeffers▲	Campbell	Xavier▲ Collins▲ Hutchison▲
19/09	A	West Ham United	0-0	1-0	8	S.G.Bennett	Gerrard	Weir	Gough	Dunne	Unsworth▲	Xavier	Collins	Hutchison▲	Bornby▲	Jeffers▲ 64	Campbell	Gemmill▲ Ball▲ Cleland▲
27/09	A	Liverpool	1-0	1-0	6	M.A.Riley	Gerrard	Weir	Gough	Dunne	Ball	Xavier	Collins	Hutchison	Bornby	Jeffers●	Campbell 4	Cadamarteri▲
02/10	H	Coventry City	1-1	1-1	5	N.S.Barry	Gerrard	Weir	Gough	Dunne▲	Ball	Xavier	Collins	Hutchison	Bornby▲	Jeffers 2	Campbell	Cadamarteri▲ Gemmill▲
16/10	A	Arsenal	1-1	1-4	7	S.W.Dunn	Gerrard	Weir	Gough	Ball	Unsworth▲	Xavier	Collins 16	Gemmill▲	Bornby▲	Hutchison	Campbell	Cleland▲ Cadamarteri▲
24/10	H	Leeds United	3-2	4-4	8	D.J.Gallagher	Gerrard	Weir 90	Gough	Watson	Unsworth▲	Ball▲	Collins	Gemmill	Bornby▲	Hutchison 37	Campbell 4 28	Johnson▲ Pembridge▲
30/10	A	Middlesbrough	1-1	1-2	9	A.P.D'Urso	Gerrard	Weir●	Gough	Dunne	Unsworth	Ball▲	Collins	Pembridge	Bornby▲	Hutchison	Campbell 4	Cadamarteri▲ Johnson▲
07/11	H	Newcastle United	0-0	1-1	10	M.D.Reed	Cleland	Weir	Cleland	Dunne	Unsworth	Ball▲	Pembridge	Pembridge	Bornby▲	Hutchison	Campbell 61	Johnson ▲
20/11	A	Chelsea	0-0	0-1	11	M.R.Halsey	Gerrard	Weir	Gough	Dunne	Unsworth	Xavier	Collins	Hutchison	Bornby▲	Jeffers	Campbell 15	Grant▲
27/11	H	Aston Villa	0-0	0-0	11	P.Jones	Gerrard	Weir	Gough	Dunne	Unsworth	Pembridge	Pembridge	Hutchison	Bornby▲	Jeffers	Campbell	Grant▲
04/12	H	Manchester United	1-3	1-5	12	G.Poll	Gerrard	Weir	Gough	Dunne▲	Unsworth 86	Xavier	Collins	Pembridge▲	Bornby▲	Jeffers 7	Campbell	Cleland▲ Grant▲
18/12	A	Watford	2-0	3-1	11	A.B.Wilkie	Gerrard	Weir	Cleland▲	Dunne	Unsworth	Xavier	Collins	Pembridge	Bornby 4	Hutchison 37	Campbell	Watson▲ Cleland▲
26/12	H	Sunderland	3-0	5-0	8	S.J.Lodge	Gerrard	Weir	Gough	Dunne	Ball 45	Xavier	Collins	Hutchison 16 25	Bornby▲	Jeffers▲ 41	Campbell 72	Moore▲ Cleland▲
28/12	A	Bradford City	2-2	2-2	9	U.D.Rennie	Gerrard	Weir	Gough	Ball	Unsworth	Pembridge	Collins 62	Moore▲	Bornby	Jeffers	Jeffers	Gemmill▲ Cadamarteri ▲
03/01	A	Leicester City	1-2	2-2	9	J.T.Winter	Gerrard	Weir	Gough	Watson	Unsworth 56	Pembridge	Collins	Hutchison 15	Bornby	Hutchison	Campbell	Gemmill▲ Moore▲
15/01	H	Tottenham Hotspur	1-2	2-2	9	A.G.Wiley	Gerrard	Weir	Dunne	Watson	Unsworth	Pembridge	Collins	Hutchison	Bornby	Jeffers	Campbell 22	Moore▲ 90 Boll▲
22/01	H	Southampton	0-0	0-2	11	A.P.D'Urso	Gerrard	Weir	Gough	Dunne▲	Unsworth▲	Pembridge	Collins	Hutchison	Moore	Jeffers	Campbell 22	Simonsen▲ Moore▲
06/02	A	Wimbledon	3-0	3-0	10	G.P.Barber	Gerrard	Weir	Gough	Dunne	Ball	Pembridge	Ball	Hutchison▲	Moore	Cadamarteri	Campbell 52 60	Xavier▲ Boll▲
12/02	H	Derby County	2-0	2-1	7	U.D.Rennie	Gerrard	Weir	Gough	Ball	Unsworth	Pembridge	Moore 23	Hutchison	Moore	Moore 70	Campbell	Collins▲ Moore▲
26/02	A	West Ham United	1-0	4-0	7	P.E.Alcock	Myhre	Weir	Gough	Ball	Boll 45	Pembridge	Collins	Xavier	Bornby▲ 7 67	Moore 70	Campbell	Word▲ Cleland▲
04/03	H	Sheffield Wednesday	1-0	1-0	8	G.P.Barber	Myhre	Weir 33	Gough	Word▲	Unsworth	Pembridge	Collins	Xavier	Bornby	Jeffers	Campbell	Dunne▲
11/03	A	Chelsea	0-1	0-1	8	D.R.Elleray	Myhre	Weir	Gough	Dunne	Xavier	Pembridge	Collins	Moore▲	Bornby	Moore	Cadamarteri 69	
15/03	H	Coventry City	0-0	0-0	8	M.R.Halsey	Gerrard	Weir	Gough	Dunne	Xavier	Pembridge	Collins	Hughes S	Bornby	Moore	Moore	Gemmill▲ Unsworth▲
19/03	H	Newcastle United	0-0	0-2	10	G.P.Barber	Gerrard	Weir	Gough	Dunne	Xavier	Pembridge	Collins	Hughes S	Bornby	Moore▲	Hughes M ▲	Boll▲ Dunne▲
25/03	A	Sunderland	1-1	1-2	10	S.G.Bennett	Gerrard	Dunne	Gough	Unsworth	Xavier	Pembridge	Collins	Hughes S	Bornby▲ 38	Moore▲	Hughes M 18	Hutchison▲ Cadamarteri▲
01/04	H	Watford	3-1	4-2	9	S.W.Dunn	Gerrard	Dunne	Gough▲	Ball	Xavier	Pembridge	Collins	Hughes S ▲	Bornby	Moore 30 36	Hughes M ▲	Moore▲
08/04	H	Leicester City	1-1	1-0	8	A.G.Wiley	Gerrard	Weir	Gough	Dunne	Xavier	Pembridge	Collins	Hughes S	Moore	Moore▲	Hutchison 27	Dunne▲ Unsworth▲
15/04	A	Bradford City	2-0	4-0	9	P.E.Alcock	Gerrard	Weir	Jevons	Unsworth▲ 15	Xavier▲	Pembridge 2	Collins 82	Hughes S ▲	Bornby 54	Hutchison	Hughes M ▲	Dunne▲ Boll▲
21/04	H	Liverpool	0-0	0-0	9	G.Poll	Gerrard	Weir	Unsworth	Dunne	Xavier	Pembridge	Collins	Hughes S	Bornby▲	Hutchison	Hughes M ▲	Boll▲ Jevons▲
29/04	A	Arsenal	0-1	0-1	10	D.J.Gallagher	Gerrard	Weir	Unsworth	Xavier	Boll	Pembridge▲	Collins	Hughes S	Bornby 60	Hutchison	Hughes M ▲	Word▲ Jeffers▲
08/05	H	Leeds United	1-1	1-1	10	A.P.D'Urso	Gerrard	Weir	Unsworth	Dunne●	Boll	Pembridge▲	Collins	Hughes S	Bornby▲	Hutchison ●	Hughes M	Word▲ Cadamarteri▲
14/05	A	Middlesbrough	0-1	0-2	13	R.J.Harris	Gerrard	Weir▲	Unsworth	Dunne	Jevons	Jevons▲	Collins	Hughes S	Bornby	Hutchison	Hughes M	Milligan▲ Jeffers▲

Goal Analysis

powered by **football.co.uk**

GOALS BY POSITION 1997/1998 - 1999/2000
for the latest stats and to share your memories go to football.co.uk

key:
■ forward   ■ defence
■ midfield   -O- final league position

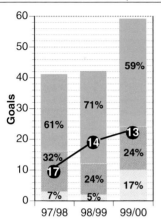

HOME

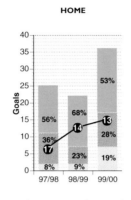

AWAY

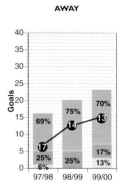

season; their 58 goals was their highest goal return for six years, a remarkable achievement given that Campbell was sidelined for a third of the season while Jeffers started only 16 games.

Campbell, whose knee injury was troubled by an infection, threatening to keep him out of the early part of this season, still managed 12 goals while Nick Barmby was called up for Euro 2000 duty after enjoying his best season for Everton. The nine goals he scored equalled his best ever League goals return,

set with Tottenham Hotspur five years previously.

Jeffers scored six and new American international Joe Max Moore, signed from New England on a free transfer in November, added an impressive half-a-dozen in just 11 starts including four in four successive Carling Premiership games.

The defence scored 17 per cent of Everton's total. David Unsworth was the chief contributor with six, including five penalties. He also missed from the spot, in the 4-0 home win over Wimbledon.

GOALS BY TIME PERIOD 1999/2000
for the latest stats and to share your memories go to football.co.uk

key:
■ goals for   ■ goals against

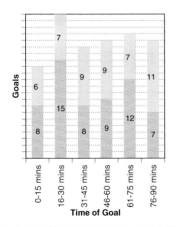

Time of Goal

HOME

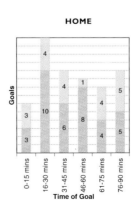

Time of Goal

AWAY

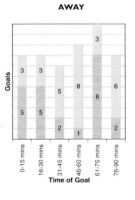

Time of Goal

What a difference a CARLING makes.

Goal Analysis

Everton

HOW GOALS WERE SCORED 1999/2000

for the latest stats and to share your memories go to football.co.uk

key:
- header
- volley
- penalty
- close range*
- free kick
- inside area
- outside area
- own goal

*inside six yard box

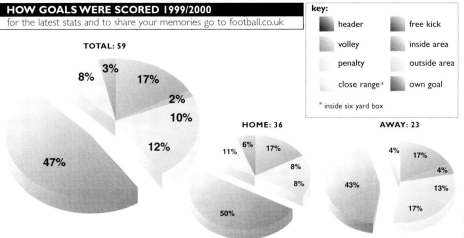

TOTAL: 59

3%
8%
17%
2%
10%
12%
47%

HOME: 36

6%
11%
17%
8%
8%
50%

AWAY: 23

4%
17%
4%
13%
17%
43%

Scotsman Hutchison scored six valuable goals from midfield including one after he had patched up his apparent differences with Smith when the pair fell out over a new contract.

Everton's strikers scored a larger percentage of their goals away from home, 70 per cent to the 53 per cent they claimed at Goodison Park.

Half the goals scored by Everton at Goodison were from inside the area while they poached 17 per cent of their away goals from inside the six-yard box.

Unsworth's penalties, plus one from Michael Ball when Unsworth was suspended, made up for no fewer than 10 per cent of Everton's goals.

Everton enjoyed the greater number of goals in the middle period of the first half, scoring 15 in between the 16th and 30th minutes; similarly, 12 of their 28 second half goals came midway through the period.

On their travels, Everton scored most goals midway through the second half though they

HOW GOALS WERE CONCEDED 1999/2000

for the latest stats and to share your memories go to football.co.uk

key:
- header
- volley
- penalty
- close range*
- free kick
- inside area
- outside area
- own goal

*inside six yard box

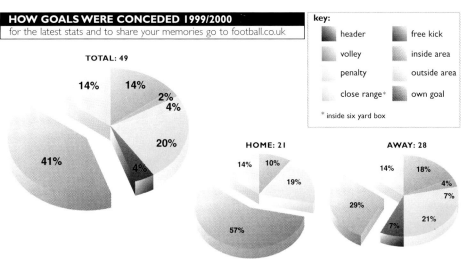

TOTAL: 49

14%
14%
2%
4%
20%
4%
41%

HOME: 21

14%
10%
19%
57%

AWAY: 28

14%
18%
4%
7%
21%
7%
29%

Squad and Performance

SQUAD LIST

for the latest stats and to share your memories go to football.co.uk

Position	Name	Appearances	Appearances as substitute	Goals	Clean Sheets	Yellow Cards	Red Cards
G	P.Gerrard	34			9	3	
G	T.Myhre	4			2		
G	S.Simonsen	1					
D	A.Cleland	3	6			1	
D	R.Dunne	27	4			4	2
D	R.Gough	29			1	3	
D	T.Phelan	1					
D	D.Unsworth	32	1	6		4	
D	M.Ward	6	4			1	
D	D.Watson	6	1			3	
D	D.Weir	34		2		2	1
M	M.Ball	14	11	1		3	
M	J.Collins	33	2	2		4	1
M	P.Degn		1				
M	S.Gemmill	6	8	1		1	
M	T.Grant		2				
M	S.Hughes	11		1			
M	D.Hutchison	28	3	6		6	1
M	P.Jevons	2	1				
M	M.Pembridge	29	2	2		2	
M	A.Xavier	18	2			1	
F	N.Barmby	37		9		6	
F	D.Cadamarteri	3	13	1		2	
F	K.Campbell	26		12		1	
F	M.Hughes	9		1		2	
F	F.Jeffers	16	5	6			1
F	T.Johnson		3	1			
F	J.Milligan		1				
F	J.Moore	11	4	6		1	

managed only two in the closing 15 minutes, Unsworth claiming late penalties at Tottenham, in the 3-2 defeat, at Watford, where they won 3-1.

Barmby was Everton's most consistent performer, missing just one game, through suspension. Scotsmen David Weir and John Collins were also regulars while goalkeeper Paul Gerrard made the position his own ahead of Norway's Thomas Myhre, who was later loaned to Birmingham for first team games ahead of Euro 2000.

Strangely, Everton struggled against the lesser teams, particularly away from home. They collected just eight per cent of their away points at clubs occupying 11th to 15th place. They were, however, successful at home to the poorest sides, beating four

TEAM PERFORMANCE TABLE

for the latest stats and to share your memories go to football.co.uk

Position	Club	Points Won	Percentage of points won at home	percentage of points won away	overall percentage of points won
1.	MANCHESTER UNITED	1/6			
2.	ARSENAL	0/6			
3.	LEEDS UNITED	2/6	27%	33%	30%
4.	LIVERPOOL	4/6			
5.	CHELSEA	2/6			
6.	ASTON VILLA	1/6			
7.	SUNDERLAND	3/6			
8.	LEICESTER CITY	2/6	60%	27%	43%
9.	TOTTENHAM HOTSPUR	1/6			
10.	WEST HAM UNITED	6/6			
11.	NEWCASTLE UNITED	1/6			
12.	MIDDLESBROUGH	0/6			
13.	EVERTON	50 pts	33%	8%	21%
14.	SOUTHAMPTON	3/6			
15.	COVENTRY CITY	1/6			
16.	DERBY COUNTY	3/6			
17.	BRADFORD CITY	4/6			
18.	WIMBLEDON	6/6	87%	67%	77%
19.	SHEFFIELD WEDNESDAY	4/6			
20.	WATFORD	6/6			

The figures show a team's performance against clubs in each quarter of the final league table. The first column represents points won from the total available against each team in the league.

What a difference a CARLING makes.

Discipline and Season Summary

powered by football.co.uk

key:
- forward
- midfield
- defence
- goalkeeper

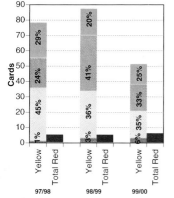

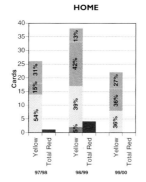

HOME

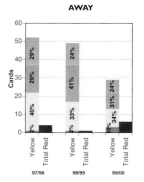

AWAY

Everton

and drawing against one of the bottom five. Everton did the double over West Ham, Wimbledon and Watford but they also lost twice to two teams – Arsenal and Middlesbrough.

Smith managed to improve his team's discipline considerably; having received nearly 90 yellow cards the previous season, Everton received just over 50 cautions, a marked improvement which cost the club far fewer missed matches through suspensions.

However, what they gained on bookings they lost on dismissals; no fewer than six red cards were received, one more than the previous season, more than any time since the 1994-95 season and worse than all their rivals apart from West Ham, who

recieved eight red cards. Interestingly, all six dismissals came away from home with defender Richard Dunne sent off twice, at Derby and Leeds. Indeed, in the game against Everton, referee Andy D'Urso set a Carling Premiership record by showing nine yellow cards and three reds.

If Everton lead at half time they do not lose; of the 13 occasions they took the lead in the opening 45 minutes, they went on to win 10 and draw the other three.

But if Everton were drawing midway through the game, a win was less likely. On the 16 occasions they were level at the interval, they went on to win just twice, losing eight and drawing the remaining six.

HOME

Number of Home Half Time Wins	Full Time Result W	L	D
9	6	0	3

Number of Home Half Time Losses	Full Time Result W	L	D
5	0	2	3

Number of Home Half Time Draws	Full Time Result W	L	D
5	1	1	3

AWAY

Number of Away Half Time Wins	Full Time Result W	L	D
4	4	0	0

Number of Away Half Time Losses	Full Time Result W	L	D
4	0	2	2

Number of Away Half Time Draws	Full Time Result W	L	D
11	1	7	3

TOTAL

Total Number of Half Time Wins	Full Time Result W	L	D
13	10	0	3

Total Number of Half Time Losses	Full Time Result W	L	D
9	0	4	5

Total Number of Half Time Draws	Full Time Result W	L	D
16	2	8	6

What a difference a CARLING makes.

Maps and Directions

Everton's Goodison Park is situated two miles north of Liverpool city centre, opposite Stanley Park, where parking is available.

From the North:
Approaching on the M6, exit at Junction 26 onto the M58 and continue until the end. At Junction 7 turn left onto the A59 Ormskirk Road. Continue on this road as it becomes Rice Lane, and cross over the roundabout into County Road. After ¼ mile turn left into Everton Valley and then Walton Lane. Goodison Road and the ground are on the left.

From the South:
Approaching on the M6, exit at Junction 21a onto the M62. Exit the M62 at Junction 4 and get onto the A5080. At the junction with the A5058 turn right and continue along this road as it becomes Queens Drive. Continue to the junction with Walton Hall Avenue and turn left onto the A580 Walton Lane. Goodison Road and the ground are on the right.

From the East:
Approaching on the M62 exit at Junction 4 and get onto the A5058. Then as route for South.

Lime Street Railway Station is in the town centre, 2 miles from Goodison Park. Kirkdale Railway Station is a 10 minute walk from the ground.

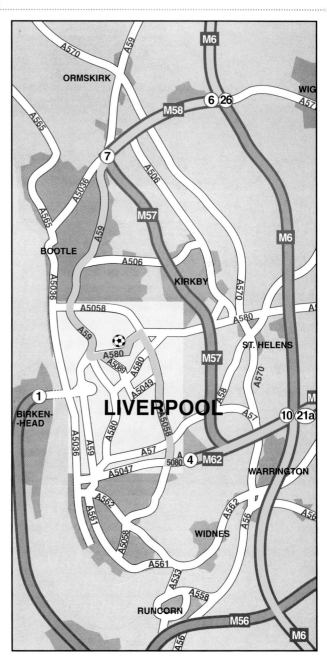

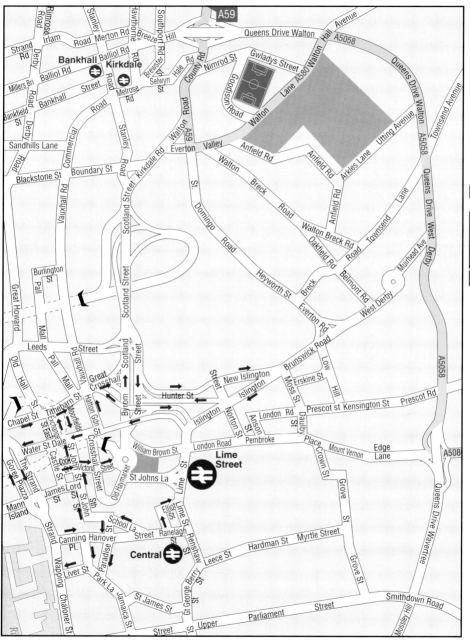

Everton

Club Honours

• Division 1 Champions: 1961-62
• Division 2 Champions: 1960-61, 1967-68, 1991-92
• Div 3 Champions: 1953-54, 1956-57
• FA Cup Winners: 1978
• UEFA Cup winners: 1981
• Texaco Cup Winners: 1973

Club Records

• Victory: 7-0 vs Portsmouth, Division 2, November 11, 1964
• Defeat: 1-10 vs Fulham, Division 1, December 26, 1963
• League goals in a season (team): 106, Division 3, 1955-56
• League goals in a season (player): : 41, Ted Phillips, Division 3, 1956-57
• Career league goals: 203, Ray Crawford, 1958-69
• League appearances: 591, Mick Mills 1966-82
• Transfer fee paid: £2,500,000 to Huddersfield for Marcus Stewart, February, 2000
• Transfer fee received: £6,500,000 from Newcastle for Kieron Dyer, July, 1999

Pos		Pld	W	D	L	F	A	Pts
3	Ipswich	46	25	12	9	71	42	87

Ipswich Town
"Town"

Portman Road, Ipswich IP1 2DA
Tel: 01473 400 500
www.itfc.co.uk

Season Review by
John Ley

The Daily Telegraph

Having reached the play-offs in the previous three seasons, Ipswich were determined to claim automatic promotion but they faded and were thrust into the drama of the play-offs again. This time, though, they got it right, beating Bolton in the semi-finals, including a crazy 5-3 home leg win against nine men, and winning the Wembley final by overcoming Barnsley.

Manager George Burley had lost Kieron Dyer to Newcastle in the previous summer and feared others might follow, particularly goalkeeper Richard Wright. In came John McGreal, Jermaine Wright and 'keeper Mike Salmon while, during the season, Gary Croft, Marcus Stewart and Martijn Reuser, on loan from Ajax, all arrived and played their part.

A sign of the tension came in a game at West Bromwich Albion where striker David Johnson had to be separated from team-mate Jim Magilton and was immediately substituted. But Ipswich kept their cool to return to the Carling Premiership at last.

Useful Information

The World of Punch

Portman Road, Club Stadium
Opening Times:
Monday-Friday: 10.00am-5.00pm
Match Saturdays: 9.30am to 4.30pm
Match Evenings: 10.00am to 7.45pm
Closed for the duration of the match.
Tel: **01473 400 501**
Mail Order service: **01473 400 501**

The World of Punch

Buttermarket Shopping Centre, Ipswich
Monday-Saturday: 9.00am to 5.30pm

The World of Punch

Abbeygate Street, Bury St Edmunds
Monday-Saturday:
9.00am to 5.30pm

Corporate Hospitality

The club offers a wide range of corporate facilities. Packages for seminars and conferences are available. Packages may include appearances from players or a tour of the stadium.
Tel: **01473 400 523**

Conference and Banqueting

Tel: **01473 400 500**

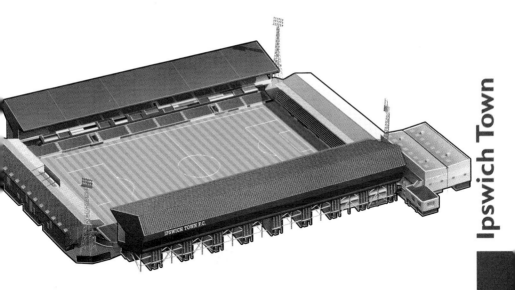

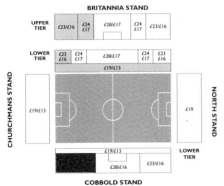

BRITANNIA STAND

UPPER TIER	£23/£16	£24 £17	£28/£17	£24 £17	£23/£16

LOWER TIER	£23 £16	£24 £17	£28/£17	£24 £17	£23 £16

£19/£13

£19/£13

CHURCHMANS STAND

£19/£13

NORTH STAND

£19

£19/£13

LOWER TIER

£28/£16 | £23/£16

COBBOLD STAND

VISITORS ENCLOSURE   FAMILY ENCLOSURE

Portman Road

Opened: August 1, 1887
Capacity: 22,600
1999/2000 highest attendance: 21,908
1999/2000 average attendance: 18,524
Record attendance: 38,010

Literature

Match Day Programme: £2.00
'About Town' Club quarterly magazine £2.50

Club Membership

Portman Plus (adults) £12.50
(for season ticket holders)
Portman Plus (adults) £15.00
Blues Crew (juniors) £12.50

Stadium Development

The South Stand development will increase the seating by 4,000, raising the overall capacity to over 26,000. New floodlights will also be introduced to meet with Premier League standards. The completion of this development work is expected to be in May 2001

Booking Information

General Enquiries
Tel: **01473 400 555**
Credit Card Ticket Line
Tel: **09068 121 069**
Ticket Recorded Information Line:
Tel: **0891 12 10 69**

Results Breakdown

POINTS WON OR LOST AT BOTH HOME AND AWAY
for the latest stats and to share your memories go to football.co.uk

key:
win · draw
loss · -0- league position
home fixtures are in red

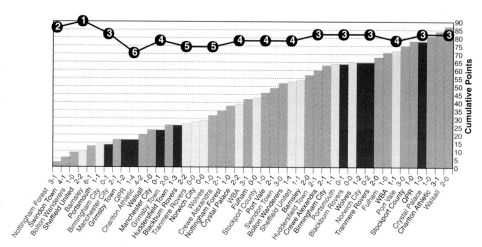

The season began well as Ipswich moved to the top of the table after four wins and a draw from their first five games. Then, though, they suffered home defeats against Birmingham and Queens Park Rangers.

The home form was impressive; only four points dropped between October and March while, away from home, they were drawing rather than losing – in 10 successive away games they were unbeaten, winning four and drawing the rest.

In February, Burley signed Marcus Stewart from Huddersfield for an initial £2.5 million and he started well by scoring in his first two games. But still Ipswich showed nerves. Charlton were walking away with the title and it became a two-way battle with Manchester City for second automatic spot, one that Ipswich lost.

Stewart, meanwhile, had failed to match his early promise but he eventually won over the Ipswich fans and made amends. His goal in the 4-2 Wembley win may have cost Ipswich a further £250,000 as per a clause in his transfer but it was to be worth around £10 million to the Suffolk club in terms of being promoted to the Carling Premiership.

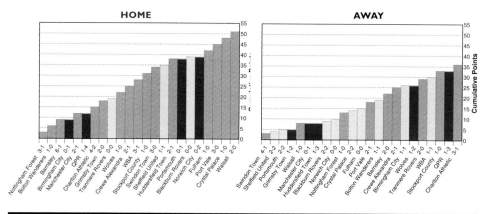

THE F.A. CARLING PREMIERSHIP
Results Table

powered by football.co.uk

Ipswich Town

Key: ● = Red Card   ◎ = Yellow Card   ▲ = Player substituted   ▲▲ = Time of goal

DATE	H/A	OPPONENT	H/T	F/T	POS	REFEREE
07/08	H	Nottingham Forest	2-0	3-1	2	P.R.Richards
15/08	A	Swindon Town	1-1	4-1	1	M.Fletcher
21/08	H	Bolton Wanderers	0-0	1-0	1	R.D.Furmandiz
28/08	A	Sheffield United	2-0	2-2	1	C.J.Foy
30/08	H	Barnsley	3-0	6-1	1	M.J.Brandwood
11/09	A	Portsmouth	0-0	1-1	1	P.E.Alcock
18/09	H	Birmingham City	0-1	0-1	3	B.Knight
26/09	H	Manchester City	1-0	2-1	2	A.P.D'Urso
02/10	H	Grimsby Town	0-1	1-2	5	M.R.Warren
16/10	A	QPR	1-1	1-4	6	P.S.Danson
19/10	A	Charlton Athletic	2-2	4-2	6	P.Lloyd
23/10	A	Walsall	0-0	0-1	4	M.J.Jones
27/10	H	Manchester City	1-0	2-0	4	J.A.Kirkby
30/10	A	Grimsby Town	1-0	2-0	4	K.A.Leach
02/11	H	Huddersfield Town	1-3	1-3	4	W.C.Burns
06/11	A	Blackburn Rovers	0-1	2-2	5	G.Laws
12/11	H	Tranmere Rovers	0-0	0-0	5	T.Heilbron
21/11	H	Norwich City	0-0	2-0	5	G.Cain
24/11	H	Wolves	0-0	0-0	5	P.S.Pike
27/11	H	Crewe Alexandra	1-0	2-1	4	R.Styles
05/12	A	Nottingham Forest	2-1	2-1	4	S.J.Baines
07/12	A	Crystal Palace	1-0	1-0	4	D.R.Crick
18/12	H	West Brom	2-0	3-1	3	A.R.Hall
26/12	A	Fulham	1-0	1-0	3	P.Jones
28/12	H	Stockport County	1-0	1-0	3	P.B.Wing
03/01	A	Port Vale	0-1	2-1	3	M.S.Pike
15/01	H	Swindon Town	2-0	3-0	2	P.B.Wing
22/01	H	Bolton Wanderers	0-0	1-1	2	G.B.Frankland
29/01	H	Sheffield United	1-0	1-1	2	A.N.Butler
05/02	A	Barnsley	2-0	3-0	2	D.Pugh
12/02	H	Stockport County	1-0	1-0	3	R.Pearson
19/02	A	Huddersfield Town	0-0	2-1	3	A.R.Leake
27/02	H	Crewe Alexandra	1-1	1-1	2	P.Taylor
04/03	A	Birmingham City	2-0	2-0	2	M.Fletcher
11/03	H	Portsmouth	1-1	1-1	3	M.J.Jones
19/03	H	Blackburn Rovers	0-0	0-0	3	R.Styles
22/03	A	Wolves	1-0	2-0	3	D.Laws
25/03	A	Norwich City	0-0	1-0	3	A.Bates
04/04	A	Tranmere Rovers	1-1	1-1	3	C.R.Wilkes
08/04	H	Fulham	2-0	3-0	3	S.J.Baines
15/04	A	West Brom	1-0	1-0	3	T.Heilbron
22/04	H	Port Vale	1-0	1-1	3	M.J.Brandwood
22/04	H	Stockport County	1-0	1-2	3	J.P.Robinson
25/04	A	QPR	1-0	1-0	3	P.R.Richards
29/04	A	Crystal Palace	3-1	3-1	3	M.Fletcher
07/05	A	Charlton Athletic	2-0	2-0	3	K.M.Lynch
07/05	A	Walsall	0-0	0-0	3	K.M.Lynch

101

Goal Analysis

powered by  football.co.uk

GOALS BY POSITION 1997/1998 - 1999/2000
for the latest stats and to share your memories go to football.co.uk

key:
- ■ forward
- ■ midfield
- ■ defence
- ◐ final league position

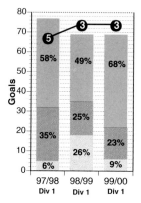

HOME

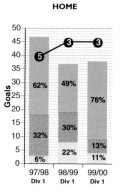

AWAY

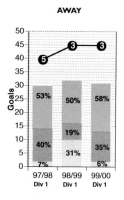

Ipswich scored 71 goals, two more than the previous season but fewer than the 77 they amassed two seasons earlier. It was also a lower total than Charlton and Manchester City, who won automatic promotion, as well as Barnsley (88). That figure, however, does not include the 11 goals they added in the play-offs, when it mattered. They scored two more home goals than the previous season and conceded two more as well. Similarly, they scored 32 away goals, equalling their total the previous term, one that was

better than at any time since the 1995-96 season.

The strikers scored a huge percentage of their goals; Johnson scored 23, his best ever return in a single season, including goals in each of the first six games, while James Scowcroft added 13, matching his total for the previous season. Add the goals of Richard Naylor and Ipswich were comfortable in attack, even though Stewart managed only two in the League.

Matt Holland was top scorer in midfield with 10 to equal his best seasonal return while in defence Ipswich

GOALS BY TIME PERIOD 1999/2000
for the latest stats and to share your memories go to football.co.uk

key:
- ■ goals for
- ■ goals against

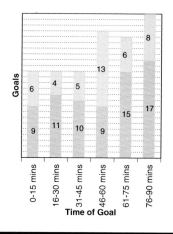

HOME

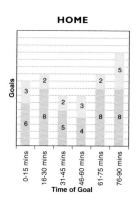

AWAY

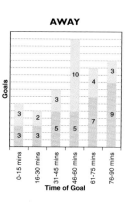

Goal Analysis

powered by football.co.uk

Ipswich Town

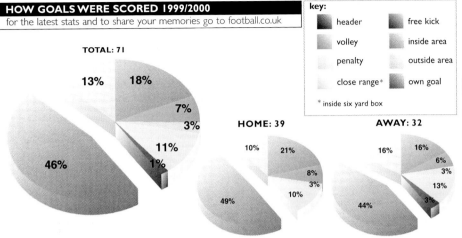

key:
- header
- volley
- penalty
- close range*
- free kick
- inside area
- outside area
- own goal

* inside six yard box

TOTAL: 71

13% · 18% · 7% · 3% · 11% · 1% · 46%

HOME: 39

10% · 21% · 8% · 3% · 10% · 49%

AWAY: 32

16% · 16% · 6% · 3% · 13% · 3% · 44%

found few goals. Jamie Clapham, whose crosses contributed to a large percentage of goals, scored twice, as did Mark Venus.

The strikers were most successful at home with 29 of Town's 39 Portman Road goals coming from the front men. Johnson scored 14 of his 23 at home, while Scowcroft claimed eight of his 13 goals at Portman Road.

Woe betide any team that treated Town lightly towards the end of games for that is when they appeared to be at their most dangerous, scoring 45 percent of their goals in the final 30 minutes, including no fewer than 17 in the last quarter of an hour. But they were at their most vulnerable just after half time, conceding 30 per cent of their goals in the first 15 minutes after the interval.

Ipswich were also susceptible to conceding penalties at Portman Road; a remarkable 12 per cent of the goals conceded at home came from the spot. Away from home, the Ipswich defence appears to be

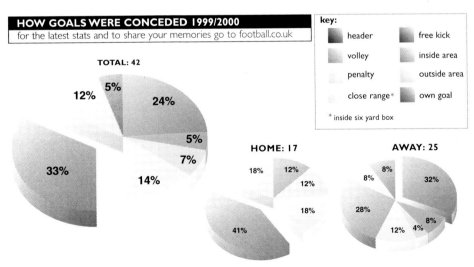

key:
- header
- volley
- penalty
- close range*
- free kick
- inside area
- outside area
- own goal

* inside six yard box

TOTAL: 42

12% · 5% · 24% · 5% · 7% · 14% · 33%

HOME: 17

18% · 12% · 12% · 18% · 41%

AWAY: 25

8% · 32% · 8% · 8% · 4% · 12% · 28%

Squad and Performance

SQUAD LIST

for the latest stats and to share your memories go to football.co.uk

Position	Name	Appearances	Appearances as substitute	Goals	Clean Sheets	Yellow Cards	Red Cards
G	R.Wright	46			18		
D	W.Brown	20	5			1	
D	J.Clapham	44	2	2		2	
D	M.Clegg	3				1	
D	G.Croft	14	7	1		2	
D	J.McGreal	34				3	1
D	T.Mowbray	35	1	1		5	
D	M.Thetis	15	1			4	1
D	M.Venus	28		2		8	
D	F.Wilnis	30	5			6	
M	M.Holland	46		10			
M	J.Magilton	33	5	3		2	1
M	M.Stockwell	21	13	2			
M	J.Wright	21	13	1		2	
F	J.Axeldal	1	14			1	
F	S.Friars		1				
F	D.Johnson	44		23		7	
F	R.Logan		1				
F	N.Midgley	1	3	1			
F	R.Naylor	19	14	8		3	
F	M.Reuser	2	6	2			
F	J.Scowcroft	40	1	13		2	
F	M.Stewart	9	1	2			

vulnerable to high balls; no fewer than 32 per cent of goals conceded on their travels were from headers.

Richard Wright would surely have left had Ipswich not won promotion; instead the goalkeeper, one of two ever-presents, kept 18 clean sheets, ended the season a full England international and a member of the Euro 2000 squad. Holland was another who played in all 46 Division One games, while Clapham and Johnson missed just two and James Scowcroft played in 40 games.

Ipswich, therefore, benefited from consistency and used it to good advantage against the better teams, taking maximum points off both Charlton and Barnsley while beating Manchester City at home. They also saw off the entire bottom six at Portman

TEAM PERFORMANCE TABLE

for the latest stats and to share your memories go to football.co.uk

Position	Club	Points Won	Percentage of points won at home	percentage of points won away	overall percentage of points won
1.	CHARLTON	6/6			
2.	MANCHESTER CITY	3/6			
3.	IPSWICH	87 pts	80%	53%	67%
4.	BARNSLEY	6/6			
5.	BIRMINGHAM	1/6			
6.	BOLTON	4/6			
7.	WOLVES	3/6			
8.	HUDDERSFIELD	3/6			
9.	FULHAM	4/6	61%	28%	44%
10.	QPR	0/6			
11.	BLACKBURN	2/6			
12.	TRANMERE	4/6			
13.	NORWICH	1/6			
14.	NOTTINGHAM FOREST	6/6			
15.	SHEFFIELD UNITED	2/6	56%	56%	56%
16.	CRYSTAL PALACE	4/6			
17.	STOCKPORT	6/6			
18.	PORTSMOUTH	1/6			
19.	CREWE	6/6			
20.	GRIMSBY	3/6			
21.	WBA	4/6	100%	72%	86%
22.	WALSALL	6/6			
23.	PORT VALE	6/6			
24.	SWINDON	6/6			

The figures show a team's performance against clubs in each quarter of the final league table. The first column represents points won from the total available against each team in the league.

What a difference a CARLING makes.

Discipline and Season Summary

BOOKINGS BY POSITION 1997/1998 - 1999/2000
for the latest stats and to share your memories go to football.co.uk

key:
- forward
- midfield
- defence
- goalkeeper

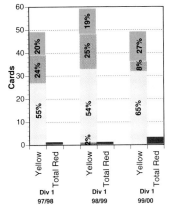

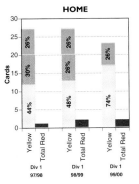

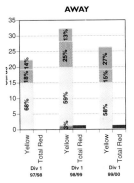

Ipswich Town

Road, where they enjoyed a 100 per cent record against the poorest clubs.

Ipswich's cautions were down but a greater per cent was collected by their defence with the worst offenders being Venus, who was booked in three successive games, Fabius Wilnis, Tony Mowbray – whose five cautions game in a 14-game, three-month period – and Manuel Thetis, with the quartet collecting no fewer than 23 cautions between them.

Few midfield cautions were received, just four, and all came away from home, though Jim Magilton, who was booked twice, was also one of three players sent-off, his red card coming in the season's biggest shock, the 4-1 home defeat by QPR in October. Thetis collected Ipswich's first red card, at home to

Bolton, while the other miscreant was McGreal, sent off at Portsmouth early in the season.

If Ipswich were ahead at the interval, they would never lose. On no fewer than 18 occasions, Burley's men led at the interval and the final result was a win for Ipswich on 15 occasions with three draws. Only once at Portman Road did Ipswich squander an interval lead, drawing with Sheffield United after leading with a David Johnson goal on the stroke of half-time.

If Town were drawing at half-time they stood a reasonable chance of finishing up with at least a point; on the 21 occasions they were level after 45 minutes, they eventually lost only four times and only once at home.

HALF TIME - FULL TIME COMPARATIVE CHART
for the latest stats and to share your memories go to football.co.uk

HOME				AWAY				TOTAL			
Number of Home Half Time Wins	Full Time Result W	L	D	Number of Away Half Time Wins	Full Time Result W	L	D	Total Number of Half Time Wins	Full Time Result W	L	D
12	11	0	1	6	4	0	2	18	15	0	3
Number of Home Half Time Losses	Full Time Result W	L	D	Number of Away Half Time Losses	Full Time Result W	L	D	Total Number of Half Time Losses	Full Time Result W	L	D
3	0	3	0	4	0	2	2	7	0	5	2
Number of Home Half Time Draws	Full Time Result W	L	D	Number of Away Half Time Draws	Full Time Result W	L	D	Total Number of Half Time Draws	Full Time Result W	L	D
8	5	1	2	13	5	3	5	21	10	4	7

Maps and Directions

South.
Take the A12 to big roundabout (by Tesco's) in the Ipswich suburbs. Take 2nd exit (s/p Ipswich West A1214) into London Road. Follow Ipswich A1214 signs for 2 ½ miles, straight over roundabout to junction at bottom of hill. Go straight on (s/p Town Centre A1214), and after a few metres at next lights turn right (s/p Cliff Quay, Football) into West End Road. There is parking on the right hand side after ½ mile . To continue to ground, all traffic turns left into Chancery Road. At T-Junction turn left into Princes Street and immediately left into Portman Road.

From North (A14)
Continue on A14 to junction with A12, and pick up route from South.

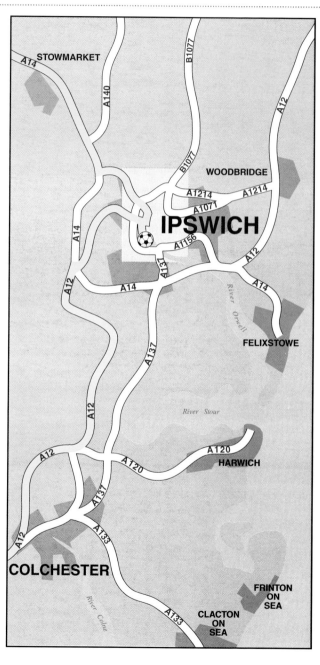

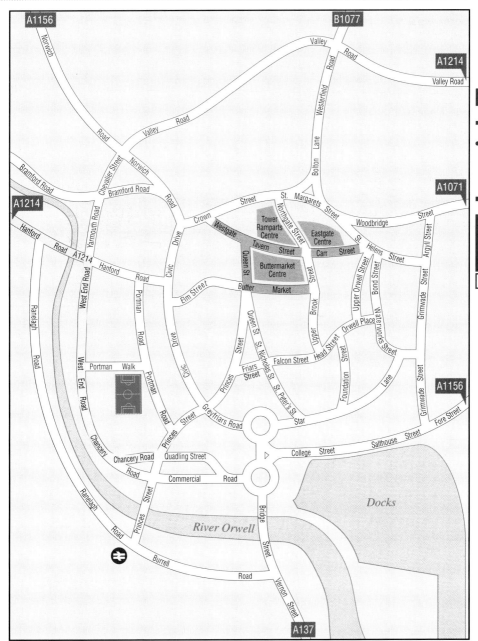

Club Honours

* Football League Champions: 1968-69, 1973-74, 1991-92
* Division 2 Champions: 1923-24, 1963-64, 1989-90
* FA Cup Winners: 1972
* League Cup Winners: 1968
* European Fairs Cup Winners: 1967-68, 1970-71

Club Records

* Victory: 10-0 v Lyn, European Cup 1st Round, 1st Leg, September 17, 1969
* Defeat: 1-8 v Stoke City, Division 1, August 27, 1934
* League goals in a season (team): 98, Division 2, 1927-28
* League goals in a season (player): 42, John Charles, Division 2, 1953-54
* Career league goals: 168, Peter Lorimer, 1965-79, 1983-86
  League appearances: 629, Jack Charlton, 1953/73
* Transfer fee paid: £7,200,000 to RC Lens for Olivier Dacourt, May, 2000
* Transfer fee received: £12,000,000 from Atletico Madrid for Jimmy Floyd Hasselbaink, August, 1999

Pos		Pld	W	D	L	F	A	Pts
3	Leeds	38	21	6	11	58	43	69

Leeds

"The Whites"

Elland Road, Leeds,
West Yorkshire LS11 0ES
Tel: 0113 226 6000

Internet: www.lufc.co.uk

Season Review by
John Ley

The Daily Telegraph

Even the most optimistic of Leeds fans could not have envisaged such a season of excitement, drama and controversy as that which followed David O'Leary's team. The departure of Jimmy Floyd Hasselbaink was offset by the arrivals of Danny Mills, Michael Bridges, Eirik Bakke, Michael Duberry and, later on, Darren Huckerby and Jason Wilcox. Add the growing maturity of O'Leary's 'babies' and Leeds had the perfect mix.

For long periods, Leeds appeared capable of winning the Carling Premiership but, ultimately, it was all too much for the players. The UEFA Cup campaign which ended in semi-final defeat and, more tragically, the death of two Leeds fans in Istanbul, made it a season never to be forgotten for many varied reasons.

After qualifying for the Champions' League, Leeds pounced in the summer for former Everton midfielder Olivier Dacourt, from Lens, though Alfie Haaland left for newcomers Manchester City.

Useful Information

Leeds United Retail Store
Elland Road
Opening Times:
Monday-Saturday: 9.00am-5.00pm
Match Saturdays: 9.00am-3.00pm
Sundays: 11.00am-3.00pm
Match Evenings: all day up to game and then an hour after full time.
Tel: 0113 225 1144 Mail Order
Service: 0113 225 1100

Leeds United Retail Store
10/11 Burton Arcade, Leeds
Opening Times:
Monday-Friday: 9.30am-5.15pm
Match Saturdays: 9.00am-5.15pm
Tel: 0113 247 0098
Fax: 0113 244 1940
There are also retail outlets at the White Rose Shopping Centre, Leeds and The Ridings Centre, Wakefield.

Stadium Tours
Contact John McClelland
(pre-book): 0113 226 6223

Corporate Hospitality
Matchday hospitality packages from £75 plus VAT
Sponsorship from £2,000 plus VAT
Matchball sponsorship from £1,850
Contact Keith Hanvey:
0113 226 1155

What a difference a _CARLING_ makes.

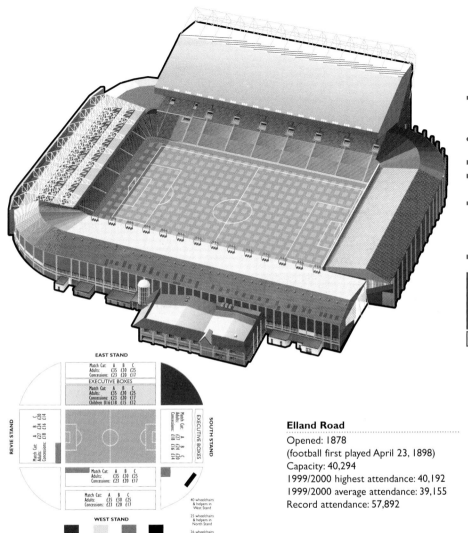

Leeds United

EAST STAND

Match Cat:	A	B	C
Adults:	£35	£30	£25
Concessions:	£23	£20	£17

EXECUTIVE BOXES

Match Cat:	A	B	C
Adults:	£35	£30	£25
Concessions:	£23	£20	£17
Children U16	£18	£15	£12

REVIE STAND

Match Cat:	A	B	C
Adults:	£27	£24	£20
Concessions:	£18	£16	£14

SOUTH STAND

EXECUTIVE BOXES

Match Cat:	A	B	C
Adults:	£27	£24	£20
Concessions:	£18	£16	£14

Match Cat:	A	B	C
Adults:	£35	£30	£25
Concessions:	£23	£20	£17

Match Cat:	A	B	C
Adults:	£35	£30	£25
Concessions:	£23	£20	£17

WEST STAND

VISITORS ENCLOSURE FAMILY ENCLOSURE DISABLED FANS JUMBO SCREEN

40 wheelchairs & helpers in West Stand

25 wheelchairs & helpers in North Stand

26 wheelchairs & helpers in SW corner

Elland Road
Opened: 1878
(football first played April 23, 1898)
Capacity: 40,294
1999/2000 highest attendance: 40,192
1999/2000 average attendance: 39,155
Record attendance: 57,892

Literature
Programme £2.50, Official magazine: Leeds Leeds Leeds £3, Super Leeds Magazine £1.50 and Leeds Expert £4.99

Pre-Match & Half Time Entertainment
Local bands, penalty shoot-out competition, guest appearances, sky diving, spot the ball, Leeds United Lottery.

Banqueting
Contact: Banqueting Department:
0113 226 1166

Matchday Creche
Tel: 0113 226 6193

Football in the Community
Tel: 0113 226 6178

Booking Information
General Enquiries:
0113 226 1000

Leeds United Travel Club
(free phone): 0500 225 151

Results Breakdown

POINTS WON OR LOST AT BOTH HOME AND AWAY

for the latest stats and to share your memories go to football.co.uk

key:
- win
- draw
- loss
- -0- league position

home fixtures are in red

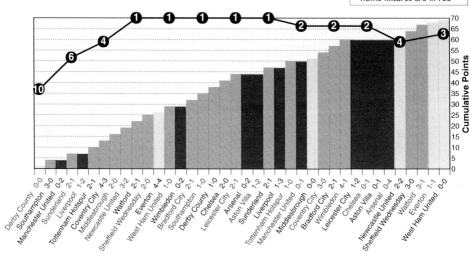

When Leeds lost the early season trip to Old Trafford there were few signs that they would become one of Manchester United's chief rivals for the title. But, after another defeat by fancied opponents, Liverpool, Leeds set off on a run of six successive victories that took them to the top of the Carling Premiership. With cup competitions, Leeds won 10 in succession, a club record beating the previous best set in 1931. Indeed, between late August and the end of the year, Leeds lost just once in 14 League games.

Despite successive defeats, by Arsenal and Aston Villa, they remained on top but four defeats in six games saw Leeds knocked off the leadership. Another run of poor results, when they lost four in succession, sent Leeds to fourth and though they rallied, it was not until the final weekend of the season that they guaranteed the place they deserved in the qualifying stages of the Champions' League over Liverpool thanks to their highest points tally (69) since 1995.

Three teams bettered Leeds's goal tally of 58 while each of the other teams in the top five finished with a better goal difference. Leeds won 11 games by

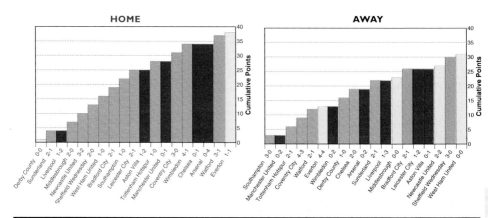

Results Table

powered by

Leeds United

Legend: ● = Red Card   ○ = Yellow Card   ▲ = Player substituted   00 = Time of goal

DATE	H/A	OPPONENT	H/T	F/T	POS	REFEREE	TEAM											SUBSTITUTES USED
07/08	H	Derby County	0-0	0-0	10	G.P.Barber	Martyn	Home	Radebe	Woodgate	Mills	Hopkin	Batty	Bowyer	Kewell	Smith	Bridges	McPhail ▲ ·
11/08	A	Southampton	3-0	3-0	4	A.G.Wiley	Martyn	Home	Radebe	Woodgate	Mills	Hopkin ▲	Batty	Bowyer	Kewell	Duberry	Bridges 11 51 72	Jones ▲ Bakke ● ▲
14/08	A	Manchester United	0-0	0-2	7	N.S.Barry	Martyn	Home ▲	Radebe	Woodgate	Mills	Duberry	Batty	Bowyer	Kewell	Huckerby	Bridges	Hidden ▲ Hopkin ▲ Bakke ▲
21/08	H	Sunderland	0-1	0-1	6	P.E.Alcock	Martyn	Home	Radebe	Woodgate	Mills	Hopkin	Batty	Bowyer 52	Kewell	Huckerby	Bridges	Smith ▲ ·
23/08	H	Liverpool	1-1	1-2	7	D.R.Elleray	Martyn	Home	Radebe	Woodgate	Mills ▲	Hopkin ▲	Batty	Bowyer	Kewell	Huckerby	Bridges	Bokke ▲ Smith ▲
28/08	A	Tottenham Hotspur	0-1	2-1	5	M.D.Reed	Martyn	Home 83	Radebe	Woodgate ▲	Mills	Duberry ▲	Batty	Bowyer 8	Kewell	Smith ● 53	Bridges	Hopkin ▲ Kelly ▲ Huckerby ▲
11/09	A	Coventry City	3-2	4-3	4	S.W.Dunn	Martyn	Home ▲ 33	Radebe	Duberry	Mills	Hopkin	Batty	Bowyer	Kewell 64	Huckerby 25	Bridges 64	Kelly ▲ Woodgate ▲
19/09	H	Middlesbrough	1-0	2-0	2	D.J.Gallagher	Martyn	Home	Radebe	Woodgate	Mills	Hopkin ▲	Batty	Bowyer	Kewell	Smith ●	Bridges ▲ 14	Kelly ▲ Huckerby ▲
25/09	H	Newcastle United	2-1	3-2	2	B.Knight	Martyn	Home	Radebe	Woodgate	Kelly	Bokke	Batty	Bowyer 11	Kewell 39	Smith	Bridges 77	Hoolond ▲ Huckerby ▲
03/10	H	Watford	1-1	2-1	1	A.P.D'Urso	Martyn	Home	Radebe	Woodgate	Kelly	Hopkin ▲	Batty	Bakke	Kewell 69	Smith 72 78	Bridges ▲ 45	Mills ▲ Hoolond ▲ Huckerby ▲
16/10	H	Sheffield Wednesday	2-0	2-0	1	G.P.Barber	Martyn	Mills	Radebe	Woodgate	Kelly	McPhail	Batty	Bowyer	Kewell	Smith	Bridges	Huckerby ▲ ·
24/10	A	Everton	2-3	4-4	1	D.J.Gallagher	Martyn	Home 57	Radebe	Woodgate 72	Kelly	McPhail	Batty	Bowyer	Kewell	Smith 77 78	Bridges 15 68	Huckerby ▲ ·
30/10	H	West Ham United	0-1	0-2	1	G.Poll	Martyn	Home	Radebe	Woodgate ▲	Kelly	McPhail	Batty	Bowyer ▲	Kewell	Smith ▲ 54	Huckerby	Duberry ▲ Bokke ▲ Hopkin ▲
07/11	A	Wimbledon	0-1	0-2	2	P.Jones	Martyn	Home 80	Radebe	Woodgate	Kelly	McPhail ▲	Batty	Bowyer	Kewell	Huckerby	Bridges	Huckerby ▲ ·
20/11	H	Bradford City	0-0	2-1	2	P.A.Durkin	Martyn	Mills	Mills	Woodgate	Kelly	McPhail ▲	Batty	Bowyer	Bokke	Bokke	Bridges 90	Bokke ▲ Smith ▲
28/11	A	Southampton	0-0	1-0	1	R.J.Harris	Martyn	Home 90	Radebe	Woodgate	Kelly	McPhail ▲ 66 88	Batty	Bowyer	Kewell	Smith	Bridges	Smith ▲ ·
05/12	A	Derby County	0-0	1-0	1	P.E.Alcock	Martyn	Home	Radebe	Woodgate	Kelly	McPhail ▲	Batty ▲	Bowyer	Kewell	Bokke	Bridges	Wilcox ▲ Jones ▲
19/12	H	Leicester City	2-1	2-1	1	J.T.Winter	Martyn	Home	Radebe	Woodgate	Kelly	McPhail	Bakke	Bowyer	Kewell	Bokke	Bridges	Wilcox ▲ Jones ▲
26/12	A	Arsenal	0-1	0-2	2	M.R.Halsey	Martyn	Home	Radebe	Woodgate	Kelly	McPhail	Bakke	Bowyer 45	Kewell 46	Bokke	Bridges	Wilcox ▲ Jones ▲
28/12	H	Aston Villa	0-1	1-2	2	G.Poll	Martyn	Home	Duberry	Woodgate	Kelly	Jones	Bakke	Bowyer ▲	Kewell	Bokke	Bridges	Wilcox ▲ Huckerby ▲
03/01	H	Middlesbrough	0-0	1-1	2	U.D.Rennie	Martyn	Home	Duberry	Woodgate	Kelly	McPhail ▲	Bakke	Hoolond	Kewell	Smith	Bridges	Bridges ▲ Jones ▲
23/01	A	Coventry City	2-0	3-0	2	J.T.Winter	Martyn	Home	Duberry	Woodgate	Kelly	McPhail ▲	Bakke	Bowyer	Kewell ▲ 23	Bokke 23 39	Bridges ▲ 50	Hoolond ▲ Huckerby ▲
05/02	A	Bradford City	2-1	2-1	2	P.A.Durkin	Martyn	Home	Duberry	Hoolond	Kelly	Jones	Wilcox	Bowyer 62	Kewell	Bokke	Smith	Jones ▲ Bridges ▲
12/02	H	Tottenham Hotspur	1-0	3-1	2	A.G.Wiley	Martyn	Home 28	Radebe	Woodgate	Kelly	Jones	Wilcox	Bowyer	Kewell 83	Bokke	Smith	Jones ▲ Huckerby ▲ Smith ▲
20/02	A	Manchester United	3-1	0-1	2	S.J.Lodge	Martyn	Home	Radebe	Woodgate	Kelly	Hopkin ▲	Wilcox	Bowyer	Kewell 38	Bokke	Bridges ▲ 12 63	Hoolond ▲ Smith ▲
26/02	H	Leicester City	1-1	1-2	2	J.T.Winter	Martyn	Home	Radebe	Woodgate	Kelly	McPhail ▲	Wilcox 24	Bowyer	Kewell	Bokke	Bridges	Huckerby ▲ ·
04/03	H	Chelsea	0-0	0-1	2	U.D.Rennie	Martyn	Home	Radebe	Woodgate	Kelly	McPhail ▲	Wilcox 85	Bowyer	Kewell 5	Bokke	Bridges ▲ 42	Jones ▲ Hopkin ▲
12/03	A	Aston Villa	2-0	2-0	2	J.T.Winter	Martyn	Home	Radebe	Woodgate	Kelly	McPhail	Wilcox	Hopkin	Bakke	Smith	Bridges ▲	Jones ▲ ·
19/03	H	Arsenal	0-1	0-1	4	P.A.Durkin	Martyn	Home	Radebe	Woodgate	Kelly	McPhail	Wilcox	Bowyer	Kewell	Hoolond	Bridges ▲ 12	Huckerby ▲ ·
26/03	A	Newcastle United	2-1	2-2	4	R.J.Harris	Martyn	Home	Radebe	Duberry	Kelly	McPhail	Wilcox	Bowyer	Kewell	Bokke	Bridges ▲ 53	Bridges ▲ Hucherby ▲ Smith ▲
01/04	A	Chelsea	0-0	0-1	3	P.E.Alcock	Martyn	Home ●	Radebe	Duberry 45	Kelly	Hopkin ▲	Wilcox	Hoolond	Kewell	Smith	Bridges	Bridges ▲ ·
09/04	H	Aston Villa	2-0	2-0	3	A.P.D'Urso	Martyn	Home ▲	Hoolond	Woodgate	Kelly	McPhail	Wilcox 17	Hopkin 1	Kewell 69	Smith	Bridges ▲ 12	Hoolond ▲ Smith ▲
16/04	H	Arsenal	0-1	0-4	3	B.Knight	Martyn	Kelly	Radebe	Woodgate	Mills	McPhail ▲	Wilcox	Bowyer	Kewell	Bokke	Bridges ▲ 33	Bowyer ▲ Hucherby ▲
23/04	A	Newcastle United	2-1	2-2	4	S.W.Dunn	Martyn	Kelly	Radebe	Hoolond	Mills	Jones	Bakke	Bowyer	Kewell	Bokke	Bridges 20	Huckerby ▲ Woodgate ▲ Smith ▲
30/04	H	Sheffield Wednesday	1-0	3-0	4	R.J.Harris	Martyn	Kelly	Radebe	Woodgate	Mills	McPhail	Wilcox ▲	Bowyer	Kewell	Huckerby 53	Bridges ▲ 53	Bowyer ▲ Hoolond ▲ Smith ▲
03/05	H	Watford	2-1	3-1	3	P.E.Alcock	Martyn	Kelly	Radebe	Woodgate	Mills	McPhail	Bakke	Bowyer	Kewell	Woodgate 20	Bridges 20	Woodgate ▲ Smith ▲ Huckerby ▲
08/05	A	Everton	1-1	1-1	3	A.P.D'Urso	Martyn	Kelly	Duberry ●	Woodgate	Mills	McPhail ▲	Wilcox ▲	Jones	Kewell	Hoolond 30	Bridges 30	Bowyer ▲ Huckerby ▲
14/05	H	West Ham United	0-0	0-0	3	G.P.Barber	Martyn	Kelly	Radebe	Woodgate	Mills	McPhail	Wilcox ▲	Bowyer	Kewell	Bokke	Bridges	Bowyer ▲ Smith ▲

THE F.A. CARLING PREMIERSHIP

Goal Analysis

GOALS BY POSITION 1997/1998 - 1999/2000
for the latest stats and to share your memories go to football.co.uk

key:
- forward
- defence
- midfield
- -0- final league position

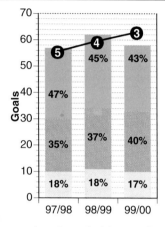

HOME

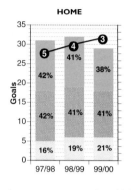

AWAY

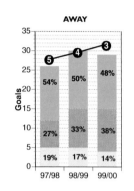

one goal, scoring 29 both home and away. The key to their success, particularly at home, was the lack of draws. Indeed, the two games they did draw at Elland Road, against Derby on the season's opening day, and Everton in their final home game, equalled their fewest number of home draws, last achieved in the 1990-91 season.

Leeds actually scored four more goals than in the 1998-99 season when Hasselbaink claimed 18. That figure, though, was beaten by Bridges who was

surprisingly sold by Sunderland and responded by scoring a hat-trick in his second appearance, at Southampton. The striker's tally, the fifth highest in the Carling Premiership, was three more than he had scored in his four seasons with Sunderland combined and the best return by a Leeds player in the Carling Premiership. It was also the highest total by a Leeds star since Lee Chapman scored 21 goals in the 1990-91 season.

Harry Kewell was next highest scorer with 10

GOALS BY TIME PERIOD 1999/2000
for the latest stats and to share your memories go to football.co.uk

key:
- goals for
- goals against

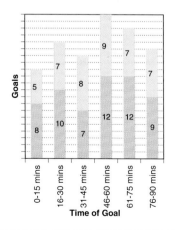

HOME AWAY

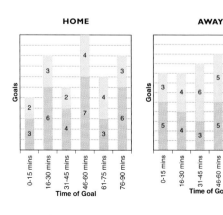

What a difference a CARLING makes.

Goal Analysis

powered by football.co.uk

HOW GOALS WERE SCORED 1999/2000
for the latest stats and to share your memories go to football.co.uk

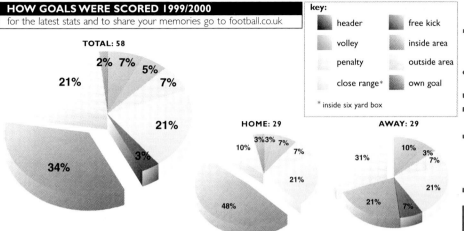

key:
- header
- free kick
- volley
- inside area
- penalty
- outside area
- close range*
- own goal

* inside six yard box

TOTAL: 58

2% 7% 5%
21%   7%
          21%
        3%
34%

HOME: 29

3% 3% 7%
10%   7%
          21%
48%

AWAY: 29

10% 3%
31%   7%
        21%
21% 7%

Leeds United

goals while the third highest was, surprisingly, a defender, Irishman Ian Harte, who claimed his best ever return, of six, though that figure did include four penalties.

Leeds's goals were evenly spread out; they scored marginally more in the second half, though away from home they were more likely to score in the second 45 minutes, particularly in the middle period.

They conceded only seven goals in the first half of home games compared to 13 in the opening period of away games.

A high percentage of their goals came from left-footed shots; no fewer than nine of Leeds's 12 goalscorers claimed at least one goal with their left boot. Leeds also scored a high percentage of their goals from outside the area, 21 per cent came from long range with Kewell probably the most successful from distance in the Carling Premiership - particularly away from home, where Leeds claimed more than 30 per cent from outside the area.

HOW GOALS WERE CONCEDED 1999/2000
for the latest stats and to share your memories go to football.co.uk

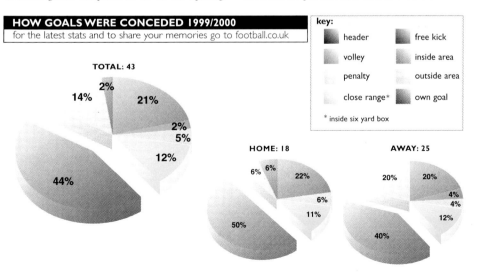

key:
- header
- free kick
- volley
- inside area
- penalty
- outside area
- close range*
- own goal

* inside six yard box

TOTAL: 43

2%
14%   21%
        2%
        5%
      12%
44%

HOME: 18

6% 6%
6%   22%
        6%
      11%
50%

AWAY: 25

20% 20%
        4%
        4%
      12%
40%

What a difference a _CARLING_ makes.

Squad and Performance

powered by **football.co.uk**

SQUAD LIST

for the latest stats and to share your memories go to football.co.uk

Position	Name	Appearances	Appearances as substitute	Goals	Clean Sheets	Yellow Cards	Red Cards
G	N.Martyn	38			13	2	
D	M.Duberry	12	1	1		4	1
D	I.Harte	33		6		8	1
D	M.Hiden		1				
D	G.Kelly	28	3			6	
D	D.Mills	16	1	1		5	
D	L.Radebe	31				2	
D	J.Woodgate	32	2			1	
M	E.Bakke	24	5	2		6	
M	D.Batty	16				4	
M	L.Bowyer	31	2	5		13	
M	A.Haaland	7	6			4	
M	D.Hopkin	10	4	1		1	
M	M.Jones	5	6			2	
M	H.Kewell	36		10		6	
M	S.McPhail	23	1			2	
M	J.Wilcox	15	5	3		1	
F	M.Bridges	32	2	19		6	
F	D.Huckerby	9	24	2			
F	A.Smith	20	6	4		5	1

Although they failed to score direct from a free kick at Elland Road they were more successful with them on their travels.

Leeds used just 20 players, fewer than any other Carling Premiership club, and fewer than at any time since the 1990-91 season. Nigel Martyn was the only ever present – in four years at Leeds the England goalkeeper has missed just six League games – while Harry Kewell missed two, one through suspension and another, strangely, because of a FIFA ban after Leeds prevented him from joining his national side.

Leeds' title challenge was halted by the fact that they could not beat the best teams. Against the other top four they won just one game – at Chelsea, while losing at home and away to Manchester United,

TEAM PERFORMANCE TABLE

for the latest stats and to share your memories go to football.co.uk

Position	Club	Points Won	Percentage of points won at home	percentage of points won away	overall percentage of points won
1.	MANCHESTER UNITED	0/6			
2.	ARSENAL	0/6			
3.	LEEDS UNITED	69 pts	0%	25%	13%
4.	LIVERPOOL	0/6			
5.	CHELSEA	3/6			
6.	ASTON VILLA	0/6			
7.	SUNDERLAND	6/6			
8.	LEICESTER CITY	3/6	80%	47%	63%
9.	TOTTENHAM HOTSPUR	6/6			
10.	WEST HAM UNITED	4/6			
11.	NEWCASTLE UNITED	4/6			
12.	MIDDLESBROUGH	4/6			
13.	EVERTON	2/6	87%	60%	73%
14.	SOUTHAMPTON	6/6			
15.	COVENTRY CITY	6/6			
16.	DERBY COUNTY	4/6			
17.	BRADFORD CITY	6/6			
18.	WIMBLEDON	3/6	87%	80%	83%
19.	SHEFFIELD WEDNESDAY	6/6			
20.	WATFORD	6/6			

The figures show a team's performance against clubs in each quarter of the final league table. The first column represents points won from the total available against each team in the league.

What a difference a CARLING makes.

Discipline and Season Summary

BOOKINGS BY POSITION 1997/1998 - 1999/2000
for the latest stats and to share your memories go to football.co.uk

key:
- forward
- midfield
- defence
- goalkeeper

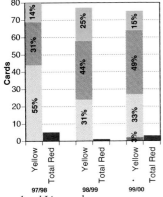

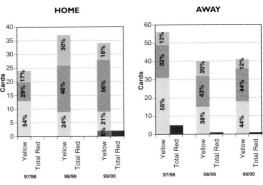

Arsenal and Liverpool.

Leeds received their lowest number of yellow cards for four seasons even though, in Lee Bowyer, they had one of the Carling Premiership's most booked players. Only Derby's Seth Johnson received as many as the 13 yellow cards shown to Bowyer, who received three separate one-match bans for his indiscipline. In the Carling Premiership their bookings total, while down, was the fifth highest in the division with Harte also receiving eight cautions. Unusually, Leeds received more bookings at home. They also collected three red cards – compared to the one the previous season – with Smith sent-off at Tottenham, Harte red-carded at home to Arsenal

and Duberry dismissed against Everton.

Like several of their rivals, Leeds never lost if they were leading at half time; on 14 occasions they led at the interval and went on to win 12 and draw two. A half time draw was also promising for Leeds fans; of the 15 times they were being held, they went on to lose only five games, though three of those defeats came at home. Manchester United were the first to turn a draw into an away win, in February, and Chelsea repeated the feat two months later. Away from home, a draw was a promising outcome at half time; of the seven occasions they were level they went on to lose just twice, at Old Trafford and Filbert Street.

HALF TIME - FULL TIME COMPARATIVE CHART
for the latest stats and to share your memories go to football.co.uk

HOME				AWAY				TOTAL			
Number of Home Half Time Wins	Full Time Result W	L	D	Number of Away Half Time Wins	Full Time Result W	L	D	Total Number of Half Time Wins	Full Time Result W	L	D
8	7	0	1	6	5	0	1	14	12	0	2
Number of Home Half Time Losses	Full Time Result W	L	D	Number of Away Half Time Losses	Full Time Result W	L	D	Total Number of Half Time Losses	Full Time Result W	L	D
3	1	2	0	6	1	4	1	9	2	6	1
Number of Home Half Time Draws	Full Time Result W	L	D	Number of Away Half Time Draws	Full Time Result W	L	D	Total Number of Half Time Draws	Full Time Result W	L	D
8	4	3	1	7	3	2	2	15	7	5	3

Maps and Directions

Elland Road is situated two miles south-west of the city centre. There are two car parks adjacent to the ground and some parking can be found in the Heath Grove area.

From the North:
Approaching on the A1, turn off onto the A58 and continue for 13 miles. Take the A58(M) for a further half mile, turning left onto the A643. Continue across the M621, turning right into Elland Road. The ground is on the right.

From the South:
Approaching from the south on the M1, continue on the M621 until Junction 2, turning left onto the A643. Then as route for North.

From the West/East:
Approaching on the M621, turn onto the A643 at Junction 2.
Then as route for North.

Leeds Railway Station is located in the city centre approximately 2 miles away. Buses operate from Sovereign Street to the ground.

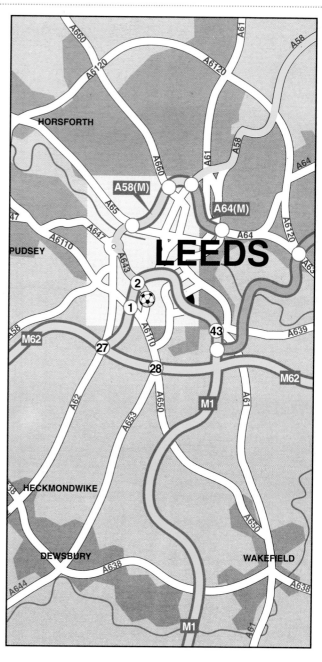

powered by football.co.uk

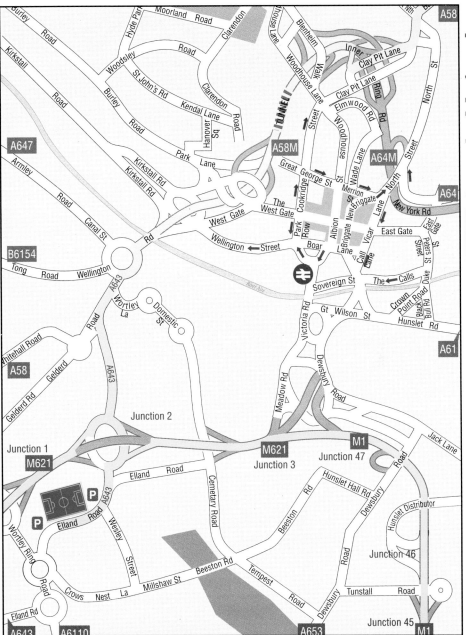

Pos		Pld	W	D	L	F	A	Pts
8	Leicester	38	16	7	15	55	55	55

Leicester City
"The Foxes"

City Stadium, Filbert Street,
Leicester LE2 7FL
Tel: 0116 291 5000
www.lcfc.co.uk

Season Review by
John Ley

The Daily Telegraph

The 1999-2000 season brought mixed emotions for Leicester's faithful fans. They lost Emile Heskey to Liverpool and manager Martin O'Neill to Celtic, but won the Worthington Cup and a place in this season's UEFA Cup. Muzzy Izzet made his Turkish debut in Euro 2000, Steve Guppy was recognised by England and Leicester finished in the top 10 for the fourth year in succession.

If the departures of Heskey and O'Neill were inevitable that did not make up for the chasm their absences left. Heskey's £11 million departure to Liverpool in March was expected and the fact that he had managed only seven goals in 23 starts, coupled with the arrival of Stan Collymore, suggested Leicester would recover.

Only time will tell if there is life after O'Neill. Leicester reacted quickly, bringing in former England Under-21 boss Peter Taylor, who in his first season back in club management, had taken Gillingham into Division One.

Useful Information
....

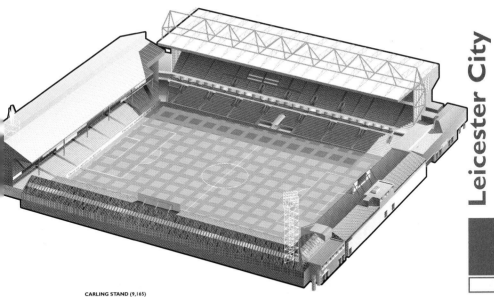

CARLING STAND (9,165)

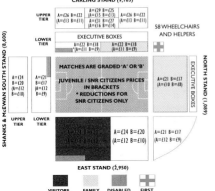

| | UPPER TIER | A=£26 B=£22 (A=£13 B=£11) | A=£29 B=£25 (A=£15 B=£13) A=£31 B=£27 (A=£16 B=£14) | A=£26 B=£22 (A=£13 B=£11) | |
| | LOWER TIER | A=£22 B=£18 *(A=£11 B=£9) | | A=£22 B=£18 (A=£11 B=£9) | 58 WHEELCHAIRS AND HELPERS |

EXECUTIVE BOXES

MATCHES ARE GRADED 'A' OR 'B'
JUVENILE / SNR CITIZENS PRICES IN BRACKETS
* REDUCTIONS FOR SNR CITIZENS ONLY

| SHANKS & McEWAN SOUTH STAND (8,600) | | | | |
| UPPER TIER | A=£24 B=£20 (A=£12 B=£10) | LOWER TIER | A=£21 B=£17 (A=£12 B=£9) | A=£21 B=£17 (A=£10 B=£8) |

NORTH STAND (1,089)

EXECUTIVE BOXES

| A=£24 B=£20 (A=£12 B=£10) | A=£24 B=£20 (A=£12 B=£10) | A=£21 B=£17 (A=£12 B=£9) |

EAST STAND (2,950)

VISITORS ENCLOSURE FAMILY ENCLOSURE DISABLED FANS FIRST AID

Filbert Street
Opened: November 7, 1891
Capacity: 22,215
1999/2000 highest attendance: 22,170
1999/2000 average attendance: 19,827
Record attendance: 47,298

---

individual players to stands. Matchball sponsorship.

Tel: **0116 291 5117**

Literature
Programme £2.50, Bi-monthly Foxes magazine £2.50,

Pre-Match & Half Time Entertainment
Leicester City mascots Filbert Fox, Vicki Vixen & Cousin Dennis. Face painting in McDonald's Family Stand. Half time presentation with Alan 'The Birch' Birchenall. Celebrity promotions.

Restaurant
Fosse Restaurant open 7 days a week, overlooks pitch.

Tel: **0116 291 5050**

Booking Information
General Enquiries:
0116 291 5296
Credit Card Bookings:
0116 291 5232
Travel Club:
0116 291 5007
Pepsi Junior Foxes:
0116 291 5006

Results Breakdown

POINTS WON OR LOST AT BOTH HOME AND AWAY
for the latest stats and to share your memories go to football.co.uk

key:
▦ win ▦ draw
■ loss -❿- league position
home fixtures are in red

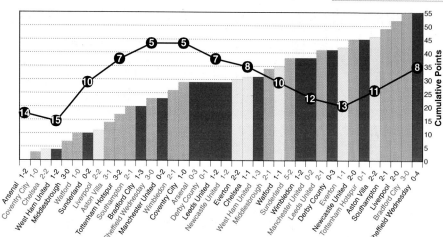

İt was a roller-coaster season for City. The remarkable spirit created by O'Neill seemed to compensate for injuries in key departments, with Steve Walsh, Andrew Impey, Neil Lennon and Steve Guppy all missing for lengthy periods. A disappointing start gave way to a good autumn run in which Leicester lost just once in seven games. By October City were fifth but a run of four straight home defeats – just one short of the club record – ruined all the good work.

City lost six home games but won 10 – their most successes at Filbert Street in the Carling Premiership

and the club's best return there for six seasons. They won more points than at any time in their Carling Premiership history, winning more home points than they had done since finishing fifth in 1996. But it was a different story away; they lost nine on their travels, they most since the 1993-94 season. Between late December and early April they went six away games without a win.

Tony Cottee's success in front of goal continued. He scored another 13 goals, his best return in a League season for five years and taking his total in Carling

HOME

AWAY

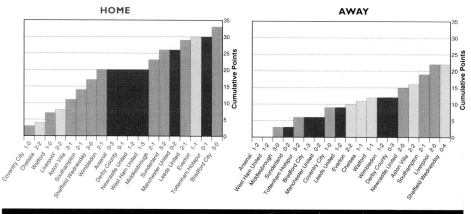

Leicester City

Legend: ● = Red Card   = Yellow Card   ▲ = Player substituted   00 = Time of goal

DATE	H/A	OPPONENT	H/T	F/T	POS	REFEREE	TEAM	SUBSTITUTES USED
07/08	A	Arsenal	0:0	1:2	14	A.B.Wilkie	Flowers, Sinclair, Elliott, Walsh▲, Impey, Guppy, Izzet, Lennon, Savage, Coffee 57, Heskey	Taggart▲ Marshall▲
11/08	H	Coventry City	1:0	1:0	12	N.S.Barry	Flowers, Sinclair, Elliott, Taggart▲, Impey, Guppy, Izzet 24, Lennon, Savage, Coffee, Heskey▲	Gilchrist▲ Campbell▲
14/08	H	Chelsea	1:0	2:2	10	S.J.Lodge	Flowers, Sinclair, Elliott, Taggart▲, Impey, Guppy, Izzet 90, Lennon, Savage▲, Coffee, Heskey 10	Gilchrist▲ Marshall▲
21/08	A	West Ham United	1:2	1:2	15	A.G.Wiley	Flowers, Sinclair, Elliott, Taggart▲, Impey, Guppy, Izzet, Lennon, Savage▲, Coffee, Heskey 2	Gilchrist▲ Marshall▲
24/08	A	Middlesbrough	2:0	3:0	6	R.J.Harris	Flowers▲, Sinclair, Elliott, Taggart, Impey, Guppy, Izzet, Lennon, Savage, Coffee▲38, Heskey 35 83	Arphexad▲ Marshall▲
30/08	H	Watford	1:0	1:0	5	N.S.Barry	Arphexad, Sinclair, Elliott, Taggart, Oakes▲, Guppy, Izzet 45, Lennon, Savage▲, Coffee▲, Heskey	Marshall▲ Zagorakis▲
11/09	A	Sunderland	0:1	0:2	5	A.P.D'Urso	Flowers, Sinclair, Elliott, Taggart●, Impey, Guppy, Izzet, Lennon, Savage▲, Coffee▲, Heskey	Marshall▲ Gilchrist▲
18/09	H	Liverpool	1:2	2:2	9	U.D.Rennie	Arphexad, Sinclair●, Elliott, Taggart▲, Impey▲, Guppy, Izzet 86, Lennon, Savage▲, Coffee ▲2, Heskey	Gilchrist▲ Oakes▲
25/09	A	Aston Villa	1:0	3:1	7	J.T.Winter	Flowers, Gilchrist▲, Elliott, Gilchrist, Impey▲, Guppy, Izzet 40, Lennon, Savage▲, Coffee ▲55, Heskey	Zagorakis▲ Marshall▲
03/10	H	Tottenham Hotspur	1:2	3:2	7	G.P.Barber	Flowers, Sinclair▲, Elliott, Taggart 76, Impey, Guppy, Izzet 25 69, Lennon, Savage▲, Coffee, Heskey	Marshall▲ Zagorakis▲
16/10	A	Southampton	2:0	2:1	5	B.Knight	Flowers, Sinclair, Elliott, Taggart▲, Impey, Guppy 8, Izzet, Lennon, Savage▲, Coffee ▲39, Heskey	Zagorakis▲ Marshall▲
23/10	A	Bradford City	1:2	1:3	6	M.D.Reed	Flowers, Sinclair, Elliott, Gilchrist, Impey 21, Guppy, Izzet, Lennon, Savage▲, Coffee ▲57, Heskey	Marshall▲ Gilchrist▲
30/10	H	Sheffield Wednesday	2:0	2:0	5	P.E.Alcock	Flowers, Sinclair, Elliott, Taggart ▲24 36, Impey, Guppy, Izzet, Lennon, Savage▲, Coffee▲, Heskey	Gilchrist▲ Walsh▲
06/11	A	Manchester United	0:1	0:2	6	P.A.Durkin	Flowers, Sinclair, Elliott, Taggart, Impey, Guppy, Izzet, Lennon, Savage▲, Coffee 21 58, Heskey	Walsh▲
20/11	H	Wimbledon	0:1	1:2	7	A.G.Wiley	Flowers, Walsh, Elliott, Taggart, Impey, Guppy, Izzet, Lennon, Savage▲, Coffee, Heskey 60	
27/11	A	Coventry City	0:0	1:0	5	S.J.Lodge	Flowers, Sinclair, Elliott, Taggart, Impey▲, Guppy, Oakes, Lennon, Savage▲, Coffee▲, Heskey	Oakes▲ Marshall▲
04/12	A	Arsenal	0:1	0:3	5	D.J.Gallagher	Flowers, Sinclair, Elliott, Taggart, Impey▲, Oakes, Izzet, Lennon, Savage▲, Eddie, Heskey	Coffee▲
18/12	H	Derby County	0:0	0:1	6	D.R.Elleray	Flowers, Walsh, Elliott, Taggart, Gilchrist, Oakes, Izzet, Zagorakis, Savage, Coffee 10, Heskey	Zagorakis▲
26/12	A	Leeds United	1:2	1:2	7	M.K.Halsey	Arphexad, Sinclair, Elliott, Taggart, Impey▲, Zagorakis 83, Izzet, Eddie, Savage, Coffee, Heskey	Campbell▲
28/12	H	Newcastle United	0:1	0:2	7	P.Durkin	Flowers, Sinclair, Elliott, Gilchrist, Oakes, Zagorakis, Izzet, Eddie, Savage, Coffee, Heskey	
03/01	H	Chelsea	2:1	2:1	8	J.T.Winter	Flowers, Sinclair, Elliott 25 31, Taggart 42, Walsh, Oakes, Zagorakis, Eddie, Savage, Eddie, Coffee	Campbell▲
15/01	A	Chelsea	1:0	1:1	8	G.P.Barber	Flowers, Sinclair, Elliott, Campbell, Gilchrist, Zagorakis, Zagorakis, Eddie, Savage▲, Marshall, Coffee 7	Guppy▲ Thomas▲
22/01	H	West Ham United	1:2	1:3	10	D.R.Elleray	Arphexad, Sinclair, Elliott, Taggart, Impey ▲41, Goodwin, Zagorakis, Eddie, Gunnlaugsson▲, Fenton, Heskey 24	Thomas▲
05/02	H	Middlesbrough	2:0	2:1	9	S.G.Bennett	Arphexad, Walsh, Elliott 39, Gilchrist, Oakes, Zagorakis, Izzet 41, Eddie, Gunnlaugsson ▲, Gilchrist, Eddie	Thomas▲
12/02	A	Watford	2:0	2:0	10	A.P.D'Urso	Flowers, Walsh, Elliott, Gilchrist, Impey, Izzet, Oakes, Lennon, Savage ▲52, Collymore, Eddie	Stewart▲
04/03	A	Sunderland	2:0	5:2	11	N.S.Barry	Arphexad, Sinclair, Elliott, Eddie▲, Guppy, Izzet, Lennon, Savage, Collymore 17 60 87, Heskey 34	Oakes▲90 Marshall▲
11/03	H	Wimbledon	0:1	1:2	11	P.E.Alcock	Flowers, Sinclair, Elliott, Impey▲, Guppy, Izzet, Lennon, Savage▲, Collymore, Eddie	Gilchrist▲ Coffee▲
18/03	H	Manchester United	0:1	0:2	12	R.J.Harris	Arphexad, Sinclair, Elliott, Oakes, Guppy, Izzet, Lennon, Eddie, Savage▲, Collymore 10, Eddie	Marshall▲ Coffee▲
26/03	A	Leeds United	1:2	1:2	11	S.J.Lodge	Arphexad, Sinclair, Elliott, Oakes, Guppy 48, Izzet, Lennon, Savage, Collymore, Eddie 14	Campbell▲ Coffee▲
02/04	H	Derby County	0:3	0:3	11	G.Poll	Arphexad, Gilchrist, Elliott, Oakes, Guppy, Izzet, Lennon, Savage, Collymore, Eddie	Zagorakis▲ Dudfield▲
08/04	A	Everton	1:1	1:1	13	A.G.Wiley	Flowers, Sinclair, Elliott, Impey, Guppy, Izzet, Lennon●, Savage, Oakes, Coffee 7	Zagorakis▲ Thomas▲
15/04	A	Newcastle United	1:0	1:0	10	U.D.Rennie	Flowers, Sinclair, Elliott, Impey, Guppy, Izzet, Lennon 67, Savage ▲52, Oakes, Coffee	Zagorakis▲ Fenton▲
19/04	H	Tottenham Hotspur	0:0	1:0	11	J.T.Winter	Arphexad, Gilchrist, Elliott 35, Gilchrist, Guppy, Izzet, Oakes, Savage, Gilchrist, Coffee	Dudfield▲ Stewart▲
22/04	A	Aston Villa	1:1	2:2	11	G.P.Barber	Flowers, Sinclair, Elliott 59 63, Eddie, Guppy, Izzet 60, Lennon, Savage▲, Gilchrist 48, Coffee ▲22	Walsh▲ Eddie▲
29/04	H	Southampton	2:1	2:1	11	M.D.Reed	Arphexad, Sinclair, Elliott, Eddie, Guppy, Izzet, Lennon, Savage▲, Gilchrist, Coffee ▲68	Walsh▲ Marshall▲
03/05	H	Liverpool	1:1	2:1	9	G.Poll	Flowers, Sinclair, Elliott, Impey▲, Oakes, Izzet, Lennon, Savage, Gilchrist 48, Coffee ▲22	Walsh▲ Oakes▲
06/05	H	Bradford City	0:0	0:0	8	S.W.Dunn	Arphexad, Gilchrist, Elliott, Impey▲, Guppy, Izzet, Lennon, Savage, Gilchrist, Coffee 68	Oakes▲ Walsh▲
14/05	A	Sheffield Wednesday	0:2	0:4	8	D.R.Elleray	Arphexad, Sinclair, Elliott, Impey▲, Guppy, Izzet, Lennon, Savage, Gilchrist, Coffee▲	Zagorakis▲ Marshall▲

Goal Analysis

powered by **football.co.uk**

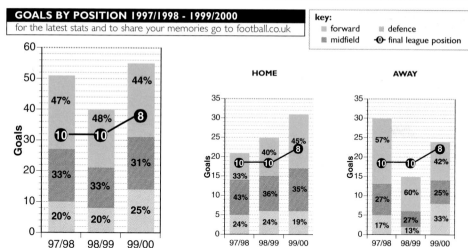

HOME   AWAY

Premiership games to 78. After the departure of Heskey, Leicester turned to Stan Collymore and the former Aston Villa striker, released on a free transfer, repaid O'Neill's faith by scoring a hat-trick in only his second game, the 5-2 home win over Sunderland. Those goals meant that Collymore had scored for four different sides in the Carling Premiership (including Forest, Liverpool and Villa) but was only the second Leicester player to score a hat-trick in the division, after Ian Marshall's three against Derby in the 1996-97 season. Sadly, after scoring just one more goal Collymore's luck was cursed again and he broke a leg, at Derby in April, which brought his season to an end. Ian Marshall stood in as a striker and a responded with three goals.

Izzet continues to improve his goal scoring achievements; having claimed three, four, then five League goals in three previous seasons he scored eight from midfield, his best ever return, to finish as the club's second top scorer. Even Robbie Savage showed

HOME   AWAY

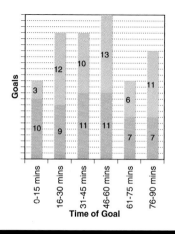
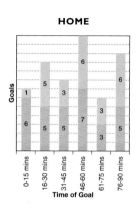
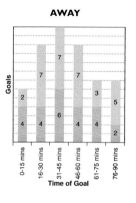

Leicester City

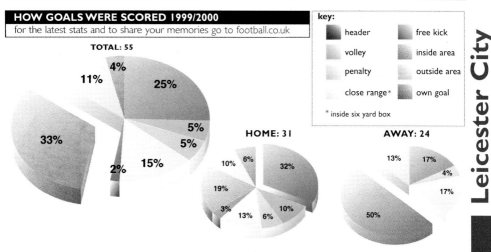

HOW GOALS WERE SCORED 1999/2000
for the latest stats and to share your memories go to football.co.uk

key:
- header
- volley
- penalty
- close range*
- free kick
- inside area
- outside area
- own goal

* inside six yard box

TOTAL: 55

4% 11% 25% 33% 5% 5% 2% 15%

HOME: 31
10% 6% 32% 19% 3% 13% 6% 10%

AWAY: 24
13% 17% 4% 17% 50%

a knack for scoring, claiming three goals from midfield, and matching his total over the previous two seasons for the Foxes.

But it was in defence that City enjoyed an unexpected contribution to their goals tally. No fewer than 25 per cent of their goals came from defence – only Middlesbrough enjoyed a greater percent contribution from their back line. Chief contributor was Gerry Taggart, who scored six, and all from open play, more than any other defender in the Carling Premiership, it was his best goals return in 13 seasons. Matt Elliott, often called upon as an emergency forward, also netted six.

At home, Leicester scored a surprisingly low number of goals from inside the penalty area. Just 19 per cent came from that area, while 32 per cent were headers thanks to the presence of Elliott and Heskey.

At Filbert Street, Leicester were far more likely to score than the opposition in the opening 15 minutes. They scored 30 of their 55 goals in the first half while

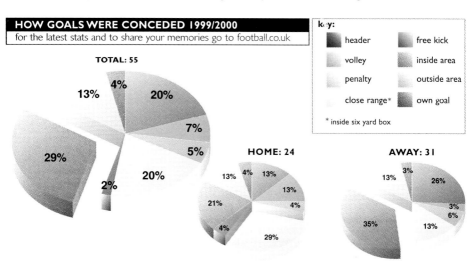

HOW GOALS WERE CONCEDED 1999/2000
for the latest stats and to share your memories go to football.co.uk

key:
- header
- volley
- penalty
- close range*
- free kick
- inside area
- outside area
- own goal

* inside six yard box

TOTAL: 55

4% 13% 20% 7% 29% 5% 2% 20%

HOME: 24
13% 4% 13% 13% 21% 4% 4% 29%

AWAY: 31
3% 13% 26% 3% 6% 35% 13%

Squad and Performance

SQUAD LIST

for the latest stats and to share your memories go to football.co.uk

Position	Name	Appearances	Appearances as substitute	Goals	Clean Sheets	Yellow Cards	Red Cards
G	P.Arphexad	9	2	3			
G	T.Flowers	29		5	2		
D	M.Elliott	37		6	2		
D	P.Gilchrist	17	10	1	1		
D	F.Sinclair	34			6		1
D	G.Taggart	30	1	6	5		1
D	D.Thomas		3				
D	S.Walsh	5	6		1		
M	S.Campbell	1	3				
M	S.Goodwin	1					
M	S.Guppy	29	1	2	2		
M	A.Impey	28	1	2			
M	M.Izzet	32		8	3		
M	N.Lennon	31		1	7	1	
M	S.Oakes	15	7	1	1		
M	R.Savage	35		1	3		
M	J.Stewart		1				
M	T.Zagorakis	6	11	1	2		
F	S.Collymore	6		4	1		
F	T.Cottee	30	3	13	1		
F	L.Dudfield		2				
F	D.Eadie	15	1		1	1	
F	G.Fenton	1	1		1		
F	A.Gunnlaugsson	2					
F	E.Heskey	23		7	5		
F	I.Marshall	2	19		1		

30 of the 55 they conceded came in the second period of the game.

Not one City player was ever-present last season though Elliott missed only one game through an FA ban imposed for an elbow, on Liverpool's Michael Owen. Savage missed only three games while Frank Sinclair missed only four. Other regulars included Taggart, Lennon and Cottee. Marshall was regular but ordinarily on the bench; only Leeds's Darren Huckerby made more appearances as a substitute.

Leicester lost home and away to the top two, while West Ham and Derby also stole maximum points. But they responded by beating Middlesbrough, Southampton and Coventry both at home and away. Strangely, they struggled away to the bottom clubs;

TEAM PERFORMANCE TABLE

for the latest stats and to share your memories go to football.co.uk

Position	Club	Points Won	Percentage of points won at home	Percentage of points won away	overall percentage of points won
1.	MANCHESTER UNITED	0/6			
2.	ARSENAL	0/6			
3.	LEEDS UNITED	3/6	33%	27%	**30%**
4.	LIVERPOOL	4/6			
5.	CHELSEA	2/6			
6.	ASTON VILLA	4/6			
7.	SUNDERLAND	3/6			
8.	LEICESTER CITY	55 pts	50%	33%	**42%**
9.	TOTTENHAM HOTSPUR	3/6			
10.	WEST HAM UNITED	0/6			
11.	NEWCASTLE UNITED	3/6			
12.	MIDDLESBROUGH	6/6			
13.	EVERTON	2/6	67%	87%	**77%**
14.	SOUTHAMPTON	6/6			
15.	COVENTRY CITY	6/6			
16.	DERBY COUNTY	0/6			
17.	BRADFORD CITY	3/6			
18.	WIMBLEDON	3/6	80%	7%	**43%**
19.	SHEFFIELD WEDNESDAY	3/6			
20.	WATFORD	4/6			

The figures show a team's performance against clubs in each quarter of the final league table. The first column represents points won from the total available against each team in the league.

What a difference a CARLING makes.

Discipline and Season Summary

BOOKINGS BY POSITION 1997/1998 - 1999/2000
for the latest stats and to share your memories go to football.co.uk

key:
- forward
- midfield
- defence
- goalkeeper

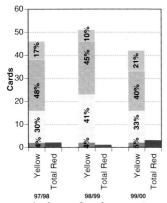

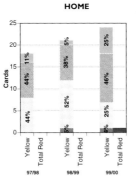

HOME

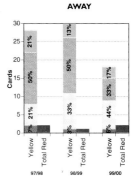

AWAY

Leicester City

against the lowest five they won just one point – against Watford.

Leicester should be applauded for their impressive behaviour; O'Neill may have ranted on the touchline but his charges were more subdued when it came to upsetting the referee. Their behaviour was the best it's ever been in the division. The bookings were shared around throughout the teams though the worst offenders were Lennon, Sinclair and Taggart, all of whom also received red cards. Darren Eadie was also sent off. At home, the midfielders were worst behaved, their figures making up nearly half of Leicester's Filbert Street cautions. Away from home, the defenders were booked more than their team-mates. For most defenders, cautions are an

occupational hazard but after being booked twice in the opening three games, Elliott avoided another yellow card.

In terms of half-time form, Leicester were fairly predictable if winning or losing. An interval lead meant a full-time victory in most cases; of their 14 half time leads, they went on to win 10 and draw four. But if they were behind after 45 minutes, they invariably lost; 13 times they went in for tea trailing – and finished up the losers 11 occasions. Only once did they turn a half time loss into a full time win and it came away, at Tottenham in October. After 25 minutes they took the lead, trailed 2-1 at half time then Taggart popped up with a 76 minute winner to make the final score 3-2 to the Foxes.

HALF TIME - FULL TIME COMPARATIVE CHART
for the latest stats and to share your memories go to football.co.uk

HOME				AWAY				TOTAL			
Number of Home Half Time Wins	Full Time Result W	L	D	Number of Away Half Time Wins	Full Time Result W	L	D	Total Number of Half Time Wins	Full Time Result W	L	D
8	7	0	1	6	3	0	3	14	10	0	4
Number of Home Half Time Losses	Full Time Result W	L	D	Number of Away Half Time Losses	Full Time Result W	L	D	Total Number of Half Time Losses	Full Time Result W	L	D
5	0	4	1	8	1	7	0	13	1	11	1
Number of Home Half Time Draws	Full Time Result W	L	D	Number of Away Half Time Draws	Full Time Result W	L	D	Total Number of Half Time Draws	Full Time Result W	L	D
6	3	2	1	5	2	2	1	11	5	4	2

What a difference a CARLING makes.

Maps and Directions

Leicester City play at Filbert Street, south of Leicester city centre. There is no matchday parking in or around Filbert Street and visiting supporters are encouraged to travel either by rail or with their club's official travel organisation.

The club actively support the "LET'S KICK RACISM OUT OF FOOTBALL" campaign and operate a 'zero tolerance' policy towards any person making racist chants or remarks in or around the ground.

From the North:
Exit M1 at Junction 22 heading for Leicester on the A50. Follow Leicester and city centre signs over five roundabouts for 6 miles until junction with Fosse Road A5125. Turn right onto the A5125 for 1 mile then left onto the A47 King Richards Road. After half a mile turn right into Narborough Road North A46. After half a mile turn left onto Upperton Road, crossing the river and taking the first right for Filbert Street.

From the South:
Exit M1 at Junction 21 and head for Leicester on the A5460. After half a mile take the second exit at the roundabout staying on the A5460 Narborough Road. After approximately 3 miles, turn right into Upperton Road, crossing the river and taking the first right for Filbert Street.

From the West:
Approaching on the M69, at Junction 21 with the M1 get onto the A5460. Then as route for South.

The main railway station is about one mile from the ground. No buses run directly to the ground and it is about a 20 minute walk.

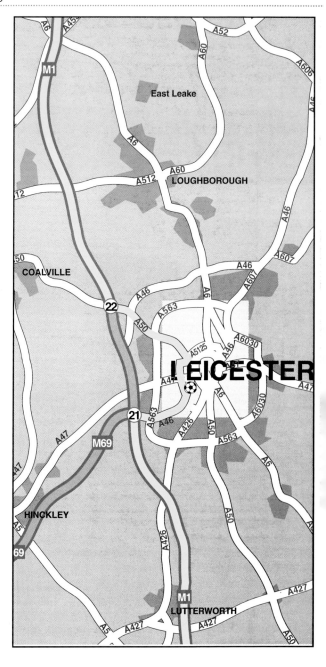

Leicester City

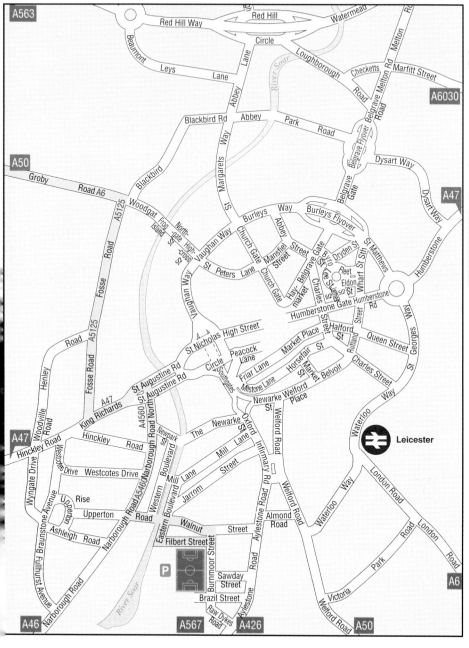

127

Pos		Pld	W	D	L	F	A	Pts
4	Liverpool	38	19	10	9	51	30	67

Liverpool

"The Reds"

Anfield Road, Liverpool L4 0TH
Tel: 0151 263 2361
www.liverpoolfc.net

Season Review by
John Ley

The Daily Telegraph

Liverpool fans who are old enough to remember standing in the Kop could have been forgiven for cursing the foreign buying policy, alien in the past to Liverpool but preferred by Gerard Houllier in the summer of 1999. He bought a German, two Dutchman, a Swiss, a Czech, a Finn and a Guinean. By the end of the season, few were complaining about the French manager's transfer policy.

The arrival of Emile Heskey, in March, to complement an attacking force already including Michael Owen, Titi Camara and Robbie Fowler, seemed ominous for the rest of the country. Injuries to Dietmar Hamann, who needed an ankle operation after just 25 minutes of his debut, Jamie Redknapp, who could miss the first half of the new season, Fowler and Owen, did not help but the early summer additions of French winger Bernard Diomede, from Auxerre for £3 million, Coventry midfielder Gary McAllister and Leicester goalkeeper Pegguy Arphexad has only strengthened Houllier's hand.

Useful Information

Liverpool Club Store

Kop Grandstand
Opening Times:
Monday-Friday: 9.00am-5.00pm
Saturdays: 9.00am-5.00pm
Sundays: 10am-4.00pm
Match Saturdays: 9.00am*
Match Sundays: 10.00am*
Match Evenings: 9.00am*
* close 45 mins after game
Tel: 0151 263 1760

LFC Official Club Store

11 Williamson Square,
Liverpool L1 1EQ
Opening Times:
Monday-Saturday: 9.00am-5.30pm
Matchday Sundays:
11.00am-5.00pm
Sundays: 10.00am-4.00pm
Tel: 0151 330 3077
Mail Order Service: 0990 532 532

Museum and Tour Centre

Admission prices for Museum and Tour; £23 family ticket (2 adults, 2 children), £8.50 adults, £5.50 children & senior citizens.
Open every day. Last admission Museum - 4.00pm (1 hour before kick-off on matchdays)
Tour Centre - 3.30pm
Tel: 0151 260 6677

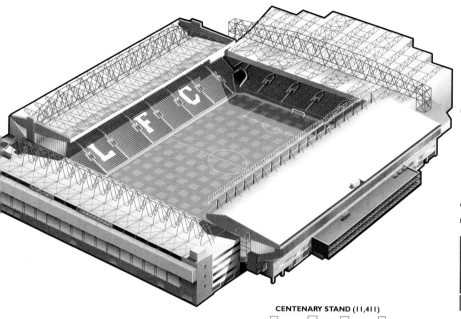

Anfield

Opened: September 28, 1884

Capacity: 45,365

1999/2000 highest attendance: 44,929

1999/2000 average attendance: 44,074

Record attendance: 61,905

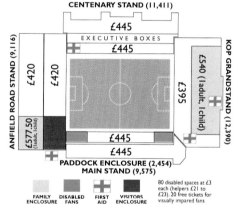

CENTENARY STAND (11,411)

£445

EXECUTIVE BOXES

£445

£420 £420

ANFIELD ROAD STAND (9,116)

£577.50 (1 adult, 1 child)

£445

£445

PADDOCK ENCLOSURE (2,454)

MAIN STAND (9,575)

KOP GRANDSTAND (12,390)

£540 (1 adult, 1 child)

£395

FAMILY ENCLOSURE

DISABLED FANS

FIRST AID

VISITORS ENCLOSURE

80 disabled spaces at £3 each (helpers £21 to £23). 20 free tickets for visually impared fans

Corporate Hospitality

A range of hospitality packages are available. Contact Sue Johnston:

0151 263 9199

Sales Conferences and Banqueting. Contact Philip Crowther:

0151 263 7744

Pre-Match & Half Time Entertainment

DJs play the latest chart music.

Liverpool International Supporters' Club

Launched in May 1992, it gives Liverpool supporters worldwide the opportunity to express their opinions and to find out the latest news on the club.

Tel: **0151 261 1444**

Booking Information

General Enquiries:

0151 260 8680

Credit Card Bookings:

0151 263 5727

Travel Club:

0151 260 8680

Recorded Info:

0151 260 9999

Results Breakdown

powered by **football.co.uk**

POINTS WON OR LOST AT BOTH HOME AND AWAY
for the latest stats and to share your memories go to football.co.uk

key:
■ win   ■ draw
■ loss   -**0**- league position
home fixtures are in red

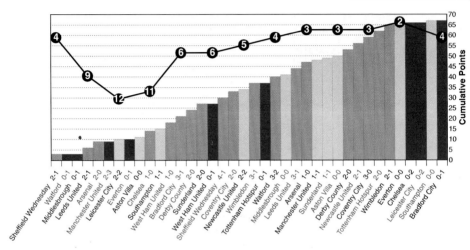

Liverpool started badly; two defeats in their opening three games dampened the early optimism but with so many changes in personnel, it should have been expected. News that Fowler needed an ankle operation after only seven games brought only greater cause for concern but, after home defeats by Manchester United and arch-rivals Everton, in September, when they finished with nine men, Liverpool began to impress. Their form at Anfield was particularly good; they won five in succession and remained unbeaten there until Leicester stole a shock win in May.

For two months Liverpool established themselves in third place behind United and Arsenal and seemed likely to take the third Champions' League place as Leeds's season appeared to be folding. They even moved into second place with a 2-1 win at Wimbledon thanks to two Heskey goals but they were to be Liverpool's last goals of the season; they drew 0-0 with Everton and three defeats and another draw to end up in a disappointing fourth place.

With so many strikers on the Anfield books, hope was high that goals would be scored in abundance;

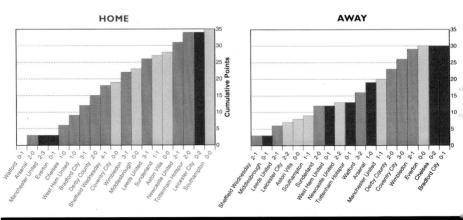

HOME   **AWAY**

What a difference a *CARLING* makes.

THE F.A. CARLING PREMIERSHIP

Results Table

Liverpool

Legend: ● = Red Card   ▲ = Player substituted   00 = Time of goal   (Yellow Card shown by marker)

DATE	H/A	OPPONENT	H/T	F/T	POS	REFEREE	TEAM											SUBSTITUTES USED
07/08	A	Sheffield Wednesday	0-0	2-1	4	G.Poll	Westerveld	Hyypia	Matteo	Heggem	Carragher	Smicer	Redknapp	Hamann	Berger	Camara 85	Fowler 75	Thompson / Staunton / Meijer
14/08	H	Watford	0-1	0-1	13	A.B.Wilkie	Westerveld	Hyypia	Matteo	Heggem ▲	Carragher	Smicer	Redknapp	Hamann	Berger	Camara	Fowler	Riedle / Song / Thompson
21/08	A	Middlesbrough	0-0	0-1	17	S.W.Dunn	Westerveld	Hyypia	Matteo	Heggem	Carragher	Staunton	Redknapp	Gerrard	Berger ▲	Camara	Fowler	Thompson ▲
23/08	A	Leeds United	1-1	2-1	9	D.R.Elleray	Westerveld	Hyypia	Matteo	Song	Carragher	Thompson	Redknapp	Gerrard	Berger	Camara 45	Fowler	
28/08	H	Arsenal	1-0	2-0	8	D.J.Gallagher	Westerveld	Hyypia	Matteo	Song	Carragher	Thompson ▲	Redknapp	Gerrard	Berger 76	Camara	Fowler 8	Owen ▲ / Heggem / Meijer
11/09	H	Manchester United	1-3	2-3	12	G.P.Barber	Westerveld	Hyypia 23	Matteo	Heggem	Carragher	Smicer	Redknapp	Gerrard	Berger 68	Owen 23 39	Fowler ▲	Smicer / Heggem / Owen
18/09	A	Leicester City	2-1	2-2	12	U.D.Rennie	Westerveld	Hyypia	Matteo	Heggem ▲	Carragher	Thompson ●	Redknapp	Gerrard	Berger	Owen 23 39	Fowler ▲	Murphy ▲ / Meijer / Meijer
27/09	H	Everton	0-1	0-1	12	M.A.Riley	Westerveld ●	Hyypia	Staunton	Heggem	Carragher	Smicer ▲	Redknapp	Hamann	Berger	Owen	Fowler ▲	Camara / Gerrard / Camara
02/10	A	Aston Villa	0-0	0-0	6	R.J.Harris	Friedel	Hyypia	Staunton	Song	Carragher	Smicer ▲	Redknapp	Hamann	Berger	Owen	Meijer	Gerrard / Carragher / Gerrard
16/10	H	Chelsea	0-0	1-0	11	M.D.Reed	Friedel	Hyypia	Staunton	Song	Henchoz	Smicer	Redknapp	Corragher	Murphy ▲	Thompson 47	Owen	Meijer / Meijer / Thompson
23/10	A	Southampton	1-1	1-1	11	N.S.Barry	Westerveld	Hyypia	Staunton	Song	Henchoz	Smicer ▲	Redknapp	Carragher	Berger	Camara 81	Meijer	Heggem / Owen / Staunton
27/10	A	West Ham United	1-0	1-0	9	S.J.Lodge	Westerveld	Hyypia	Staunton	Song	Henchoz	Thompson ▲	Redknapp	Carragher	Berger	Camara 43	Meijer	Smicer / Heggem / Staunton
01/11	H	Bradford City	2-1	3-1	6	J.T.Winter	Westerveld	Hyypia	Matteo	Song	Henchoz	Smicer ▲	Redknapp	Hamann 78	Berger	Thompson	Camara 20	Corragher / Murphy 65 / Heggem
06/11	A	Derby County	0-0	2-0	5	U.D.Rennie	Westerveld	Hyypia	Matteo	Heggem	Henchoz	Smicer ▲	Redknapp 69	Hamann	Berger 85	Owen ▲62	Owen	Murphy ▲65 / Murphy ▲62 / Gerrard
20/11	H	Sunderland	0-0	2-0	5	D.J.Gallagher	Westerveld	Hyypia	Matteo	Song	Henchoz	Heggem	Redknapp	Homann	Berger	Thompson	Owen	Thompson / Meijer / Meijer
27/11	A	West Ham United	0-1	0-1	6	G.P.Barber	Westerveld	Hyypia	Matteo	Corragher	Henchoz	Song	Gerrard	Homann	Berger ▲41	Murphy ▲41	Owen	Thompson / Fowler / Fowler
05/12	H	Sheffield Wednesday	2-1	4-1	5	P.A.Durkin	Westerveld	Hyypia	Matteo	Heggem	Henchoz	Gerrard 69	Thompson	Homann	Berger	Camara	Owen 45	Corragher / Heggem / Staunton
18/12	H	Coventry City	1-0	2-0	5	A.P.D'Urso	Westerveld	Hyypia 21	Matteo	Song ▲	Henchoz	Gerrard	Thompson 79	Homann	Berger	Camara ▲74	Owen 31 53	Smicer / Murphy / Heggem
26/12	A	Newcastle United	1-1	2-2	5	D.R.Elleray	Westerveld	Hyypia	Matteo	Corragher	Henchoz	Gerrard	Murphy ▲	Homann	Berger 68	Corragher	Owen 31 58	Fowler / Carragher / Song
28/12	H	Wimbledon	0-0	3-1	5	N.S.Barry	Westerveld	Hyypia	Matteo	Heggem	Henchoz	Corragher	Thompson ▲	Corragher	Berger 10	Camara	Owen 45	Fowler ▲79 / Owen / Thompson
03/01	A	Tottenham Hotspur	0-1	0-1	5	A.B.Wilkie	Westerveld	Hyypia	Matteo	Heggem ▲	Henchoz	Smicer	Gerrard	Corragher	Berger	Corragher	Camara	Staunton ▲71 / Camara / Shaunton
15/01	H	Watford	0-1	3-2	5	S.J.Lodge	Westerveld	Hyypia	Matteo	Corragher	Henchoz	Thompson 41	Gerrard	Homann	Berger	Owen	Owen 17	Smicer / Camara / Shaunton
22/01	H	Middlesbrough	0-0	0-0	4	P.Durkin	Westerveld	Hypic	Matteo ▲	Corragher	Henchoz	Thompson	Gerrard	Homann	Berger	Smicer	Meijer	Murphy / Meijer / Newby
05/02	A	Leeds United	1-0	0-3	4	M.D.Reed	Westerveld	Hyypia	Matteo	Corragher	Henchoz	Smicer ▲	Gerrard	Homann	Berger 69	Corragher	Meijer	Corragher / Meijer
13/02	H	Arsenal	1-0	1-0	3	P.A.Durkin	Westerveld	Hyypia	Matteo	Corragher	Henchoz	Smicer	Corragher	Homann	Berger	Camara ▲85	Meijer	Smicer / Heggem / Owen
04/03	A	Manchester United	0-1	0-1	4	A.P.D'Urso	Westerveld	Hyypia	Matteo	Heggem ▲	Henchoz	Gerrard	Gerrard	Homann	Berger 27	Corragher 18	Owen	Heggem / Song / Owen
11/03	H	Sunderland	0-0	1-0	4	G.Poll	Westerveld	Hyypia	Matteo	Song ▲	Henchoz	Thompson	Gerrard	Homann	Berger 2	Heskey	Meijer	Song / Murphy / Owen
18/03	A	Derby County	0-0	2-0	3	S.G.Bennett	Westerveld	Hyypia	Matteo	Corragher	Henchoz	Thompson	Gerrard	Corragher	Berger	Heskey	Meijer	Thompson / Camara / Redknapp
25/03	H	Newcastle United	0-0	2-1	3	B.Knight	Westerveld	Hyypia	Matteo	Corragher	Henchoz	Thompson 41	Gerrard	Homann	Berger 10	Heskey	Owen 17	Thompson / Camara
01/04	A	Coventry City	2-0	3-0	3	M.D.Read	Westerveld	Hyypia	Matteo	Corragher	Henchoz	Thompson	Gerrard	Homann	Berger	Heskey	Camara 51	Redknapp / Camara / Camara 86
09/04	H	Tottenham Hotspur	1-0	2-0	2	S.J.Lodge	Westerveld	Hyypia	Matteo	Corragher	Henchoz	Thompson	Gerrard	Homann	Berger 34	Heskey 78	Owen ▲23 37	Murphy / Redknapp ▲23 37
16/04	A	Wimbledon	1-0	2-1	2	M.A.Riley	Westerveld	Hyypia	Matteo	Corragher	Henchoz	Murphy	Murphy	Homann	Berger	Heskey ▲36 62	Owen ▲61	Camara / Camara / Smicer
21/04	H	Everton	0-0	0-0	4	G.Poll	Westerveld	Hyypia	Matteo	Corragher	Henchoz	Thompson ▲	Thompson	Homann	Berger	Heskey ▲36 62	Owen ▲90	Heggem / Fowler / Smicer
29/04	A	Chelsea	0-2	0-2	3	G.P.Barber	Westerveld	Hyypia	Matteo	Corragher	Henchoz	Murphy	Murphy	Homann	Berger	Heskey	Owen	Camara / Camara
03/05	H	Leicester City	0-1	0-2	4	G.Poll	Westerveld	Hyypia	Matteo	Corragher	Henchoz	Thompson	Thompson	Homann	Berger	Heskey	Owen	Fowler / Murphy / Camara
07/05	H	Southampton	0-0	0-0	3	P.E.Alcock	Westerveld	Hyypia	Matteo ▲	Corragher	Henchoz	Song ▲	Song	Homann	Berger	Heskey	Fowler ▲	Hamann / Thompson / Meijer
14/05	A	Bradford City	0-1	0-1	4	D.J.Gallagher	Westerveld	Hyypia	Matteo	Corragher	Henchoz	Gerrard	Gerrard	Homann	Berger ▲	Heskey	Owen	Camara / Meijer / Meijer

131

Goal Analysis

powered by  football.co.uk

GOALS BY POSITION 1997/1998 - 1999/2000

for the latest stats and to share your memories go to football.co.uk

key:
- forward
- midfield
- defence
- final league position

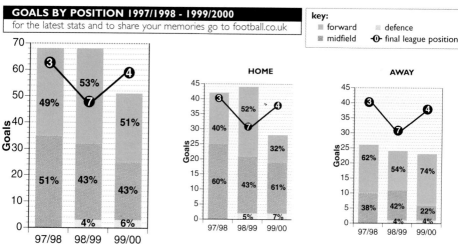

instead they scored 51, fewer than 10 Carling Premiership opponents and their worst tally since they scored 47 in the 1991-92 season. Most worrying was their goal return at Anfield where they scored 28 goals, two fewer than relegated Wimbledon got at Selhurst Park. It was their worst goal return at home since the 1950-51 season, though they did balance the figures by conceding only 13 home goals, the lowest scored against Liverpool at Anfield for four years.

Liverpool failed to score in 34 per cent of their games (13 out of 38), including their final five outings. Indeed, they start the season having gone four minutes short of eight hours since Heskey scored their last goal, at Wimbledon on April 16.

New goalkeeper Sander Westerveld did well in keeping 14 clean sheets but Liverpool's highest scorer, Owen, claimed only 11 goals – his lowest total in three seasons as an Anfield striker and, of more concern, the lowest total by a Liverpool player for eight years since Dean Saunders finished with 10.

Perhaps, Liverpool's forwards were worried about

GOALS BY TIME PERIOD 1999/2000

for the latest stats and to share your memories go to football.co.uk

key:
- goals for
- goals against

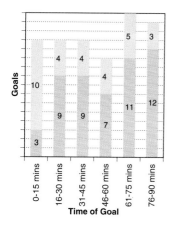
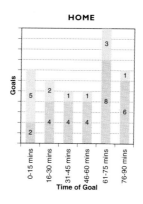
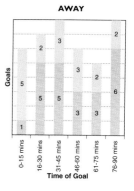

Goal Analysis

powered by football.co.uk

HOW GOALS WERE SCORED 1999/2000
for the latest stats and to share your memories go to football.co.uk

key:

- ■ header
- ■ free kick
- ■ volley
- ■ inside area
- ■ penalty
- ■ outside area
- ■ close range*
- ■ own goal

* inside six yard box

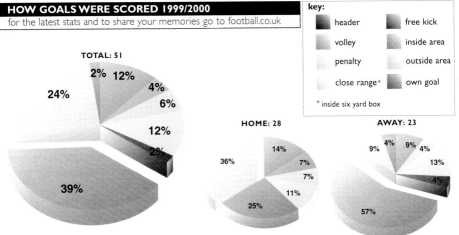

Liverpool

upsetting the natives; at Anfield the goals from the recognised strikers accounted for only 32 per cent of their goals scored at home. Owen scored only three of his 11 at Anfield while Camara claimed only four of his nine at home. The midfielders were happier at home; Patrik Berger scored six of his nine at Anfield.

Liverpool were at their most dangerous in the final 30 minutes, scoring 33 of their 51 goals after the 60th minute. They also showed a strange weakness for conceding early goals; exactly a third of the 30 goals they let in were scored within the opening 15 minutes.

And at home Liverpool scored more goals from outside the area than inside, 10 of their 28 coming from long range efforts with Patrik Berger claiming most of them.

Headed goals were also a rarity; only six (four at Anfield) were scored off the heads of Liverpool players while penalties were not in abundance. Owen scored one penalty – but missed two, against Chelsea and Aston Villa. Berger and Redknapp were successful from the spot.

Only one player, Sami Hyypia, played in every

HOW GOALS WERE CONCEDED 1999/2000
for the latest stats and to share your memories go to football.co.uk

key:

- ■ header
- ■ free kick
- ■ volley
- ■ inside area
- ■ penalty
- ■ outside area
- ■ close range*
- ■ own goal

* inside six yard box

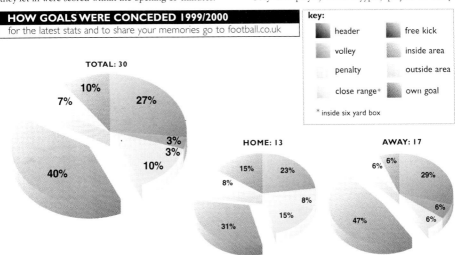

Squad and Performance

powered by football.co.uk

SQUAD LIST

for the latest stats and to share your memories go to football.co.uk

Position	Name	Appearances	Appearances as substitute	Goals	Clean Sheets	Yellow Cards	Red Cards
G	B.Friedel	2			1		
G	S.Westerveld	36			14		1
D	V.Heggem	10	12				
D	S.Henchoz	29				8	
D	S.Hyypia	38			2	2	
D	D.Matteo	32				2	
D	R.Song	14	3			2	
D	S.Staunton	7	5			2	1
M	P.Berger	34		9		2	
M	J.Carragher	33	2			4	
M	S.Gerrard	26	3	1		5	1
M	D.Hamann	27	1	2		6	
M	D.Murphy	9	13	3		3	
M	J.Redknapp	18	3	3		4	
M	V.Smicer	13	7	1		1	
M	D.Thompson	19	8	3		7	1
M	D.Traore		1				
F	T.Camara	22	11	9		7	
F	R.Fowler	8	6	3		1	
F	E.Heskey	12		3			
F	E.Meijer	7	13			2	
F	J.Newby		1				
F	M.Owen	22	5	11		2	
F	K.Riedle		1				

Carling Premiership game for Liverpool though four others made more than 30 appearances. Others had their appearances shortened by injuries, including Robbie Fowler, who was involved in 14 games – his fewest appearances in a season since he made his Liverpool debut in 1993.

Against the best and the worst of the Carling Premiership, Liverpool were strong; it was against the middle echelon of clubs that they seemed to struggle. They did the double over both Arsenal and Leeds while also beating Chelsea at home. Only against Manchester United did they fail to win at all. They also claimed six points off Coventry, Wimbledon and Sheffield Wednesday while also claiming points from Bradford and Watford.

TEAM PERFORMANCE TABLE

for the latest stats and to share your memories go to football.co.uk

Position	Club	Points Won	Percentage of points won at home	percentage of points won away	overall percentage of points won
1.	MANCHESTER UNITED	1/6			
2.	ARSENAL	6/6			
3.	LEEDS UNITED	6/6	75%	58%	67%
4.	LIVERPOOL	67 pts			
5.	CHELSEA	3/6			
6.	ASTON VILLA	2/6			
7.	SUNDERLAND	4/6			
8.	LEICESTER CITY	1/6	53%	33%	43%
9.	TOTTENHAM HOTSPUR	3/6			
10.	WEST HAM UNITED	3/6			
11.	NEWCASTLE UNITED	4/6			
12.	MIDDLESBROUGH	1/6			
13.	EVERTON	1/6	53%	40%	47%
14.	SOUTHAMPTON	2/6			
15.	COVENTRY CITY	6/6			
16.	DERBY COUNTY	6/6			
17.	BRADFORD CITY	3/6			
18.	WIMBLEDON	6/6	80%	80%	80%
19.	SHEFFIELD WEDNESDAY	6/6			
20.	WATFORD	3/6			

The figures show a team's performance against clubs in each quarter of the final league table. The first column represents points won from the total available against each team in the league.

What a difference a CARLING makes.

Discipline and Season Summary

BOOKINGS BY POSITION 1997/1998 - 1999/2000

for the latest stats and to share your memories go to football.co.uk

key:
- forward
- midfield
- defence
- goalkeeper

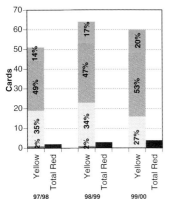

HOME

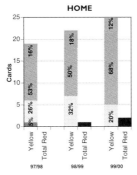

AWAY

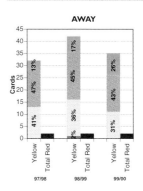

Liverpool

Liverpool collected four red cards; however, one of those dismissals, administered by referee Rob Harris to Steve Staunton in the goalless draw at Villa Park against Aston Villa, was later reduced to a yellow, one of seven issued to Liverpool players in that game. Gerrard was one whose dismissal stood when he and Westerveld failed to finish the derby game against Everton in September. Thompson was another Liverpool player to be dismissed.

A majority of Liverpool's cautions were against midfielders; Hamann received six, David Thompson saw seven while Steven Gerrard received five. Twelve more bookings were issued to other Liverpool midfielders. Defender Stephane Henchoz was also a regularly breaker of the rules, seeing eight yellow cards,

while the worst offender in attack was Camara, who was cautioned seven times.

Liverpool led at half time on 14 occasions; only Arsenal, Manchester United and Tottenham led Carling Premiership games more times at the interval. The confidence of a half time advantage was enough to inspire them to success; they went on to win 12 and draw two, against Leicester, at Filbert Street, and at home to Sunderland where the Carling Premiership's top-scorer Kevin Phillips's late spot kick cancelled Berger's second minute penalty. When Liverpool were level at the interval they had a good chance of winning; of the 15 times they were all square at the break, they went on to win seven, draw seven and lose only once, at Middlesbrough.

HALF TIME - FULL TIME COMPARATIVE CHART

for the latest stats and to share your memories go to football.co.uk

HOME				AWAY				TOTAL			
Number of Home Half Time Wins	Full Time Result W	L	D	Number of Away Half Time Wins	Full Time Result W	L	D	Total Number of Half Time Wins	Full Time Result W	L	D
8	7	0	1	6	5	0	1	14	12	0	2
Number of Home Half Time Losses	Full Time Result W	L	D	Number of Away Half Time Losses	Full Time Result W	L	D	Total Number of Half Time Losses	Full Time Result W	L	D
4	0	4	0	5	0	4	1	9	0	8	1
Number of Home Half Time Draws	Full Time Result W	L	D	Number of Away Half Time Draws	Full Time Result W	L	D	Total Number of Half Time Draws	Full Time Result W	L	D
7	4	0	3	8	3	1	4	15	7	1	7

What a difference a CARLING makes.

Maps and Directions

Liverpool's Anfield Road ground is situated two miles north of Liverpool city centre, close to Stanley Park.

From the North:
Approaching on the M6, exit at Junction 26 onto the M58 and continue until the end. At Junction 7 turn left onto the A59 Ormskirk Road. Continue on this road as it becomes Rice Lane, and cross over the roundabout into County Road. After ¼ mile turn left into Everton Valley and then right into Anfield Road.
The ground is on the right.

From the South:
Approaching on the M6, exit at Junction 21a onto the M62. Exit the M62 at Junction 4 and get onto the A5080. At the junction with the A5058 turn right and continue along this road as it becomes Queens Drive. Continue to the junction with Walton Hall Avenue and turn left onto the A580 Walton Lane. Turn left into Anfield Road and the ground is on the right.

From the East:
Approaching on the M62 exit at Junction 4 and get onto the A5058. Then as route for South.

Lime Street Railway Station is in the town centre, 2 miles from Anfield. Kirkdale Railway Station is 30 minutes walk from the ground.

Frequent Soccerbus shuttles run from Sandhills Station two hours before each match and 50 minutes after the final whistle.

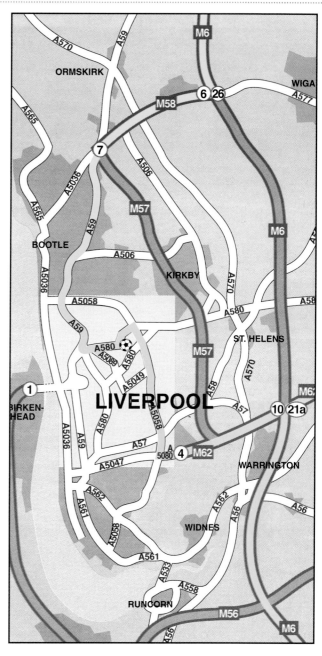

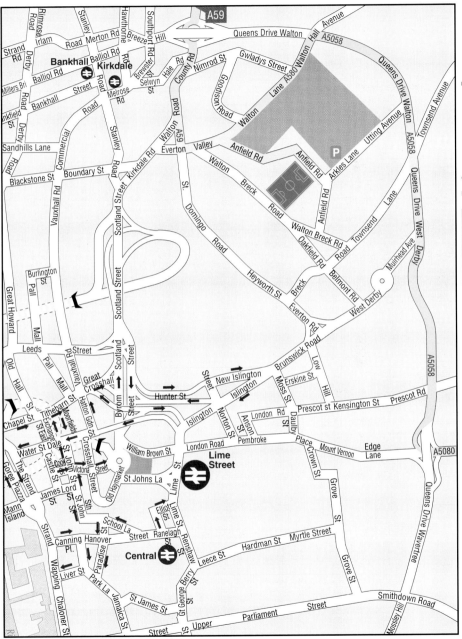

Liverpool

Pos		Pld	W	D	L	F	A	Pts
2	Manchester City	46	26	11	9	78	40	89

Manchester City
"City"

Maine Road, Moss Side, Manches
M14 7WN
Tel: 0161 232 3000
www.mcfc.co.uk

Season Review by
John Ley

The Daily Telegraph

Manchester City fans will insist that their club is back in its rightful place; given the magnificent support City enjoyed during the dark days of the Second Division and, last season, in the First, few could argue. They return to the Carling Premiership following an absence of four years and City, who featured in the first four seasons of the competition before being relegated, are back in confident mood after winning automatic promotion at the first attempt.

Manager Joe Royle signed Wimbledon winger Mark Kennedy before last season's start and then added important players throughout the campaign, as promotion became a distinct possibility. In came Leeds's defender Danny Granville followed by strikers Lee Peacock and Robert Taylor, Everton midfielder Tony Grant and Derby defender Spencer Prior. He made his first foray into the summer transfer market by signing Leeds's Alfie Haaland.

Useful Information

City Store (Maine Road)
Maine Rd, Manchester, Lancashire M14 7WW
Opening Times:
Monday-Sat: 9.00am-5.00pm
Closed Sundays
Match Saturdays: 9.00am-kick off.*
Match weekdays: 9.00am-kick off.*
Match Sundays: 9.00am-kick off.*
*Plus half an hour after the game.

Tel: 0161 232 1111
Mail Order Service: 0161 226 6000
Stadium Tours
Contact 0161 226 1782
Corporate Hospitality
Suites and executive boxes are available in the Kippax Stand for conferences, meetings, exhibitions and dinners. Maine Road specialises in all kinds of celebrity occasions

including birthday parties, wedding anniversaries and even full-scale marriage ceremonies.
Contact: 0161 232 3030
Conference and Banqueting.
Tel: 0161 232 3007
Literature
Programme £2
Manchester City Magazine £2.50

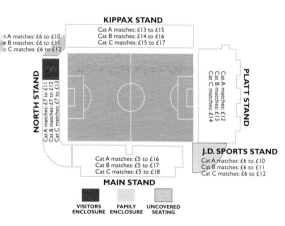

KIPPAX STAND
Cat A matches: £13 to £15
Cat B matches: £14 to £16
Cat C matches: £15 to £17

t A matches: £6 to £10
B matches: £6 to £11
C matches: £6 to £12

NORTH STAND
Cat A matches: £7 to £11
Cat B matches: £7 to £12
Cat C matches: £7 to £13

PLATT STAND
Cat A matches: £12
Cat B matches: £13
Cat C matches: £14

Cat A matches: £5 to £16
Cat B matches: £5 to £17
Cat C matches: £5 to £18
MAIN STAND

J.D. SPORTS STAND
Cat A matches: £6 to £10
Cat B matches: £6 to £11
Cat C matches: £6 to £12

VISITORS ENCLOSURE   FAMILY ENCLOSURE   UNCOVERED SEATING

Maine Road
Opened: August 1, 1922
Capacity: 33,148
1999/2000 highest attendance: 33,027
1999/2000 average attendance: 32,088
Record attendance: 84,569

Pre-Match & Half Time Entertainment
Club mascot, 'Moonchester' usually keeps goal in a five-a-side competition.

Advertising & Sponsorship
Contact Richard Aldridge
Commercial Department:
0161 232 3060, Marketing
Department: **0161 232 3064**

Junior Supporters
Junior Blues Annual Membership £12.00, Junior Blues 0-5 Club (cost for 5 years) £40.00, Family Membership (UK Only) two children £22.00 three children £34.00 (children must be from same family) Tel: **0161 232 3061**
E-mail: juniorblues@mcfc.co.uk

Booking Information
General Enquiries:
0161 232 3000
Credit Card Bookings:
0161 232 3061
Junior Blues
0161 224 5000
Travel Club:
0161 226 2224

Results Breakdown

POINTS WON OR LOST AT BOTH HOME AND AWAY

for the latest stats and to share your memories go to football.co.uk

key:
■ win   ■ draw
■ loss   -⓪- league position
home fixtures are in red

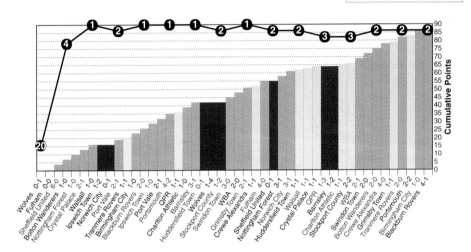

City's march back to the Carling Premiership was a lesson in self-belief; even in August Royle was insisting his club reach at least the play-offs but, within seven games, City had moved to the top of the First Division after winning 1-0 at Walsall. Their impressive home form meant they remained there until December; eight straight home wins at Maine Road was halted by successive defeats by Huddersfield and Stockport but they lost only one more home game, winning a further nine. Indeed, the 17 home wins was City's best return since 1968.

Their away form was not as impressive, though City still won nine and drew nine while losing only five. Only the superlative form of Charlton prevented City from taking charge but successive March defeats by QPR and Barnsley saw City drop to third. However, they resisted Ipswich's challenge with seven wins and two draws from their final nine games to confirm their elevation.

City fans were treated to 78 goals, the club's best total since the 1988-89 season when they netted 80. No fewer than 48 were scored at Maine Road, their

HOME   AWAY

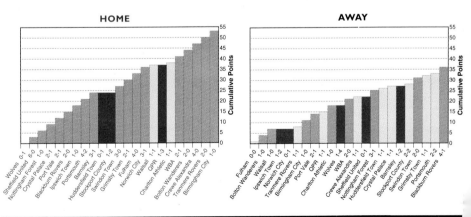

Manchester City

Legend: ● = Red Card = Yellow Card ▲ = Player substituted 00 = Time of goal

DATE	H/A	OPPONENT	H/T	F/T	POS	REFEREE	TEAM											SUBSTITUTES USED
08/08	H	Wolves	0-1	0-1	20	T.Heilbron	Weaver	Edghill	Wiekens	Morrison	Horlock	Whitley Jeff	Granville	Kennedy	Cooke	Dickov	Goater	Crooks ▲, Taylor G ▲
14/08	A	Fulham	0-0	0-0	21	P.Rejer	Weaver	Crooks	Wiekens	Morrison ●	Horlock	Whitley Jeff	Tiatto	Kennedy	Bishop	Dickov	Goater	Vaughan ▲, Jobson ▲
21/08	H	Sheffield United	2-0	6-0	8	P.R.Richards	Weaver	Edghill	Wiekens	Jobson	Horlock 37 41	Whitley Jeff	Tiatto	Kennedy 62	Cooke	Dickov 71	Goater ▲66	Jobson ▲, Taylor G ▲86, Crooks ▲
28/08	A	Bolton Wanderers	1-0	1-0	4	R.Pearson	Weaver	Edghill	Jobson	Morrison	Horlock	Whitley Jeff	Tiatto	Kennedy 30	Cooke	Dickov	Goater ▲13	Bishop ▲, Taylor G ▲13, Crooks ▲
30/08	H	Nottingham Forest	1-0	1-0	2	C.B.Frankland	Weaver	Edghill	Jobson 44	Morrison	Horlock	Whitley Jeff	Tiatto	Kennedy	Cooke	Dickov	Goater	Bishop ▲, Taylor G ▲, Crooks ▲
11/09	A	Crystal Palace	1-0	1-0	2	P.Dowd	Weaver	Edghill	Jobson	Morrison	Horlock	Whitley Jeff	Tiatto	Kennedy	Cooke	Dickov	Goater	Bishop ▲, Taylor G ▲60, Crooks ▲
18/09	H	Walsall	1-0	1-0	1	D.R.Elleray	Weaver	Edghill	Wiekens	Jobson	Horlock	Whitley Jeff	Tiatto	Kennedy	Bishop	Dickov	Goater 33	Granville ▲, Crooks ▲
26/09	A	Ipswich Town	0-1	1-2	3	A.P.D'Urso	Weaver	Crooks	Jobson	Morrison	Horlock	Whitley Jeff	Granville	Kennedy	Bishop	Dickov	Goater 50	Granville ▲, Allsopp ▲
28/09	A	Norwich City	0-1	0-1	4	M.Fletcher	Weaver	Crooks	Crooks	Morrison	Horlock	Whitley Jeff	Granville	Kennedy	Bishop	Dickov	Goater	Cooke ▲, Allsopp ▲
02/10	H	Port Vale	2-0	2-1	2	S.J.Barnes	Weaver	Crooks	Jobson 47	Morrison	Horlock	Whitley Jeff	Granville	Kennedy	Bishop	Dickov	Goater	Cooke ▲, Crooks ▲
16/10	A	Tranmere Rovers	0-0	1-1	4	D.J.Gallagher	Weaver	Edghill	Jobson	Morrison	Horlock ●50	Whitley Jeff	Granville	Kennedy	Bishop 30 36	Dickov	Taylor G	Allsopp ▲, Edghill ▲
19/10	H	Birmingham City	0-0	1-0	2	D.Laws	Weaver	Edghill	Jobson	Morrison	Horlock	Whitley Jeff	Granville	Kennedy	Bishop	Dickov	Goater	Taylor G ▲, Crooks ▲
23/10	A	Blackburn Rovers	0-0	2-0	1	A.N.Butler	Weaver	Edghill	Jobson	Morrison	Horlock	Whitley Jeff	Granville	Kennedy	Bishop	Dickov	Goater	Taylor G ▲, Cooke ▲
27/10	H	Ipswich Town	1-3	1-4	2	J.A.Kirkby	Weaver	Edghill	Jobson	Morrison	Horlock 58	Whitley Jeff	Granville	Kennedy	Bishop	Dickov	Goater	Crooks ▲, Tiatto ▲
30/10	A	Port Vale	0-1	2-1	2	G.Laws	Weaver	Edghill	Wiekens	Morrison	Crooks	Whitley Jeff	Granville	Kennedy	Cooke	Pollock	Taylor G	Taylor G ▲
03/11	H	Portsmouth	0-1	4-2	1	A.R.Hall	Weaver	Edghill	Wiekens 49	Jobson	Horlock 61	Whitley Jeff 46	Granville	Kennedy	Bishop	Wright-Phillips ▲90	Taylor G 66 69	Pollock ▲90, Peacock ▲
06/11	A	QPR	1-0	3-0	1	R.Styles	Weaver	Edghill	Wiekens	Jobson	Horlock	Whitley Jeff	Tiatto	Kennedy	Bishop	Wright-Phillips	Taylor G	Pollock ▲, Cooke ▲
20/11	A	Charlton Athletic	0-0	1-0	1	C.R.Wilkes	Weaver	Edghill	Jobson	Morrison	Horlock 73	Whitley Jeff	Tiatto	Kennedy	Pollock	Taylor R	Goater 48	Cooke ▲, Tiatto ▲
24/11	H	Barnsley	1-1	2-1	1	R.D.Furnandiz	Weaver	Crooks 8	Wiekens	Jobson	Horlock 5 90	Whitley Jeff	Tiatto	Kennedy	Pollock	Taylor R ▲10	Goater ▲10	Crooks ▲, Cooke ▲
27/11	A	Wolves	1-3	1-4	2	A.R.Leake	Weaver	Edghill	Jobson	Morrison	Horlock 87	Whitley Jeff	Tiatto	Kennedy	Pollock	Taylor R	Goater	Peacock ▲, Cooke ▲
03/12	A	Crewe Alexandra	0-0	0-1	2	K.A.Leach	Weaver	Edghill	Jobson	Morrison	Pollock	Grant	Tiatto	Kennedy	Bishop	Taylor R	Pollock	Pollock ▲, Taylor G ▲
07/12	H	Swindon Town	1-0	3-0	1	S.G.Bennett	Wright	Edghill	Wiekens 49	Jobson	Pollock 29	Whitley Jeff	Granville	Kennedy	Bishop	Taylor R 47	Goater 31	Taylor G ▲, Peacock ▲
18/12	A	Swindon Town	2-0	3-0	1	M.J.Brandwood	Weaver	Edghill	Jobson	Morrison	Horlock	Whitley Jeff	Granville 50	Kennedy	Bishop	Taylor R 47	Goater ▲59	Grant ▲, Peacock ▲
26/12	H	West Brom	0-0	2-0	1	W.C.Burns	Weaver	Edghill	Jobson	Morrison	Peacock 5 90	Whitley Jeff 84	Granville	Tiatto	Pollock	Pollock	Goater 71	Grant ▲, Whitley Jeff ▲
28/12	A	Grimsby Town 79	1-1	2-1	1	D.Pugh	Weaver	Edghill	Jobson	Morrison	Horlock 5 90	Whitley Jeff	Granville	Kennedy	Bishop	Taylor R	Goater 29 77 85	Tiatto ▲, Dickov ▲
16/01	A	Fulham	1-0	4-0	1	P.S.Danson	Weaver	Edghill	Wiekens	Jobson	Horlock	Grant	Tiatto	Kennedy	Bishop	Taylor R ▲31	Goater 35 83	Granville ▲, Dickov ▲
22/01	H	Sheffield United	0-1	1-1	1	N.S.Barry	Weaver	Crooks	Wiekens	Jobson	Horlock	Whitley Jeff	Granville	Kennedy	Bishop	Dickov	Goater 2	Allsopp ▲, Pollock ▲
05/02	A	Nottingham Forest	0-1	0-1	1	P.Dowd	Weaver	Edghill	Wiekens	Jobson	Horlock	Whitley Jeff	Granville	Kennedy 82 83	Bishop	Dickov	Goater 45	Whitley Jim ▲, Cooke ▲
12/02	H	Norwich City	3-1	3-1	1	A.Bates	Weaver	Edghill	Jobson	Morrison	Horlock	Whitley Jeff	Granville	Kennedy	Bishop	Dickov	Goater 71	Tiatto ▲, Cooke ▲
18/02	A	Huddersfield Town	1-1	1-1	1	C.R.Wilkes	Weaver	Edghill	Wiekens	Jobson	Horlock	Whitley Jeff	Granville	Kennedy	Bishop	Peacock	Taylor R 8	Wright-Phillips ▲, Tiatto ▲
26/02	A	Walsall	1-1	1-1	1	D.R.Crick	Weaver	Edghill	Jobson	Morrison	Horlock	Whitley Jeff	Granville	Kennedy	Horlock	Peacock	Dickov	Dickov ▲, Horlock ▲
04/03	A	Crystal Palace	1-1	1-1	2	K.M.Lynch	Weaver	Edghill	Jobson	Morrison	Pollock	Whitley Jeff	Granville	Kennedy	Horlock	Mills	Goater 10	Taylor R ▲, Horlock ▲
08/03	H	QPR	0-2	1-3	2	A.R.Hall	Weaver	Edghill	Jobson	Morrison	Pollock	Whitley Jeff	Granville	Kennedy	Horlock	Dickov	Goater 86	Dickov ▲, Bishop ▲
11/03	A	Barnsley	2-1	2-2	4	G.Laws	Weaver	Edghill	Jobson	Morrison	Horlock	Whitley Jeff	Granville	Kennedy	Bishop	Dickov	Goater 32	Granville ▲, Dickov ▲
19/03	H	Charlton Athletic	1-1	1-1	2	J.A.Kirkby	Weaver	Edghill	Jobson	Morrison	Horlock 7	Whitley Jeff	Tiatto	Kennedy 57	Bishop	Taylor R	Goater 86	Granville ▲, Bishop ▲
21/03	H	Stockport County	2-2	2-2	2	J.T.Winter	Weaver	Edghill	Jobson	Morrison	Pollock	Whitley Jeff	Tiatto	Kennedy	Bishop	Taylor R	Goater 32	Dickov ▲, Granville ▲
25/03	A	West Brom	0-0	0-0	3	T.Jones	Weaver	Prior	Jobson	Morrison	Pollock	Whitley Jeff	Granville	Kennedy 77	Bishop	Taylor R	Goater	Dickov ▲, Grant ▲
01/04	H	Swindon Town	1-0	2-0	3	S.G.Bennett	Weaver	Edghill	Wiekens	Jobson	Horlock	Whitley Jeff	Tiatto	Kennedy	Grant 57	Dickov	Goater ▲43	Wiekens ▲, Bishop ▲
05/04	H	Bolton Wanderers	2-0	4-0	2	P.Taylor	Weaver	Edghill	Jobson	Morrison	Horlock	Whitley Jeff	Tiatto	Kennedy 82 83	Horlock 18	Dickov 23	Goater 68 90	Mills ▲, Bishop ▲
08/04	A	Tranmere Rovers	2-0	4-0	2	P.Rejer	Weaver	Edghill	Jobson	Morrison	Pollock	Whitley Jeff	Granville	Kennedy	Horlock	Dickov	Goater	Bishop ▲, Grant ▲
15/04	H	Grimsby Town	1-1	2-1	2	D.Laws	Weaver	Edghill	Jobson	Morrison	Pollock	Whitley Jeff	Granville	Kennedy 86	Horlock	Peacock	Taylor R 8	Bishop ▲, Cooke ▲
22/04	A	Portsmouth	2-1	2-2	4	A.R.Leake	Weaver	Edghill	Jobson	Morrison	Pollock	Whitley Jeff	Granville	Kennedy	Horlock	Peacock	Goater 10	Horlock ▲, Taylor R ▲
24/04	H	Birmingham City	2-2	2-2	4	P.E.Alcock	Weaver	Edghill	Jobson	Morrison	Pollock	Whitley Jeff 77	Tiatto	Kennedy	Horlock	Taylor R ▲40	Goater 40	Granville ▲, Pollock ▲
28/04	A	Birmingham City	1-0	1-0	2	A.N.Butler	Weaver	Edghill	Wiekens	Jobson	Pollock	Whitley Jeff	Tiatto	Kennedy	Horlock	Taylor R ▲40	Goater 60	Granville ▲, Dickov ▲
07/05	A	Blackburn Rovers	0-1	4-1	2	T.Heilbron	Weaver	Pollock	Pollock ▲	Jobson	Pollock	Whitley Jeff	Tiatto	Kennedy ▲75	Horlock	Dickov ▲75	Goater ▲81	Dickov ▲81, Granville ▲

141

Goal Analysis

GOALS BY POSITION 1997/1998 - 1999/2000
for the latest stats and to share your memories go to football.co.uk

key:
- forward
- midfield
- defence
- ⟨0⟩ final league position

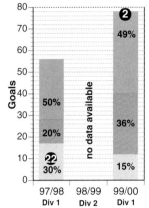

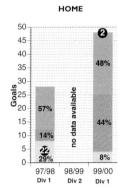

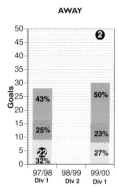

best home tally since they scored 50 at Maine Road 11 years ago. and in doing so, City seemed to have struck the perfect balance with 50 per cent of goals, both home and away, coming from their strikers. Shaun Goater, once of Manchester United, had spent seven years at Rotherham and two more at Bristol City until Royle invested £400,000 in the striker; the response has been amazing. In his first full season Goater scored 17 goals but last season he finished with 23 with a further six in other competitions. In addition he scored a hat-trick for Bermuda, while missing the trip to Crystal Palace. He started the season with Paul Dickov, who scored five, but finished it alongside Robert Taylor. Taylor had scored 18 goals for Gillingham in their quest for promotion from Division Two and added a further five for City in 16 games. In midfield, Kevin Horlock scored 10, his best total for four years with a further eight from Kennedy who had scored only twice in his previous six seasons with Liverpool and Wimbledon.

GOALS BY TIME PERIOD 1999/2000
for the latest stats and to share your memories go to football.co.uk

key:
- goals for
- goals against

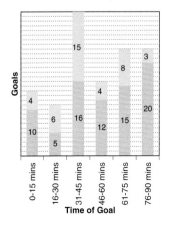

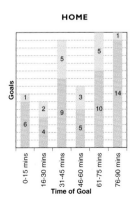

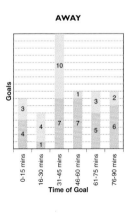

Goal Analysis

Manchester City

HOW GOALS WERE SCORED 1999/2000
for the latest stats and to share your memories go to football.co.uk

key:
- header
- volley
- penalty
- close range*
- free kick
- inside area
- outside area
- own goal

* inside six yard box

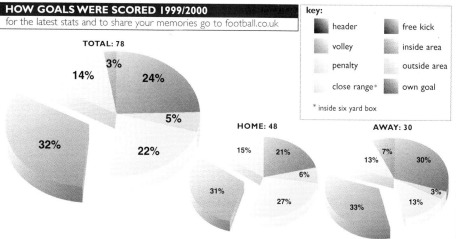

TOTAL: 78

3%
14%
24%
32%
5%
22%

HOME: 48

15% 21%
13%
6%
31%
27%
33%

AWAY: 30

7%
30%
3%
13%
13%

City scored more goals in the second period of games; in particular they were most dangerous in the final 30 minutes, scoring 35 goals – 45 percent of their total – in the last half an hour. At Maine Road, City fans knew it was unwise to leave before the final whistle because 28 home goals came in the final third. But, once they got over that period, they were comfortable, particularly away because they conceded just six second half goals on their travels.

Their busiest period was the final 15 minutes of the first half; not only did City score 16 goals but they also conceded 15 just before the interval, 10 of those coming away from home, an aspect they will need to keep under control when on their Carling Premiership travels.

City's goals were well balances though they scored slightly more from within the penalty box; perhaps Joe Royle might want to practice free kicks before the big kick-off; not one of their 78 goals came from free kicks.

HOW GOALS WERE CONCEDED 1999/2000
for the latest stats and to share your memories go to football.co.uk

key:
- header
- volley
- penalty
- close range*
- free kick
- inside area
- outside area
- own goal

* inside six yard box

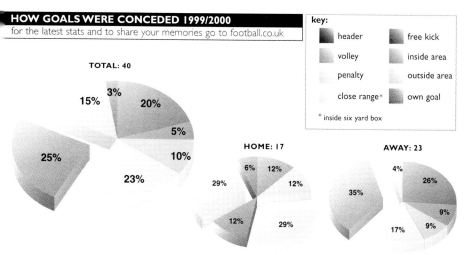

TOTAL: 40

3%
15% 20%
5%
25% 10%
23%

HOME: 17

6% 12%
29% 12%
12%
12% 29%

AWAY: 23

4%
26%
35%
9%
17% 9%

Squad and Performance

powered by football.co.uk

SQUAD LIST

for the latest stats and to share your memories go to football.co.uk

Position	Name	Appearances	Appearances as substitute	Goals / Clean Sheets	Yellow Cards	Red Cards
G	N.Weaver	45		17	1	
G	T.Wright	1		1		
D	R.Edghill	40	1		5	
D	D.Granville	28	7	2	3	
D	R.Jobson	43	1	3	4	
D	A.Morrison	12			2	1
D	S.Prior	9			3	
D	T.Vaughan		1		1	
D	G.Wiekens	32	1	1	3	
M	I.Bishop	25	11	2	1	
M	L.Crooks	9	11	1	4	
M	T.Grant	4	4			
M	K.Horlock	36	2	10	4	1
M	M.Kennedy	41		8	3	
M	J.Pollock	17	7	3	4	
M	D.Tiatto	26	9		5	
M	Jeff Whitley	41	1	3	3	
M	Jim Whitley		1			
F	D.Allsopp		4			
F	T.Cooke	6	7			
F	P.Dickov	22	12	5	4	
F	S.Goater	40		23		
F	L.Mills	1	2			
F	L.Peacock	4	4			
F	G.Taylor	8	9	5		
F	R.Taylor	14	2	5	4	
F	S.Wright-Philips	2	1			

England Under-21 goalkeeper Nicky Weaver, the hero of Wembley 12 months earlier, played in all but one Division One games, missing only the 3-0 home win over Swindon. Weaver kept 17 clean sheets; of the goalkeepers he will face this season, only Ipswich's Richard Wright kept more (18). City had a further five players who featured in 40 games or more, showing just how important consistency can be. Sadly, captain Andy Morrison was troubled by a knee injury, limiting him to only 12 appearances. City, meanwhile, did the double over seven teams, claiming at least one win off each of the bottom nine, none of who managed to beat City.

The fact that Morrison missed three-quarters of the season meant that City's disciplinary record was

TEAM PERFORMANCE TABLE

for the latest stats and to share your memories go to football.co.uk

Position	Club	Points Won	Percentage of points won at home	Percentage of points won away	overall percentage of points won
1.	CHARLTON	4/6			
2.	MANCHESTER CITY	89 pts			
3.	IPSWICH	3/6			
4.	BARNSLEY	3/6	87%	60%	73%
5.	BIRMINGHAM	6/6			
6.	BOLTON	6/6			
7.	WOLVES	0/6			
8.	HUDDERSFIELD	1/6			
9.	FULHAM	4/6	50%	39%	44%
10.	QPR	1/6			
11.	BLACKBURN	6/6			
12.	TRANMERE	4/6			
13.	NORWICH	3/6			
14.	STOCKPORT	1/6			
15.	SHEFFIELD UNITED	3/6	83%	33%	58%
16.	NOTTINGHAM FOREST	6/6			
17.	PORTSMOUTH	4/6			
18.	CRYSTAL PALACE	4/6			
19.	CREWE	4/6			
20.	GRIMSBY	4/6			
21.	WBA	6/6	89%	78%	83%
22.	WALSALL	4/6			
23.	PORT VALE	6/6			
24.	SWINDON	6/6			

The figures show a team's performance against clubs in each quarter of the final league table. The first column represents points won from the total available against each team in the league.

What a difference a CARLING makes.

Discipline and Season Summary

 powered by football.co.uk

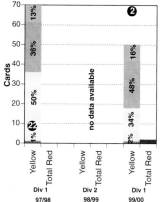

BOOKINGS BY POSITION 1997/1998 - 1999/2000
for the latest stats and to share your memories go to football.co.uk

key:
- forward
- defence
- midfield
- goalkeeper

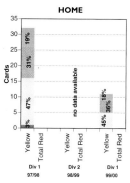

HOME

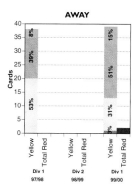

AWAY

Manchester City

highly impressive. They received 51 cautions, 25 less than the previous season, while their total of two red cards was considerably improved on the six they received in the 1998-99 term. Morrison, traditionally one of City's worst behaved players, collected two cautions in his 12 games, though he still managed a red card – in the second game of the season, the goalless draw at Fulham. The only other player to be dismissed was Horlock, who was controversially sent off at Tranmere, a decision that, on appeal, brought only a one-match ban. City's worst offenders were Richard Edghill, who collected three of his five bookings in a spell of five games, and Danny Tiatto, who was also shown five yellow

cards. Crooks received four yellows, but in only nine starts, clearly the frustration of not being able to break into the first team.

On 10 occasions City led at half time at Maine Road; put your money on a win if that happens this season because that's what happened every time last term. Similarly, away from home, when City were ahead, they never lost, though they did relinquish their lead twice, going on to draw at Crewe and Portsmouth. Even a half time deficit was clawed back on several occasions. They were trailing at the interval in 13 games yet lost only seven of those. A successful season in the top flight awaits if they can maintain that kind of fighting spirit.

HALF TIME - FULL TIME COMPARATIVE CHART
for the latest stats and to share your memories go to football.co.uk

				AWAY					TOTAL			
Number of Home Half Time Wins	Full Time Result W	L	D	Number of Away Half Time Wins	Full Time Result W	L	D	Total Number of Half Time Wins	Full Time Result W	L	D
10	10	0	0	6	4	0	2	16	14	0	2
Number of Home Half Time Losses	Full Time Result W	L	D	Number of Away Half Time Losses	Full Time Result W	L	D	Total Number of Half Time Losses	Full Time Result W	L	D
4	1	2	1	9	2	5	2	13	3	7	3
Number of Home Half Time Draws	Full Time Result W	L	D	Number of Away Half Time Draws	Full Time Result W	L	D	Total Number of Half Time Draws	Full Time Result W	L	D
9	5	2	2	8	3	0	5	17	8	2	7

What a difference a CARLING makes.

Maps and Directions

From the North and West, M61 becomes M60, and exit at Junction 5 following the signs to Manchester (A5103); turn right at the crossroads (2 ³/₄ miles) into Claremont Road, after ¹/₃ mile turn right into Maine Road.

From the South, exit M6 at Junction 19 following A556 joining M56 at Junction 8, follow M56 into M60. Then same as from north.

By Rail
Arrive at Manchester Piccadilly or Victoria Stations and then catch the regular bus service to the Ground.

By Bus
Catch No.111 from Piccadilly Square to the Ground.

powered by **football.co.uk**

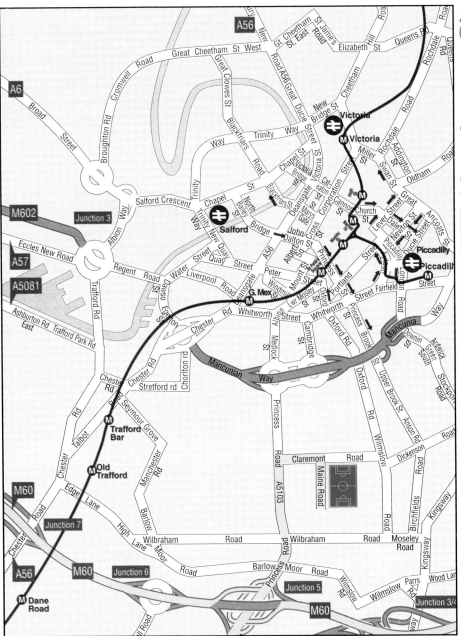

147

Club Honours

- F.A. Carling Premiership Champions: 1992-93, 1993-94, 1995-96, 1996-97, 1998-99, 1999-00
- Football League Champions: 1907-08, 1910-11, 1951-52, 1955-56, 1956-57, 1964-65, 1966-67
- Division 2 Champions: 1935-36, 1974-75
- FA Cup Winners: 1909, 1948, 1963, 1977, 1983, 1985, 1990, 1994, 1996, 1999
- League Cup Winners: 1992
- European Cup Winners: 1967-68, 1998-99
- European Cup Winners' Cup Winners: 1990-91
- European Super Cup Winners: 1991
- Inter-Continental Champions: 1999-00

Club Records

- Victory: 10-0 v RSC Anderlecht, European Cup Preliminary Round, 2nd Leg, September 26, 1956
- Defeat: 0-7 v Blackburn Rovers, Division 1, April 10, 1926
- League goals in a season (team): 103, Division 1, 1956-57 and 1958-59
- League goals in a season (player): 32, Dennis Viollet, 1959-60
- Career league goals: 199, Bobby Charlton, 1956-73
- League appearances: 606, Bobby Charlton, 1956-73
- Transfer fee paid: £12,600,000 to Aston Villa for Dwight Yorke, August, 1998
- Transfer fee received: £7,000,000 from Internazionale for Paul Ince, June, 1995

Pos		Pld	W	D	L	F	A	Pts
1	Manchester United	38	28	7	3	97	45	91

Manchester United
"The Red Devils"

Sir Matt Busby Way, Old Trafford
Manchester M16 0RA
Tel: 0161 868 8000
www.manutd.com

Season Review by
John Ley

𝕿𝖍𝖊 𝕯𝖆𝖎𝖑𝖞 𝕿𝖊𝖑𝖊𝖌𝖗𝖆𝖕𝖍

What do you give the team that has everything? United had the treble and though their withdrawal from the FA Cup meant they could not repeat that feat, their march to yet another Carling Premiership crown was masterly and a tribute to the staying power of England's best team. The Carling Premiership has existed for eight seasons; United have won it six times and their latest success produced a pot of records. United started as favourites, adding only Mark Bosnich, as replacement for Peter Schmeichel. Later another goalkeeper, Massimo Taibi, arrived but finished the season on loan at Reggiana. Quinton Fortune and Mickael Silvestre arrived to supplement the squad. Gary Neville was troubled by a groin problem while Ronny Johnsen missed all but the last month of the season but there were few down sides to a season interrupted by a winter's break in Brazil, where United participated in the FIFA World Club Championship. The summer arrival of goalkeeper Fabian Barthez will put pressure on Bosnich.

Useful Information

Megastore
21-26 United Road, Old Trafford
Opening Times:
Monday-Saturday: 10.00am-6.00pm
Match Saturdays: 9.00am-6.00pm
Sundays: 10.00am-4.00pm
Match Evenings: 9.00am-10.30pm
Tel: 0161 868 8567
Fax: 0161 868 8874
Mail Order Service: 0161 868 7000

Red Cafe
Manchester United themed restaurant in North Stand.
Opening Times:
Monday-Sunday 9.00am-5.00pm
not opened match days
Tel: 0161 868 8303

Stadium Tours
Museum & Tour Centre
Tel: 0161 868 8631

Corporate Hospitality
Function suites of varying sizes are available at Old Trafford for either business or social occasions.
Contact Commercial Department:
0161 868 8200

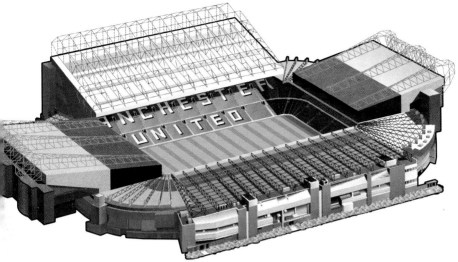

Old Trafford

Opened: February 19, 1910
Capacity: 67,400
1999/2000 highest attendance: 61,619
1999/2000 average attendance: 57,569
Record attendance: 76,962

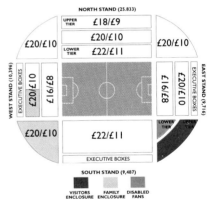

Manchester United holds Sportsman's Dinners at Old Trafford. Previous guest speakers include Sir Bobby Charlton and George Best.
For further information or to have your name put on the Events database contact the Manchester United Events Team:
Tel: **0161 868 8300**

Literature
Programme £2

Pre-Match & Half Time Entertainment
Manchester United's own radio station broadcasts direct from Old Trafford on 1413 AM every matchday. Programmes include full match commentary, team interviews, music etc.

Booking Information
General Enquiries:
0161 868 8000
Text Phone:
(for deaf and hard of hearing)
0161 868 8668
Travel Club:
0161 868 8000
Recorded Info:
0161 868 8020

149

Results Breakdown

powered by football.co.uk

POINTS WON OR LOST AT BOTH HOME AND AWAY
for the latest stats and to share your memories go to football.co.uk

key:
- win
- draw
- loss
- -0- league position

home fixtures are in red

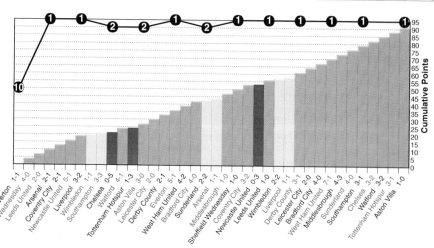

United went top after three games and were never out of the top two. They remained unbeaten at Old Trafford, for only the seventh time in their history and second time in the Carling Premiership. They also won more away games than any other, 13, while losing only three times away, including the shock 5-0 reverse at Chelsea. They won 49 points from a possible 57 at Old Trafford; after their opening day draw with Everton they won their next six. Two draws and two defeats from their next six games was their only hiccup. They beat Palmeiras to win the Toyota Cup in

Japan and returned to stamp their authority on the Carling Premiership before leaving for Brazil. In their absence no team could take advantage and, after drawing with Arsenal, United went on to lose just one of their remaining 18 games, setting yet another Carling Premiership record by winning their final 11 games and claiming the title by 18 points – an all-time English record.

United scored more goals, just three short of a century, than any team had previously claimed in the Carling Premiership. They averaged more than three

HOME

AWAY

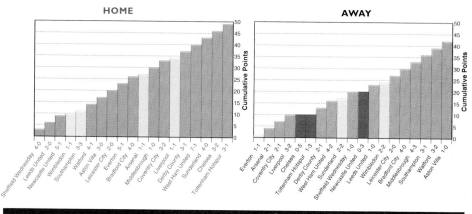

What a difference a CARLING makes.

Results Table

Manchester United

Key: ● = Red Card · = Yellow Card · ▲ = Player substituted · 00 = Time of goal

DATE	H/A	OPPONENT	H/T	F/T	POS	REFEREE	TEAM (1–11)	SUBSTITUTES USED
08/08	A	Everton	1-0	1-1	10	D.J.Gallagher	Bosnich, Neville P, Berg, Stam, Irwin, Keane, Beckham, Scholes, Giggs ▲, Cole, Yorke 6	Butt ▲, Sheringham ▲, Solskjaer ▲84
11/08	H	Sheffield Wednesday	2-0	4-0	3	M.D.Reed	Bosnich, Neville P, Berg, Stam, Irwin, Keane, Beckham, Scholes 9, Giggs, Cole 54, Yorke ▲35	Butt ▲, Sheringham ▲
14/08	H	Leeds United	0-0	2-0	1	N.S.Barry	Bosnich, Neville P, Berg, Stam, Irwin, Keane, Beckham, Scholes, Giggs, Cole, Yorke ▲76 80	Von der Gouw ▲, Butt ▲, Sheringham ▲
22/08	A	Arsenal	2-1	2-1	1	G.Poll	Van der Gouw, Neville P, Berg, Stam, Irwin, Keane 58 88, Beckham, Butt, Giggs, Cole, Yorke	Culkin ▲, Yorke
25/08	H	Coventry City	0-0	2-1	1	A.B.Wilkie	Van der Gouw, Neville P, Berg, Silvestre, Irwin, Keane, Beckham, Butt, Giggs 81, Sheringham, Yorke 75	Curtis ▲, Scholes ▲62
30/08	A	Newcastle United	1-1	5-1	1	J.T.Winter	Van der Gouw, Neville P, Berg, Silvestre, Neville G, Butt, Beckham, Scholes, Giggs, Sheringham 14 46 64 71, Cole ●18	Clegg ▲, Sheringham ▲
11/09	A	Liverpool	3-1	3-2	1	G.P.Barber	Taibi, Silvestre, Berg, Stam, Irwin, Butt ▲, Beckham, Scholes, Giggs, Sheringham, Solskjaer	Clegg ▲, Wallwork ▲
18/09	H	Wimbledon	1-1	1-1	2	R.J.Harris	Taibi, Neville P ▲, Berg, Silvestre, Irwin, Silvestre, Beckham, Scholes, Giggs, Solskjaer, Cole ●18	Wallwork ▲, Cruyff ▲73
25/09	H	Southampton	2-1	3-3	2	S.W.Dunn	Taibi, Silvestre, Berg, Taibi, Irwin, Butt, Sheringham, Scholes, Silvestre, Solskjaer 34, Cole	Clegg ▲, Cruyff ▲73
03/10	A	Chelsea	0-2	0-5	3	D.J.Gallagher	Taibi, Neville P, Berg, Taibi, Irwin, Butt ●, Beckham, Scholes, Silvestre, Sheringham, Cole	Wilson ▲, Solskjaer ▲
16/10	H	Watford	3-0	4-1	2	P.Jones	Bosnich, Neville P, Berg, Silvestre, Irwin 44, Butt, Beckham, Scholes, Giggs, Cole 42 54, Yorke 40	Keane ▲, Greening ▲
23/10	A	Tottenham Hotspur	1-2	1-3	3	J.T.Winter	Bosnich, Neville P, Berg, Silvestre, Irwin ▲, Keane, Beckham, Scholes 30, Giggs 23, Cole, Yorke	Greening ▲, Solskjaer ▲
30/10	H	Aston Villa	2-0	3-0	2	A.B.Wilkie	Bosnich, Neville P, Berg, Silvestre, Irwin, Keane 65, Beckham, Scholes, Giggs 45, Cole 30 83, Yorke	Wilson ▲, Solskjaer ▲
06/11	A	Leicester City	0-1	2-0	2	P.A.Durkin	Bosnich, Neville P, Higginbottom ▲, Silvestre, Irwin, Keane, Beckham, Solskjaer, Giggs, Cole 30 83, Yorke	Berg ▲, May ▲
20/11	H	Derby County	0-0	2-1	2	M.D.Reed	Bosnich, Neville P, Berg, Silvestre, Neville G, Keane, Beckham, Butt 53, Giggs, Cole 83, Yorke	Berg ▲, Solskjaer ▲
04/12	A	Everton	5-1	5-1	1	G.Poll	Van der Gouw, Neville P, Berg, Silvestre, Irwin 25, Keane, Butt, Scholes, Giggs, Sheringham, Yorke	Neville P ▲, Butt ▲
18/12	H	West Ham United	3-1	4-2	1	U.D.Rennie	Bosnich, Neville P, Stam, Silvestre, Irwin ▲, Keane, Beckham, Scholes, Giggs 12 19, Sheringham, Solskjaer 29 43 52 59	Von der Gouw ▲, Butt ▲
26/12	H	Bradford City	3-1	4-0	1	P.Jones	Bosnich, Neville P, Silvestre, Silvestre, Neville P, Keane 88, Beckham, Scholes, Giggs 8 62, Sheringham, Yorke 8 62	Scholes ▲, Yorke ▲79
28/12	A	Sunderland	1-2	2-2	1	J.T.Winter	Bosnich, Neville P, Stam, Silvestre, Neville P, Keane 88, Butt 87, Beckham, Fortune 74, Sheringham, Cole	Cruyff ▲, Solskjaer ▲
24/01	A	Arsenal	1-1	1-1	2	P.A.Durkin	Bosnich, Neville P, Silvestre, Silvestre, Irwin, Keane 27, Beckham, Butt, Giggs, Cole, Yorke	Scholes ▲, Neville P ▲
29/01	H	Middlesbrough	0-0	1-0	1	A.P.D'Urso	Bosnich, Neville G, Berg, Silvestre, Irwin ▲, Keane, Beckham 87, Butt, Sheringham 73, Cole, Giggs 73	Scholes ▲, Sheringham ▲73
02/02	A	Sheffield Wednesday	0-0	1-0	1	S.W.Dunn	Bosnich, Neville G, Silvestre, Silvestre, Irwin, Keane, Beckham, Butt, Giggs, Sheringham, Cole 45	Scholes ▲, Cole ▲
05/02	H	Coventry City	3-2	3-2	1	A.B.Wilkie	Bosnich, Neville G, Stam, Silvestre, Irwin ▲, Keane, Beckham, Scholes 77, Solskjaer, Cole 39 54, Yorke	Cruyff ▲, Cole ▲79
12/02	A	Newcastle United	0-1	0-3	1	S.J.Lodge	Bosnich, Neville G, Stam, Silvestre, Irwin, Keane ●, Beckham, Scholes, Solskjaer, Sheringham, Cole 52	Solskjaer ▲, Neville P ▲
20/02	A	Leeds United	0-0	0-1	1	P.Jones	Van der Gouw, Neville G, Silvestre, Silvestre, Neville P, Keane, Butt, Scholes, Giggs, Cole, Sheringham	Sheringham ▲, Sheringham ▲73
26/02	H	Wimbledon	1-1	2-2	2	D.R.Elleray	Bosnich, Neville G, Stam, Silvestre, Neville P ▲, Cruyff ▲30, Beckham, Butt, Giggs, Cole 80, Sheringham	Beckham ▲, Cole ▲
04/03	A	Liverpool	0-0	1-0	2	D.J.Gallagher	Van der Gouw, Neville G, Silvestre, Johnsen, Irwin, Keane, Beckham, Butt, Giggs, Solskjaer 45, Cole	Cole ▲, Sheringham ▲
11/03	H	Derby County	1-0	3-1	1	J.T.Winter	Bosnich, Neville G, Berg, Johnsen, Berg, Keane, Beckham, Scholes, Fortune, Yorke 12 70 72, Cole	Butt ▲, Sheringham ▲
18/03	A	Leicester City	1-0	2-0	1	R.J.Harris	Bosnich, Neville G, Berg, Johnsen, Irwin, Keane, Beckham 33, Scholes, Giggs, Yorke 83, Cole	Silvestre ▲, Sheringham ▲
25/03	H	Bradford City	2-0	4-0	1	G.Poll	Bosnich, Neville G, Berg, Silvestre, Neville P, Keane, Beckham 80, Scholes 71, Giggs 75, Yorke 37 40, Cole	Wallwork ▲, Silvestre ▲
01/04	A	West Ham United	3-1	7-1	1	M.A.Riley	Bosnich, Neville G, Stam, Johnsen, Irwin 26, Keane, Beckham 66, Scholes 24 51 62, Fortune, Yorke, Cole 45	Butt ▲, Sheringham ▲
10/04	A	Middlesbrough	0-1	4-3	1	P.A.Durkin	Van der Gouw, Neville G, Silvestre, Johnsen, Irwin, Keane, Butt 66, Scholes 74, Giggs ▲46, Yorke, Cole 60	Butt ▲, Beckham ▲
15/04	H	Sunderland	1-0	4-0	1	P.Jones	Van der Gouw, Neville P, Stam, Johnsen, Irwin, Keane, Beckham, Scholes, Fortune, Solskjaer 3 51, Yorke	Von der Gouw ▲, Sheringham ▲
22/04	A	Southampton	3-0	3-1	1	N.S.Barry	Van der Gouw, Neville P, Stam, Johnsen, Irwin, Keane, Beckham 7, Silvestre, Fortune, Solskjaer ▲29, Cole	Sheringham ▲, Beckham ▲
24/04	H	Chelsea	2-2	3-2	1	S.W.Dunn	Van der Gouw, Neville P, Stam, Johnsen, Silvestre, Keane, Beckham, Scholes, Giggs, Solskjaer ▲39, Cole	Sheringham ▲, Scholes ▲
29/04	A	Watford	0-1	3-2	1	S.J.Lodge	Van der Gouw, Neville P, Stam, Silvestre, Berg, Greening, Wilson, Scholes, Giggs, Sheringham, Cole	Higginbottom ▲, Berg ▲
06/05	H	Tottenham Hotspur	3-1	3-1	1	A.G.Wiley	Van der Gouw, Neville P, Stam, Silvestre, Irwin, Butt ●, Beckham 34, Scholes, Giggs, Solskjaer 5, Sheringham 36	Berg ▲, Cruyff ▲
14/05	A	Aston Villa	0-0	1-0	1	P.A.Durkin	Van der Gouw, Neville P, Berg, Silvestre, Irwin, Higginbottom ▲, Scholes, Giggs, Yorke, Sheringham 65, Solskjaer	Wallwork ▲, Cruyff ▲

151

Goal Analysis

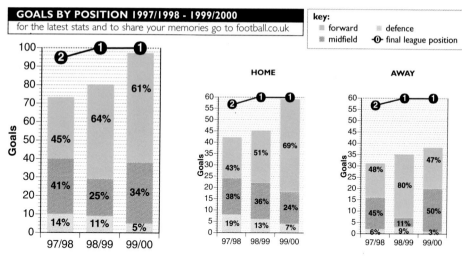

GOALS BY POSITION 1997/1998 - 1999/2000
for the latest stats and to share your memories go to football.co.uk

key:
■ forward   ■ defence
■ midfield   -●- final league position

goals a home game where both leading scorers Dwight York and Andy Cole scored the majority of their goals. Yorke scored 20, his best League return in 12 seasons with Aston Villa and United while Cole scored 19 and Ole Gunnar Solskjaer claimed 12, in only 15 starts and a further 13 substitute appearances. Yorke scored 12 of his 20 goals at Old Trafford, including a hat-trick against Derby, while Cole scored 14 there and only five away.

Cole's haul included four in the 5-1 win over former club Newcastle. With Teddy Sheringham adding five more, and then confirming he was staying for another year, the forwards' goals made up for 61 percent of the club's total haul, actually a lower figure than in the previous season. Encouragingly, the contribution from midfield was improved, especially away from home where half of United's goals came from the middle.

United scored 33 goals from midfield, more than any other Carling Premiership team. The best

GOALS BY TIME PERIOD 1999/2000
for the latest stats and to share your memories go to football.co.uk

key:
■ goals for   ■ goals against

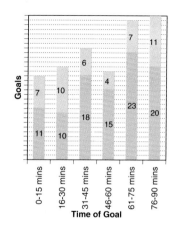

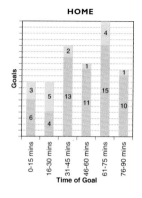

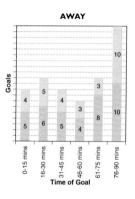

What a difference a CARLING makes.

Goal Analysis

powered by **football.co.uk**

Manchester United

HOW GOALS WERE SCORED 1999/2000
for the latest stats and to share your memories go to football.co.uk

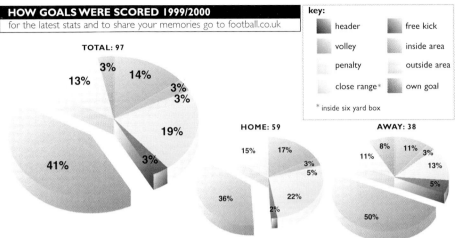

key:
- header
- volley
- penalty
- close range*
- free kick
- inside area
- outside area
- own goal

* inside six yard box

TOTAL: 97

3% · 14% · 3% · 3% · 19% · 3% · 13% · 41%

HOME: 59

15% · 17% · 3% · 5% · 22% · 2% · 36%

AWAY: 38

8% · 11% · 3% · 13% · 5% · 50% · 11%

contributor from that position was Paul Scholes, who was the third player to score a hat-trick, in the 7-1 win over West Ham, taking his tally to nine – his best League return for four years. David Beckham and Ryan Giggs claimed six while Roy Keane, voted both the Players' Player and Writers' Footballer of the Year, scored five.

Of United's 97 goals, 14 were headers, with Yorke claiming a high percentage of that number. Only three penalties were scored but Yorke missed

from the spot against Derby – perhaps he felt sympathy having claimed a hat-trick – and Denis Irwin was also thwarted when West Ham's Craig Forrest saved his kick in the 7-1 rout. Interestingly, Andy D'Urso became the first referee to award a penalty at Old Trafford to the visiting team for five years when he gave one to Middlesbrough. Bosnich saved Juninho's kick and Beckham went on to claim a dramatic winner two minutes from time. Indeed, United scored plenty of late goals with 43 coming in

HOW GOALS WERE CONCEDED 1999/2000
for the latest stats and to share your memories go to football.co.uk

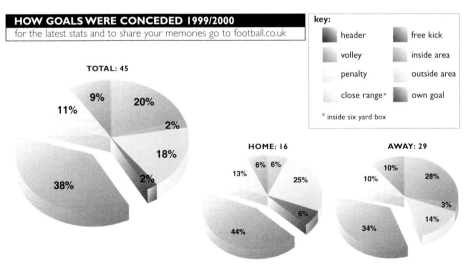

key:
- header
- volley
- penalty
- close range*
- free kick
- inside area
- outside area
- own goal

* inside six yard box

TOTAL: 45

9% · 20% · 2% · 18% · 2% · 11% · 38%

HOME: 16

6% · 6% · 25% · 13% · 6% · 44%

AWAY: 29

10% · 28% · 3% · 14% · 10% · 34%

What a difference a *CARLING* makes.

153

Squad and Performance

SQUAD LIST

for the latest stats and to share your memories go to football.co.uk

Position	Name	Appearances	Appearances as substitute	Goals	Clean Sheets	Yellow Cards	Red Cards
G	M.Bosnich	23			11		
G	N.Culkin		1				
G	M.Taibi	4					
G	R.Van der Gouw	11	3		1		
D	H.Berg	16	6	1		2	
D	M.Clegg	2					
D	J.Curtis	1					1
D	D.Higginbottom	2	1				
D	D.Irwin	25				3	1
D	R.Johnsen	2	1				
D	D.May	1					
D	G.Neville	22					
D	P.Neville	25	4			4	
D	M.Silvestre	30	1				
D	J.Stam	33				5	
D	R.Wallwork		5				
M	D.Beckham	30	1	6		6	
M	N.Butt	21	11	3		3	2
M	Q.Fortune	4	2	2			
M	R.Giggs	30		6		2	
M	R.Keane	28	1	5		7	1
M	P.Scholes	27	4	9		6	
M	M.Wilson	1	2				
F	A.Cole	23	5	19		2	1
F	J.Cruyff	1	7	3		1	
F	J.Greening	1	3				
F	T.Sheringham	15	12	5			
F	O.Solskjaer	15	13	12		2	
F	D.Yorke	29	3	20		1	

the final 30 minutes. If United showed any vulnerability it was in the final 15 minutes of away games with 10 out of 29 coming in that period.

United used three goalkeepers and not one of their talented squad played in all 38 Carling Premiership games, which is not a surprise given that other competitions took their number of games played last season to 59 and that without participation in the FA Cup.

For a team with so many points it is not surprising that they beat half the Carling Premiership clubs both home and away. There was only one team they failed to register at least one win against, and that, remarkably, was relegated Wimbledon. They stole an Old Trafford draw only after Jordi Cruyff had

TEAM PERFORMANCE TABLE

for the latest stats and to share your memories go to football.co.uk

Position	Club	Points Won	Percentage of points won at home	percentage of points won away	overall percentage of points won
1.	MANCHESTER UNITED	91 pts			
2.	ARSENAL	4/6			
3.	LEEDS UNITED	6/6	67%	75%	71%
4.	LIVERPOOL	4/6			
5.	CHELSEA	3/6			
6.	ASTON VILLA	6/6			
7.	SUNDERLAND	4/6			
8.	LEICESTER CITY	6/6	100%	67%	83%
9.	TOTTENHAM HOTSPUR	3/6			
10.	WEST HAM UNITED	6/6			
11.	NEWCASTLE UNITED	3/6			
12.	MIDDLESBROUGH	6/6			
13.	EVERTON	4/6	87%	67%	77%
14.	SOUTHAMPTON	4/6			
15.	COVENTRY CITY	6/6			
16.	DERBY COUNTY	6/6			
17.	BRADFORD CITY	6/6			
18.	WIMBLEDON	2/6	87%	87%	87%
19.	SHEFFIELD WEDNESDAY	6/6			
20.	WATFORD	6/6			

The figures show a team's performance against clubs in each quarter of the final league table. The first column represents points won from the total available against each team in the league.

Discipline and Season Summary

powered by

Manchester United

BOOKINGS BY POSITION 1997/1998 - 1999/2000
for the latest stats and to share your memories go to football.co.uk

key:
- forward
- midfield
- defence
- goalkeeper

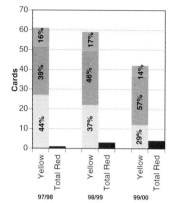

HOME

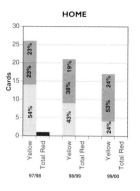

AWAY

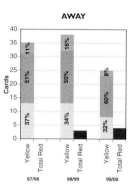

equalised and then drew 2-2 at Selhurst Park when the Dons threw away the lead twice.

Those who criticised United's siege mentality will be surprised to discover that they were, generally, a referee's dream. The fact is that they received only 42 yellow cards, the fewest in the Carling Premiership, and their lowest number since the 1993-94 season, when only 31 yellow cards were shown to United players. The worst offender was Keane, with seven, while Beckham and Scholes received six, hence the fact that 57 per cent of their cautions were given to midfielders. But in the red card stakes, United were no angels, collecting four. Two of those went to Nicky Butt, who was dismissed in the 5-0 defeat at Chelsea

and went again at Watford towards the end of the season. Keane was also sent off, at Newcastle, while Cole was given an early bath against Liverpool.

If United are not losing at the interval this season, expect them to finish as the winners – if last season's form can be used as a guide. On no fewer than 17 occasions they led at half time and went on to win 15 and draw two. And of the 12 times they were level after 45 minutes, they went on to win 10 and draw the others. Even when they were losing at half time they had a fair chance of rescuing the situation; of the nine times they were behind (seven of them away) they lost only three, which were their only three defeats of the campaign.

HALF TIME · FULL TIME COMPARATIVE CHART
for the latest stats and to share your memories go to football.co.uk

HOME				AWAY				TOTAL			
Number of Home Half Time Wins	Full Time Result W L D			Number of Away Half Time Wins	Full Time Result W L D			Total Number of Half Time Wins	Full Time Result W L D		
11	10	0	1	6	5	0	1	17	15	0	2
Number of Home Half Time Losses	Full Time Result W L D			Number of Away Half Time Losses	Full Time Result W L D			Total Number of Half Time Losses	Full Time Result W L D		
2	0	0	2	7	3	3	1	9	3	3	3
Number of Home Half Time Draws	Full Time Result W L D			Number of Away Half Time Draws	Full Time Result W L D			Total Number of Half Time Draws	Full Time Result W L D		
6	5	0	1	6	5	0	1	12	10	0	2

What a difference a CARLING makes.

Maps and Directions

Manchester United play at Old Trafford, two miles south-west of Manchester city centre. Parking is available at several paying car parks in the immediate vicinity of the ground.

From the North:
Approaching on the M61, at Junction 1 continue onto the M602 and keep on this road for 4 miles. At Junction 3 turn right onto Trafford Road and after one mile turn right again into Trafford Park Road. Sir Matt Busby Way and Old Trafford are on the left.

From the South:
Take the M6 to Junction 19, turning onto the A556 Stockport Road which becomes the A56 at Altrincham. This becomes the Chester Road. After 9 miles, turn left onto the the A5063 Trafford Road, left onto the A5081 Trafford Park Road and left again into Sir Matt Busby Way. Old Trafford is on the right.

From the West:
Approaching on the M62, at Junction 12 continue on the M602, keeping to this road for 4 miles. Then as route for North.

From the East:
Get onto the M63 and at Junction 7 turn onto the A556. Then as route for South.

The nearest Metrolink stations are Old Trafford and Trafford Bar.

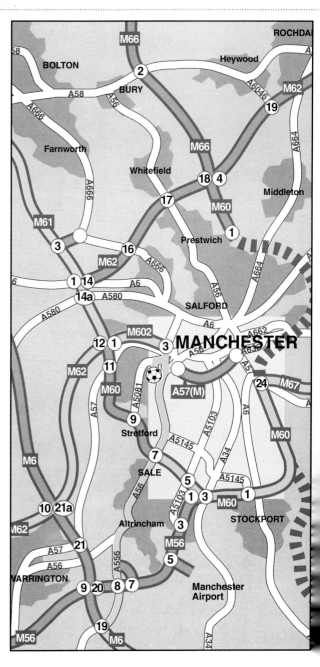

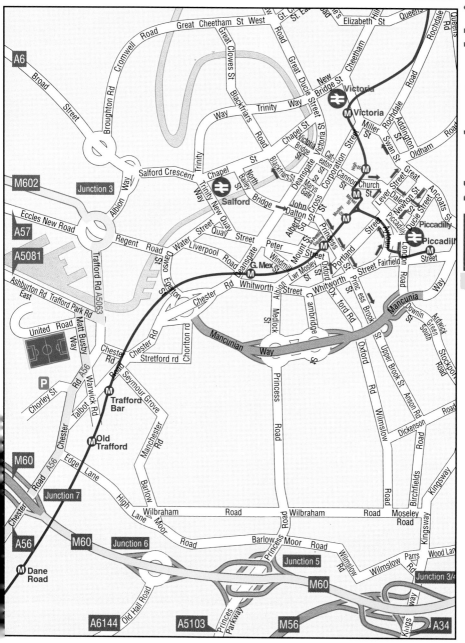

Pos		Pld	W	D	L	F	A	Pts
12	Middlesbrough	38	14	10	14	46	52	52

Middlesbrough "Boro"

BT Cellnet Riverside Stadium,
Middlesbrough TS3 6RS
Tel: 01642 877 700
www.mfc.co.uk

Season Review by
John Ley

The Daily Telegraph

It is not many years ago that Middlesbrough's old Ayresome Park was taken over by administrators and the club were forced to play at Hartlepool. Now, at their splendid Riverside Stadium, Middlesbrough's expectations are high enough for the fans to be disappointed that their club finished in 12th place. The fact they ended up behind Sunderland and Newcastle might also rank as an annoyance, but Bryan Robson's team continued to progress after returning to the Carling Premiership two years ago.

Robson made two impressive signings; Christian Ziege came from AC Milan while Liverpool's Paul Ince teamed up with his former Manchester United team-mate. Both players featured in Euro 2000, suggesting they are still in the prime of their careers. He added young Argentine Carlos Marinelli while Juninho returned on loan from Atletico Madrid and Middlesbrough finished three places lower but one point better off than the previous season.

Useful Information

Stadium Store
BT Cellnet Riverside Stadium
Opening Times:
Monday-Friday: 9.30am-5.00pm
Match Saturdays: 10.00am-2.30pm, 5.00pm-6.00pm
Match Sundays: 10.00am-3.30pm
Match Eves: open until 30 mins before kick off
Tel: 01642 877 720

MFC Retail
Captain Cook Square,
Middlesbrough
Opening Times:
Monday-Saturday: 9.00am-5.00pm
Match Saturdays: 9.00am-5.00pm
Tel: 01642 877 849
Fax: 01642 877 723
Mail Order Service: 01642 866 622

Stadium Tours
Tours of ground, dressing room etc.
Contact Heather Machon:
01642 877 730

Corporate Hospitality
Facilities include 26 executive boxes, Riverside Restaurant, BT Cellnet Club, Middlehaven Suite, Fenton Lounge, Hardwick Suite, Ayresome Lounge.

What a difference a CARLING makes.

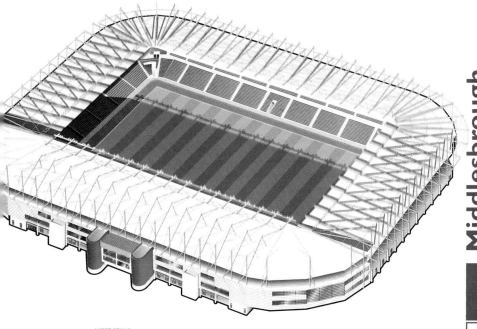

WEST STAND

Disabled upper inc helper	UPPER TIER		
£430 (£22.63 per match)		£470 (£24.73 per match)	£430 (£22.63 per match)
Disabled lower inc helper	EXECUTIVE BOXES		£294 (£15.47 per match)
£294 (£15.47 per match)	LOWER TIER £382 (£20.10 per match)		
	concessions £186 (£9.79 per match)		

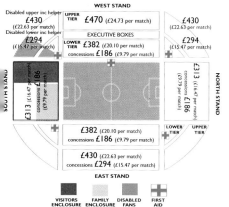

£313 (£16.47 per match)
concessions £186 (£9.79 per match)

SOUTH STAND

NORTH STAND

£313 (£16.47 per match)
concessions £186 (£9.79 per match)

£382 (£20.10 per match)
concessions £186 (£9.79 per match)

LOWER TIER   UPPER TIER

£430 (£22.63 per match)
concessions £294 (£15.47 per match)

EAST STAND

VISITORS ENCLOSURE   FAMILY ENCLOSURE   DISABLED FANS   FIRST AID

BT Cellnet Riverside Stadium
Opened: August 26, 1995
Capacity: 35,049
1999/2000 highest attendance: 34,800
1999/2000 average attendance: 33,393
Record attendance: 34,687

Sponsorship Packages: Match, matchball, team, programme and man of the match.
Contact Michelle Coulton:
01642 877 700
Conference & Banqueting:
01642 877750

Literature
Programme Riverside Red £2
Riverside Roar £2.50

Other publications include The Boro Alphabet, The Riverside Rollercaoster, The Boro Bible and Yer Jokin' Aren't Yer

Pre-Match & Half Time Entertainment
Starting 45 minutes before kick off: Cheerleaders, quizzes, music, bands. Half time draw.

Booking Information
General Enquiries:
01642 877 745
Recorded Info:
01642 877 809
Credit Card Bookings:
01642 877 745
Travel Club:
01642 877 745

Results Breakdown

POINTS WON OR LOST AT BOTH HOME AND AWAY
for the latest stats and to share your memories go to football.co.uk

key:
- win
- draw
- loss
- **-0-** league position
- home fixtures are in red

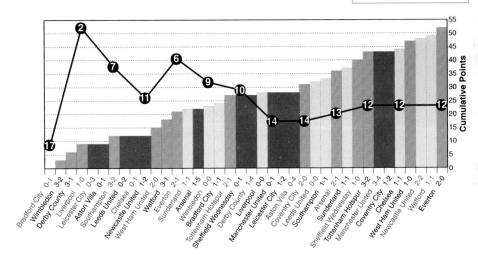

Middlesbrough started with a shock home defeat against newcomers Bradford City but they made amends with three successive wins to move into second place. Five defeats from their next six spoiled the good start but a run of three victories saw Boro back in sixth place. Another run of five defeats from six outings sent Boro down again, as low as 14th place but their zig-zag season took to the up-curve again with a seven-match unbeaten run halted by successive December defeats by Sheffield Wednesday and Derby County – before finishing with another unbeaten

sequence of five games. In five Carling Premiership seasons Boro have never won more than eight home games so their eight victories this time around was par for the course. But while six home defeats was their worst number of losses for three years, they did manage six wins, one more than the previous season. Boro were ultimately undone by their constant struggle to win away games; in an amazing period between October and April they went eight games on their travels without a win, including a 5-1 drubbing at Highbury by Arsenal.

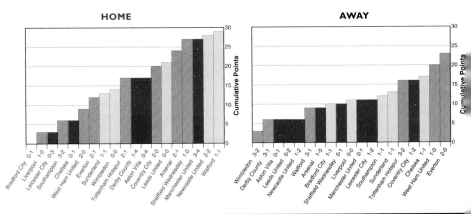

Results Table

powered by football.co.uk

Middlesbrough

Legend: ● = Red Card   ○ = Yellow Card   ▲ = Player substituted   00 = Time of goal

DATE	H/A	OPPONENT	H/T	F/T	POS	REFEREE	TEAM (line-up)	SUBSTITUTES USED
07/08	H	Bradford City	0-0	0-1	17	N.S.Barry	Schwarzer, Gordon, Vickers▲, Festo, Ziege, Mustoe, Goscoigne, O'Neill, Stamp, Deane, Campbell▲	Townsend▲, Ricard▲
10/08	A	Wimbledon	2-1	3-2	10	B.Knight	Schwarzer, Gordon▲, Vickers, Festo, Ziege▲23, Ince●, Goscoigne, O'Neill, Stamp, Deane, Ricard▲27 63	O'Neill▲, Mustoe▲, Campbell▲
14/08	H	Derby County	2-1	3-1	4	S.G.Bennett	Schwarzer, Gordon▲, Vickers, Festo, Ziege 20, Ince, Mustoe, Townsend, Stamp, Deane 9, Ricard▲66	Townsend▲, Armstrong▲
21/08	A	Liverpool	0-0	1-0	2	S.W.Dunn	Schwarzer, Pallister, Vickers, Festo, Ziege, Ince, Goscoigne▲, O'Neill, Stockdale, Deane 49, Ricard	Mustoe▲, O'Neill▲, Campbell▲
24/08	A	Leicester City	0-2	0-3	4	R.J.Harris	Schwarzer, Pallister, Vickers, Festo, Ziege, Ince, Mustoe, Townsend▲, Stockdale, Deane, Ricard	Maddison▲, Campbell▲
28/08	H	Aston Villa	0-1	0-1	10	M.R.Halsey	Schwarzer, Pallister 17, Vickers, Govin, Stockdale, Ince, Mustoe, Townsend▲, Stamp▲, Deane, Ricard	Summerbell▲, Campbell▲
11/09	A	Southampton	1-1	3-2	7	S.J.Lodge	Schwarzer, Pallister, Vickers▲, Cooper, Ziege, Ince, Mustoe, Goscoigne 67, Juninho, Deane▲78, Ricard	Stockdale▲, Govin▲, Goscoigne●
19/09	H	Leeds United	0-1	0-2	11	D.J.Gallagher	Schwarzer, Pallister, Vickers, Festo, Ziege, Ince, Mustoe, O'Neill, Stamp▲, Deane, Armstrong▲	Ricard▲, Govin▲
25/09	A	Chelsea	0-0	0-1	11	P.E.Alcock	Schwarzer, Pallister, Fleming, Festo, Ziege, Ince▲, Cooper, O'Neill, Juninho, Deane, Armstrong▲	Armstrong▲
03/10	H	Newcastle United	0-2	1-2	11	S.J.Lodge	Schwarzer, Pallister, Fleming, Festo, Ziege, Ince, Mustoe, O'Neill, Juninho▲, Deane 89, Ricard	Armstrong▲, Campbell▲
17/10	H	West Ham United	0-0	2-0	11	U.D.Rennie	Schwarzer, Pallister, Vickers, Festo, Ziege, Ince, Cooper, Cooper, Juninho▲, Deane 52, Vickers▲	Armstrong▲89
24/10	A	Watford	2-0	3-1	10	A.G.Wiley	Schwarzer, Pallister▲, Vickers, Fleming, Ziege, Ince 83, Cooper, O'Neill, Juninho▲18, Deane, Ricard	Armstrong▲, Stamp▲
30/10	H	Everton	1-1	2-1	6	A.P.D'Urso	Schwarzer, Pallister, Vickers, Fleming, Ziege 15, Ince, Stamp, O'Neill, Juninho, Deane 61, Ricard	Armstrong▲
06/11	A	Sunderland	0-0	1-1	7	G.P.Barber	Schwarzer, Pallister, Vickers, Cooper, Ziege, Ince, Stamp, O'Neill, Juninho, Deane, Ricard 76	Stamp▲
20/11	A	Arsenal	0-0	1-5	8	N.S.Barry	Schwarzer, Pallister, Vickers▲, Cooper, Ziege, Ince, Goscoigne, Govin, Juninho▲, Deane, Ricard 68	Stockdale▲, Armstrong▲, Campbell▲
27/11	H	Wimbledon	0-0	0-0	9	P.Durkin	Schwarzer, Pallister, Vickers, Cooper, Ziege, Ince, Mustoe, O'Neill, Juninho▲, Deane, Ricard 13	Armstrong▲, Summerbell▲
04/12	A	Bradford City	1-0	1-0	10	R.J.Harris	Schwarzer, Pallister, Fleming▲, Fleming, Ziege, Mustoe, Goscoigne, Stamp, Juninho, Deane, Ricard 13	Maddison▲, Armstrong▲
18/12	H	Tottenham Hotspur	1-1	2-1	8	S.W.Dunn	Schwarzer, Maddison, Maddison, Festo, Ziege▲35, Mustoe, Stockdale, O'Neill, Juninho, Deane 67, Ricard	Maddison▲, Armstrong▲
26/12	A	Sheffield Wednesday	0-1	0-1	10	B.Knight	Schwarzer, Maddison, Maddison, Festo, Fleming, Mustoe, Stockdale, Stamp, Juninho▲, Deane, Armstrong▲	Govin▲, Armstrong▲
15/01	A	Derby County	0-1	1-4	13	M.R.Halsey	Schwarzer, Pallister, Vickers, Festo, Ziege, Ince, Stockdale, Mustoe▲18, Juninho, Deane, Ricard	Maddison▲, Govin▲, Ricard▲71
22/01	H	Liverpool	0-0	0-0	13	A.G.Wiley	Schwarzer, Cooper, Vickers, Festo, Fleming, Ince, Cooper, Summerbell, Juninho, Armstrong, Campbell▲	Maddison▲, Govin▲, Campbell▲
29/01	H	Manchester United	0-0	0-1	14	S.W.Dunn	Schwarzer, Pallister▲, Vickers▲, Festo, Ziege, Ince, Cooper, Summerbell, Juninho, Campbell, Govin▲	Govin▲, Maddison▲
05/02	A	Leicester City	0-2	1-2	15	S.G.Bennett	Schwarzer, Pallister, Vickers, Festo, Ziege, Ince, Cooper, Goscoigne, Juninho, Campbell, Campbell 52	Ricard▲, Ricard▲
14/02	A	Aston Villa	1-0	1-4	16	A.B.Wilkie	Beresford, Pallister, Vickers, Festo, Ziege, Ince, Goscoigne▲, O'Neill, Juninho, Summerbell, Campbell	Maddison▲, Stamp▲
19/02	H	Coventry City	2-0	2-0	14	G.P.Barber	Schwarzer, Cooper▲, Vickers, Festo, Cooper, Ince 86, Cooper, Summerbell, Campbell 18, Summerbell, Ricard 20	Campbell 18, Maddison▲
26/02	A	Leeds United	0-0	0-0	13	U.D.Rennie	Schwarzer, Festo, Vickers, Cooper, Ziege, Ince, Stockdale, Summerbell, Campbell, Deane 60, Ricard 44	Cummins▲, Armstrong▲
04/03	H	Southampton	1-1	1-1	13	S.W.Dunn	Schwarzer, Pallister, Fleming, Festo, Ziege▲82, Maddison, Maddison, Summerbell, Juninho 5, Deane, Ricard 63	Govin▲, Ricard▲, Armstrong▲
12/03	A	Arsenal	0-0	0-0	13	R.J.Harris	Schwarzer, Pallister, Fleming, Festo, Ziege, Maddison 49, Cooper, Summerbell, Juninho, Deane, Ricard	Maddison▲, Govin▲
18/03	H	Sunderland	0-0	0-1	14	D.R.Elleray	Schwarzer, Pallister, Fleming, Festo, Ziege, Ince, Cooper, Summerbell, Juninho, Deane, Campbell 11	Campbell▲, Festo▲
25/03	H	Sheffield Wednesday	1-0	1-0	12	D.J.Gallagher	Schwarzer, Cooper, Fleming, Festo, Ziege, Ince, Mustoe, Summerbell, Campbell, Deane, Ricard 63 78	Mustoe▲, Juninho▲90
03/04	A	Tottenham Hotspur	1-1	3-2	12	P.A.Durkin	Schwarzer, Pallister, Fleming, Festo, Ziege, Ince, Mustoe▲, Goscoigne, Campbell 18, Deane, Ricard	Festo▲, Juninho▲, Stamp▲
10/04	H	Manchester United	1-0	3-4	13	N.S.Barry	Schwarzer, Festo, Fleming, Festo, Ziege 64, Maddison, Mustoe, Summerbell, Cooper, Deane, Ricard 37	Juninho▲, Campbell▲, Stamp▲
15/04	A	Coventry City	0-1	1-2	13	U.D.Rennie	Schwarzer, Fleming, Festo, Fleming, Ziege, Ince, Mustoe, Summerbell, Juninho, Campbell, Campbell	Cummins▲, Campbell▲
22/04	H	Chelsea	1-1	1-1	12	B.Knight	Schwarzer, Festo, Fleming, Festo, Cooper, Ince, Mustoe▲, Summerbell, Juninho, Campbell, Ricard	Gordon▲, Ricard▲
29/04	A	West Ham United	1-2	2-2	13	M.A.Riley	Schwarzer, Fleming, Vickers, Festo 78, Ziege, Ince, Mustoe, Summerbell, Juninho 5, Deane, Campbell	Stockdale▲, Mustoe▲
02/05	H	Newcastle United	1-2	2-2	12	B.Knight	Schwarzer, Fleming, Vickers, Festo, Ziege, Ince, Mustoe, Stockdale 27, Juninho, Campbell, Ricard	Stockdale▲, Mustoe▲, Kilgannon▲
06/05	A	Watford	1-0	1-1	13	P.Jones	Schwarzer, Cooper, Vickers, Festo, Cooper, Ince, Mustoe, Stamp, Juninho, Campbell▲, Ricard	Marinelli▲
14/05	A	Everton	1-0	2-0	12	R.J.Harris	Schwarzer, Fleming, Vickers, Festo, Mustoe, Ince, Stamp▲, Cooper, Juninho 86, Deane 8, Campbell	Maddison▲

Goal Analysis

powered by **football.co.uk**

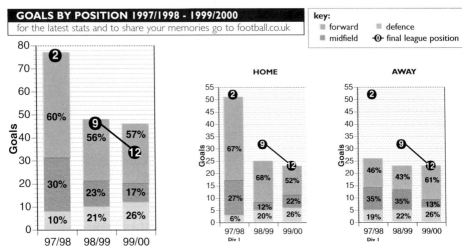

GOALS BY POSITION 1997/1998 - 1999/2000
for the latest stats and to share your memories go to football.co.uk

key:
■ forward   ■ defence
■ midfield   -◐- final league position

Middlesbrough's tally of just 23 goals at the Riverside was their lowest at home for 15 years, when they scored 22. Two seasons previously, on winning promotion from Division One, Boro scored more goals at home than they did last season in total; their 46 was their poorest return in front of goal for four years. Boro also conceded more home goals than they have for four years but if there is any good to come from the figures they can at least take some heart from the fact that the 26 they conceded on their travels was

10 fewer than the previous season. Worryingly, Boro conceded four goals or more on four occasions, including the 5-1 thrashing at Arsenal along with 4-1 and 4-0 Riverside drubbings by Derby and Aston Villa respectively.

They were let down generally in midfield, an area that provided just eight goals, three less than the previous season and well below the 23 the Boro midfielders poached in the 1997-98 season. Juninho had scored 12 in his previous season at Boro but

GOALS BY TIME PERIOD 1999/2000
for the latest stats and to share your memories go to football.co.uk

key:
■ goals for   ■ goals against

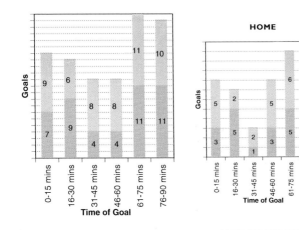

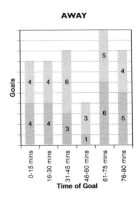

Goal Analysis

Middlesbrough

HOW GOALS WERE SCORED 1999/2000
for the latest stats and to share your memories go to football.co.uk

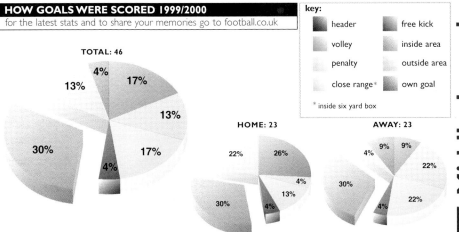

key:
- header
- volley
- penalty
- close range*
- free kick
- inside area
- outside area
- own goal

inside six yard box

TOTAL: 46
4% · 17% · 13% · 13% · 17% · 4% · 30% · 4%

HOME: 23
22% · 26% · 4% · 13% · 4% · 30%

AWAY: 23
4% · 9% · 9% · 22% · 30% · 4% · 22%

managed four in 27 appearances – and missed two penalties – while Ince scored three. Colombian Hamilton Ricard failed to match his 15 League goals in the 1998-99 season but still finished as the highest scorer with 12. Brian Deane scored half a dozen, as he had the previous term, while the promising Andy Campbell became an England Under-21 international, scoring in the UEFA Championship play-off against Yugoslavia in Barcelona, and adding his first four goals for Boro, in 16 starts.

Boro seemed to reserve their best for the final 30 minutes; 22 of their 46 goals came in the closing period, though they were also most vulnerable in that period, conceding 21 in the final third. At the Riverside they were extremely exposed; 17 of the 26 goals they conceded at home (65 per cent) were scored in the second half.

Middlesbrough were awarded nine penalties but of the three that came their way at home, two were missed with Ricard failing against Derby and Juninho

HOW GOALS WERE CONCEDED 1999/2000
for the latest stats and to share your memories go to football.co.uk

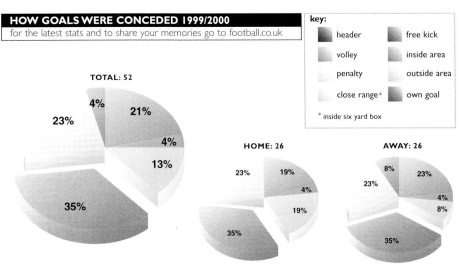

key:
- header
- volley
- penalty
- close range*
- free kick
- inside area
- outside area
- own goal

inside six yard box

TOTAL: 52
4% · 21% · 23% · 4% · 13% · 35%

HOME: 26
23% · 19% · 4% · 19% · 35%

AWAY: 26
8% · 23% · 23% · 4% · 8% · 35%

Squad and Performance

SQUAD LIST

for the latest stats and to share your memories go to football.co.uk

Position	Name	Appearances	Appearances as substitute	Goals	Clean Sheets	Yellow Cards	Red Cards
G	M.Beresford	1					
G	M.Schwarzer	37			9	1	
D	J.Beresford						
D	C.Cooper	26				5	
D	G.Festa	27	2	2		6	1
D	C.Fleming	27				6	
D	J.Gavin	2	4				
D	D.Gordon	3	1			1	
D	G.Pallister	21		1		5	
D	R.Stockdale	6	5	1			
D	S.Vickers	30	2			5	
D	C.Ziege	29		6		9	1
M	M.Cummins		1				
M	P.Gascoigne	7	1	1		1	1
M	P.Ince	32			3	8	
M	.Juninho	24	3	4		1	
M	N.Maddison	6	7			1	
M	C.Marinelli		2				
M	R.Mustoe	18	9			3	
M	K.O'Neill	14	2			5	
M	A.Ormerod		1				
M	P.Stamp	13	3			6	
M	M.Summerbell	16	3			4	
M	A.Townsend	3	2			1	
F	A.Armstrong	3	9	1			
F	A.Campbell	16	9	4			
F	B.Deane	29		9		6	
F	W.Kilgannon		1				
F	H.Ricard	28	6	12		7	

missing against Sheffield Wednesday – after the Brazilian had squandered another, at Old Trafford. Strangely, five of the six they converted were scored away, contributing 22 per cent of their away goals.

It was easy to forget that Paul Gascoigne remained a Boro player. Not since he suffered serious injury with Lazio had Gazza played so few games in a season. He managed just eight through a combination of rest for personal reasons, a succession of injuries – the worst a broken arm – and suspensions. Goalkeeper Mark Schwarzer missed only one game, while with Australia in February. Boro managed at least one win against half of the Premiership and six points were taken off three teams, while they failed to glean a single point off

TEAM PERFORMANCE TABLE

for the latest stats and to share your memories go to football.co.uk

Position	Club	Points Won	Percentage of points won at home	percentage of points won away	overall percentage of points won
1.	MANCHESTER UNITED	0/6			
2.	ARSENAL	3/6			
3.	LEEDS UNITED	1/6	47%	13%	30%
4.	LIVERPOOL	4/6			
5.	CHELSEA	1/6			
6.	ASTON VILLA	0/6			
7.	SUNDERLAND	2/6			
8.	LEICESTER CITY	0/6	47%	47%	47%
9.	TOTTENHAM HOTSPUR	6/6			
10.	WEST HAM UNITED	6/6			
11.	NEWCASTLE UNITED	1/6			
12.	MIDDLESBROUGH	52 pts			
13.	EVERTON	6/6	83%	33%	58%
14.	SOUTHAMPTON	4/6			
15.	COVENTRY CITY	3/6			
16.	DERBY COUNTY	3/6			
17.	BRADFORD CITY	1/6			
18.	WIMBLEDON	4/6	33%	67%	50%
19.	SHEFFIELD WEDNESDAY	3/6			
20.	WATFORD	4/6			

The figures show a team's performance against clubs in each quarter of the final league table. The first column represents points won from the total available against each team in the league.

What a difference a CARLING makes.

Discipline and Season Summary

powered by football.co.uk

BOOKINGS BY POSITION 1997/1998 - 1999/2000
for the latest stats and to share your memories go to football.co.uk

key:
- forward
- defence
- midfield
- goalkeeper

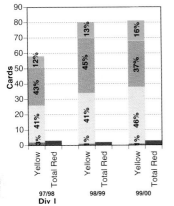

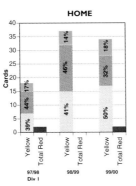

HOME

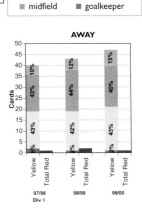

AWAY

Middlesbrough

another three. Strangely, their home form against the bottom five was poor with only one win, over Wednesday, at the Riverside.

Middlesbrough's discipline was disappointing; they collected 81 yellow cards – only Derby and Tottenham received more. Those cautions, three sendings off and a three match ban given to Gascoigne for the use of an elbow, cost Boro a total of 16 games lost through bans, something a squad of their size can ill afford to lose. Ziege may have enjoyed a fine first season in English football, operating usually from the wing-back position, but he showed little respect for the laws, collecting nine yellow cards and one red – against Manchester United at Old Trafford.

No fewer than five more Boro defenders collected five cautions or more, representing a total of 46 per cent of their total cautions. In midfield, Ince was booked eight times, though that was better than his last season at Liverpool when he collected nine yellow cards. Strikers Brian Deane and Hamilton Ricard were also in trouble, collecting a combined 13 bookings. Others to be sent off were Gascoigne, for swearing in the last minute of the home defeat by Chelsea, and Gianluca Festa, who left early in front of the Riverside's record attendance against Leeds.

Boro rarely led at half time at the Riverside and when they did it was no guarantee they would win. Of the four occasions they were ahead after 45 minutes they won twice, losing one and drawing the other.

HALF TIME - FULL TIME COMPARATIVE CHART
for the latest stats and to share your memories go to football.co.uk

HOME				AWAY				TOTAL			
Number of Home Half Time Wins	Full Time Result W	L	D	Number of Away Half Time Wins	Full Time Result W	L	D	Total Number of Half Time Wins	Full Time Result W	L	D
4	2	1	1	5	4	0	1	9	6	1	2
Number of Home Half Time Losses	Full Time Result W	L	D	Number of Away Half Time Losses	Full Time Result W	L	D	Total Number of Half Time Losses	Full Time Result W	L	D
4	0	3	1	7	0	7	0	11	0	10	1
Number of Home Half Time Draws	Full Time Result W	L	D	Number of Away Half Time Draws	Full Time Result W	L	D	Total Number of Half Time Draws	Full Time Result W	L	D
11	6	2	3	7	2	1	4	18	8	3	7

What a difference a *CARLING* makes.

Maps and Directions

Middlesbrough play at the BT Cellnet Riverside Stadium in the Middlehaven development area, 15 minutes walk from the town centre.

Although fans are encouraged to park in the town centre and walk to the ground, there is some room available at the nearby Readman Car Park.

From the North:
Approaching Middlesbrough on the A19, cross over the River Tees.
Turn left onto the A66 Middlesbrough bypass, continuing for 3 miles until the first roundabout. Turn left into Forest Road and the ground is straight ahead.

From the South:
Approaching from the South on the M1, exit where signposted to Teesside onto the A19. After 30 miles turn right onto the A66 Middlesbrough bypass. Then as route for North.

From the West:
From the A1(M) exit at Junction 57 onto the A66(M), following it until the end, turning onto the A66 for approximately 20 miles, turning left at the roundabout into Forest Road. The ground is straight ahead.

Middlesbrough Station is located on Albert Road, 10 minutes walk from the ground.

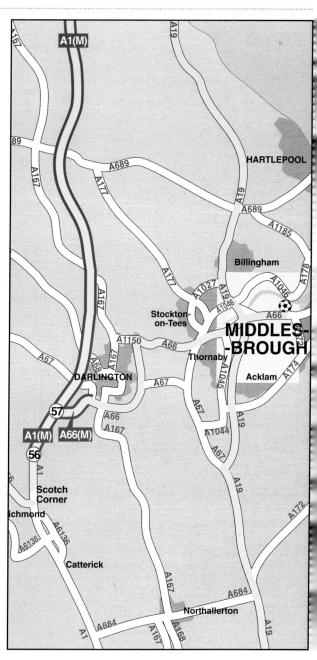

Middlesbrough

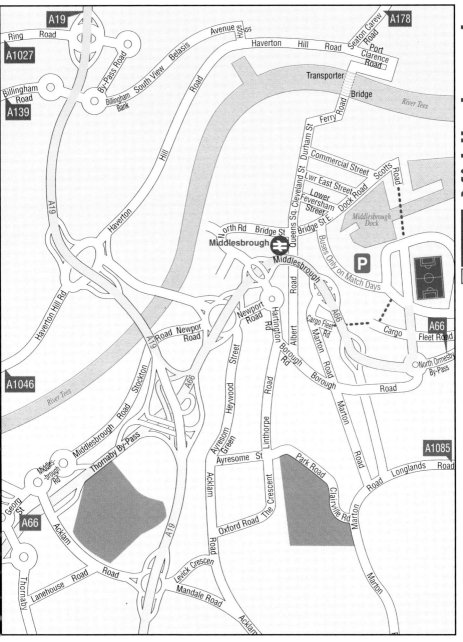

Club Honours

- Football League Champions: 1904-05, 1906-07, 1908-09, 1926-2?
- Division I Champions: 1992-93
- Division 2 Champions: 1964-65
- FA Cup Winners: 1910, 1924, 1932, 1951, 1952, 1955
- Texaco Cup Winners: 1974, 1975
- European Fairs Cup Winners: 1968-69
- Anglo-Italian Cup Winners: 1972-73

Club Records

- Victory: 13-0 v Newport County, Division 2, October 5, 1946
- Defeat: 0-9 v Burton Wanderers, Division 2, April 15, 1895
- League goals in a season (team): 98, Division 1, 1951-52
- League goals in a season (player): 36, Hughie Gallacher, Division 1, 1926-27
- Career league goals: 178, Jackie Milburn, 1946-57
- League appearances: 432, Jim Lawrence, 1904-1922
- Transfer fee paid: £15,000,000 to Blackburn Rovers for Alan Shearer, July, 1996
- Transfer fee received: £8,000,000 from Liverpool for Dietmar Hamann, July, 1999

Pos		Pld	W	D	L	F	A	Pts
11	Newcastle	38	14	10	14	63	54	52

Newcastle United
"The Magpies"

St James' Park,
Newcastle-Upon-Tyne NE1 4ST
Tel: 0191 201 8400
www.nufc.co.uk

Season Review by
John Ley

The Daily Telegraph

Nothing is ever straight-forward when you are a member of the Toon Army. At the start of the previous season fans saw Kenny Dalglish in charge for just two games; last season new manager Ruud Gullit lasted five matches until he resigned, leaving the Newcastle board with the task of finding a successor. This time, Bobby Robson was available and the great man was lured home to his 'dream job'. Immediately Robson earned the respect Gullit could never command; when he arrived Newcastle were 19th, having won one point from six games – Steve Clarke was caretaker for one game – but Robson, in charge of several new players signed by his predecessor, turned the club's fortunes around.

Kieron Dyer soon proved to be one of the few good things left behind by Gullit; the midfielder enjoyed a dazzling season when he was not injured. Several others suffered long term injuries but for the Toon Army the future is looking bright.

Useful Information

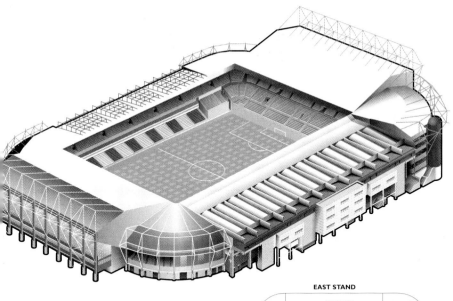

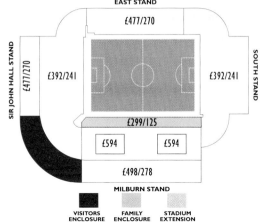

EAST STAND

£477/270

SIR JOHN HALL STAND

£477/270

£392/241

£392/241

SOUTH STAND

£299/125

£594   £594

£498/278

MILBURN STAND

VISITORS ENCLOSURE   FAMILY ENCLOSURE   STADIUM EXTENSION

St James' Park

Opened: October 16, 1880
Capacity: 52,000
1999/2000 highest attendance: 36,619
1999/2000 average attendance: 36,328
Record attendance: 68,387

Literature

Programme £2
Magazine Black & White £2.30

Restaurant

Magpie Restaurant.
Tel: **0191 201 8439**

Stadium Redevelopment

Newcastle United are redeveloping St James' Park at a cost of £42 million the stadium will eventually hold 52,000 people. Facilities will include restaurants, executive boxes, club business centre, Directors' entertainment suites, shops and a police station.

Booking Information

General Enquiries :
0191 201 8401
Credit Card Bookings:
0191 261 1571
Travel Club:
0191 201 8550
Recorded Info:
0191 201 8400

Results Breakdown

POINTS WON OR LOST AT BOTH HOME AND AWAY

for the latest stats and to share your memories go to football.co.uk

key:
■ win ■ draw
■ loss -0- league position
home fixtures are in red

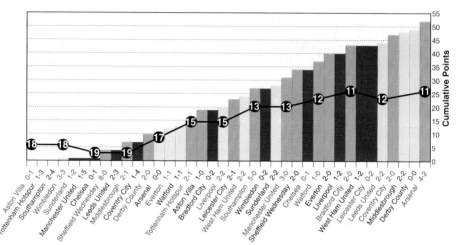

Until mid-September and the arrival of Robson Newcastle were 19th but after losing his first game, at Chelsea, the new boss turned things around and by midway through the season they had been elevated to 13th place. The fans were singing 'Walking in a Robson Wonderland' as they romped to an 8-0 win over Sheffield Wednesday – the first time they had scored eight since the 8-2 win over Everton in 1959 and the largest margin of victory since 1946, when a debut-making Len Shackleton scored six in a 13-0 win over Newport County. From that victory, Newcastle

were unbeaten at St James' Park until they lost 1-0 to Chelsea in March but they lost their first six away games – two short of the record worst start set 70 years earlier – and managed to win just four away games all season. Interestingly, Newcastle continued to struggle in London; they have now failed to win in their last 18 League and Cup visits to the capital.

If results were sometimes disappointing, nobody could complain about the number of goals Newcastle scored. They scored 63, 15 more than the previous season and their best goalscoring return for three

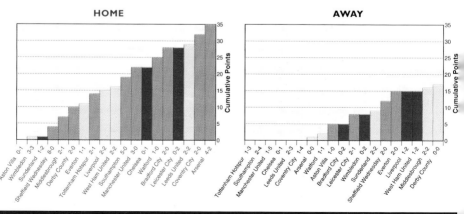

What a difference a CARLING makes.

THE F.A. CARLING PREMIERSHIP
Results Table

powered by football.co.uk

Newcastle United

● = Red Card   ○ = Yellow Card   ▲ = Player substituted   00 = Time of goal

DATE	H/A	OPPONENT	H/T	F/T	POS	REFEREE
07/08	H	Aston Villa	0-0	0-1	18	U.D.Rennie
09/08	A	Tottenham Hotspur	1-2	1-3	19	R.J.Harris
15/08	A	Southampton	1-0	2-4	20	D.R.Ellery
21/08	H	Wimbledon	2-1	3-3	18	M.D.Reed
25/08	H	Sunderland	1-0	1-2	19	G.Poll
30/08	A	Manchester United	1-1	1-5	19	J.T.Winter
11/09	A	Chelsea	0-1	0-1	19	G.Poll
19/09	H	Sheffield Wednesday	4-0	8-0	19	N.S.Barry
25/09	A	Leeds United	1-2	2-3	19	B.Knight
03/10	A	Middlesbrough	2-0	2-1	19	S.J.Lodge
16/10	H	Derby County	0-3	1-4	19	A.G.Wiley
25/10	A	Arsenal	1-0	2-0	17	S.W.Dunn
30/10	H	Arsenal	0-0	0-0	17	P.Jones
20/11	H	Everton	0-0	1-1	16	M.D.Reed
20/11	A	Watford	0-0	1-1	16	S.W.Dunn
28/11	H	Tottenham Hotspur	1-1	2-1	15	P.E.Alcock
04/12	A	Aston Villa	1-0	1-0	14	M.A.Riley
18/12	H	Bradford City	0-0	2-1	15	N.S.Barry
26/12	A	Liverpool	1-1	2-2	15	D.R.Ellery
28/12	H	Leicester City	1-0	2-1	14	P.Durkin
03/01	H	Manchester United	1-0	0-2	14	P.Jones
16/01	A	Southampton	4-0	5-0	13	N.S.Barry
22/01	A	Wimbledon	0-0	0-2	13	D.J.Gallagher
05/02	H	Sunderland	2-1	2-2	13	D.J.Gallagher
12/02	A	Manchester United	1-0	3-0	12	S.J.Lodge
26/02	H	Sheffield Wednesday	1-0	2-0	12	M.A.Riley
04/03	H	Chelsea	0-1	0-1	12	M.A.Riley
19/03	A	Watford	0-0	1-0	12	A.G.Wiley
19/03	A	Everton	0-0	0-0	12	P.Durkin
25/03	H	Liverpool	0-0	1-2	12	A.P.D'Urso
01/04	H	Bradford City	1-0	2-0	10	P.E.Alcock
12/04	H	West Ham United	0-0	1-0	10	U.D.Rennie
15/04	A	Leicester City	0-1	0-2	11	D.R.Ellery
23/04	A	Leeds United	1-2	2-2	11	D.R.Ellery
29/04	H	Coventry City	0-0	2-0	12	P.Jones
02/05	H	Middlesbrough	2-1	2-2	12	M.A.Riley
06/05	A	Derby County	0-0	0-0	12	A.G.Wiley
14/05	H	Arsenal	2-1	4-2	11	G.Poll

171

Goal Analysis

powered by football.co.uk

GOALS BY POSITION 1997/1998 - 1999/2000
for the latest stats and to share your memories go to football.co.uk

key:
- forward
- midfield
- defence
- ⓿ final league position

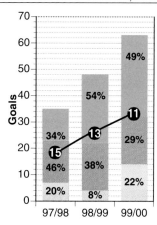

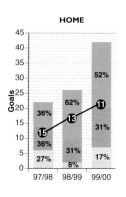

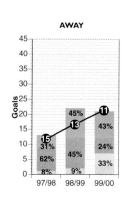

seasons. Only Manchester United and Arsenal scored more and once again it was Shearer who led the way, scoring 23 goals to take his tally in the Carling Premiership to 176, a record in the division, and 199 in League football. It was his best League goal return for three seasons while with cup goals he reached 30, his best ever seasonal tally for Newcastle. Shearer boosted his total by scoring five in one game, against Wednesday in the remarkable 8-0 victory. Shearer's feat matched Andy Cole's Carling Premiership record,

for Manchester United in the 9-0 win against Ipswich Town four years earlier. Shearer scored 70 percent of his goals at St James' Park while Newcastle's attack overall scored 52 percent of the home goals but only 43 percent of those claimed away. However, few other goals came from strikers; Duncan Ferguson added six and Kevin Gallacher, signed from Blackburn in September for £700,000, scored two more.

The midfield goals were led by Gary Speed with the Welsh skipper's nine proving to be his best return

GOALS BY TIME PERIOD 1999/2000
for the latest stats and to share your memories go to football.co.uk

key:
- goals for
- goals against

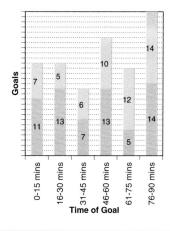

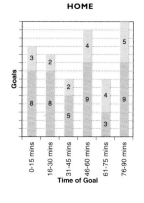

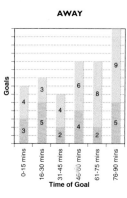

Goal Analysis

powered by football.co.uk

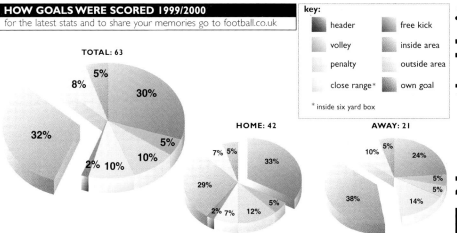

HOW GOALS WERE SCORED 1999/2000
for the latest stats and to share your memories go to football.co.uk

key:
header · free kick · volley · inside area · penalty · outside area · close range* · own goal
* inside six yard box

TOTAL: 63

HOME: 42

AWAY: 21

for four years. From defence, Newcastle scored a greater percentage of their goals than at any time in the Carling Premiership with Nikos Dabizas and Didier Domi leading the way.

The best time to watch United games if you wanted goals was in the last 15 minutes. Newcastle scored 14 and so did the opposition. But they were highly effective in the opening 30 minutes of games, scoring 24. At St James' Park, Newcastle scored the same amount in either half but they conceded only seven at home in the first half compared to 13 in the second period. But away from home they were at their most vulnerable in the final 30 minutes, letting in 17 goals during that period.

Newcastle scored more headed goals in last season's Carling Premiership than any other team; a total of 19 headers were scored, representing 30 per cent of their goals. Shearer made a massive contribution but Speed and Ferguson were also major contributors with headed goals.

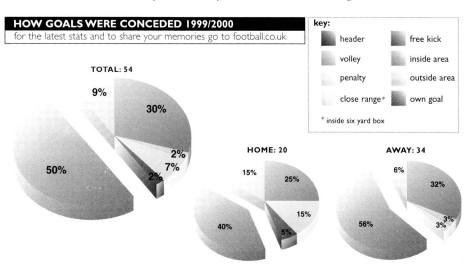

HOW GOALS WERE CONCEDED 1999/2000
for the latest stats and to share your memories go to football.co.uk

key:
header · free kick · volley · inside area · penalty · outside area · close range* · own goal
* inside six yard box

TOTAL: 54

HOME: 20

AWAY: 34

What a difference a CARLING makes.

Newcastle United

Squad and Performance

powered by football.co.uk

SQUAD LIST

for the latest stats and to share your memories go to football.co.uk

Position	Name	Appearances	Appearances as substitute	Goals / Clean Sheets	Yellow Cards	Red Cards
G	S.Given	14		6		
G	S.Harper	18		5	1	
G	J.Karelse	3		1		
G	T.Wright	3				
D	W.Barton	33	1		5	1
D	D.Beharall		2			
D	H.Cristovao	3			1	
D	N.Dabizas	29		4	5	1
D	D.Domi	19	8	3	2	
D	A.Goma	14			5	
D	A.Griffin	1	2	1		
D	R.Helder	5			1	1
D	S.Howey	7	2		1	
D	A.Hughes	22	5	2		
D	E.Marcelino	10	1		2	
D	A.Pistone	15			1	1
D	C.Serrant	2				
M	L.Charvet	1	1			
M	F.Dumas	6			1	
M	K.Dyer	27	3	3	1	
M	J.Fumaca	1	4			
M	D.Gavilan	2	4	1		
M	S.Glass	1	6	1		
M	R.Lee	30			5	
M	S.Maric	3	10			
M	J.McClen	3	6		2	
M	N.Solano	29	1	3	6	
M	G.Speed	36		9	6	
F	D.Ferguson	17	6	6	1	
F	K.Gallacher	15	5	2		
F	T.Ketsbaia	11	10			
F	P.Robinson	2	8			
F	A.Shearer	36	1	23	2	1

Newcastle used 33 players, more than any other Carling Premiership squad. The most regular performers were Shearer and Speed who, with 36 appearances, took his total of Carling Premiership appearances to 288; only Wednesday's Peter Atherton (291) has made more appearances in the competition. Warren Barton and Robert Lee also made 30 appearances or more; when the season began Lee had not even been assigned a squad number by Gullit but went on to become one of the Magpies's most consistent performers. Newcastle managed to enjoy at least one win against 13 different teams but they only succeeded in taking all six points off Wednesday; after the 8-0 home win they won 2-0 at Hillsborough.

TEAM PERFORMANCE TABLE

for the latest stats and to share your memories go to football.co.uk

Position	Club	Points Won	Percentage of points won at home	percentage of points won away	overall percentage of points won
1.	MANCHESTER UNITED	3/6			
2.	ARSENAL	4/6			
3.	LEEDS UNITED	1/6	53%	7%	30%
4.	LIVERPOOL	1/6			
5.	CHELSEA	0/6			
6.	ASTON VILLA	3/6			
7.	SUNDERLAND	1/6			
8.	LEICESTER CITY	3/6	27%	47%	37%
9.	TOTTENHAM HOTSPUR	3/6			
10.	WEST HAM UNITED	1/6			
11.	NEWCASTLE UNITED	52 pts			
12.	MIDDLESBROUGH	4/6			
13.	EVERTON	4/6	83%	33%	58%
14.	SOUTHAMPTON	3/6			
15.	COVENTRY CITY	3/6			
16.	DERBY COUNTY	4/6			
17.	BRADFORD CITY	3/6			
18.	WIMBLEDON	1/6	87%	33%	60%
19.	SHEFFIELD WEDNESDAY	6/6			
20.	WATFORD	4/6			

The figures show a team's performance against clubs in each quarter of the final league table. The first column represents points won from the total available against each team in the league.

What a difference a CARLING makes.

Discipline and Season Summary

Newcastle United

BOOKINGS BY POSITION 1997/1998 - 1999/2000
for the latest stats and to share your memories go to football.co.uk

key:
- forward
- midfield
- defence
- goalkeeper

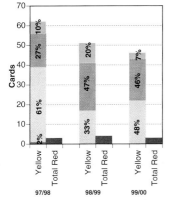

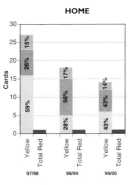

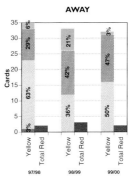

In common with several other Carling Premiership rivals, Newcastle increased their goal tally while reducing their number of cautions. They collected 46 yellow cards, their lowest number of bookings since the 1993-94 season and fewer than all but three of the other Carling Premiership teams. Shearer collected only two cautions, a marked improvement on the six he collected a season earlier, while Ferguson was the only other striker to be yellow carded. The worst offenders were the defence with Barton (with four yellow cards in the first seven games), Dabizas and Alain Goma all picking up five cautions; in midfield Speed and Solano offended the most. The bookings chart shows that Newcastle were

almost angelic at home but were given considerably more cautions away.

Just 14 bookings were issued to Newcastle players at St James' Park, in eight games. In the other 11, Newcastle avoided a booking; either that reflects their duty at home or the power of persuasion from the vocal Toon Army. Shearer was sent off there in the opening game of the season while but Barton and Nikos Dabozas also saw red.

Newcastle's standing at half time was rarely a pointer to the final outcome. On 15 occasions they led at the interval but went on to win nine. Similarly, at half time they were level in 16 games but they managed to win five and lose six.

HALF TIME - FULL TIME COMPARATIVE CHART
for the latest stats and to share your memories go to football.co.uk

HOME

Number of Home Half Time Wins	Full Time Result W	L	D
10	7	1	2

Number of Home Half Time Losses	Full Time Result W	L	D
3	0	2	1

Number of Home Half Time Draws	Full Time Result W	L	D
6	3	1	2

AWAY

Number of Away Half Time Wins	Full Time Result W	L	D
5	2	1	2

Number of Away Half Time Losses	Full Time Result W	L	D
4	0	4	0

Number of Away Half Time Draws	Full Time Result W	L	D
10	2	5	3

TOTAL

Total Number of Half Time Wins	Full Time Result W	L	D
15	9	2	4

Total Number of Half Time Losses	Full Time Result W	L	D
7	0	6	1

Total Number of Half Time Draws	Full Time Result W	L	D
16	5	6	5

What a difference a *CARLING* makes.

Maps and Directions

Newcastle United play at St James' Park, half a mile from Newcastle city centre. The metro system is very efficient and there is a station by the ground. There is no car parking at the ground although limited car parking is available on Barrack Road.

From the North:
Exit A1 onto the A167 Ponteland Road heading towards the city centre. At the fourth roundabout after approximately 1½ miles, turn left onto Jedburgh Road. Take the first exit, turning right onto Grandstand Road and then left onto the A189 Ponteland Road. Keep on this road which becomes Barrack Road until the roundabout. The ground is on the left.

From the South:
From the A1(M) turn off at the junction with the A1 and continue on the A1 until the junction with the A184. Turn onto the the A184 and continue along this road, bearing left onto the A189. Continue over the River Tyne on the Redheugh Bridge, go straight over the roundabout onto Blenheim Street and continue until you meet Bath Lane. Turn left into Bath Lane, right into Corporation Street, and left at the roundabout into Gallowgate. At the next roundabout Barrack Road and the ground are straight ahead.

Newcastle Central Railway Station is half a mile from St James' park. The metro runs every 3-4 minutes to St James' Station.

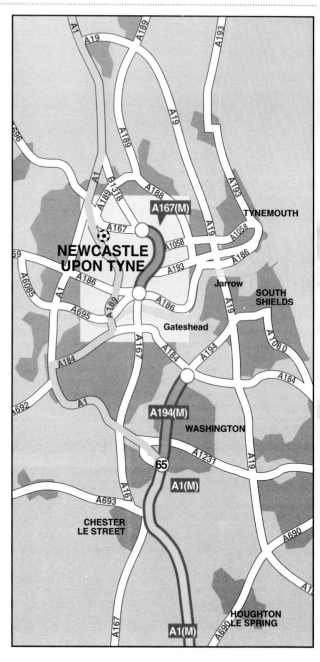

powered by football.co.uk

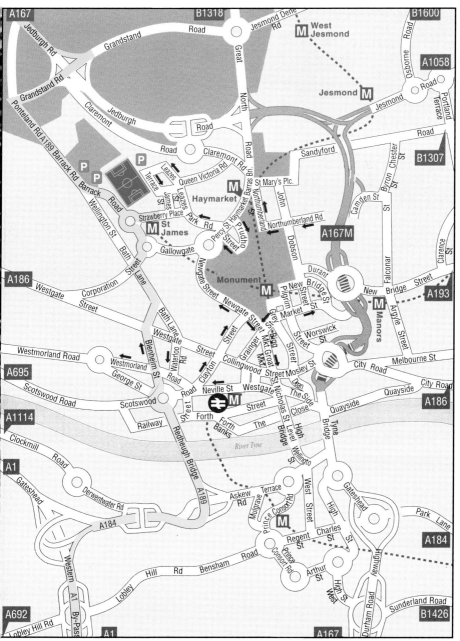

Newcastle United

177

Club Honours

- Division 3 Champions: 1921-22 (South), 1959-60
- FA Cup Winners: 1976

Club Records

- Victory: 9-3 v Wolverhampton Wanderers, Division 2, September 18, 1965
- Defeat: 0-8 v Tottenham Hotspur, Division 2, March 28, 1936; 0-8 v Everton, Division 1, November 20, 1971
- League goals in a season (team): 112, Division 3 (South), 1957-58
- League goals in a season (player): 39, Derek Reeves, Division 3, 1959-60
- Career league goals: 185, Mike Channon, 1966-77, 1979-82
- League appearances: 713, Terry Paine, 1956-74
- Transfer fee paid: £2,000,000 to Sheffield Wednesday for David Hirst, October, 1997
- Transfer fee received: £7,250,000 from Blackburn Rovers for Kevin Davies, May, 1998

Pos		Pld	W	D	L	F	A	Pts
15	Southampton	38	12	8	18	45	62	44

Southampton
"The Saints"

The Dell, Milton Road,
Southampton SO15 2XH
Tel: 01703 220 505
www.saintsfc.co.uk

Season Review by
John Ley

The Daily Telegraph

Manager Dave Jones signed Wolves' Dean Richards then Coventry's Trond Soltvedt and former Saint Kevin Davies arrived. Soon afterwards Arsenal's Luis Boa Morte was signed and three wins from the opening five games represented a healthy start for one of the perennial strugglers in the Carling Premiership. At one stage Southampton were sixth but it was to turn into a traumatic season with Jones given a year's leave of absence for personal reasons and former England boss Glenn Hoddle drafted in, in January. By then, Saints were 17th and facing their annual battle to stay in the top flight. Injuries affected Stuart Ripley, Paul Jones, David Hughes, Richard Dryden, John Beresford, David Howells and David Hirst, who eventually retired in January, but the arrivals of Jo Tessem and Tahar El Khalej strengthened the squad while Marian Pahars's improvement continued. Mark Hughes left, for Everton, but Southampton were safe before the end of the season.

Useful Information

The Saints Shop
The Dell, Milton Road,
Southampton
Opening Times:
Monday-Friday: 9.00am-5.00pm
Match Saturdays: 9.00am-5.00pm
Match Evenings: 9.00am-10.00pm
Tel: **01703 236 400**
Mail Order Service: **01703 236 400**

The Saints Shop
Unit 29, The Bargate Centre,
Southampton
Opening Times:
Monday-Friday: 9.00am-5.00pm
Match Saturdays: 9.00am-5.00pm
Tel: **01703 333 105**

New Stadium
New stadium is open to the public on the 19th August 2001.

Stadium Tours
Visit dressing rooms, boardroom and pitch. Contact Terry Marshall:
01703 225 921

Literature
Programme £2
Saints magazine £2.50

Social Activities
Children's Social Club.
Tel: **01703 334 172**

What a difference a CARLING makes.

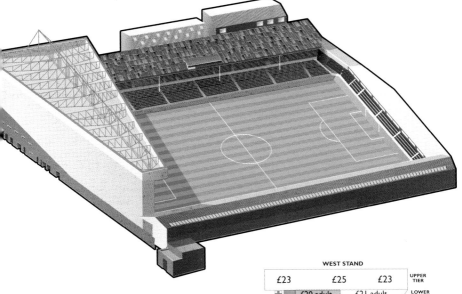

The Dell

Opened: September 3, 1898
Capacity: 15,525
1999/2000 highest attendance: 15,257
1999/2000 average attendance: 15,132
Record attendance: 31,044

WEST STAND

			UPPER TIER
£23	£25	£23	
£20 adult £8 child	£21 adult £8 child		LOWER TIER

MILTON ROAD STAND — £23 adult £8 child

ARCHERS ROAD STAND — £23 adult £8 child

LOWER TIER	£21 adult £8 child	
UPPER TIER	£23	£25	£21 / £23

EAST STAND

| VISITORS ENCLOSURE | FAMILY ENCLOSURE | DISABLED FANS | FIRST AID |

Corporate Hospitality

Executive Club includes hospitality with seat for match, lunch, half time and full time refreshments. Matchday sponsorship for 12 people includes seats in Directors Box, 4-course lunch and advertising opportunities. Matchball package for 4 people Includes seats in Executive Box, 4-course lunch and advertising opportunities.
Contact Kim Lawford:
01703 331 417

Pre-Match & Half Time Entertainment

Local bands and junior soccer competitions. Super Saint mascot.

Booking Information

General Enquiries:
01703 220 505
Credit Card Bookings:
01703 337 171
Travel Club and Young Saints:
01703 334 172
Recorded Information:
01703 228 575

Results Breakdown

POINTS WON OR LOST AT BOTH HOME AND AWAY

for the latest stats and to share your memories go to football.co.uk

key:
- win
- draw
- loss
- -0- league position
- home fixtures are in red

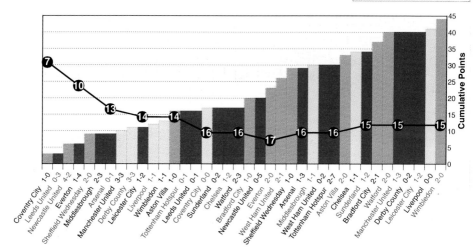

Three wins in five games were followed by a sequence of seven games without a win that saw Saints slump to 14th place. Egil Ostenstad was swapped with Davies but with James Beattie missing the start with broken ribs, Southampton were limited in attack. Matt Le Tissier started the first three but injury caused Saints' favourite son to struggle to make the side. Meanwhile, the results got worse with five defeats and a draw, against Coventry, and the pressure was building on Jones. The Saints, though, were rallying after beating Everton but the

board decided to release their manager and brought in Hoddle, who started with a 2-1 win over West Ham and 1-0 victory at Sheffield Wednesday. Jones had won six games in 22; Hoddle won the same number in 16 with victories over Bradford and Watford giving them the edge over their rivals fighting against relegation. Their away form was again disappointing, a poor run of form saw them losing seven out of eight consecutive away games.

Overall they claimed fewer goals at The Dell but Hoddle's men improved away, doubling the club's

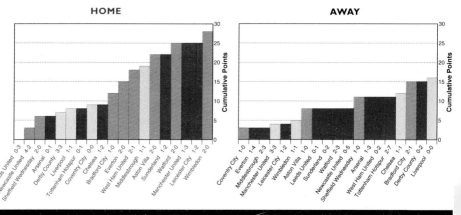

THE F.A. CARLING PREMIERSHIP

Results Table

Southampton

Legend: ● = Red Card ◣ = Yellow Card ▲ = Player substituted 00 = Time of goal

DATE	H/A	OPPONENT	H/T	F/T	POS	REFEREE	TEAM (line-up)	SUBSTITUTES USED
07/08	A	Coventry City	0-0	1-0	7	P.Jones	Jones, Richards, Benali, Dodd, Marsden▲, Lundekvam, Kachloul◣, Le Tissier▲, Hughes, Osterstad 85, Pahars	Ripley▲, Beresford▲
11/08	H	Leeds United	0-1	0-3	14	A.G.Wiley	Jones, Richards, Benali, Dodd, Marsden▲, Lundekvam, Kachloul◣, Le Tissier▲, Hughes, Osterstad, Pahars	Oakley▲, Ripley▲
15/08	A	Newcastle United	0-1	4-2	6	D.R.Elleray	Jones, Richards, Benali, Hiley, Oakley▲, Lundekvam, Kachloul, Le Tissier▲, Hughes 78, Osterstad, Pahars 66	Soltvedt▲, Bridge▲, Bradley▲
21/08	A	Everton	0-1	1-4	10	B.Knight	Jones, Richards, Benali, Dodd, Soltvedt, Lundekvam, Kachloul◣, Ripley, Hughes, Oakley 84, Pahars ▲70	Bridge▲, Oakley▲, Bradley▲
28/08	H	Sheffield Wednesday	0-0	2-0	9	P.E.Alcock	Jones, Richards, Benali, Dodd, Soltvedt, Lundekvam, Kachloul 53, Ripley▲, Hughes, Boo Monte 84, Pahars	Boo Monte▲
11/09	H	Middlesbrough	1-1	2-3	13	S.J.Lodge	Jones, Richards, Benali, Dodd, Soltvedt, Lundekvam, Kachloul 15, Ripley▲, Hughes, Boo Monte ●, Pahars ▲55	Beattie▲, Beattie▲
18/09	H	Arsenal	0-0	0-1	13	G.P.Barber	Jones, Richards, Benali, Dodd, Soltvedt, Lundekvam, Kachloul, Oakley▲, Hughes, Bridge▲, Pahars	Oakley▲, Le Tissier▲, Almeida▲
25/09	A	Manchester United	1-2	3-3	13	S.W.Dunn	Jones, Richards, Benali, Dodd, Soltvedt, Lundekvam, Kachloul, Ripley, Hughes, Oakley, Pahars ▲17	Marsden▲, Le Tissier▲57 73, Beattie▲
04/10	H	Derby County	2-1	3-3	13	G.Poll	Jones, Richards, Benali, Dodd, Hiley, Oakley 35, Kachloul◣, Ripley 66, Hughes, Le Tissier▲, Pahars 22	Beattie▲, Boo Monte▲
16/10	A	Leicester City	0-2	1-2	14	B.Knight	Jones, Richards, Benali, Dodd, Marsden, Lundekvam, Kachloul, Ripley▲, Hughes, Le Tissier▲, Pahars 84	Boo Monte▲, Le Tissier▲, Davies●
23/10	H	Liverpool	1-0	1-1	14	N.S.Barry	Jones, Richards, Benali, Dodd, Soltvedt ▲39, Lundekvam, Kachloul, Le Tissier▲, Hughes, Oakley, Pahars ▲63	Ripley▲, Beattie▲
30/10	A	Wimbledon	0-0	1-1	14	S.J.Lodge	Jones, Richards 84, Benali, Dodd, Soltvedt, Lundekvam, Kachloul, Ripley▲, Hughes, Oakley, Pahars	Oakley▲, Beattie▲
06/11	A	Aston Villa	0-0	0-1	14	A.P.D'Urso	Jones, Colleter, Colleter, Tessem, Oakley, Lundekvam ●, Kachloul, Ripley▲, Hughes, Beattie▲, Pahars	Boo Monte▲, Beattie▲, Soltvedt▲
20/11	H	Tottenham Hotspur	0-0	0-1	14	S.G.Bennett	Jones, Richards, Colleter ●, Tessem, Oakley, Lundekvam, Kachloul, Ripley▲, Hughes, Soltvedt, Pahars	Beattie▲, Boo Monte▲
28/11	A	Leeds United	0-0	0-1	16	R.J.Harris	Jones, Richards, Benali, Dodd, Tessem, Lundekvam, Kachloul◣, Ripley▲, Hughes, Beattie, Pahars	Davies▲
04/12	H	Coventry City	0-0	0-0	16	J.T.Winter	Jones▲, Richards, Benali, Dodd, Tessem▲, Lundekvam, Kachloul, Ripley, Coleter, Beattie, Pahars	Moss▲, Le Tissier▲, Beattie▲
18/12	A	Sunderland	0-2	1-2	16	M.D.Reed	Jones, Richards, Benali, Dodd, Soltvedt▲, Lundekvam, Kachloul◣, Le Tissier, Oakley▲, Soltvedt, Pahars	Tessem▲, Boo Monte▲, Davies▲80
26/12	H	Chelsea	1-2	0-2	16	P.E.Alcock	Jones▲, Richards, Benali, Dodd, Tessem, Lundekvam, Kachloul◣, Oakley, Hughes▲, Beattie, Davies 61	Davies▲, Boo Monte▲, Kachloul▲
28/12	A	Watford	0-2	2-3	16	M.A.Riley	Jones, Richards, Benali, Marsden, Tessem, Lundekvam, Soltvedt, Le Tissier, Boo Monte 61, Boo Monte, Davies 63	Ripley▲▲
03/01	H	Bradford City	0-0	1-1	16	D.R.Elleray	Jones, Richards, Marsden, Dryden▲, Colleter, Lundekvam, Bridge, Ripley, Boo Monte, Davies 55, Pahars	Beresford▲, Benali▲, Monk▲
16/01	A	Newcastle United	0-4	0-5	17	N.S.Barry	Jones, Richards, Colleter▲, Monk, Tessem, Soltvedt, Boo Monte ◣, Ripley, Hughes, Beattie, Beattie	Beresford▲, Soltvedt▲, Beattie▲
22/01	H	Everton	0-0	2-0	17	A.P.D'Urso	Jones, Richards, Benali, Dodd, Tessem 47, Lundekvam, Oakley ◣56, Marsden, Boo Monte▲, Davies, Pahars	Soltvedt▲, Beattie▲, Beresford▲
05/02	H	West Ham United	1-0	1-0	14	B.Knight	Jones, Richards, Benali, Bridge, Colleter▲, Tessem, Kachloul, Marsden, Boo Monte▲, Davies, Pahars ▲54	Bridge▲, Soltvedt▲, Hughes▲
12/02	A	Sheffield Wednesday	1-0	1-0	14	A.G.Wiley	Jones, Richards, Benali, Dodd, Colleter▲, Tessem 28, Kachloul, Marsden, Oakley, Davies, Pahars	Beattie▲, Hughes▲, Boo Monte▲
26/02	H	Arsenal	0-2	1-3	16	J.T.Winter	Jones, Richards 51, Benali, Dodd, Colleter▲, Tessem, Kachloul, Marsden, Oakley, Beattie ▲44, Pahars	Hughes▲, Boo Monte▲
04/03	A	Middlesbrough	1-1	1-1	15	S.J.Lodge	Jones, Bridge, Benali, Dodd, Tessem, Lundekvam, Kachloul 4, Marsden, Oakley, Davies, Pahars 44	Boo Monte▲
08/03	A	West Ham United	0-2	0-2	15	M.R.Halsey	Jones, Oakley, Benali, El-Khalej 33, Tessem 26, Oakley, Kachloul, Marsden, Bridge, Davies, Pahars	Le Tissier▲, Rodrigues▲
11/03	H	Tottenham Hotspur	2-4	2-7	15	M.A.Riley	Jones, Richards, Benali, El-Khalej, Tessem 67, Oakley, Kachloul◣, Marsden, Hughes▲, Davies 39 63, Pahars	Soltvedt▲
18/03	H	Aston Villa	0-0	0-0	15	M.A.Riley	Jones, Richards, El-Khalej, Dodd, Tessem▲, Lundekvam, Kachloul ●, Marsden, Bridge, Davies, Pahars	Soltvedt▲
25/03	A	Chelsea	0-1	1-2	15	D.J.Gallagher	Jones▲, Richards, El-Khalej, Dodd, Tessem 67, Oakley, Kachloul, Marsden, Bridge, Davies, Pahars	Moss▲, Le Tissier▲90, Kachloul▲
01/04	H	Sunderland	0-1	1-2	15	P.A.Durkin	Moss, Richards, El-Khalej, Dodd, Tessem▲, Lundekvam, Oakley◣, Marsden 56, Bridge, Davies, Pahars	Le Tissier▲, Pahars ▲76
08/04	A	Bradford City	0-2	2-1	15	D.R.Elleray	Moss, Richards, El-Khalej, Benali, Tessem, El-Khalej, Marsden 56, Ripley, Bridge, Davies, Le Tissier	Soltvedt▲, Pahars ▲75
15/04	H	Watford	1-0	2-0	15	A.B.Wilkie	Moss, Richards, El-Khalej, Bridge, Tessem, Lundekvam, Marsden, Le Tissier, Bridge, Davies 4, Beattie ▲75	Kachloul▲, Oakley▲
22/04	A	Manchester United	0-3	1-3	15	N.S.Barry	Moss, Richards, Benali◣, Dodd, Tessem, Lundekvam, Kachloul, Bridge, Bridge, Davies, Pahars ▲84	Oakley▲, Oakley▲, Le Tissier▲
24/04	H	Derby County	0-2	2-0	15	P.Jones	Moss, Richards, El-Khalej, Dodd, Marsden▲, Oakley, Kachloul◣4, Ripley▲, Soltvedt, Beattie▲, Beattie	Davies▲, Tessem▲, Boo Monte▲
29/04	A	Leicester City	1-2	1-2	15	M.D.Reed	Moss, Richards ●, El-Khalej, Dodd, Tessem, El-Khalej, Kachloul, Ripley▲, Bridge, Davies, Pahars	Rodrigues▲, Oakley▲
07/05	H	Liverpool	0-0	0-0	15	P.E.Alcock	Moss, Richards, El-Khalej, Dodd, Tessem, Lundekvam, Soltvedt◣, Soltvedt▲, Bridge, Davies, Pahars	Marsden▲
14/05	A	Wimbledon	2-0	2-0	15	S.J.Lodge	Oakley, Oakley, El-Khalej, Dodd, Tessem, Lundekvam, Kachloul◣, Soltvedt▲, Bridge 57, Davies, Pahars 79	Rodrigues▲

181

Goal Analysis

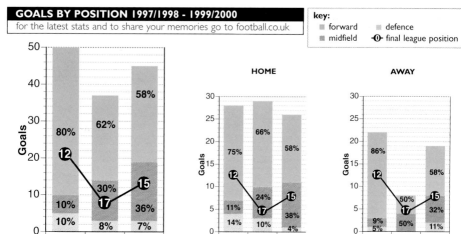

GOALS BY POSITION 1997/1998 - 1999/2000
for the latest stats and to share your memories go to football.co.uk

key:
- forward
- midfield
- defence
- final league position

HOME | AWAY

worst ever away day goal tally the previous season. The 26 goals they scored at home was their poorest total at The Dell for four seasons – only four teams scored fewer at home. However, they also conceded fewer goals there than at any time since the 1995-96 term. But away from home they conceded 40 goals; only the three teams who were relegated to Division One let in more on their travels. The man who led the way with goals was Pahars. The little Latvian quickly developed a taste for the Carling

Premiership after scoring three goals in six games the previous season and the 13 goals he added was the highest haul by a Southampton player since Le Tissier scored the same amount in the 1996-97 season. Kevin Davies scored six goals on his return to the south coast while Le Tissier stole two against Manchester United at Old Trafford after coming on as a substitute, and when he added a penalty in the 2-1 home defeat it was his 100th goal in the Carling Premiership, allowing Le Tissier to join an elite band

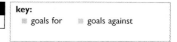

GOALS BY TIME PERIOD 1999/2000
for the latest stats and to share your memories go to football.co.uk

key:
- goals for
- goals against

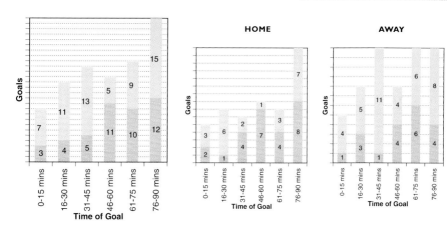

Goal Analysis

powered by football.co.uk

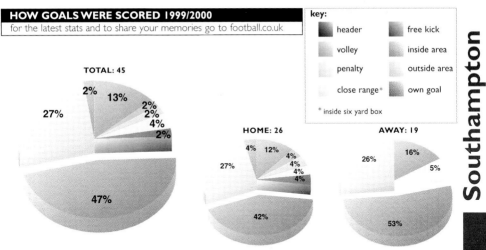

HOW GOALS WERE SCORED 1999/2000

for the latest stats and to share your memories go to football.co.uk

key:
- header
- volley
- penalty
- close range*
- free kick
- inside area
- outside area
- own goal

* inside six yard box

TOTAL: 45
- 2%
- 13%
- 2%
- 2%
- 4%
- 2%
- 27%
- 47%

HOME: 26
- 4%
- 12%
- 4%
- 4%
- 4%
- 27%
- 42%

AWAY: 19
- 16%
- 26%
- 5%
- 53%

Southampton

of players who have reached a century in the competition – Alan Shearer, Ian Wright, Les Ferdinand, Robbie Fowler and Andy Cole. Le Tissier actually scored fewer League goals than at any time since the 1987-88 season but his overall League total is now 161.

Encouragingly for Hoddle, more Saints' players scored goals than at any time for 20 years; not since the days of Phil Boyer, Mick Channon, Charlie George and Nick Holmes have the goals been shared by so many with no fewer than 16 players scoring Southampton's 45 goals.

The Saints rarely got going early on; only two goals were scored in the opening 15 minutes while just 12 of their 45 came in the first half; the remaining 33 second half strikers represents 73 per cent of their goals. But they showed a vulnerability to concede goals before half time; of the 62 they conceded, 24 were scored in the final half an hour of the first half.

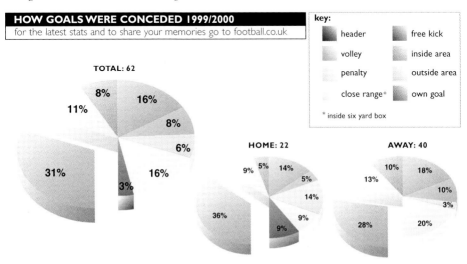

HOW GOALS WERE CONCEDED 1999/2000

for the latest stats and to share your memories go to football.co.uk

key:
- header
- volley
- penalty
- close range*
- free kick
- inside area
- outside area
- own goal

* inside six yard box

TOTAL: 62
- 8%
- 16%
- 11%
- 8%
- 6%
- 31%
- 3%
- 16%

HOME: 22
- 5%
- 14%
- 9%
- 5%
- 14%
- 36%
- 9%
- 9%

AWAY: 40
- 10%
- 18%
- 13%
- 10%
- 3%
- 28%
- 20%

Squad and Performance

SQUAD LIST

for the latest stats and to share your memories go to football.co.uk

Position	Name	Appearances	Appearances as substitute	Goals	Clean Sheets	Yellow Cards	Red Cards
G	P.Jones	31			8		
G	N.Moss	7	2		3		
D	M.Almeida		1				
D	F.Benali	25	1			4	
D	J.Beresford		3				
D	P.Colleter	8				2	1
D	J.Dodd	30	1			5	
D	R.Dryden	1					
D	S.Hiley	3					
D	G.Monk	1	1				
D	D.Richards	35			2	4	1
M	T.El-Khalej	11		1		2	
M	H.Kachloul	29	3	5		8	
M	C.Lundekvam	25	1			3	1
M	C.Marsden	19	2	1		7	
M	M.Oakley	26	5	3		3	
M	S.Ripley	18	5	1		1	
M	T.Soltvedt	17	6	1			
M	J.Tessem	23	2	4			
F	J.Beattie	8	10			2	
F	L.Boa Morte	6	8	1		1	1
F	S.Bradley		1			1	
F	W.Bridge	15	3	1			
F	K.Davies	19	4	6		6	1
F	M.Hughes M	18	2	1		8	
F	M.Le Tissier	9	9	3		3	
F	E.Ostenstad	3		1		2	
F	M.Pahars	31	2	13		5	
F	D.Rodrigues		2				

Not only were goals shared around; Southampton used 29 players with goalkeeper Paul Jones deprived of a full season because of a back injury while Pahars, Jason Dodd and Hassan Kachloul were all regular performers. Matt Le Tissier started only nine games and came on as a substitute in another nine; his 18 appearances were his fewest appearances in 14 seasons at The Dell.

Not for the first time, Saints were comfortable against the poorer teams but struggled against the best. They beat only one of the top nine teams, winning both at home and away against Aston Villa. But they failed to glean a single point against five different teams, all in the top nine. They did, however, get one point against the champions.

TEAM PERFORMANCE TABLE

for the latest stats and to share your memories go to football.co.uk

Position	Club	Points Won	Percentage of points won at home	percentage of points won away	overall percentage of points won
1.	MANCHESTER UNITED	1/6			
2.	ARSENAL	0/6			
3.	LEEDS UNITED	0/6	7%	20%	13%
4.	LIVERPOOL	2/6			
5.	CHELSEA	1/6			
6.	ASTON VILLA	6/6			
7.	SUNDERLAND	0/6			
8.	LEICESTER CITY	0/6	40%	20%	30%
9.	TOTTENHAM HOTSPUR	0/6			
10.	WEST HAM UNITED	3/6			
11.	NEWCASTLE UNITED	3/6			
12.	MIDDLESBROUGH	1/6			
13.	EVERTON	3/6	67%	25%	46%
14.	SOUTHAMPTON	44 pts			
15.	COVENTRY CITY	4/6			
16.	DERBY COUNTY	1/6			
17.	BRADFORD CITY	6/6			
18.	WIMBLEDON	4/6	87%	47%	67%
19.	SHEFFIELD WEDNESDAY	6/6			
20.	WATFORD	3/6			

The figures show a team's performance against clubs in each quarter of the final league table. The first column represents points won from the total available against each team in the league.

What a difference a CARLING makes.

Discipline and Season Summary

BOOKINGS BY POSITION 1997/1998 - 1999/2000

for the latest stats and to share your memories go to football.co.uk

key:
- ■ forward
- ■ defence
- ■ midfield
- ■ goalkeeper

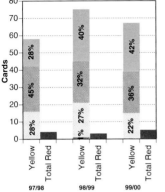

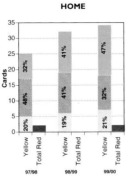

HOME

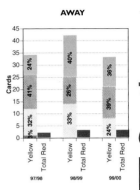

AWAY

Southampton

Typically, bookings were also shared around with 18 Southampton players collecting 67 cautions and five dismissals. The bookings total was lower than the previous season but the five red cards was their worst number of early baths in the Carling Premiership with only Everton and West Ham collecting more. The first to be dismissed was Luis Boa Morte, sent off on his full debut, at Middlesbrough, for handling on the line. Davies was next, dismissed just nine minutes after coming on, after a bad challenge on Leicester's Gerry Taggart. Claus Lundekvam and Patrick Colleter were next and then Saints went five months without a red card until Richards went, at home to

Leicester, in added time after kicking Welshman Robbie Savage.

Given Southampton's scarcity of early goals it is not surprising that they led at the interval on only five occasions throughout the season and of that total they actually went on to win only three – against Sheffield Wednesday, Aston Villa and Watford. Five times they were behind at half time and twice they had conceded four goals in the first 45 minutes. At Newcastle they were 4-0 down by half time, while at White Hart Lane, they were leading 2-1 with Spurs' strike coming from a Richards own goal! But by half time they were 4-2 down and went on to lose 7-2.

HALF TIME - FULL TIME COMPARATIVE CHART

for the latest stats and to share your memories go to football.co.uk

HOME

	Full Time Result		
	W	L	D
Number of Home Half Time Wins			
4	2	0	2
Number of Home Half Time Losses			
5	1	4	0
Number of Home Half Time Draws			
10	5	3	2

AWAY

	Full Time Result		
	W	L	D
Number of Away Half Time Wins			
1	1	0	0
Number of Away Half Time Losses			
10	0	9	1
Number of Away Half Time Draws			
8	3	2	3

TOTAL

	Full Time Result		
	W	L	D
Total Number of Half Time Wins			
5	3	0	2
Total Number of Half Time Losses			
15	1	13	1
Total Number of Half Time Draws			
18	8	5	5

Maps and Directions

Southampton play at The Dell, half a mile from the city centre.
It is usually possible to park near the ground.

From the North:
Follow the M3 to the end exiting at s/p M27 west, Southampton docks. After 3/4 of a mile where the road forks bear left onto the A33 s/p Southampton. At second roundabout take the first exit into Bassett Avenue which becomes the Avenue. After 1 1/4 miles turn right s/p County Cricket and the Dell. The ground is at the T junction.

From the West:
From the M27 exit at Junction 3, turning right onto the M271. At roundabout after 1 1/2 miles turn left onto the A35. Straight on over the flyover s/p city centre A3024. After 1 1/4 turn left s/p Shirley/Portswood into Paynes Rd. Carry straight on over two crossroads into Archers Rd.

From the East:
From the M27 exit at Junction 5 left onto the Swaythling Link Road A335 and on onto the High Road. Turn right where the road divides onto the A35 Burgess Road for 1 mile. Turn left onto The Avenue and the same as North.

Southampton Central Railway Station is a 10 minute walk from the ground.

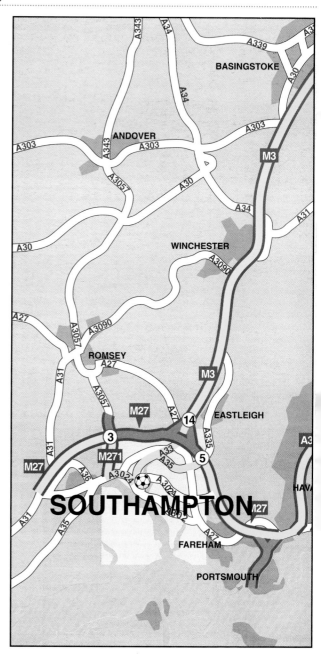

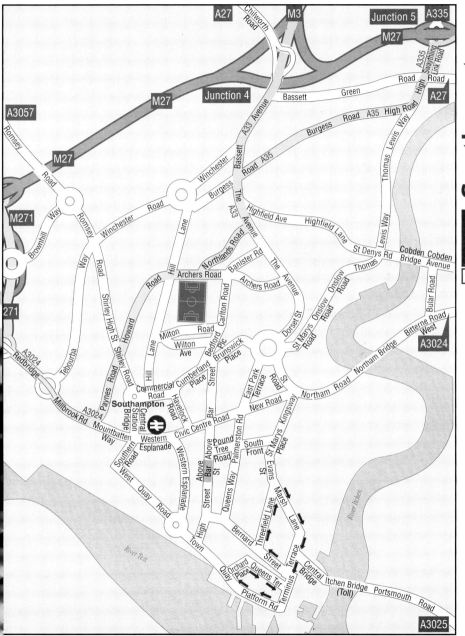

Southampton

187

Club Honours

- Football League Champions: 1891-92, 1892-93, 1894-95, 1901-02, 1912-13, 1935-36
- Division 1 Champions: 1995-96, 1998-99
- Division 2 Champions: 1975-76
- Division 3 Champions: 1987-88
- FA Cup Winners: 1937, 1973

Club Records

- Victory: 11-1 v Fairfield, FA Cup 1st Round, February 2, 1895
- Defeat: 0-8 v West Ham United, Division 1, October 19, 1968
- League goals in a season (team): 109, Division 1, 1935-36
- League goals in a season (player): 43, Dave Halliday, Division 1, 1928-29
- Career league goals: 209, Charlie Buchan, 1911-25
- League appearances: 537, Jim Montgomery, 1962-77
- Transfer fee paid: £4,000,000 to Valencia for Stefan Schwarz, August, 1999
- Transfer fee received: £5,000,000 from Leeds for Michael Bridges, July, 1999

Pos		Pld	W	D	L	F	A	Pts
7	Sunderland	38	16	10	12	57	56	58

Sunderland
"The Black Cats"

Sunderland Stadium of Light,
Sunderland, Tyne-and-Wear SR
Tel: 0191 551 5000
www.sunderland-afc.com

Season Review by
John Ley

The Daily Telegraph

Sunderland arrived on the back of a record season in the First Division, where they had scored 91 goals and won 105 points. Peter Reid, who celebrated 200 games in charge against Chelsea in December, signed Stefan Schwarz and Steve Bould and although he sold Michael Bridges and Lee Clark, he also added Marseille's Erik Roy and Kevin Kilbane from West Bromwich Albion. The season owed much to two strikers; one a tried and trusted forward and another former shelf packer who had come from non league football only five years earlier. Niall Quinn and Kevin Phillips respectively proved to be the answer to any critics who thought Sunderland, like so many predecessors, would tumble back from whence they came. With Schwarz and Bould outstanding, Sunderland shot into second place by October and, but for a disappointing patch of away form, could have finished higher than seventh. The deadline arrival of Honduran international Milton Nunez will add weight to the attack.

Useful Information

Stadium of Light
Sunderland SR5 1SU
Opening Times:
Monday-Saturday: 9.00am 5.00pm
Sundays: 11.00am-5.00pm
Match Saturdays: 9.00am-5.30pm
Match Sundays: 11.00am-30
minutes after final whistle
Match Evenings: 9.00am-10.00pm
Tel: **0191 551 5050**

City Centre
10 Market Square,
Sunderland SR1 3HL
Opening Times:
Monday-Saturday: 9.00am-5.00pm
Tel: **0191 564 0002**
Mail Order Service: **0191 385 2778**
also: Metro Centre Store, 62
Garden Walk, Gateshead
Tel: **0191 461 0582**

Stadium Tours
Every day except matchdays and
Bank Holidays.
Tel: **0191 551 5055**

Corporate Hospitality
Space for 3,000 guests, and a wide
variety of sponsorship packages.
The Stadium of Light includes an
extensive range of hospitality
facilities incorporating:

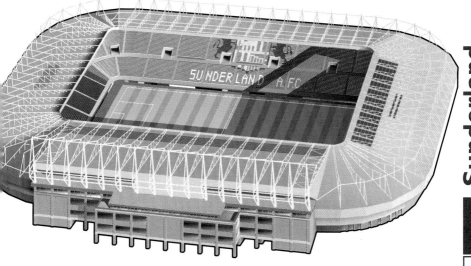

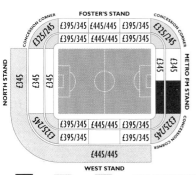

FOSTER'S STAND

CONCESSION CORNER

CONCESSION CORNER

| £395/345 | £445/445 | £395/345 |
| £395/345 | £445/445 | £395/345 |

£325/245

£325/245

£345

£345

£345

£345

£345

NORTH STAND

METRO FM STAND

£325/245

£325/245

CONCESSION CORNER

| £395/345 | £445/445 | £395/345 |
| £395/345 | | £395/345 |

£445/445

WEST STAND

VISITORS ENCLOSURE

FAMILY ENCLOSURE

STADIUM EXTENSION

SEASON TICKET PRICES 2000-2001
First listed price is for adult
second price for under 16

Stadium of Light

Opened: July 30, 1997
Capacity: 48,300
1999/2000 highest attendance: 42,026
1999/2000 average attendance: 41,323
Record attendance: 42,026

---

54 Executive boxes
Executive club membership
Directors Suite
Matchday sponsorship
Themed Bar
Tel: **0191 551 5555**

Literature

Programme £2
Monthly magazine Legion of
Light £2.95

Pre-Match & Half Time Entertainment

Arts-orientated programs before each game, e.g. Scottish Opera, Northern Symphonia, Republica Live, contemporary dance groups.

Restaurants

Sports theme restaurant, carveries and bar.
Tel: **0191 551 5555**

Booking Information

General Enquiries:
0191 551 5000
Ticket Office:
0191 551 5151
SAFC 24-7:
0191 551 5247

Results Breakdown

powered by **football**.co.uk

POINTS WON OR LOST AT BOTH HOME AND AWAY

for the latest stats and to share your memories go to football.co.uk

key:
- win
- draw
- loss
- -0- league position

home fixtures are in red

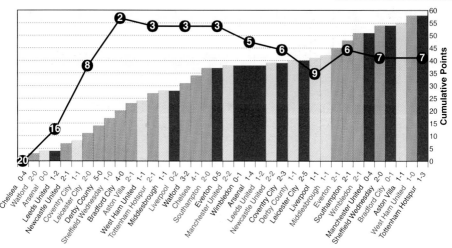

Sunderland began with a 4-0 defeat at but their first day nerves quickly gave way to a confidence propelled by the Phillips-Quinn combination and enforced by the experience of Bould. Five straight wins took Sunderland to second and at Upton Park they were one minute from going top for the first time since 1953 until West Ham's Trevor Sinclair stole a late equaliser. Though Kevin Ball left for Fulham and Thomas Helmer, after one full appearance, returned to Germany on loan, Sunderland were enjoying life. They won 5-0 and 4-0 against Derby and Bradford

respectively, and only a 2-0 defeat by Liverpool at the Stadium of Light spoiled an otherwise impressive home record. However, the 5-0 defeat at Everton – Phillips is out with an ankle injury – was the catalyst for a drop in form. Sunderland went on to lose six and draw five of their next 11 games and dropped to ninth. They rallied to finish seventh – their highest league position since1956 when they took ninth spot.

Sunderland scored 57 goals, well down on the previous record-breaking season in Division One but still bettered by only five rival Carling Premiership

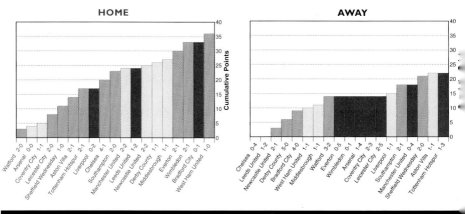

Results Table

powered by football.co.uk

Legend: ● = Red Card   ▲ = Yellow Card   ▲ = Player substituted   00 = Time of goal

Sunderland

DATE	H/A	OPPONENT	H/T	F/T	POS	REFEREE	TEAM											SUBSTITUTES USED
07/08	A	Chelsea	0-2	0-4	20	M.A.Riley	Sorensen	Makin	Bould▲	Butler P	Ball	Lumsden▲	Gray	Summerbee	Roe	Quinn	Phillips	Fredgaard▲ McCann▲ ·
10/08	H	Watford	0-0	2-0	11	J.T.Winter	Sorensen	Makin	Bould▲	Butler P	Oster▲	Schwarz	Gray	Summerbee	Roe	Quinn	Phillips 62 85	Dichio▲ McCann▲ ·
14/08	H	Arsenal	0-0	0-0	11	U.D.Rennie	Sorensen	Makin	Bould▲	Butler P	Ball▲	Schwarz	Gray▲	Summerbee	Oster▲	Quinn	Phillips	Helmer▲ McCann▲ Quinn▲
21/08	A	Leeds United	1-0	1-2	16	P.E.Alcock	Sorensen	Makin	Helmer	Butler P	McCann	Schwarz▲	Gray	Summerbee	Roe●	Quinn	Phillips 38	Quinn Holloway▲ Dichio▲
25/08	A	Newcastle United	0-1	2-1	11	G.Poll	Sorensen	Makin	Bould	Butler P	McCann	Schwarz▲	Gray	Summerbee	Roe	Quinn 64	Phillips 74	Ball▲ Boll▲ ·
29/08	H	Coventry City	0-1	1-1	12	S.J.Lodge	Sorensen	Makin	Bould	Butler P	McCann	Schwarz▲	Gray	Summerbee	Roe	Quinn	Phillips 72	Oster▲ · ·
11/09	H	Leicester City	1-0	2-0	8	A.P.D'Urso	Sorensen	Makin	Bould	Butler P	McCann 82	Schwarz▲	Gray	Summerbee	Roe	Quinn	Phillips	Williams▲ Dichio▲ ·
18/09	A	Derby County	2-0	5-0	4	P.Jones	Sorensen	Makin	Bould	Butler P 28	McCann▲24	Schwarz	Gray	Summerbee	Ball▲	Quinn▲55	Phillips 42 52 85	Roe▲ Dichio▲ Dichio▲
25/09	H	Sheffield Wednesday	0-0	1-0	4	A.G.Wiley	Sorensen	Makin	Bould	Butler P	McCann	Schwarz 50	Gray	Summerbee	Ball▲	Quinn	Phillips	Roe▲ Dichio▲ ·
02/10	A	Bradford City	1-0	4-0	2	S.G.Bennett	Sorensen	Makin	Bould	Butler P	McCann	Schwarz	Gray	Summerbee▲	Roe▲	Quinn▲68	Phillips 88 90	Williams▲ Williams▲ Roy▲
16/10	H	Aston Villa	1-0	2-1	3	D.R.Elleray	Sorensen	Makin	Bould	Butler P	McCann	Schwarz	Gray▲	Summerbee	Roe▲	Quinn	Phillips 59 82	Dichio▲ Roy▲ Boll▲
24/10	A	West Ham United	1-0	1-1	3	M.R.Halsey	Sorensen	Makin	Bould●	Butler P	McCann	Schwarz	Gray▲	Summerbee▲	Roy▲	Quinn	Phillips 23	Dichio▲ Williams▲ Boll▲
31/10	A	Tottenham Hotspur	2-0	2-1	3	M.A.Riley	Sorensen	Makin	Bould	Butler P	McCann	Schwarz 10 21	Gray	Summerbee▲	Roy▲	Quinn 10 21	Phillips	Williams▲ Dichio▲ ·
06/11	H	Middlesbrough	0-0	1-1	3	G.P.Barber	Sorensen	Makin●	Bould	Butler P	McCann	Roe	Gray▲	Summerbee	Roy	Quinn	Phillips	Reddy▲77 Boll▲ Williams▲
20/11	H	Liverpool	0-0	0-2	4	D.J.Gallagher	Sorensen	Williams	Croddock	Butler P	McCann	Schwarz	Gray	Summerbee	Roy	Quinn 14	Phillips	· · ·
27/11	A	Watford	2-1	3-2	3	U.D.Rennie	Sorensen	Makin	Croddock	Butler P	McCann 70	Schwarz	Gray	Summerbee	Roy	Quinn	Phillips 33 24	Reddy▲ Williams▲ ·
04/12	A	Chelsea	4-0	4-1	4	S.W.Dunn	Sorensen	Makin	Croddock	Thirlwell	Williams	Schwarz	Gray▲	Summerbee▲	Roy▲	Quinn 1 38	Phillips 23 35	Holloway▲ Roy▲ ·
18/12	A	Southampton	1-0	2-0	3	M.D.Reed	Sorensen	Makin	Bould	Butler P	McCann	Schwarz▲	Williams▲	Summerbee	Roy	Quinn	Phillips 30 90	Kilbone▲ Williams▲ ·
26/12	H	Everton	0-3	0-5	3	S.J.Lodge	Sorensen	Makin	Bould	Butler P	McCann 2	Schwarz	Gray▲	Summerbee	Roe▲	Kilbone	Quinn 14	Reddy▲ Williams▲ ·
28/12	H	Manchester United	2-1	2-2	4	J.T.Winter	Marriott	Makin▲	Croddock	Butler P	McCann	Schwarz	Gray	Summerbee	Roe	Kilbone	Phillips 53	Williams▲ Reddy▲ Williams▲
03/01	A	Wimbledon	0-3	1-4	4	G.Poll	Sorensen	Makin▲	Bould	Williams	McCann	Schwarz	Gray	Summerbee▲	Kilbone	Quinn 47	Phillips 77	Oster▲ Williams▲ ·
15/01	A	Arsenal	0-1	0-4	5	P.E.Alcock	Sorensen	Williams	Bould▲	Williams	Holloway	Schwarz	Gray▲	Summerbee▲	Roy	Kilbone	Phillips	Williams▲ Kilbone▲ ·
23/01	H	Leeds United	0-1	1-2	5	P.Jones	Sorensen	Makin	Croddock	Butler P	Holloway	Schwarz	Gray▲	Roe	Kilbone	Quinn	Phillips 52	Holloway▲ Croddock▲ Reddy▲
05/02	H	Newcastle United	1-2	2-2	6	D.J.Gallagher	Sorensen	Makin	Croddock	Butler P	McCann	Schwarz▲	Gray	Summerbee▲	Kilbone	Quinn	Phillips 22 82	Reddy▲ Holloway▲ ·
12/02	A	Coventry City	0-3	2-3	6	P.E.Alcock	Sorensen	Makin	Croddock	Butler P	McCann	Roe 61	Williams▲	Roy▲	Kilbone	Quinn	Phillips 57	Holloway▲ Reddy▲ Roy▲
26/02	H	Derby County	0-2	2-5	7	A.G.Wiley	Sorensen	Makin	Croddock▲	Butler P	Thirlwell	Schwarz	Williams▲	Roy▲	Kilbone	Quinn	Phillips 86 90	Holloway▲ Williams▲ ·
04/03	A	Leicester City	0-2	2-5	7	N.S.Barry	Sorensen	Makin	Croddock▲	Williams	Holloway▲	Schwarz	Gray	Roy▲	Kilbone	Quinn 75	Phillips 53	Summerbee▲ Oster▲ ·
11/03	A	Liverpool	0-1	1-1	9	G.Poll	Sorensen	Makin	Croddock▲	Butler P	Williams	Schwarz	Gray	Thirlwell	Roe	Quinn	Phillips 77	Summerbee▲ · ·
18/03	H	Middlesbrough	0-0	1-1	8	D.R.Elleray	Sorensen	Makin	Croddock	Williams	Holloway	Schwarz	Gray	Roe	Kilbone	Quinn 66	Phillips 77	Summerbee▲ · ·
25/03	H	Everton	1-2	1-2	6	S.G.Bennett	Sorensen	Makin	Croddock	Williams	Holloway	Schwarz▲	Gray	Summerbee 7	Kilbone	Quinn 14	Phillips 86	Gray▲ · ·
01/04	A	Southampton	1-0	2-1	6	P.A.Durkin	Sorensen	Makin	Croddock	Williams	Holloway	Roy▲	Gray▲	Summerbee▲	Kilbone	Quinn 56	Phillips	Nunez▲ Thirlwell▲ ·
08/04	H	Wimbledon	0-0	2-1	6	G.P.Barber	Sorensen	Makin	Croddock	Williams	Holloway	Roy▲	Grey▲	Roe	Kilbone 81	Quinn	Phillips 86	Butler P▲ Summerbee▲ ·
15/04	A	Manchester United	0-4	0-4	7	P.Jones	Sorensen	Makin	Croddock▲	Williams▲	Holloway	Grey	Grey	Roe	Kilbone	Quinn	Phillips	Butler P▲ Summerbee▲ Dichio▲
22/04	H	Sheffield Wednesday	0-0	2-0	7	M.D.Reed	Sorensen	Makin	Croddock	Butler P	McCann	Roy	Grey	Roe	Kilbone	Quinn 86 90	Phillips 86 90	Williams▲ Oster▲ ·
24/04	A	Bradford City	0-1	0-1	7	S.J.Lodge	Sorensen	Makin	Croddock▲	Butler P	McCann	Roy	Grey	Roe	Kilbone	Quinn 86	Phillips	Oster▲ Dichio▲ ·
29/04	H	Aston Villa	0-0	1-1	7	A.P.D'Urso	Sorensen	Makin	Croddock	Butler P	Thirlwell	Roy	Grey	Summerbee	Oster▲	Quinn	Phillips	Butler I▲ Oster▲ ·
06/05	H	West Ham United	1-0	1-0	7	N.S.Barry	Sorensen	Makin	Croddock	Butler P	Thirlwell	Roy	Grey	Summerbee	Oster▲	Quinn	Phillips 14	Butler I▲ Dichio▲ Holloway▲
14/05	A	Tottenham Hotspur	1-1	1-3	7	M.A.Riley	Sorensen	Makin▲20	Croddock	Butler P	Thirlwell	Roy	Grey	Summerbee	Oster▲	Quinn	Phillips	Holloway▲ Roe● Kilbone▲

Goal Analysis

GOALS BY POSITION 1997/1998 - 1999/2000
for the latest stats and to share your memories go to football.co.uk

key:
- forward
- midfield
- defence
- **-0-** final league position

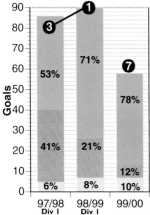

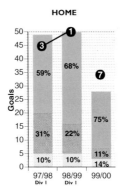
HOME

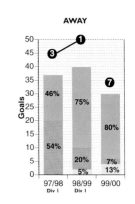
AWAY

outfits. It was also their highest total in the top division for 33 years while they scored more home goals in the top-flight (28) than they had done since they netted 30 at Roker Park in the 1982-83 season. They also claimed their highest away total (29) in the top division since they scored 36 on their travels during the 1955-56 season. Phillips' 30 goals came in 3,197 minutes meaning he averaged a goal every 107 minutes in the Carling Premiership – not bad for a player who was operating with Baldock Town as

recently as 1994. When he scored the winner against West Ham he became only the third player to score 30 or more Carling Premiership goals, following in the boots of Alan Shearer and Andy Cole. Phillips scored more goals away, 16 to 14, though that was helped by a hat-trick at Derby and the good services of the Carling Premiership's Dubious Goal Committee, who awarded Phillips two goals at Watford, rather than a Robert Page own goal, after studying video evidence. Phillips could also afford to miss two penalties – one

GOALS BY TIME PERIOD 1999/2000
for the latest stats and to share your memories go to football.co.uk

key:
- goals for
- goals against

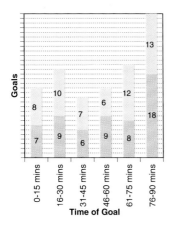

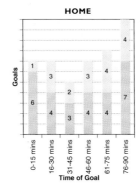
HOME

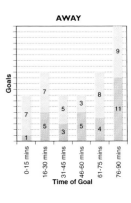
AWAY

What a difference a *CARLING* makes.

Goal Analysis

powered by football.co.uk

Sunderland

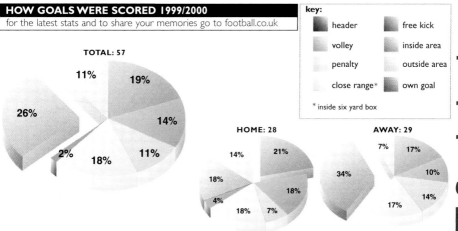

HOW GOALS WERE SCORED 1999/2000
for the latest stats and to share your memories go to football.co.uk

key:

- header
- volley
- penalty
- close range*
- free kick
- inside area
- outside area
- own goal

* inside six yard box

TOTAL: 57

11% · 19% · 14% · 11% · 18% · 2% · 26%

HOME: 28

14% · 21% · 18% · 7% · 18% · 4% · 18%

AWAY: 29

7% · 17% · 10% · 14% · 17% · 34%

at Middlesbrough that cost Sunderland a win and another at home to Southampton that denied him another hat-trick.

Phillips capitalised on his brilliant first touch to score goals from every department, though he seemed to enjoy long range attempts. Quinn scored 14 but had to wait until the last day of October before scoring his first home goal of the season, though he finished the season with seven at home and seven away.

The manner of Sunderland's goals was shared around; a quarter came from inside the area while 11 were headers and 10 were close range efforts. But Sunderland reserved a large percentage of their goals for the final 15 minutes; no fewer than 18 of their 57 came in the closing stages. Phillips scored 12 of them, including two in the last two minutes at Bradford and a brace in the final four minutes to clinch a 2-0 win at Hillsborough. Indeed, Phillips took time to warm up, scoring only a third of his 30

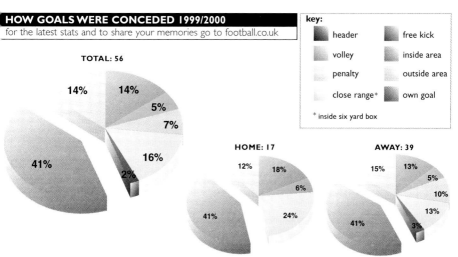

HOW GOALS WERE CONCEDED 1999/2000
for the latest stats and to share your memories go to football.co.uk

key:

- header
- volley
- penalty
- close range*
- free kick
- inside area
- outside area
- own goal

* inside six yard box

TOTAL: 56

14% · 14% · 5% · 7% · 16% · 2% · 41%

HOME: 17

12% · 18% · 6% · 41% · 24%

AWAY: 39

15% · 13% · 5% · 10% · 13% · 3% · 41%

Squad and Performance

SQUAD LIST

for the latest stats and to share your memories go to football.co.uk

Position	Name	Appearances	Appearances as substitute	Goals / Clean Sheets	Yellow Cards	Red Cards
G	A.Marriott	1				
G	T.Sorensen	37		9	2	
D	S.Bould	19	1		2	1
D	P.Butler	31	1	1	5	
D	J.Craddock	18	1		1	
D	T.Helmer	1			1	
D	D.Holloway	8	7		1	
D	C.Makin	34		1	8	1
D	G.McCann	21	3	4	8	
D	D.Williams	13	12		3	
M	K.Ball	6	4		6	
M	T.Butler		1			
M	M.Gray	32	1			
M	K.Kilbane	17	3	1	2	
M	C.Lumsden	1				
M	J.Oster	4	6		1	
M	A.Rae	22	4	3	6	2
M	E.Roy	19	4		2	
M	S.Schwarz	27		1	10	
M	N.Summerbee	29	3	1	2	
M	P.Thirlwell	7	1		2	
F	D.Dichio		11		1	
F	C.Fredgaard		1			
F	M.Nunez		1			
F	K.Phillips	36		30	5	
F	N.Quinn	35	2	14	5	
F	M.Reddy		6		1	

in the first period.

Thomas Sorensen, their goalkeeper, missed one game, with 'flu, while the front men missed only five games between them. The ever-improving Chris Makin was also regular as was Paul Butler, Michael Gray and Nicky Summerbee. But they were left to wonder what would have happened had they enjoyed a better return against the best in the country. Sunderland's record against all but the top four was pretty impressive; of that group they failed to beat only Coventry and Middlesbrough. But against Manchester United, Arsenal, Leeds and Liverpool, they collected only three points from a possible 12. Only Leeds did the double over Sunderland while they won maximum points off Southampton,

TEAM PERFORMANCE TABLE

for the latest stats and to share your memories go to football.co.uk

Position	Club	Points Won	Percentage of points won at home	percentage of points won away	overall percentage of points won
1.	MANCHESTER UNITED	1/6			
2.	ARSENAL	1/6			
3.	LEEDS UNITED	0/6	33%	7%	20%
4.	LIVERPOOL	1/6			
5.	CHELSEA	3/6			
6.	ASTON VILLA	4/6			
7.	SUNDERLAND	58 pts			
8.	LEICESTER CITY	3/6	100%	17%	58%
9.	TOTTENHAM HOTSPUR	3/6			
10.	WEST HAM UNITED	4/6			
11.	NEWCASTLE UNITED	4/6			
12.	MIDDLESBROUGH	2/6			
13.	EVERTON	3/6	60%	47%	53%
14.	SOUTHAMPTON	6/6			
15.	COVENTRY CITY	1/6			
16.	DERBY COUNTY	4/6			
17.	BRADFORD CITY	3/6			
18.	WIMBLEDON	3/6	67%	80%	73%
19.	SHEFFIELD WEDNESDAY	6/6			
20.	WATFORD	6/6			

The figures show a team's performance against clubs in each quarter of the final league table. The first column represents points won from the total available against each team in the league.

What a difference a CARLING makes.

Discipline and Season Summary

powered by football.co.uk

BOOKINGS BY POSITION 1997/1998 - 1999/2000

for the latest stats and to share your memories go to football.co.uk

key:
■ forward   ■ defence
■ midfield   ■ goalkeeper

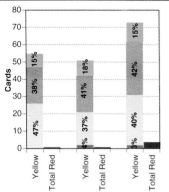

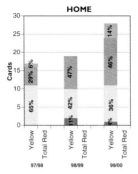

HOME

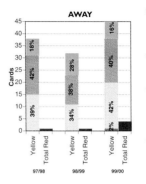

AWAY

Sunderland

Sheffield Wednesday and Watford.

Sunderland may have scored a lot of goals but they also collected a lot of cards with Schwarz the worst offender. The Swedish former Arsenal star was booked no fewer than 10 times including a caution in the early season game against Leeds in which he was one of six Sunderland players to be punished when five were booked and another, Alex Rae, dismissed. Such a repeat this season could see clubs punished, for the Football Association plan to follow UEFA and fine clubs who collect a certain number of bookings per game. Makin and Gavin McCann were also regular miscrants though the 10 yellow cards collected by Quinn and Phillips (plus one for

Danielle Dichio) represented only 15 per cent of their total.

Rae was sent-off twice, both against Leeds and, on the final day of the season at Tottenham, for which he will miss the start of the 2000-01 campaign. But he was also suspended for two games after video evidence confirmed that he had elbowed Derby's Darryl Powell in February.

If Sunderland were drawing at half time it was virtually impossible to determine the outcome. Of the 14 times they were level after half a game, they won six, lost three and drew the remaining five. At home they were particularly difficult to read; of their 10 half time leads, they won only five.

HALF TIME - FULL TIME COMPARATIVE CHART

for the latest stats and to share your memories go to football.co.uk

HOME				AWAY				TOTAL			
Number of Home Half Time Wins	Full Time Result W	L	D	Number of Away Half Time Wins	Full Time Result W	L	D	Total Number of Half Time Wins	Full Time Result W	L	D
6	5	0	1	6	4	1	1	12	9	1	2
Number of Home Half Time Losses	Full Time Result W	L	D	Number of Away Half Time Losses	Full Time Result W	L	D	Total Number of Half Time Losses	Full Time Result W	L	D
3	0	1	2	9	1	7	1	12	1	8	3
Number of Home Half Time Draws	Full Time Result W	L	D	Number of Away Half Time Draws	Full Time Result W	L	D	Total Number of Half Time Draws	Full Time Result W	L	D
10	5	2	3	4	1	1	2	14	6	3	5

What a difference a CARLING makes.

Maps and Directions

Sunderland play at the Stadium of Light, half a mile from the city centre. There are some car parking facilities at the ground.

From the South:
Exit the A1 at Junction 64, signposted to Washington, Birtley A195. Get on to the Western Highway. At the roundabout, after 1 ½ miles, follow signs for Sunderland A1231 on the Washington Highway. Take the second exit for the A1231 and follow the road for 4 ½ miles, heading for the city centre. Follow signs for the Queens Road B1289 and turn right at the roundabout. Follow signs for Stadium of Light.

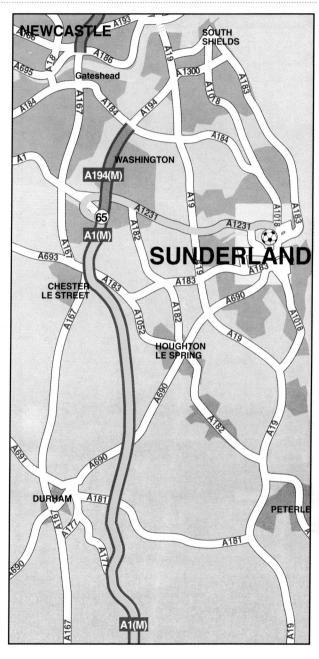

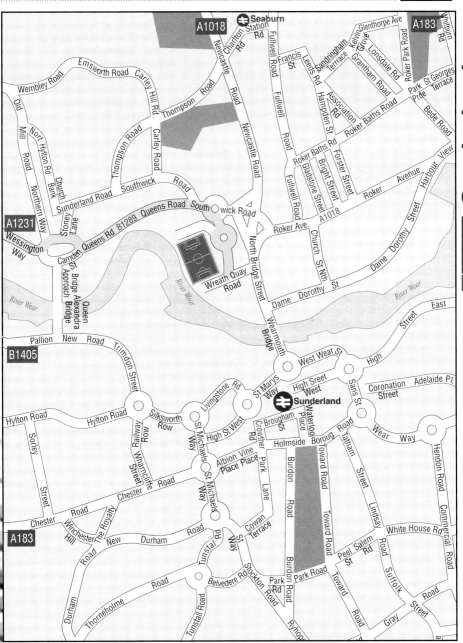

Sunderland

A1018

A183

Seaburn
Station

A1231

B1405

A183

Sunderland

Club Honours

- Football League Champions: 1950-51, 1960-61
- Division 2 Champions: 1919-20, 1949-50
- FA Cup Winners: 1901, 1921, 1961, 1962, 1967, 1981, 1982, 1991
- League Cup Winners: 1971, 1973, 1999
- European Cup Winners' Cup Winners: 1962-63
- UEFA Cup Winners: 1971-72, 1983-84

Club Records

- Victory: 13-2 v Crewe Alexandra, FA Cup 4th Round (replay), February 3, 1960
- Defeat: 0-8 v Cologne, UEFA Inter Toto Cup, July 22, 1995
- League goals in a season (team): 115, Division 1, 1960-61
- League goals in a season (player): 37, Jimmy Greaves, Division 1, 1962-63
- Career league goals: 220, Jimmy Greaves, 1961-70
- League appearances: 655, Steve Perryman, 1969-86
- Transfer fee paid: £11,000,000 to Dynamo Kiev for Sergei Rebrov, July, 2000
- Transfer fee received: £5,500,000 from Lazio for Paul Gascoigne, July, 1991

Pos		Pld	W	D	L	F	A	Pts
10	Tottenham	38	15	8	15	57	49	53

Tottenham "Spurs" Hotspur

Bill Nicholson Way, 748 High Rd
Tottenham, London N17 0AP
Tel: 020 8365 5000
www.spurs.co.uk

Season Review by
John Ley

The Daily Telegraph

Every season expectations are high that White Hart Lane will witness a season of entertainment and success. But after winning the Worthington Cup and qualifying for Europe in his first season, it was difficult to know how manager George Graham could improve, particularly with a squad of limited attacking options. In the summer he brought in Wimbledon defender Chris Perry and Willem Korsten, from Vitesse Arnhem and later added youngsters from the lower leagues rather than a big name the fans wanted. Spurs' form was erratic with Graham developing a love-hate relationship with the supporters' favourite, David Ginola. Graham himself missed several games towards the end of the season with illness, but in the summer signed Wimbledon goalkeeper Neil Sullivan and Sergei Rebrov, the Dynamo Kiev striker, for a club record £11 million. Villa showed interest in Ginola over the summer while Graham still has much to do to win over the fans.

Useful Information

Spurs Megastore

1-3 Park Lane, Tottenham, N17 0HJ
Opening Times:
Monday-Saturday 9.30am - 5.30pm
Midweek Match days 9.30am-
7.45pm and 9.45pm-10.15pm
Saturday Matches 9.30am-3.00pm
and 4.45pm-6.00pm
Tel: **020 8365 5042**
Mail Order: **020 8804 7888**

Spurs Store

776 High Road, Tottenham, N17 0AP
Opening Times:
Monday-Saturday 9.30am - 5.30pm
Midweek Match days 9.30am-
7.45pm and 9.45pm-10.15pm
Saturday Matches 9.30am-3.00pm
and 4.45pm-6.00pm
Tel: **020 8365 5041**
Mail Service: **020 8804 7888**

Stadium Tours

Tel: **020 8365 5056**

Corporate Hospitality

120 executive boxes (72 × 8 seaters, 15 × 10 seaters, 21 × 12 seaters, 12 × 18 seaters). Eight executive clubs of various sizes. Matchday hospitality packages. Match, associate match, matchball and match programme sponsorship

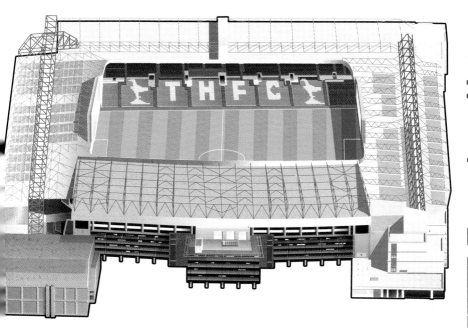

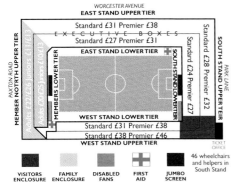

WORCESTER AVENUE
EAST STAND UPPER TIER

Standard £31 Premier £38

E X E C U T I V E   B O X E S

Standard £27 Premier £31

EAST STAND LOWER TIER

MEMBER NOTRTH UPPER TIER

MEMBERS LOWER TIER

PAXTON ROAD

Adults £20/£16 Juniors £11/£13

SOUTH STAND LOWER TIER

SOUTH STAND UPPER TIER

Standard £24 Premier £27

Standard £28 Premier £32

PARK LANE

WEST STAND LOWER TIER

Standard £31 Premier £38

Standard £38 Premier £46

WEST STAND UPPER TIER

TICKET OFFICE

46 wheelchairs and helpers in South Stand

VISITORS ENCLOSURE   FAMILY ENCLOSURE   DISABLED FANS   FIRST AID   JUMBO SCREEN

White Hart Lane

Opened: September 4, 1899
Capacity: 36,289
1999/2000 highest attendance: 36,233
1999/2000 average attendance:34,912
Record attendance: 75,038

packages available.

Contact Commercial Office:
020 8365 5010

Literature

Programme £2
Official magazine £2.50

Pre-Match & Half Time Entertainment

Spurs TV on Jumbotron.
'Chirpy' mascot.

Conference Centre

Conferences, training and banqueting on non-match days from small meetings to a gala dinners for 250 people.
Contact Philip Cartwright:
020 8365 5006

Booking Information

General Enquiries:
020 8365 5000
Ticket Line:
020 8365 5050
Club Fax:
020 8365 5005
Junior Clubline:
020 8365 5050

199

Results Breakdown

powered by football.co.uk

POINTS WON OR LOST AT BOTH HOME AND AWAY

for the latest stats and to share your memories go to football.co.uk

key:
- win
- draw
- loss
- -0- league position

home fixtures are in red

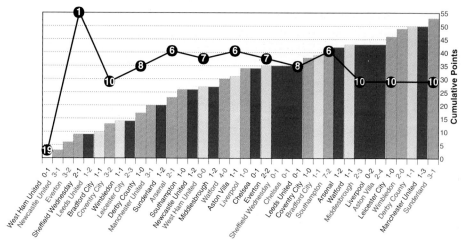

Spurs went top after four games – the first time they had occupied pole position for 13 years. But the joy was short-lived with Spurs losing at home to Graham's former club Leeds and by the time they won again they had slumped to 10th. Throughout the season, Spurs reached a low when they were beaten 6-1 by Newcastle in the FA Cup but responded by beating Southampton 7-2 – their best win for 23 years. In between, Tottenham went through a spell in which they won just two and lost eight in 13 games.

They went on to finish 10th – their best position for three years – while winning 10 home games, more than at any time since the 1994-95 season. On their travels Spurs won only five games. Only twice did they win successive games but one point from 15, starting in March at Arsenal with a 2-1 defeat, ruined any hopes Spurs had of qualifying again for the UEFA Cup.

With Steffen Iversen continuing to improve and Chris Armstrong finally finding his scoring touch, Spurs' strikers made light of the fact that Graham

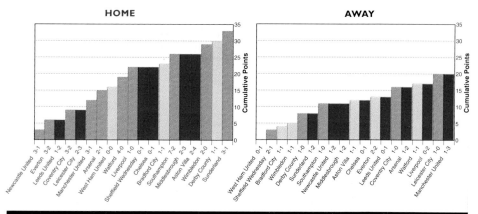

THE F.A. CARLING PREMIERSHIP

Results Table

powered by football.co.uk

Tottenham Hotspur

Legend: ● = Red Card ○ = Yellow Card ▲ = Player substituted 00 = Time of goal ▲ = Substitute used

DATE	H/A	OPPONENT	H/T	F/T	POS	REFEREE	TEAM											SUBSTITUTES USED
07/08	A	West Ham United	0-1	0-1	19	P.A.Durkin	Walker	Carr	Campbell ▲	Perry	Edinburgh	Freund ●	Sherwood	Anderton	Ginola ▲	Dominguez ▲	Iversen	Scales ▲ Leonhardsen ▲ Ferdinand ▲
09/08	H	Newcastle United	2-1	3-1	2	R.J.Harris	Walker	Carr	Scales	Perry	Torrico ▲	Leonhardsen 82	Sherwood 60	Anderton	Ginola	Ferdinand ▲44	Iversen 28	Young ▲ Dominguez ▲ Freund ▲
14/08	A	Everton	1-1	3-2	5	P.E.Alcock	Walker ○	Scales	Perry	Torrico	Leonhardsen 42	Sherwood 35	Anderton ○	Ginola	Ferdinand	Iversen 85		Freund ▲
21/08	H	Sheffield Wednesday	2-1	2-1	1	A.P.D'Urso	Walker	Carr	Young	Perry	Torrico	Leonhardsen 42	Sherwood 36	Freund	Ginola	Ferdinand 18	Iversen	Dominguez ▲ Nielsen ▲
28/08	A	Leeds United	1-0	1-2	7	M.D.Reed	Walker	Carr	Young	Perry	Torrico	Leonhardsen	Sherwood 36	Freund	Ginola	Ferdinand ▲	Iversen	Dominguez ▲▲ Nielsen ▲
12/09	H	Bradford City	0-0	1-1	6	A.B.Wilkie	Walker	Carr	Young ○	Perry 76	Torrico	Leonhardsen	Sherwood	Freund	Ginola	Ferdinand ▲	Iversen	Armstrong ▲ Nielsen ▲
19/09	A	Coventry City	3-2	3-2	10	A.P.D'Urso	Walker	Carr	Young	Perry	Torrico	Leonhardsen 52	Sherwood	Freund	Ginola	Armstrong ▲50	Iversen 7	Dominguez ▲ Nielsen ▲
26/09	H	Wimbledon	1-1	1-1	8	G.Poll	Walker	Carr 75	Campbell ▲	Perry	Torrico	Leonhardsen	Sherwood	Nielsen	Ginola ▲	Armstrong	Iversen	Dominguez ▲
03/10	H	Leicester City	2-1	2-3	9	G.P.Barber	Walker	Carr ○	Campbell	Perry	Torrico	Leonhardsen	Sherwood ○	Freund	Ginola	Armstrong	Iversen ●26 35	Vega ▲ Nielsen ▲ Vega ▲
16/10	A	Derby County	1-0	1-0	8	P.A.Durkin	Walker	Carr ○	Campbell	Perry	King	Leonhardsen	Sherwood	Nielsen	Ginola	Armstrong ▲37	Iversen	Sherwood ▲ Piercy ▲ Vega ▲
23/10	H	Manchester United	2-1	3-1	5	J.T.Winter	Walker	Carr 70	Campbell	Perry ▲	Torrico	Leonhardsen ▲	Sherwood	Freund	Ginola	Fox ▲	Iversen 35	Sherwood ▲ Piercy ▲ Dominguez ▲
31/10	A	Sunderland	0-2	1-2	7	M.A.Riley	Walker	Carr	Campbell	Young ▲	Vega	Clemence	Sherwood 20	Freund	Ginola	Armstrong	Iversen 63	Dominguez ▲ Sherwood ▲ Perry ▲
07/11	A	Arsenal	0-2	1-2	7	D.R.Elleray	Walker	Carr ○	Campbell	Perry	Edinburgh	Leonhardsen	Clemence	Freund	Ginola	Piercy ▲	Iversen 7	Armstrong ▲
20/11	H	Southampton	0-0	0-0	6	S.G.Bennett	Walker	Carr	Campbell	Perry	Torrico	Leonhardsen	Sherwood	Freund	Ginola	Armstrong	Iversen	Dominguez ▲
28/11	A	Newcastle United	1-1	1-2	7	P.E.Alcock	Walker	Edinburgh	Campbell	Perry	Torrico	Leonhardsen ▲	Sherwood	Freund ▲	Ginola	Armstrong ▲43	Iversen	Clemence ▲ Dominguez ▲
06/12	H	West Ham United	0-0	0-0	7	P.Jones	Walker	Edinburgh	Campbell	Perry	Torrico	Leonhardsen	Sherwood	Freund ▲	Ginola	Dominguez ▲	Iversen	Nielsen ▲ Armstrong ▲
18/12	A	Middlesbrough	1-1	1-2	6	S.W.Dunn	Walker	Young	Campbell	Perry	Vega 8	Nielsen ▲	Sherwood ●	Freund	Ginola ○27	Armstrong	Iversen	Sherwood ▲ Edinburgh ▲ Fox ▲
29/12	H	Aston Villa	4-0	4-0	6	M.D.Reed	Walker	Carr	Campbell ▲	Perry	Torrico	Nielsen ▲	Sherwood 55 82	Clemence	Ginola	Armstrong	Iversen 32	Dominguez ▲ Armstrong ▲
03/01	A	Liverpool	1-0	1-0	6	A.B.Wilkie	Walker	Carr	Campbell	Perry ○	Torrico	Young	Sherwood 44	Clemence	Ginola	Armstrong 23	Iversen	Young ▲
12/01	H	Chelsea	0-0	0-1	7	N.S.Barry	Walker	Carr	Campbell	Perry	Edinburgh	Clemence	Sherwood	Anderton	Ginola	Armstrong	Iversen	
15/01	A	Everton	2-2	2-2	7	A.G.Wiley	Walker	Carr	Campbell	Perry	Edinburgh ▲	Clemence	Sherwood	Anderton	Ginola ▲28	Armstrong 24	Iversen	Young ▲ Nielsen ▲
22/01	H	Sheffield Wednesday	0-1	1-1	7	M.A.Riley	Walker	Carr	Campbell	Perry ○	Edinburgh ▲	Clemence ▲	Sherwood	Anderton	Ginola	Armstrong	Iversen	Young ▲ Korsten ▲ Nielsen ▲
05/02	H	Chelsea	0-0	0-1	7	G.Poll	Walker	Carr	Campbell	Perry	Torrico	Clemence	Sherwood	Anderton	Ginola	Armstrong	Iversen	Nielsen ▲ Korsten ▲
12/02	A	Leeds United	0-1	0-1	8	D.J.Gallagher	Walker	Carr ●	Campbell	Perry	Torrico ▲	Clemence ▲	Sherwood ▲	Anderton	Ginola	Korsten	Armstrong 82	Nielsen ▲ Dominguez ▲
26/02	H	Coventry City	0-0	1-0	9	P.A.Durkin	Walker	Carr	Campbell	Perry ○	Torrico	Leonhardsen ○	Sherwood ▲	Anderton	Ginola 82	Freund	Iversen 14	Young ▲ Clemence ▲
04/03	A	Bradford City	4-2	7-2	8	P.Jones	Walker	Carr	Campbell	Perry ○	Torrico ▲	Leonhardsen	Freund	Anderton 38	Ginola	Armstrong 41 63	Iversen 45 77 90	Young ▲ Ferdinand ▲
11/03	H	Southampton	4-2	7-2	10	M.R.Halsey	Walker	Carr	Campbell	Perry	Torrico	Leonhardsen	Freund	Anderton	Ginola ▲	Armstrong 29	Iversen	Young ▲ Ferdinand ▲
19/03	A	Arsenal	0-0	0-0	8	P.A.Durkin	Walker	Carr	Campbell ▲	Perry	Torrico	Leonhardsen	Freund	Anderton	Ginola	Armstrong 51	Iversen	Young ▲ Ferdinand ▲
25/03	H	Watford	0-0	1-0	8	U.D.Rennie	Walker	Carr	Scales	Perry	Torrico	Leonhardsen ▲	Freund	Anderton	Ginola	Armstrong 30	Iversen	Clemence ▲ Korsten ▲
03/04	A	Middlesbrough	1-1	2-3	10	A.G.Wiley	Walker	Carr ○	Campbell	Perry	Torrico	Korsten ○	Freund	Anderton	Ginola ▲	Armstrong	Iversen	Clemence ▲ Etherington ▲
09/04	H	Liverpool	0-1	0-2	11	S.J.Lodge	Walker	Carr	Campbell	Perry	Torrico	Clemence	Freund	Anderton	Ginola 82	Armstrong	Iversen	Davies ▲ Etherington ▲
15/04	A	Aston Villa	1-0	2-4	12	R.J.Harris	Walker	Carr	Campbell	Perry	Torrico	Clemence	Freund	Anderton	Ginola 90	Armstrong 47	Iversen 16	Young ▲ Korsten ▲
19/04	A	Leicester City	0-1	0-1	12	J.T.Winter	Walker	Carr	Campbell	Perry	Korsten	Clemence	Freund	Anderton	Ginola	Armstrong ▲	Iversen	Etherington ▲
22/04	H	Wimbledon	2-0	2-0	10	D.J.Gallagher	Walker	Carr	Campbell	Perry ○	Young	Clemence	Freund	Anderton 36	Ginola	Armstrong 7	Iversen	Etherington ▲
29/04	A	Derby County	0-0	1-1	9	N.S.Barry	Walker	Carr	Campbell	Perry	Young	Clemence 90	Korsten ▲	Anderton	Ginola ▲	Armstrong ▲20	Iversen	McEwen ▲ Davies ▲ Etherington ▲
06/05	H	Manchester United	1-3	1-3	10	A.G.Wiley	Walker	Carr	Campbell	Perry	Davies	Clemence	Etherington	Anderton	Ginola ▲	Armstrong	Iversen	Korsten ▲ Doherty ▲ King ▲
14/05	A	Sunderland	1-3	1-3	10	M.A.Riley	Walker	Carr 82	Campbell	Perry	King	Leonhardsen ▲	Freund	Anderton 11	Ginola	Armstrong	Iversen	Doherty ▲ Sherwood ▲72

Goal Analysis

GOALS BY POSITION 1997/1998 - 1999/2000

for the latest stats and to share your memories go to football.co.uk

key:
- forward
- midfield
- defence
- final league position

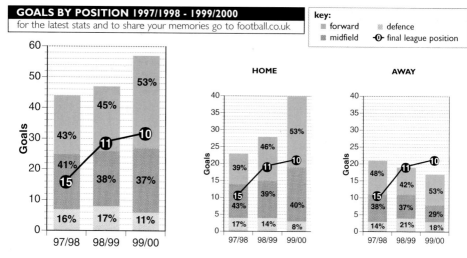

spent most of the season searching for a new goalscorer. Spurs scored 57 goals, more than five teams who finished higher, and their best return since the 1994-95 season. While only 17 were scored away from home – their worst for nine years – they scored more home goals than at any time since the first season of the Carling Premiership.

Armstrong and Iversen both scored 14, the best by a Spurs player since the 1995-96 season when Teddy Sheringham finished with 16. For Armstrong,

it represented his best league return since he scored one goal less than Sheringham four years earlier, while Iversen enjoyed his best ever return in his fourth season in north London. If Armstrong felt under pressure from the Spurs crowd he didn't show it, scoring seven at home and the same number away. Having missed the start of the season with a groin problem, Armstrong scored only three goals before Christmas but improved with nine from his final 13 appearances of the season. But

GOALS BY TIME PERIOD 1999/2000

for the latest stats and to share your memories go to football.co.uk

key:
- goals for
- goals against

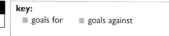

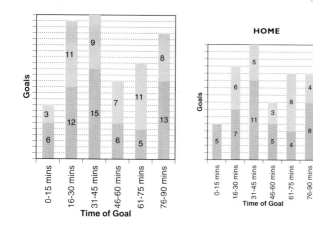

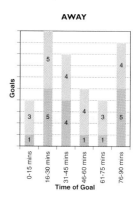

Goal Analysis

Tottenham Hotspur

HOW GOALS WERE SCORED 1999/2000
for the latest stats and to share your memories go to football.co.uk

key:

■ header		■ free kick	
■ volley		■ inside area	
penalty		outside area	
close range*		■ own goal	

* inside six yard box

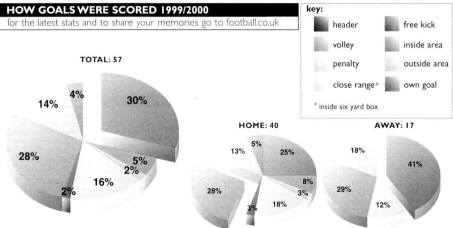

TOTAL: 57

30% 4% 14% 28% 5% 2% 2% 16%

HOME: 40

5% 25% 13% 8% 3% 28% 3% 18%

AWAY: 17

18% 41% 29% 12%

Iversen clearly preferred the comforts of home; he scored 13 of his 14 goals at White Hart Lane, with only one away goal, at Sunderland.

Les Ferdinand missed most of the season with injury though he did score twice before being burdened with calf and Achilles problems. Those three, however, collected 53 per cent of Tottenham's goals while, in midfield, Darren Anderton scored three while Tim Sherwood collected eight – his best return for 13 seasons –

before a groin operation halted his season. Oyvind Leonhardsen scored four but his season was also hindered by injuries. Stephen Carr led the defensive scoring with three including a lightening bolt against Manchester United that helped them beat the champions for the first time in three years.

Tottenham were dangerous at corners, scoring a high percentage of goals from within the area. They also claimed a fifth of their goals with headers but they had to wait until the final game of the season

HOW GOALS WERE CONCEDED 1999/2000
for the latest stats and to share your memories go to football.co.uk

key:

■ header		■ free kick	
■ volley		■ inside area	
penalty		outside area	
close range*		■ own goal	

* inside six yard box

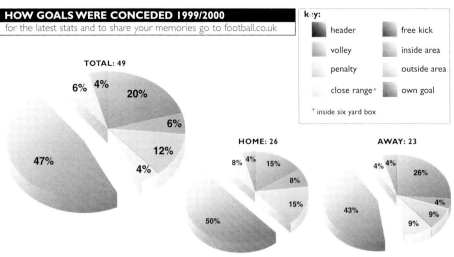

TOTAL: 49

6% 4% 20% 6% 47% 12% 4%

HOME: 26

8% 4% 15% 8% 50% 15%

AWAY: 23

4% 4% 26% 4% 43% 9% 9%

Squad and Performance

SQUAD LIST

for the latest stats and to share your memories go to football.co.uk

Position	Name	Appearances	Appearances as substitute	Goals	Clean Sheets	Yellow Cards	Red Cards
G	I.Walker	38			8	1	
D	S.Campbell	29				6	
D	S.Carr	34		3		6	
D	G.Doherty			2			
D	J.Edinburgh	7	1			3	
D	S.Freund	24	3			9	
D	L.King	2	1				
D	C.Perry	36	1	1		8	
D	J.Scales	3	1				
D	M.Tarrico	29				9	
D	R.Vega	2	3	1		1	
M	D.Anderton	22		3		5	
M	S.Clemence	16	4	1		4	
M	S.Davies	1	2				
M	J.Dominguez	2	10				
M	M.Etherington	1	4				
M	R.Fox	1	2			1	
M	D.Ginola	36		4		3	
M	W.Korsten	4	5			1	
M	O.Leonhardsen	21	1	4		2	
M	A.Nielsen	5	9			2	1
M	J.Piercy	1	2				
M	T.Sherwood	23	4	8		9	
M	L.Young	11	9			2	
F	C.Armstrong	29	2	14		4	
F	L.Ferdinand	5	4	2		1	
F	S.Iversen	36		14		5	
F	D.McEwen			1			

before scoring a penalty with Anderton successful from the spot against Sunderland. Interestingly, the first 12 of Spurs' 15 defeats were by a single goal.

If Walker is concerned about losing his place to Sullivan he can point out that he was Tottenham's only ever present. Ginola started 36 of the 38 – but finished only 19 and was substitute in the other 17. Indeed, following the arrival of Graham, Ginola had started 60 League games – and been substituted in 28 of them. Injuries were damaging; 12 players missed at least a month.

The table shows clearly where Spurs failed. Against the lower teams they were relatively successful; against the bottom 10 they won at least one game, apart from Middlesbrough. But they

TEAM PERFORMANCE TABLE

for the latest stats and to share your memories go to football.co.uk

Position	Club	Points Won	Percentage of points won at home	percentage of points won away	overall percentage of points won
1.	MANCHESTER UNITED	3/6			
2.	ARSENAL	3/6			
3.	LEEDS UNITED	0/6	60%	0%	30%
4.	LIVERPOOL	3/6			
5.	CHELSEA	0/6			
6.	ASTON VILLA	1/6			
7.	SUNDERLAND	3/6			
8.	LEICESTER CITY	3/6	33%	33%	33%
9.	TOTTENHAM HOTSPUR	53 pts			
10.	WEST HAM UNITED	1/6			
11.	NEWCASTLE UNITED	3/6			
12.	MIDDLESBROUGH	0/6			
13.	EVERTON	4/6	80%	47%	63%
14.	SOUTHAMPTON	6/6			
15.	COVENTRY CITY	6/6			
16.	DERBY COUNTY	4/6			
17.	BRADFORD CITY	2/6			
18.	WIMBLEDON	4/6	53%	60%	57%
19.	SHEFFIELD WEDNESDAY	3/6			
20.	WATFORD	4/6			

The figures show a team's performance against clubs in each quarter of the final league table. The first column represents points won from the total available against each team in the league.

What a difference a CARLING makes.

Discipline and Season Summary

Tottenham Hotspur

BOOKINGS BY POSITION 1997/1998 - 1999/2000
for the latest stats and to share your memories go to football.co.uk

key:
- forward
- defence
- midfield
- goalkeeper

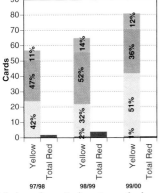

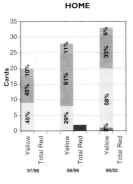

HOME

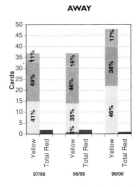

AWAY

failed to take a single point at the homes of any of the top five.

Tottenham were the last team to receive a red card in the 1999-2000 season and when they did, Allan Nielsen receiving his marching orders in the last minute at Middlesbrough in December, Graham complained bitterly – but then he was prone to argue over most refereeing decisions against his side. It was an improvement on the previous season when they had four dismissed. But the number of bookings they received was not as impressive; they received 82 yellow cards, the most they have ever collected, with no fewer than nine players receiving nine cautions – Steffen Freund,

Tarrico and Sherwood. Perry was also booked eight times; he took 29 games to collect his first three then was booked in five of six games towards the end of the season. Spurs had no fewer than 20 of their 28 players cautioned at some stage.

If Spurs were losing at half time, nothing Graham could say in the dressing room seemed to inspire his team for they went on to lose each of the seven in which they were trailing at the interval. But of the six games they lost at White Hart Lane, they were leading three times and drawing twice at half time. An interval lead was no guarantee of a full time win; of the 15 occasions Spurs led after 45 minutes they went on to win only 10.

HALF TIME - FULL TIME COMPARATIVE CHART
for the latest stats and to share your memories go to football.co.uk

HOME

Number of Home Half Time Wins	Full Time Result W	L	D
11	8	3	0

Number of Home Half Time Losses	Full Time Result W	L	D
1	0	1	0

Number of Home Half Time Draws	Full Time Result W	L	D
7	2	2	3

AWAY

Number of Away Half Time Wins	Full Time Result W	L	D
4	2	0	2

Number of Away Half Time Losses	Full Time Result W	L	D
6	0	6	0

Number of Away Half Time Draws	Full Time Result W	L	D
9	3	3	3

TOTAL

Total Number of Half Time Wins	Full Time Result W	L	D
15	10	3	2

Total Number of Half Time Losses	Full Time Result W	L	D
7	0	7	0

Total Number of Half Time Draws	Full Time Result W	L	D
16	5	5	6

Maps and Directions

White Hart Lane is situated in North London, 6 miles from the city centre. Limited parking is available near the ground.

From the North:
From the M1, turn off onto the A1 at Junction 2/3. Join the A406 North Circular Road eastbound and continue for 7 miles. At the Edmonton traffic lights turn right onto the A1010 Fore Street. Continue for 1 mile and White Hart Lane is on the left.

From the North-West:
Approaching London on the M40, at Junction 1 stay on the A40 for 10 miles before turning onto the A406 North Circular Road for 13 miles until reaching the Edmonton traffic lights. Then as route for North.

From the West:
Approaching London on the M4, turn off onto the A406 North Circular Road at Junction 1 and continue for 16 miles until reaching the Edmonton traffic lights. Then as route for North.

From the South-West:
From the M3 turn off onto the M25 at Junction 2. Continue for 10 miles until you reach Junction 15 at which point turn off onto the M4. Then as route for West.

From the East:
From the M11 turn off onto the A406 at Junction 4 and continue for 6 miles. At the Edmonton traffic lights turn left onto the A1010 Fore Street. Continue for 1 mile and White Hart Lane is on the left.

Seven Sisters tube station is 1½ miles from the ground; White Hart Lane Main Line is a 3 minute walk away; Northumberland Park is a 7 minute walk.

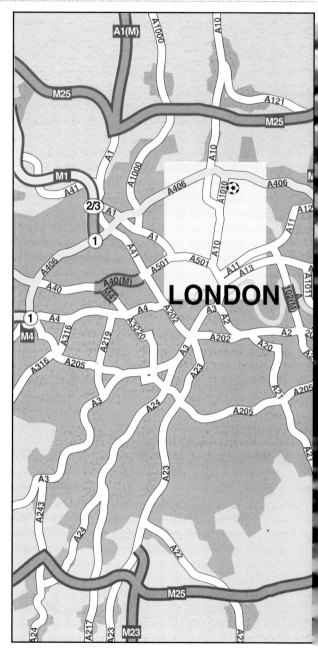

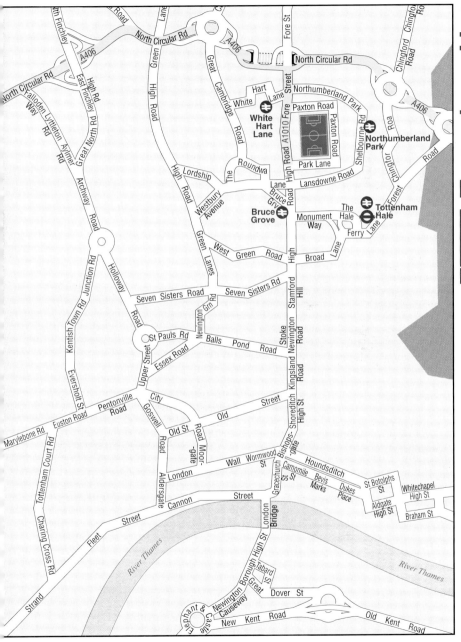

Pos		Pld	W	D	L	F	A	Pts
9	West Ham	38	15	10	13	52	53	55

West Ham United
"The Hammers"

Boleyn Ground, Green Street
Upton Park, London E13 9AZ
Tel: 020 8548 2748
www.whufc.co.uk

Season Review by
John Ley

The Daily Telegraph

Sometimes, one wondered how seriously West Ham took themselves; they could be world-beaters or surrender too easily. Harry Redknapp gave the fans some smashing entertainment, even though he lost a lot of players through injuries and suspensions, and for the third time in three years they finished in the top half of the Carling Premiership. Redknapp brought in striker Paulo Wanchope to partner Paolo di Canio, while introducing Stuart Pearce in defence. After the season began Gary Charles arrived from Benfica while Derby's Igor Stimac joined the defence. Later Frederic Kanoute was signed on loan from Lyon before making the move permanent in the summer, with Marc Vivien Foe going to France. Pearce broke his leg twice while Steve Potts, Neil Ruddock, Scott Minto and Ian Pearce all suffered bad injuries, as did Joe Cole whose impressive season ended with a broken leg. The arrival of Nigel Winterburn and Davor Suker from Arsenal will strengthen the team.

Useful Information

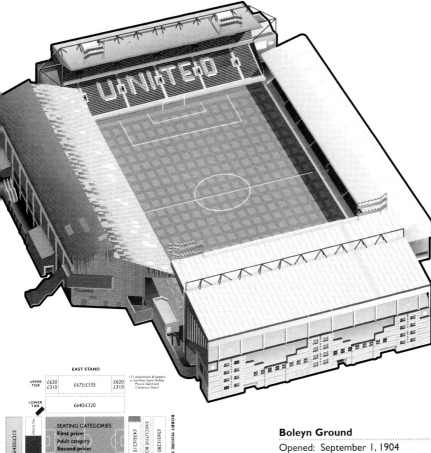

EAST STAND

| UPPER TIER | £620 £310 | £675/£335 | £620 £310 | 117 wheelchairs & helpers in the West Stand: Bobby Moore Stand and Centenary Stand |
| LOWER TIER | | £640/£320 | | |

SEATING CATEGORIES
First price:
Adult category
Second price:
Junior/OAP category

£435/£215   BOBBY MOORE STAND   EXECUTIVE BOXES £565/£280   £435/£215

| £580 £290 | £620 £310 | £675/£335 | £620 £310 | £580 £290 | LOWER TIER | UPPER TIER |
| £620 £310 | | £675/£335 | | £620 £310 | | |

WEST STAND

VISITORS ENCLOSURE   FAMILY ENCLOSURE   DISABLED FANS   FIRST AID   JUMBO SCREEN

Boleyn Ground

Opened: September 1, 1904
Capacity: 26,500
1999/2000 highest attendance: 26,044
1999/2000 average attendance: 25,095
Record attendance: 42,322

Literature

rogramme price £2, Official
lagazine Hammers News £2.75

Corporate Hospitality

latchball, programme
ponsorship.

latch sponsorship for 20 people,
cludes exclusive use of Trevor
rooking Suite.

estaurant and conference

facilities also available.

Contact Commercial Department:
020 8548 2777

Pre-Match & Half Time Entertainment

Hammerettes sports dance team.
50/50 cash prize draw.

The official West Ham website
broadcasts full live matchday
commentary.

Booking Information

General Enquiries :
020 8548 2700
Credit Card Bookings:
020 8548 2700
Travel Club:
020 8548 2700
Junior Club:
020 8548 2727

Results Breakdown

powered by **football.co.uk**

POINTS WON OR LOST AT BOTH HOME AND AWAY
for the latest stats and to share your memories go to football.co.uk

key:
- win
- draw
- loss
- ⦿ league position
- home fixtures are in red

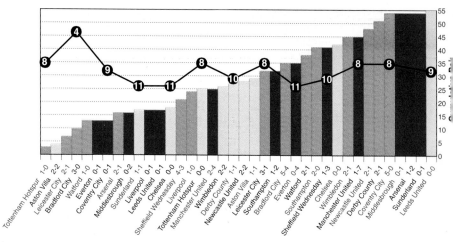

After finishing fifth the previous season it was difficult to know how West Ham could improve. Four wins and a draw in their opening five games took the Hammers into fourth place suggesting the extra practice they had received from entering the InterToto Cup – they started in Mid-July – was paying off. Then they lost five from the next seven games and began to wobble. Stuart Pearce had started well but broke his leg against Watford in September and, when he returned in the spring, he lasted three games before breaking the same bone. West Ham's away form was poor with only 17 points gleaned from 1? away games. In between their 3-0 victory at Bradford in August and the 3-1 January win at Leicester, the Hammers lost five in succession followed by four straight draws. They also suffered the humiliation of a 7-1 thrashing at Old Trafford – the first time the? had conceded so many goals in a League game since 1963 when they lost 8-2 to Blackburn Rovers.

West Ham's 52 goals was six better than the? previous season when they had finished fifth. Ofte? it became the Paulo and Paolo show with Wanchop?

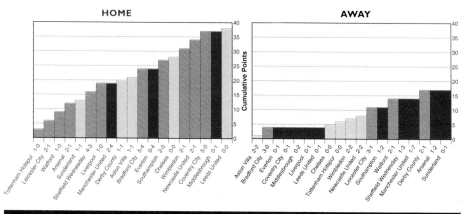

What a difference a *CARLING* makes.

Results Table

powered by **football.co.uk**

West Ham United

Legend: ● = Red Card ■ = Yellow Card ▲ = Player substituted 00 = Time of goal

DATE	H/A	OPPONENT	H/T	F/T	POS	REFEREE	TEAM											SUBSTITUTES USED
07/08	H	Tottenham Hotspur	1-0	1-0	8	P.A.Durkin	Hislop	Ferdinand	Potts	Pearce S	Minto	Foe	Pearce ▲	Lampard 45	Sinclair	Wanchope	di Canio ▲	Keller ▲, Cole ▲
16/08	A	Aston Villa	1-1	2-2	9	M.A.Riley	Hislop	Ferdinand	Potts	Pearce S	Minto	Foe	Moncur ▲	Lampard	Sinclair 90	Wanchope	di Canio	Kitson ▲
21/08	H	Leicester City	1-1	2-1	7	A.G.Wiley	Hislop	Ferdinand	Potts	Pearce S	Lomas	Foe	Moncur	Lampard	Sinclair	Wanchope 28	di Canio 52	
28/08	A	Bradford City	2-0	3-0	4	P.Jones	Hislop	Ferdinand ▲	Potts	Pearce S	Lomas	Keller	Moncur ▲	Lampard	Sinclair 44	Wanchope 48	di Canio 34	Carrick ▲
11/09	H	Watford	0-0	1-0	3	D.J.Gallagher	Hislop	Stimac	Potts	Pearce S ▲	Lomas	Keller	Moncur ▲	Lampard	Sinclair	Wanchope	di Canio 47	Carrick ▲, Margas ▲
19/09	A	Everton	0-0	0-1	9	S.G.Bennett	Hislop	Stimac	Potts	Margas	Lomas	Keller	Moncur	Lampard	Sinclair	Wanchope	di Canio	Newton ▲
25/09	H	Coventry City	0-1	0-1	9	D.R.Elleray	Hislop	Stimac	Potts	Keller ▲	Lomas	Foe ●	Moncur ▲	Lampard	Sinclair	Wanchope	di Canio	Newton ▲
03/10	A	Arsenal	1-0	2-1	9	M.D.Reed	Hislop	Stimac	Potts	Ruddock	Lomas	Foe ●	Moncur ▲	Lampard	Sinclair	Wanchope	di Canio 29 72	Margas ▲, Kitson ▲
17/10	H	Middlesbrough	0-0	0-2	10	U.D.Rennie	Hislop	Ferdinand	Stimac	Ruddock	Lomas	Keller ■	Cole	Lampard	Sinclair	Wanchope	di Canio	Cole ▲, Forrest ▲
24/10	A	Sunderland	0-1	1-1	11	M.R.Halsey	Hislop	Ferdinand	Stimac	Margas	Lomas	Keller	Cole	Lampard	Sinclair 88	Wanchope	di Canio	Ruddock ▲, Moncur ▲	Kitson ▲
27/10	A	Liverpool	0-1	0-1	12	S.J.Lodge	Hislop	Ferdinand	Potts	Ruddock	Lomas	Keller	Cole	Lampard	Sinclair	Kitson	di Canio	Kitson
30/10	A	Leeds United	0-0	0-1	12	G.Poll	Hislop	Ferdinand	Margas	Ruddock	Lomas	Foe ▲	Moncur	Lampard	Sinclair	Wanchope	Kitson	Cole ▲
07/11	H	Chelsea	0-0	0-0	11	M.A.Riley	Forrest	Ferdinand	Margas ●	Stimac	Lomas	Keller ■	Cole ▲	Lampard	Sinclair	Wanchope	Foe	Ruddock ▲
21/11	H	Sheffield Wednesday	1-1	4-3	10	A.B.Wilkie	Hislop	Ferdinand	Potts	Ruddock	Keller	Foe ●	Cole	Lampard 76	Sinclair	Wanchope 27	di Canio 62	Kitson ▲
27/11	A	Liverpool	1-0	1-0	8	G.P.Barber	Hislop	Ferdinand	Margas ●	Ruddock	Lomas	Foe	Cole ▲	Lampard	Sinclair 44	Wanchope ▲	di Canio ▲	Kitson ▲
06/12	A	Tottenham Hotspur	0-0	0-0	8	P.Jones	Hislop	Ferdinand	Keller	Margas	Minto	Foe	Cole	Lampard	Sinclair	Kitson ▲	di Canio ▲	Potts ▲, Minto ▲
18/12	H	Manchester United	1-3	2-4	9	U.D.Rennie	Hislop	Ferdinand	Margas	Ruddock	Minto ▲	Foe	Lomas	Lampard 80	Sinclair 45	Wanchope	di Canio 23 52	Wanchope ▲
26/12	A	Wimbledon	1-1	2-2	11	S.W.Dunn	Hislop	Ferdinand	Margas	Margas	Minto ▲	Foe	Cole	Lampard	Sinclair	Wanchope	di Canio	Keller ▲
28/12	H	Derby County	0-1	2-1	10	A.G.Wiley	Hislop	Ferdinand	Potts	Simoc 87	Lomas	Keller	Cole	Lampard	Sinclair 21	Wanchope	Carrick	Byrne ▲
03/01	A	Newcastle United	0-1	0-2	11	R.J.Harris	Hislop	Ferdinand	Margas	Simoc	Lomas	Keller ■	Cole	Lampard 84	Sinclair	Wanchope	di Canio 77	
15/01	H	Aston Villa	2-1	3-1	8	G.Poll	Hislop ▲	Ferdinand	Margas	Ruddock	Lomas ▲	Keller ■	Cole	Lampard	Sinclair	Wanchope 13 45	di Canio 60	Forrest ▲, Cole ▲
22/01	A	Leicester City	2-1	3-1	8	D.R.Elleray	Forrest	Ferdinand	Stimac	Simoc	Minto	Lomas	Cole	Lampard 66	Sinclair	Charles	Wanchope	Moncur ▲, Kitson ▲
05/02	H	Southampton	0-0	1-2	10	B.Knight	Hislop ▲	Ferdinand	Stimac	Charles ▲	Minto	Lomas	Cole 69	Lampard	Sinclair 35	Moncur 45	di Canio 65	Bywater ▲
12/02	A	Bradford City	2-2	5-4	9	N.S.Barry	Ilic	Ferdinand	Stimac	Pearce S	Lomas	Keller	Cole	Moncur	Sinclair	Wanchope	Kitson	
26/02	A	Everton	0-1	0-4	11	P.E.Alcock	Forrest	Ferdinand	Stimac	Simoc	Minto ■	Foe	Moncur ▲	Lampard	Sinclair	Lomas 3	Wanchope 35	Minto ▲
04/03	H	Watford	2-0	2-0	10	M.D.Reed	Forrest	Ferdinand	Stimac	Simoc	Lomas	Cole ▲	Moncur	Lampard	Sinclair 48	Moncur	Wanchope 17	Cole ▲
08/03	A	Southampton	1-0	2-0	6	S.J.Lodge	Forrest	Ferdinand	Stimac	Simoc	Lomas	Moncur	Moncur	Lampard 10	Sinclair	Wanchope	di Canio	Cole ▲, Kitson ▲
11/03	H	Sheffield Wednesday	1-0	1-3	10	P.Jones	Forrest	Ferdinand	Stimac	Minto	Minto	Moncur	Moncur ■	Lampard	Sinclair	Kanoute 59	di Canio	Kitson ▲
18/03	H	Chelsea	0-0	0-0	9	S.W.Dunn	Forrest	Ferdinand	Stimac	Simoc ●	Lomas	Moncur ▲	Moncur ▲	Lampard	Sinclair	Kanoute	di Canio 8	Cole ▲, Ruddock ▲
26/03	A	Wimbledon	2-1	2-1	9	R.J.Harris	Forrest	Ferdinand	Stimac	Minto	Minto	Moncur ▲	Moncur	Lampard	Sinclair	Kanoute	Wanchope 11	Keller ▲
01/04	H	Manchester United	1-3	1-7	8	M.A.Riley	Forrest	Ferdinand	Stimac ▲	Ruddock ▲	Lomas	Cole	Moncur	Lampard	Sinclair	Wanchope	di Canio	Wanchope 60 89 ▲
12/04	H	Newcastle United	0-0	2-1	8	P.E.Alcock	Feuer	Ferdinand	Stimac	Margas	Minto ▲	Kanoute 80	Cole ▲	Lampard	Sinclair 83	Wanchope 15 32	di Canio	Charles ▲, Margas ▲
15/04	A	Derby County	2-0	3-0	8	M.R.Halsey	Feuer	Ferdinand	Stimac	Margas 13	Minto ▲	Kanoute	Carrick 6	Lampard	Sinclair	Wanchope	di Canio 49 67	Charles ▲
22/04	A	Coventry City	2-0	5-0	8	A.P.D'Urso	Feuer	Ferdinand	Stimac	Margas	Lomas	Kanoute	Cole ▲	Lampard	Sinclair	Wanchope	di Canio	Newton ▲
29/04	H	Middlesbrough	0-1	0-1	8	B.Knight	Feuer	Ferdinand	Simoc	Margas	Keller	Kanoute	Moncur ▲	Lampard	Sinclair	Moncur	di Canio	
02/05	H	Arsenal	1-0	1-2	8	P.A.Durkin	Bywater	Potts	Simoc	Potts	Keller	Kanoute	Foe ●	Carrick	Sinclair ●	Wanchope	di Canio 41	
06/05	A	Sunderland	0-1	0-1	9	N.S.Barry	Bywater	Ferdinand	Simoc	Potts	Moncur	Kanoute	Foe	Carrick	Sinclair	Wanchope	di Canio	
14/05	H	Leeds United	0-0	0-0	9	G.P.Barber	Bywater	Ferdinand	Simoc	Potts	Margas	Moncur	Foe ●	Kanoute	Sinclair	Wanchope	di Canio	

211

Goal Analysis

GOALS BY POSITION 1997/1998 - 1999/2000

for the latest stats and to share your memories go to football.co.uk

key:
- forward
- defence
- midfield
- -0- final league position

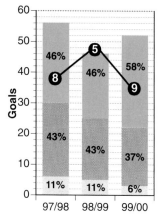

HOME

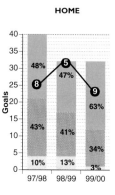

AWAY

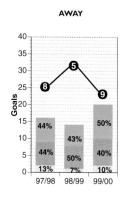

and di Canio combining superbly. Wanchope finished with 12 goals while di Canio got 16 and though the Italian remained the firm favourite with the Hammers fans, there was no doubting that Wanchope scored some valuable goals. The 16 goals that di Canio scored was the best return by a Hammer since Tony Morley scored 20 in the old Second Division (1992-93) but the first time any West Ham player had scored so many in the top flight since Tony Cottee netted 23 First Division goals 13

years ago. In addition, Kanoute added two goals to suggest he will feature more regularly this season. O~ di Canio's 16, 13 were scored at Upton Park and he rarely scored an easy goal. By contrast, Wanchope scored seven of his 12 away.

Frank Lampard and Trevor Sinclair enjoyec impeccable seasons and both finished with seven goals apiece. For Lampard, it was his best ever League goal return and two more than in the previous Carling Premiership season. and Cole

GOALS BY TIME PERIOD 1999/2000

for the latest stats and to share your memories go to football.co.uk

key:
- goals for
- goals against

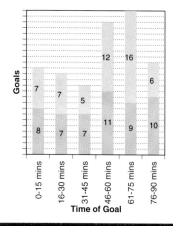

HOME

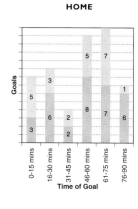

AWAY

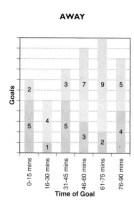

Goal Analysis

West Ham United

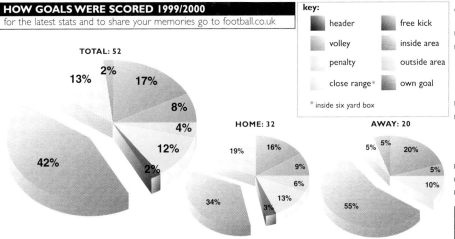

HOW GOALS WERE SCORED 1999/2000

for the latest stats and to share your memories go to football.co.uk

key:
- header
- volley
- penalty
- close range*
- free kick
- inside area
- outside area
- own goal

* inside six yard box

TOTAL: 52 — 2%, 13%, 17%, 8%, 4%, 12%, 2%, 42%

HOME: 32 — 19%, 16%, 9%, 6%, 13%, 3%, 34%

AWAY: 20 — 5%, 5%, 20%, 5%, 10%, 55%

cored his first Carling Premiership goal, in the thrilling 5-4 win over Bradford. That was not the first time West Ham starred in a goal-fest; they beat Sheffield Wednesday 4-3, played their part in the nine-goal spectacle against Bradford, lost 7-2 at Old Trafford – and beat Coventry 5-0. Strangely, however, they finished the season by scoring just once in the final four games.

Clearly, West Ham must be on their guard in the second period of games this season. Of the 53 they

conceded last term, 34 were in the second half with 21 coming away from home. United also scored more in the second half, with 30 of their 52 coming after the interval. But they tended to be sharper in the second half, particularly at home where 11 were scored in the opening 45 minutes and a further 21 in the second period overall.

Most goals came from inside the area where West Ham's patient approach work often paid dividends. But they also scored nine headers and

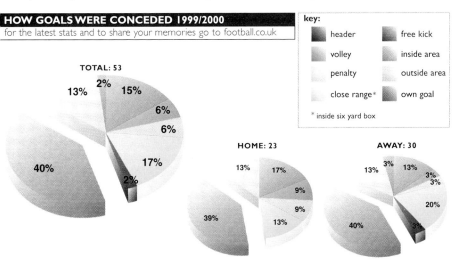

HOW GOALS WERE CONCEDED 1999/2000

for the latest stats and to share your memories go to football.co.uk

key:
- header
- volley
- penalty
- close range*
- free kick
- inside area
- outside area
- own goal

* inside six yard box

TOTAL: 53 — 2%, 13%, 15%, 6%, 6%, 17%, 2%, 40%

HOME: 23 — 13%, 17%, 9%, 9%, 13%, 39%

AWAY: 30 — 3%, 13%, 13%, 3%, 3%, 20%, 3%, 40%

Squad and Performance

powered by **football.co.uk**

SQUAD LIST

for the latest stats and to share your memories go to football.co.uk

Position	Name	Appearances	Appearances as substitute	Goals	Clean Sheets	Yellow Cards	Red Cards
G	S.Bywater	3	1		1		
G	I.Feuer	3			1	1	
G	C.Forrest	9	2		3		
G	S.Hislop	22			5		1
G	S.Ilic	1					
D	S.Byrne		1				
D	G.Charles	2	2			1	
D	R.Ferdinand	33				2	
D	J.Margas	15	3	1		1	1
D	S.Minto	15	3			2	
D	A.Newton		2				
D	I.Pearce	1					
D	S.Pearce	8				2	
D	S.Potts	16	1			1	
D	N.Ruddock	12	3			4	
D	I.Stimac	24		1		8	1
M	M.Carrick	4	4	1			
M	J.Cole	17	4	1		1	
M	M.Foe	25		1		6	2
M	M.Keller	19	3			4	
M	F.Lampard	34		7		4	
M	S.Lomas	25		1		5	1
M	J.Moncur	20	2	1		7	1
M	T.Sinclair	36		7		5	1
F	P.di Canio	29	1	16		6	
F	F.Kanoute	8		2		1	
F	P.Kitson	4	6				
F	P.Wanchope	33	2	12		6	

seven from outside the area, with Lampard collecting a good percentage of those.

West Ham used more goalkeepers than any other team in the Premiership; Shaka Hislop began as first choice but suffered the Hammers hoodoo when he broke his leg after just two minutes of the 5-4 win over Bradford. In came Stephen Bywater, who suffered a difficult debut but made amends at Arsenal in May when he was outstanding. Craig Forrest came in, saved a penalty from Denis Irwin during the 7-1 thumping at Old Trafford and then suffered injury. In came Ian Feuer, a colourful American, while Charlton's on-loan Yugoslav Sasa Ilic also got a game.

The Hammers failed to beat Manchester United,

TEAM PERFORMANCE TABLE

for the latest stats and to share your memories go to football.co.uk

Position	Club	Points Won	Percentage of points won at home	percentage of points won away	overall percentage of points won
1.	MANCHESTER UNITED	0/6			
2.	ARSENAL	3/6			
3.	LEEDS UNITED	1/6	53%	7%	**30%**
4.	LIVERPOOL	3/6			
5.	CHELSEA	2/6			
6.	ASTON VILLA	2/6			
7.	SUNDERLAND	1/6			
8.	LEICESTER CITY	6/6	67%	42%	**54%**
9.	TOTTENHAM HOTSPUR	4/6			
10.	WEST HAM UNITED	55 pts			
11.	NEWCASTLE UNITED	4/6			
12.	MIDDLESBROUGH	0/6			
13.	EVERTON	0/6	60%	7%	**33%**
14.	SOUTHAMPTON	3/6			
15.	COVENTRY CITY	3/6			
16.	DERBY COUNTY	4/6			
17.	BRADFORD CITY	6/6			
18.	WIMBLEDON	4/6	87%	67%	**77%**
19.	SHEFFIELD WEDNESDAY	3/6			
20.	WATFORD	6/6			

The figures show a team's performance against clubs in each quarter of the final league table. The first column represents points won from the total available against each team in the league.

What a difference a *CARLING* makes.

Discipline and Season Summary

powered by **football.co.uk**

West Ham United

BOOKINGS BY POSITION 1997/1998 - 1999/2000

for the latest stats and to share your memories go to football.co.uk

key:
- ■ forward
- □ defence
- ■ midfield
- ■ goalkeeper

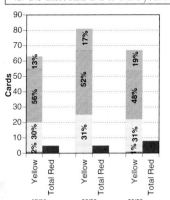

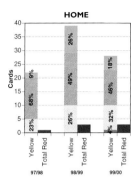

HOME

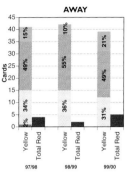

AWAY

Middlesbrough or Everton but did the double over Leicester, Bradford and Watford.

Given that West Ham started the season without three players because of suspension one could reasonably expect that their behaviour could not get any worse; in the 1998-99 season they collected 81 yellow cards and five red. But, though cautions were down, to 67, they collected no fewer than eight red cards – a Carling Premiership record. Their record was such that they averaged a dismissal every five games; 18 games were lost to suspensions – and Sinclair will miss the start of this season after being sent-off at Arsenal. Foe will also miss the start of the season – with Lyon – after collecting his second

dismissal in last season's final game, at home to Leeds. West Ham actually avoided a red card until the end of September when John Moncur was dismissed but in the next two games, Foe and Hislop departed early. Margas and Steve Lomas were next, followed by Stimac, Sinclair and Foe again.

No fewer than 19 of the 28 players used were booked at least once; the worst offender was Stimac, with eight cautions, while Moncur received seven and both di Canio and Wanchope collected six.

On 17 occasions West Ham were level at the interval but only seven times did the game finish level, with five ending in wins and a further five ending in defeats.

HALF TIME - FULL TIME COMPARATIVE CHART

for the latest stats and to share your memories go to football.co.uk

HOME				AWAY				TOTAL			
Number of Home Half Time Wins	Full Time Result W L D			Number of Away Half Time Wins	Full Time Result W L D			Total Number of Half Time Wins	Full Time Result W L D		
6	6	0	0	6	4	2	0	12	10	2	0
Number of Home Half Time Losses	Full Time Result W L D			Number of Away Half Time Losses	Full Time Result W L D			Total Number of Half Time Losses	Full Time Result W L D		
4	0	2	2	5	0	4	1	9	0	6	3
Number of Home Half Time Draws	Full Time Result W L D			Number of Away Half Time Draws	Full Time Result W L D			Total Number of Half Time Draws	Full Time Result W L D		
9	5	1	3	8	0	4	4	17	5	5	7

What a difference a *CARLING* makes.

Maps and Directions

Upton Park is in London's East End, approximately 7 miles from the city centre. There is usually ample parking in streets around the ground.

From the North:
From the M1, turn off onto the A1 at Junction 2/3. Join the A406 North Circular Road and continue east for 17 miles until the junction with the A124 Barking Road. Turn right into Barking Road and continue for 2 miles, turning right into Green Street. Upton Park is on the right.

From the North-West:
Approaching London on the M40, at Junction 1 stay on the A40 for 10 miles before turning onto the A406 North Circular Road eastbound. Stay on this road for 23 miles until the junction with the A124 Barking Road. Then as route for North.

From the West:
Approaching London on the M4, turn off onto the A406 North Circular Road eastbound. Stay on this road for 26 miles until the junction with the A124 Barking Road. Then as route for North.

From the South-West:
From the M3 turn off onto the M25 at Junction 2. Continue for 10 miles until you reach Junction 15 at which point turn off onto the M4.
Then as route for West.

From the East:
From the M11 turn off onto the A406 at Junction 4 for 4 miles until the junction with the A124 Barking Road. Then as route for North.

The nearest tube stations are Upton Park and East Ham.

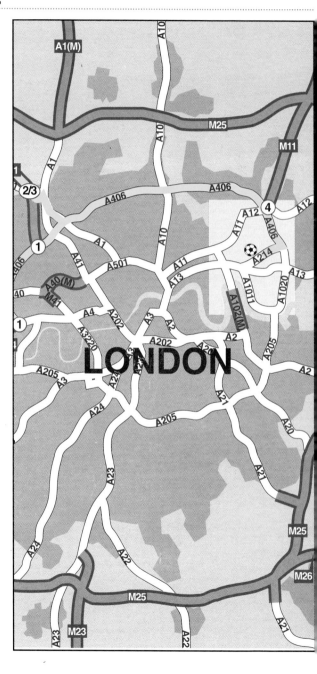

West Ham United

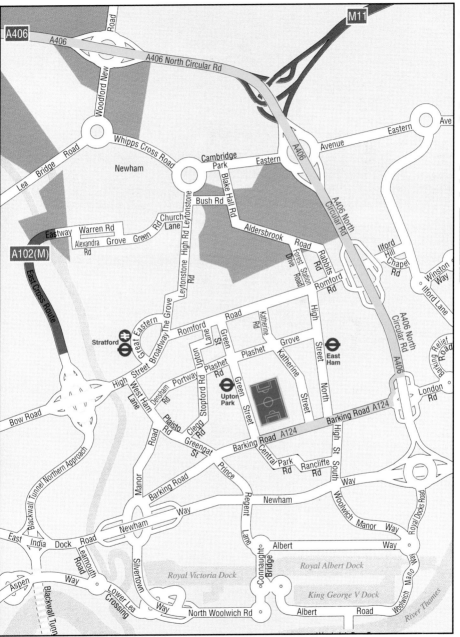

Maps and Directions

Leave the M1 at Junction 37 and following the road signs to the ground. At motorway roundabout follow "Barnsley F.C." signs into Dodworth Road. After 1/4 mile turn left at the traffic lights into Pogmoor Road. After 1 mile turn right into Gawber Road and after 1/3 mile follow road round sharp bend into Victoria Road and continue straight on into Old Mill Lane travelling down hill for 1/3 mile to traffic lights. Continue straight on taking the right hand lane. Follow signs "Pontefract A628" turning right at B&Q roundabout (McDonald's/Asda on left) into Harborough Hill Road. Travel uphill and in approximately 1/2 mile branch left (sign posted Pontefract A628) then immediately left into Queens Road. The visitors car park is at the top of Queens Road on the right hand side.

Barnsley railway station is within walking distance.

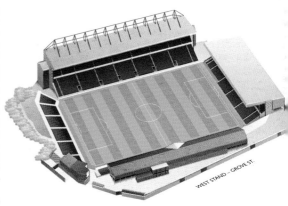

WEST STAND - GROVE ST.

Barnsley

Oakwell Ground, Barnsley,
South Yorkshire S71 1ET
Tel: 01226 211211

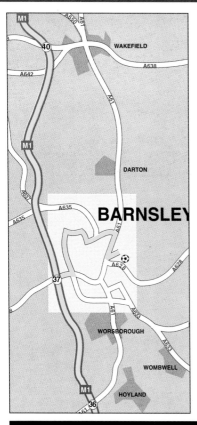

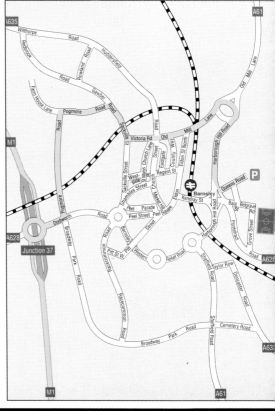

Maps and Directions

Exit M6 at Junction 6 and take the A38(M) (Aston Expressway). Leave at 2nd exit then take first exit at roundabout along Dartmouth Middleway. After 1 ¼ miles turn left into St. Andrew's Street.

Car Parking is available in the streets surrounding the stadium.

Bus Services:
Service 97 from Birmingham; Services 98 & 99 from Digbeth.

Nearest Railway Station:
Birmingham New Street or Birmingham Moor Street (20 minutes walk).

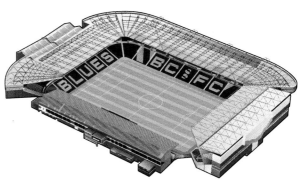

Birmingham City

St Andrews Ground,
Birmingham B9 4NH
Tel: 0121 772 0101

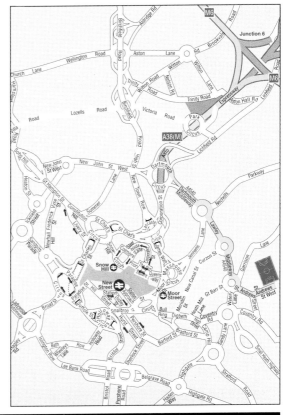

Maps and Directions

From The North and South:
Exit M6 at junction 31 onto A59/A677 towards Blackburn. After 1 1/2 miles the road splits. Keep to the A677. After approximately 5 miles turn right at the Esso garage onto Montague Street, cross over King Street into Byron Street, left into Canterbury Street and follow the one-way system until the T-junction with the Bolton Road A666. Turn right for Ewood Park.

From The South:
Exit M61 junction 8 onto A674. After 5 miles turn right onto the A6062 for 3 miles until the Bolton Road A666. Turn right and Ewood Park is 1/4 mile down on your left.

From The East:
Exit M65 junction 6, turn left onto the A6119 Whitebirk Road for 1/2 mile, turn right onto the A677 for 1/2 mile and then bear left onto the A679 for 1 mile, then left onto the A666 for 1 1/4 miles. Ewood Park is on the left.

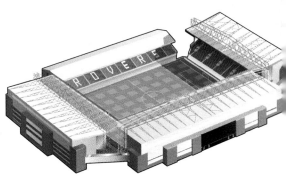

Blackburn Rovers

Ewood Park, Blackburn,
Lancashire, BB2 4JF
Tel: 01254 698888

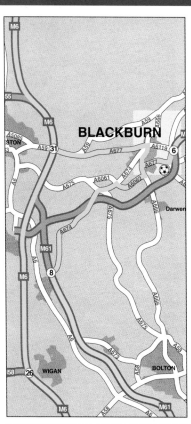

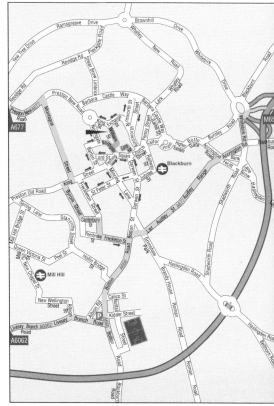

Maps and Directions

From the North West:
Take M61 to Junction 6.
From the North East
Take M62 to Junction 14 then same as directions from South.

From the South:
Travel on the M1 until Junction 19, then take the M6 to Junction 10, turn onto the M62 until Junction 14 and take M61 to Junction 6.

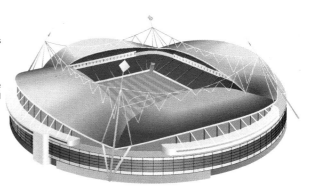

Bolton Wanderers

The Reebok Stadium, Burnden Way,
Horwich, Bolton, BL6 6JW
Tel: 01204 673673

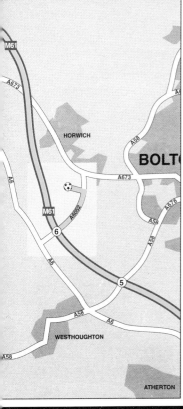

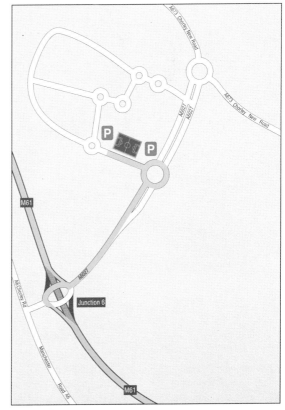

Maps and Directions

From all points:

Leave M6 at junction 29 and follow signs to the M65 eastbound. Get onto the M65 and at junction 10 s/p Burnley A671 get off. At the roundabout take the fifth exit s/p burnley A671. At the next roundabout adjacent to the Little Chef turn left for Burnley Town Centre. At the lights turn right into Trafalgar St. Keep going following signs for Rochdale A671 onto Centenary Way. After 1/2 mile go straight over at roundabout. After 1/3 mile turn right into Ormerod Rd (by Sparrowhawk Hotel). At the junction turn right into Belvedere Rd. Turf Moor is on the left handside after 1/2 mile.

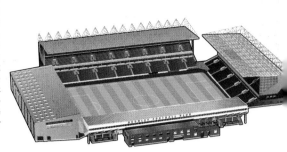

Burnley

Turf Moor, Brunshaw Road,
East Lancashire, BB10 4BX
Tel: 01282 700000

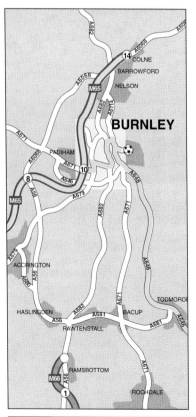

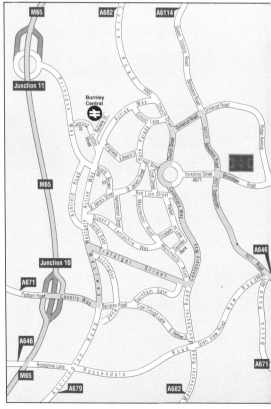

Maps and Directions

From North:
Leave M6 at junction 17 (A534). At T-junction turn right for Crewe and follow A534 (signposted Crewe, Nantwich). Continue for about 6 miles. Gresty Road is the first left after Crewe Station.

From South and East:
Exit M6 at junction 16 (A500). At roundabout follow signs for Crewe. After two miles turn right at roundabout (A5020) towards Crewe. Turn left at the next roundabout, straight on at the next, passing the Brocklebank pub on the left, then left at the next and final roundabout, taking you into Nantwich Road, passing Crewe Station on your left.

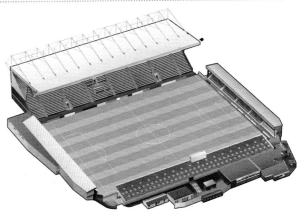

Crewe Alexandra

Gresty Road, Crewe,
Cheshire, CW2 6EB
Tel: 01270 213014

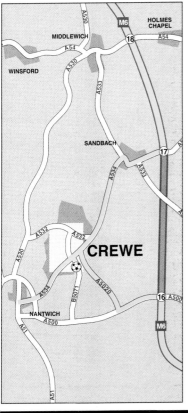

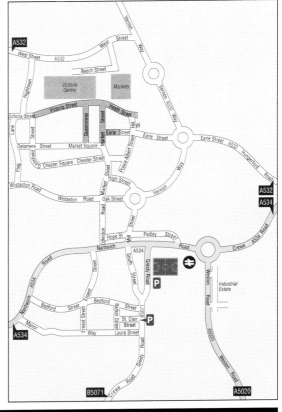

223

Maps and Directions

North: Approaching on the M1, exit at Junction 1 onto the A406 North Circular Road. Keep on the North Circular until Chiswick roundabout, then take the A205 South Circular which joins the A3 to Wandsworth. Follow the one-way system and turn right onto the A214 Trinity Road, through Tooting Bec to Streatham. Turn onto the A23 Streatham High Road and left onto the A214 Crown Lane. Turn right onto the A215 Beulah Hill and then right into Whitehorse Lane.

North West: arrive on the M40/A40 continue until you meet the A406 North Circular. Then as route for North.

West: Approaching on the M4, exit at Junction 1 Chiswick Roundabout onto the A205 South Circular. Then as route for North.

South West: Approaching on the M3, continue onto the A316 until the junction with the A205 South Circular. Then as route for North.

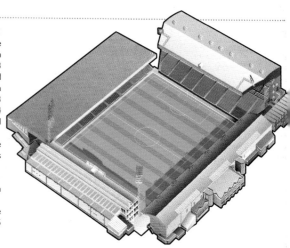

Crystal Palace

Selhurst Park Stadium
South Norwood, London SE25 6PY
Tel: 020

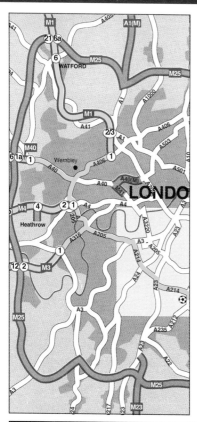

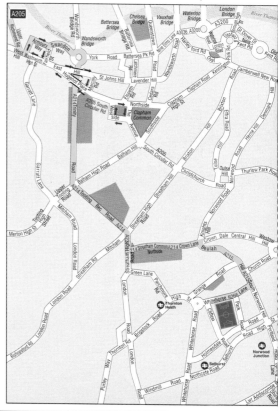

What a difference a *CARLING* makes.

Maps and Directions

Drive into London on the M4, following signs to Central London (A4). After 10 miles you come to the Hogarth roundabout. Take the second exit (signposted Central London, Hammersmith, A4) remain on the A4, passing the Griffin Brewery. At the Hammersmith flyover junction keep in left hand lane and exit the A4 (signposted Hammersmith (A306, A313, A219). Follow signs to Oxford (A40) to T-Junction. This is the Hammersmith roundabout. Continue round to where road runs underneath and parallel to the A4 and turn left (signposted alternative route via Putney Bridge) into Fulham Palace Road. Go straight on for 1 ¼ miles, and turn right into Bishops Park Road, which leads to the ground.

From the South: Go over Putney Bridge, and go straight on at the junction (signposted the West and West End) - at mini roundabout by the Kings Head pub, go straight on into Fulham Palace Road.

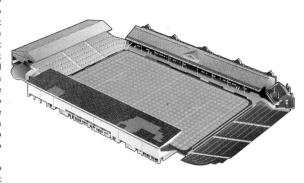

Fulham

Craven Cottage, Stevenage Road,
London, SW6 6HH
Tel: 020 7893 8383

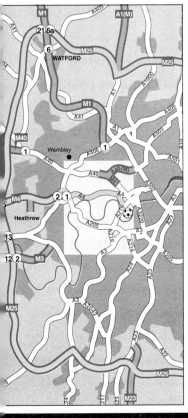

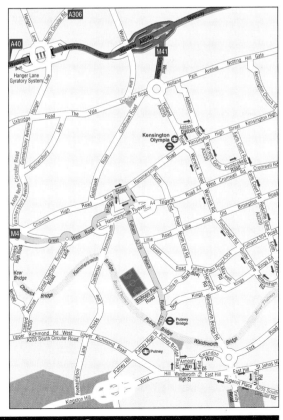

225

Maps and Directions

Leave the M2 at junction 4 and at roundabout follow signs to Gillingham 'A278' onto the A278. Continue on this road for approx 2 miles (over two roundabouts) to a third roundabout. Here take the left turning that is sign posted Gillingham/Chatham 'A2' onto the A2. Continue along this road for half a mile, straight over one roundabout turning right at the traffic lights (will be sign posted Strand Leisure Park / Riverside Country Park). This will take you onto Woodlands Road. After 3/4 miles you should turn left (opposite Mayfair Cars centre) into Chicago avenue. You should be able to see the floodlights now so this is the ideal opportunity to look for parking spaces. To go on to the ground, turn right at the end of Chicago Avenue and then quickly left into Redfern Avenue.

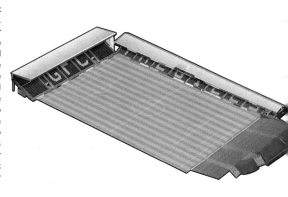

Gillingham

Priestfield Stadium, Redfern Avenue
Gillingham, Kent ME7 4DD
Tel: 01643 851854

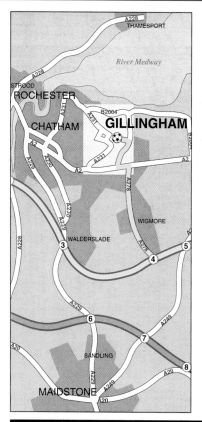

Maps and Directions

All routes:
Follow the M180 onto the A180 towards Grimsby. At first roundabout go straight on then follow signs for Cleethorpes (A180) onto Grimsby Road. Blundell Park is situated behind the Drive Thru' McDonald's

From A46 (Lincoln):
Follow A46 into Grimsby, go straight on at the roundabout after duel carriageway, following signs to Cleethorpes. At Grimsby College, get in right hand lane and keep following signs for Cleethorpes. At Isaac's Hill roundabout turn left onto Grimsby Road, Blundell Park is situated behind the Drive Thru' McDonald's

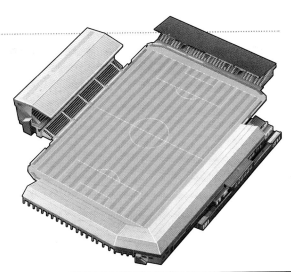

Grimsby Town

Blundell Park, Cleethorpes,
North East Lincolnshire DN35 7PY
Tel: 01472 605050

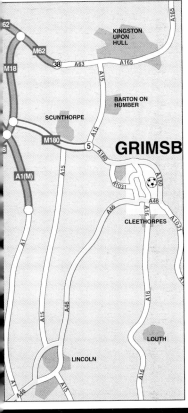

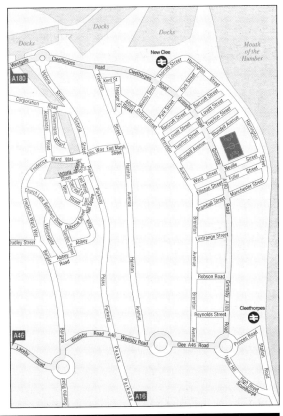

227

Maps and Directions

From the North and East: Exit M62 at junction 25. At motorway roundabout follow signs to Huddersfield A644. After 1 1/4 miles turn right at roundabout into Leeds Road (A62). Follow Huddersfield A62 signs through several sets of lights for 3 miles, and then turn left into St. Andrews Road, and then left into the Stadium at the next set of lights.

From the South: Keep on the M1 all the way up to Leeds, turning on to the M62. Then as North and East.

From the West: Leave M62 at junction 24. At motorway roundabout follow signs to Huddersfield (A629) into the Town Centre. Follow the Ring Road round and exit onto Leeds Road (A62), then take 2nd right down Gasworks Street. At the crossroads go straight across to get to the Stadium.

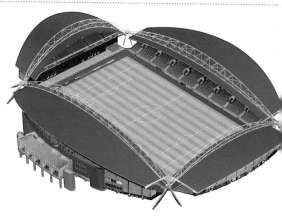

Huddersfield Town

The Alfred McAlpine Stadium
Huddersfield, HD1 6PX
Tel: 01484 484100

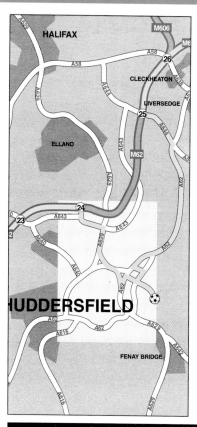

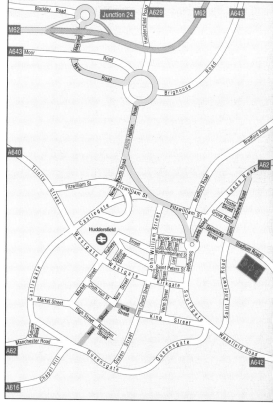

Maps and Directions

From the West:
Head to Norwich on the A47, this becomes the Norwich southern bypass. Keep on the A47 for 10 miles. At junction with the A146 turn left (s/p Norwich). At T junction after 3/4 mile turn right into Martineau Rd (A 1054). At Roundabout take first exit for car park second exit for stadium. Keep in the right hand lane and after 1/4 mile turn right into King St (s/p Ring road A47). After 1/4 mile bend right with the road, go over the river straight over at lights and the ground is on the right hand side.

From South: Head to Norwich on the A11 until you reach the junction with the A47, get onto the A47 following signs to Norwich East and Great Yarmouth. After 4 miles exit at junction A146 and follow route from West.

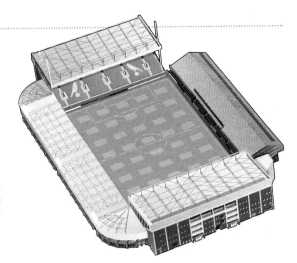

Norwich City

Carrow Road,
Norwich, NR1 1JE
Tel: 01603 760760

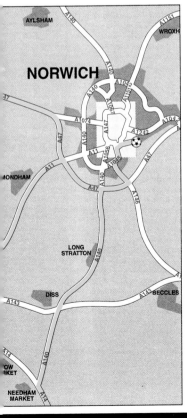

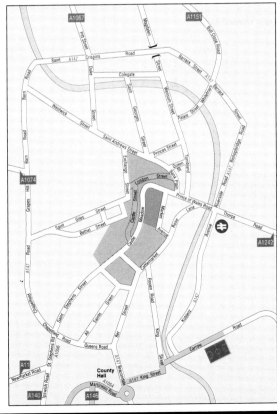

229

Maps and Directions

From the North: Leave M1 at junction 26, following the signs to Nottingham via the A610 Nuthall Road until you meet the Nottingham Ring Road A6514 at Western Boulevard. Turn right and follow the Ring Road South, passing the Queens Medical Centre where the Ring Road becomes the A52. Continue South on the A52 s/p Grantham over Clifton Bridge, past the Nottingham Knight Island to join the Lings Bar Road at the next traffic island. Continue to the Gamston Island and then turn left into Radcliffe Road (A6011). Turn right into Colwick Road.

From the South: Leave the M1 at junction 24, on the A453 towards Nottingham. At the Clifton Bridge complex follow signs A52 Grantham past Nottingham Knight Island to join the Lings Bar Road at the next traffic island. Follow the A52 signposted Grantham to the Gamston Island and then turn left into Radcliffe Road (A6011). Turn right into Colwick Road.

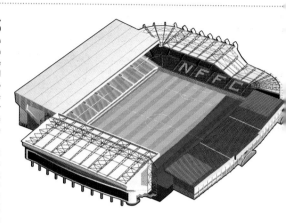

Nottingham Forest

The City Ground,
Nottingham NG2 5FJ
Tel: 0115 9824444

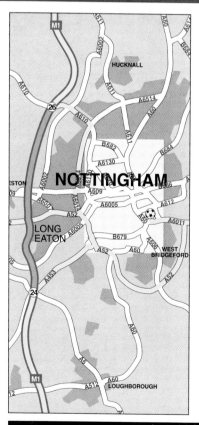

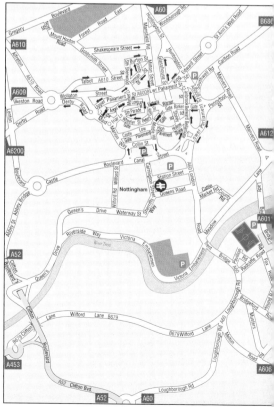

Maps and Directions

Take the M3 and M27. Travel east on the M27 until it becomes the A27. Continue until you come to the Southsea turn-off (A2030). Take this road (Eastern Road), through various sets of traffic lights, until you reach the roundabout at the end of Velder Avenue. Fratton Park is directly ahead.

There is limited parking available in Rodney Road and Velder Avenue. There is also a Pay and Display car park in the grounds of St Mary's Hospital in Milton Road, but this fills up early on match days.

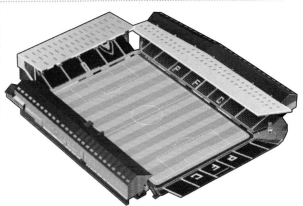

Portsmouth

Fratton Park, Frogmore Road
Portsmouth, POA 8RA
Tel: 01705 731204

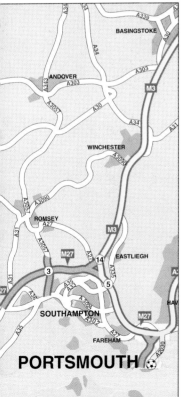

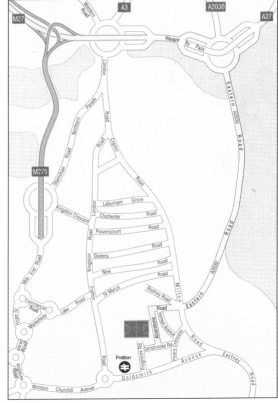

231

Maps and Directions

From North, South and East:
Exit M6 at junction 31. At the roundabout take the first exit (s/p Preston A59) onto the A59. At mini-roundabout after 1 mile, by the Hesketh Arms, take the second exit (s/p Ring road, Blackpool A583, Football Ground) onto the Blackpool Road A5085. Go straight on for just over a mile and bear left before the lights (s/p Town Centre, Football Ground) into Sir Tom Finney Way. The ground is on the left-hand-side.

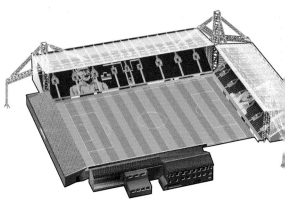

Preston North End

Sir OM Finney Way, Deepdale
Preston, Lancs PR1 6RU
Tel: 01772 902020

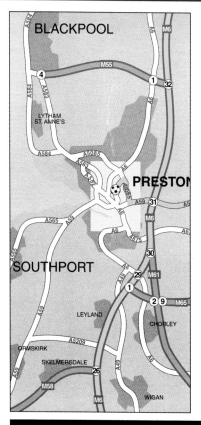

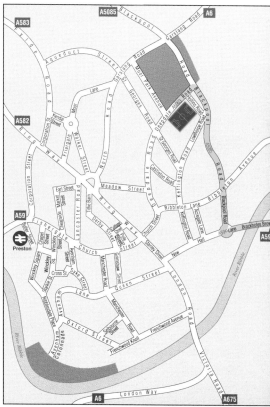

Maps and Directions

From North:
Take the M1 onto the A406 West, then the A40 at Hanger Lane towards Central London. Turn off to White City, right into Wood Lane, then right again into South Africa Road.

From the East:
Take the A40(M) Westway, then turn off to White City, left into Wood Lane, then right into South Africa Road.

From the South:
Take the A3 and follow signs for Hammersmith, then the A219 to Shepherds Bush, then towards White City (Wood Lane), and left into South Africa Road.

From the West:
Take the M4 to Chiswick, A315 and A402 to Shepherds Bush, then towards White City (Wood Lane), and left into South Africa Road.

Parking is available for £5.00 in the BBC car park on match days.

Queens Park Rangers

Loftus Road Stadium,
South Africa Road, London W12 7PA
Tel: 020 8743 0262

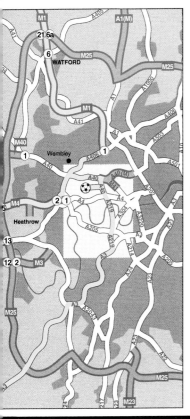

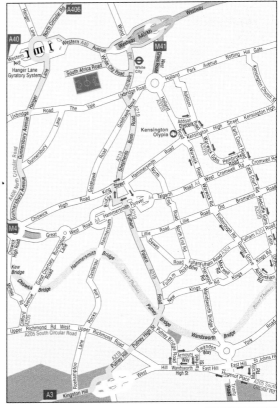

233

Maps and Directions

Sheffield Wednesday's stadium is situated 2 miles from the city centre. All visitors are advised to approach via the M1/A61 route and avoid the city centre. Parking is possible in the area just north of Hillsborough around Doe Royd Lane as well as next to the stadium in Parkside Road.

All Routes:

Approaching on the M1, exit at Junction 36 onto the A61. Keep on this road for 7 miles, crossing over the roundabout onto Pennistone Road. The ground is on the right.

Sheffield Railway Station is situated in the town centre, approximately 2 miles from the ground. Buses run to the ground from nearby Pond Street.

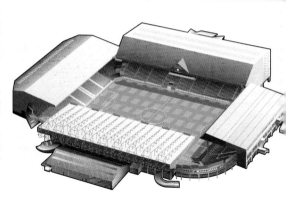

Sheffield Wednesday

Penistone Road, Hillsborough,
Sheffield S6 1SW
Tel: 0114 221 2121

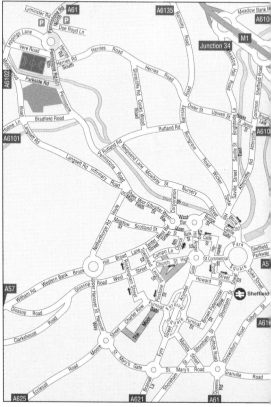

234   What a difference a *CARLING* makes.

Maps and Directions

From all directions:
Exit the M1 at junction 33 and follow the signs at roundabout towards Sheffield City Centre onto the A630 dual carriageway. After 5½ miles, at Park Square roundabout take 3rd exit (Ring Road, Chesterfield A16). Pass railway station on the left hand side and move into the middle lane for Sheaf Square roundabout. Take 1st exit (Ring Road, Chesterfield A61) and keep in right hand lane, turning right at lights (Ring Road, Bakewell A621, also the Leadmill) into Shoreham Street. Go straight through at the first and second set of lights (ignoring signpost to Bramall Lane). The ground is on the right hand side.

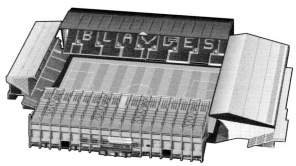

Sheffield United

Bramall Lane,
Sheffield, S2 4SU
Tel: 0114 221 5757

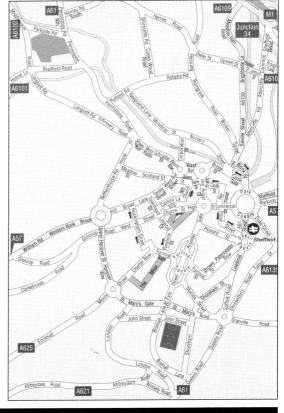

235

Maps and Directions

From the North, South and West:
Exit the M63 at junction 11 and join the A560 towards Stockport. After half a mile, turn right into Edgeley Road. After one mile turn right into Caroline Street.

From the East:
Take the A6 into Stockport town centre, then turn left into Greek Street. At roundabout take the second exit into Castle Street then left into Caroline Street.

There is limited street parking around the stadium. There are also council car parks off Mercian Way.

Stockport County

Edgeley Park, Hardcastle Road, Stockport, SK3 9DD
Tel: 0161 286 8888

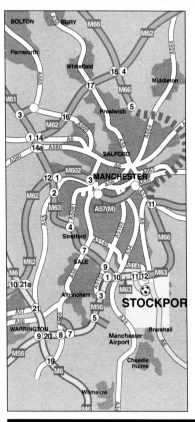

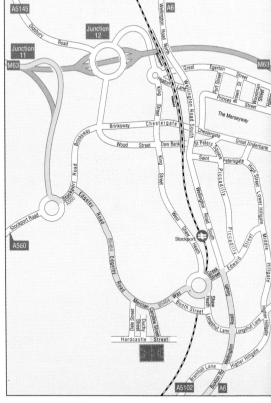

What a difference a *CARLING* makes.

Maps and Directions

From the North:

From Liverpool city centre, travel through Queensway Mersey Tunnel (signposted Birkenhead) and after the toll booths, bear right onto the flyover. The ground is signposted from here. Travel along Borough Road for 3 miles, the ground is directly ahead.

From the South and East:

Take M53 to Junction 4. Take the fourth exit from the roundabout onto the B5151 Mount Road. Continue for 2 1/2 miles when Mount Road becomes Shoreton Road, then turn right into Prenton Road West.

For street parking, head away from the ground up Prenton Road East. Turn right at the junction and take the second exit at the roundabout into Bebington Road.

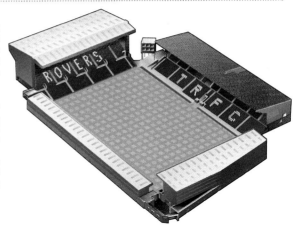

Tranmere Rovers

Prenton Park, Prenton Road West,
Prenton, Wirral, CH42 9PY
Tel: 0151 608 4194

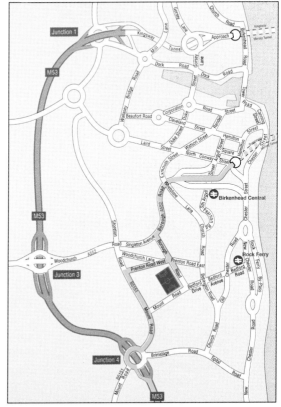

Maps and Directions

From the North:
Head south on M1. At M1 Junction 5, turn right onto A41 towards Hemel Hempstead. Continue onto A4008 for 1 1/2 miles. Turn right onto A411 towards Watford for 1/2 mile. Continue west onto A4145 towards Croxley Green for 1/3 miles. Turn left for Watford.

From the South:
Head north on M3 towards Staines. At M3 Junction 2, turn left onto M25. Continue on M25 for 18 miles. At M25 Junction 17, turn right onto A412 towards Maple Cross for 2 miles. Turn right onto A404 at Rickmansworth and continue for 1 mile. Turn left onto A4145 at Batchworth and continue for 3 1/2 miles towards Watford. Turn right for Watford.

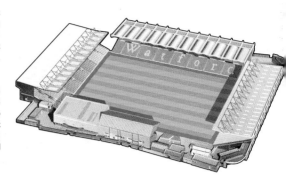

Watford

Vicarage Road Stadium, Vicarage R[
Watford WD1 8ER
Tel: 01923 496 000

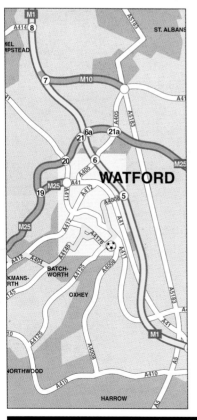

Maps and Directions

From all Directions:
Exit the M5 at junction 1. Take the A41 road signposted Birmingham. The stadium is visible immediately after the motorway island is cleared, and stands about 600 metres to the Birmingham side of junction 1.
Turn right into Halfords Lane for stadium and car parking.

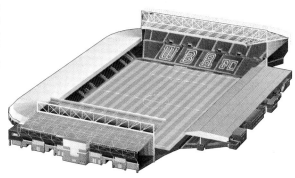

West Bromwich Albion

The Hawthorns, Halfords Lane,
West Bromwich, West Midlands
Tel: 0121 525 8888

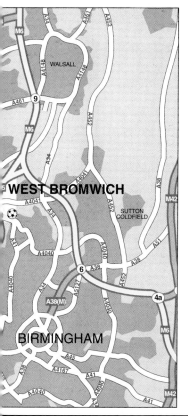

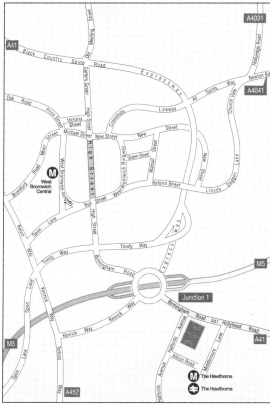

Maps and Directions

North: Approaching on the M1, exit at Junction 1 onto the A406 North Circular Road. Keep on the North Circular until Chiswick roundabout, then take the A205 South Circular which joins the A3 to Wandsworth. Follow the one-way system and turn right onto the A214 Trinity Road, through Tooting Bec to Streatham. Turn onto the A23 Streatham High Road and left onto the A214 Crown Lane. Turn right onto the A215 Beulah Hill and then right into Whitehorse Lane.

North West: arrive on the M40/A40 continue until you meet the A406 North Circular. Then as route for North.

West: Approaching on the M4, exit at Junction 1 Chiswick Roundabout onto the A205 South Circular. Then as route for North.

South West: Approaching on the M3, continue onto the A316 until the junction with the A205 South Circular. Then as route for North.

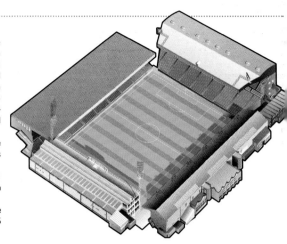

Wimbledon

Selhurst Park Stadium
South Norwood, London SE25 6PY
Tel: 020 8771 2233

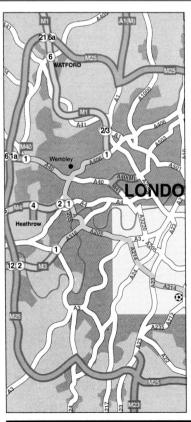

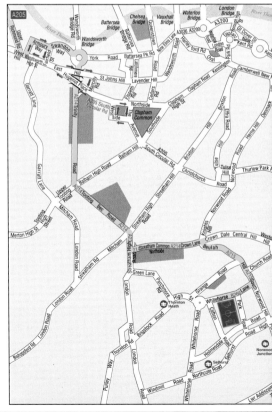

Maps and Directions

Travel North on M6, exit at junction 10A, then junction 2 on the M54.
Take the A449 Stafford Road to Wolverhampton. As you approach the Town Centre, take the 3rd exit at the island (not the town centre exit) into Waterloo Road. The stadium is approximately half a mile along the road on the left signposted 'Molineux Centre'.

Street parking is available around the ground. There are multi-storey car parks in the town centre, which is about a 10 minute walk away.

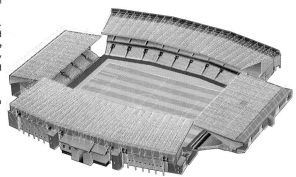

Wolverhampton Wanderers

Molineux Stadium, Waterloo Road
Wolverhampton, WV1 4QR
Tel: 01902 655000

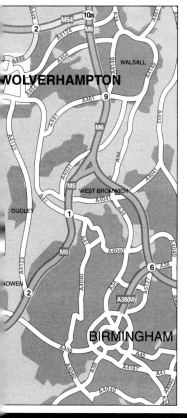

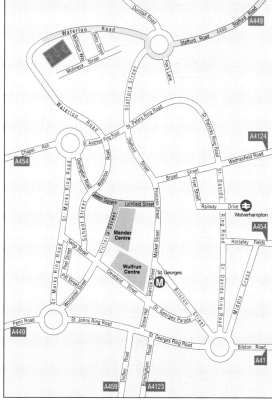

What a difference a *CARLING* makes.

241

Final League Tables 1999/2000

THE F.A. CARLING PREMIERSHIP

Pos	Team	Pld	W	D	L	F	A	Points
1	Manchester United	38	28	7	3	97	45	91
2	Arsenal	38	22	7	9	73	43	73
3	Leeds United	38	21	6	11	58	43	69
4	Liverpool	38	19	10	9	51	30	67
5	Chelsea	38	18	11	9	53	34	65
6	Aston Villa	38	15	13	10	46	35	58
7	Sunderland	38	16	10	12	57	56	58
8	Leicester City	38	16	7	15	55	55	55
9	West Ham United	38	15	10	13	52	53	55
10	Tottenham Hotspur	38	15	8	15	57	49	53
11	Newcastle United	38	14	10	14	63	54	52
12	Middlesbrough	38	14	10	14	46	52	52
13	Everton	38	12	14	12	59	49	50
14	Coventry City	38	12	8	18	47	54	44
15	Southampton	38	12	8	18	45	62	44
16	Derby County	38	9	11	18	44	57	38
17	Bradford City	38	9	9	20	38	68	36
18	Wimbledon	38	7	12	19	46	74	33
19	Sheffield Wednesday	38	8	7	23	38	70	31
20	Watford	38	6	6	26	35	77	24

DIVISION ONE

Pos	Team	Pld	W	D	L	F	A	Points
1	Charlton Athletic	46	27	10	9	79	45	91
2	Manchester City	46	26	11	9	78	40	89
3	Ipswich Town	46	25	12	9	71	42	87
4	Barnsley	46	24	10	12	88	67	82
5	Birmingham City	46	22	11	13	65	44	77
6	Bolton Wanderers	46	21	13	12	69	50	76
7	Wolverhampton Wanderers	46	21	11	14	64	48	74
8	Huddersfield Town	46	21	11	14	62	49	74
9	Fulham	46	17	16	13	49	41	67
10	Queens Park Rangers	46	16	18	12	62	53	66
11	Blackburn Rovers	46	15	17	14	55	51	62
12	Norwich City	46	14	15	17	45	50	57
13	Tranmere Rovers	46	15	12	19	57	68	57
14	Nottingham Forest	46	14	14	18	53	55	56
15	Crystal Palace	46	13	15	18	57	67	54
16	Sheffield United	46	13	15	18	59	71	54
17	Stockport County	46	13	15	18	55	67	54
18	Portsmouth	46	13	12	21	55	66	51
19	Crewe Alexandra	46	14	9	23	46	67	51
20	Grimsby Town	46	13	12	21	41	67	51
21	West Bromwich Albion	46	10	19	17	43	60	49
22	Walsall	46	11	13	22	52	77	46
23	Port Vale	46	7	15	24	48	69	36
24	Swindon Town	46	8	12	26	38	77	36